IMMANUEL KANT

The Metaphysics of Morals

EDITED BY

LARA DENIS

Agnes Scott College

TRANSLATED BY

MARY GREGOR

CAMBRIDGE
UNIVERSITY PRESS

CAMBRIDGE
UNIVERSITY PRESS

University Printing House, Cambridge CB2 8BS, United Kingdom

Cambridge University Press is part of the University of Cambridge.

It furthers the University's mission by disseminating knowledge in the pursuit of education, learning, and research at the highest international levels of excellence.

www.cambridge.org
Information on this title: www.cambridge.org/9781107451353

© Cambridge University Press 2017

First published 2017
4th printing 2020

Printed in the United Kingdom by TJ International Ltd. Padstow Cornwall

A catalogue record for this publication is available from the British Library.

Library of Congress Cataloguing in Publication Data
Names: Kant, Immanuel, 1724–1804, author. | Gregor, Mary J., editor.
Title: The metaphysics of morals / Immanuel Kant ; translated and edited by Mary Gregor ; with an introduction by Lara Denis, Agnes Scott College.
Other titles: Metaphysik der Sitten. English
Description: New York : Cambridge University Press, 2017. | Series: Cambridge texts in the history of philosophy | Previously published: 1996. | Includes index.
Identifiers: LCCN 2016056476 | ISBN 9781107451353
Subjects: LCSH: Ethics – Early works to 1800. | Duty – Early works to 1800. | Virtue – Early works to 1800.
Classification: LCC B2785.E5 G7413 2017 | DDC 170–dc23
LC record available at https://lccn.loc.gov/2016056476

ISBN 978-1-107-08639-5 Hardback
ISBN 978-1-107-45135-3 Paperback

CAMBRIDGE TEXTS IN THE
HISTORY OF PHILOSOPHY

IMMANUEL KANT
The Metaphysics of Morals

CAMBRIDGE TEXTS IN THE HISTORY OF PHILOSOPHY

Series editors
KARL AMERIKS
Professor of Philosophy at the University of Notre Dame

DESMOND M. CLARKE
Emeritus Professor of Philosophy, University College Cork

The main objective of Cambridge Texts in the History of Philosophy is to expand the range, variety and quality of texts in the history of philosophy which are available in English. The series includes texts by familiar names (such as Descartes and Kant) and also by less well-known authors. Wherever possible, texts are published in complete and unabridged form, and translations are specially commissioned for the series. Each volume contains a critical introduction together with a guide to further reading and any necessary glossaries and textual apparatus. The volumes are designed for student use at undergraduate and postgraduate level and will be of interest not only to students of philosophy, but also to a wider audience of readers in the history of science, the history of theology and the history of ideas.

For a list of titles published in the series, please see end of book.

Contents

Preface to the Second Edition

This second edition of Immanuel Kant's *The Metaphysics of Morals* within Cambridge Texts in the History of Philosophy (CTHP) contains a new Introduction and a new Further Reading section. The index has been updated. There are only minimal changes, however, to Mary J. Gregor's translation from the first CTHP edition (Cambridge University Press, 1996). Consequently, that edition's Translator's Note on the Text has been retained, albeit with a few new editorial notes and small alterations.

Footnotes to the text of *The Metaphysics of Morals* that are new to this edition or revised from the first edition are indicated by my initials, unless they are merely providing German words translated or making minor editorial changes. In this edition, the German words cited in translation notes are inflected and spelled as they are within the Academy Edition of the text edited by Paul Natorp (Berlin: Walter de Gruyter, 1907), on which Gregor's translation is based.

I flag revisions to Gregor's translation in footnotes, except where the changes seem too insignificant to warrant it. Where I am aware that Gregor's translation is controversial, I have usually retained it and alerted readers to the issue or offered an alternative translation in a footnote. When a problem with, or an alternative to, Gregor's translation came to my attention through (or is helpfully explained by) a particular article or book, I have cited the source. I hope that, in addition to giving credit where it is due, those citations will encourage inquisitive readers to seek out the sources cited and explore their discussions of the terms, text, and interpretive or philosophical stakes.

I wish to thank several people for their help with various aspects of this project. Frederick Rauscher, Eric Entrican Wilson, and Allen W. Wood gave me valuable feedback on drafts of the Introduction and Further Reading section. Suggestions or consultation concerning the translation and notes were provided by Paul Guyer, Arthur Ripstein, Barbara Sattler, Jens Timmermann, Helga Varden, and Allen W. Wood. I thank Hilary Gaskin and Karl Ameriks for inviting me to undertake this project, and Agnes Scott College for a sabbatical leave during which I completed most of my work on it. Finally, I thank my husband, Roger Wertheimer, for his enduring support, encouragement, patience, and sense of humor.

My first sustained encounter with *The Metaphysics of Morals* was through Gregor's 1991 translation in the Cambridge Texts in German Philosophy series. Indeed, the copy I acquired during my first year of graduate school remains a treasured (if tattered) possession. It is an honor to have the opportunity to bring this important work, through a descendant of that translation, to a new generation of readers.

L.D.

Introduction

Kant's *Metaphysics of Morals* is a complex and important work, reflecting Kant's mature legal and ethical thought. It contains the system of duties Kant takes to hold for human beings as such, as well as his accounts of will, right, obligation, virtue, and other fundamental moral concepts.

The Project and its Evolution

The Metaphysics of Morals is likely far different from what Kant originally envisaged. Letters indicate that Kant had planned a work roughly like *The Metaphysics of Morals* from at least as far back as the mid-1760s (see 10:56)[1]; such aspirations were expressed periodically until *The Metaphysics of Morals* finally emerged.[2] Kant's moral thought had changed significantly by the late 1790s. During the mid-1760s, it was heavily influenced by British moral sense theorists and, increasingly, Rousseau. Kant had yet to develop transcendental idealism, with its profound implications for freedom and morality.

Yet *The Metaphysics of Morals* differs also from what Kant's *Critique of Pure Reason* (1781, 1787) and *Groundwork of the Metaphysics of Morals* (1785) might lead us to expect. The first *Critique* and the *Groundwork* describe a metaphysics of morals as a system of pure moral philosophy, containing *a priori* concepts and principles.[3] For concepts and principles to be *a priori* as opposed to *a posteriori* is for them to be inherent in reason and revealed through its operation rather than

---

[1] References to Kant's works are by Academy Edition volume and page number, save for references to the *Critique of Pure Reason*, in which the page numbers of the first and second edition are preceded by "A" and "B" respectively.

[2] See Manfred Kuehn, "Kant's *Metaphysics of Morals*: The History and Significance of its Deferral," in Lara Denis (ed.), *Kant's Metaphysics of Morals: A Critical Guide* (Cambridge University Press, 2010), 9–27, especially 11–16.

[3] Additionally, the *Groundwork* anticipates a more accessible work than what Kant eventually produced: "a metaphysics of morals, despite its intimidating title, is yet capable of a great degree of popularity and suitability for the common understanding" (4:391; cf. 6:206).

derived from experience or observation. For a moral philosophy to be pure, it must be based only on *a priori* principles (see 4:388), "completely cleansed of everything that may be only empirical and that belongs to anthropology" (4:389).[4]

The first *Critique* says, "the metaphysics of morals is really the pure morality, which is not grounded on any anthropology (no empirical condition)" (A 841/B 869). That a metaphysics of morals is a species of "pure philosophy" – and as such the principal part of moral philosophy – is explicit in the *Groundwork* too, where Kant explains that only a pure philosophy can reveal "the moral law in its purity and genuineness" (4:390; cf. 410f.). Kant also says there, "a metaphysics of morals has to examine the idea and the principles of a possible *pure* will and not the actions and conditions of human volition generally, which for the most part are drawn from psychology" (4:390f.). As a pure will is non-empirical, determinable completely and only through *a priori* principles, it does not seem that its principles would encompass the array of moral principles binding finite, embodied human beings that are featured in *The Metaphysics of Morals* (cf. 4:421).[5]

The Metaphysics of Morals does present a system containing *a priori* practical principles and pure concepts. Yet it is characterized by a concern for their application to human beings. It often draws on empirical cognition of human nature in order to ascertain what our rights and duties are, what dispositions we must fight, which feelings we should cultivate, and so on. To that extent, *The Metaphysics of Morals* seems "impure" and thus at odds with Kant's characterization of a metaphysics of morals in his earlier critical works.

In its Introduction, Kant explains why *The Metaphysics of Morals* contains the empirical elements it does. After reminding readers that moral laws are necessary *a priori* (see 6:215) and that morality commands everyone irrespective of their inclinations (see 6:216), Kant says this:

> If, therefore, a system of *a priori* cognition from concepts alone is called *metaphysics*, a practical philosophy, which has not nature but freedom of choice as its object, will presuppose and require a metaphysics of morals. ... But just as there must be principles in a metaphysics of nature for applying those highest universal principles of a nature in general to objects of experience, a metaphysics of morals cannot dispense with principles of application, and we shall often have to take as our object the particular *nature* of human beings, which is cognized only by experience, in order to *show* in it what can be inferred from universal moral principles. But this will in no way detract from the purity of these principles or cast doubt on their *a priori* source. –

---

[4] Quotations from Kant's works are from the Cambridge Edition translations, except for those from *The Metaphysics of Morals*, which are from this volume.
[5] See Jens Timmermann, *Kant's Groundwork of the Metaphysics of Morals: A Commentary* (Cambridge University Press, 2007), 168–72, 170.

This is to say, in effect, that a metaphysics of morals cannot be based upon anthropology but can still be applied to it. (6:216f.; cf. 205f.)

This passage offers several considerations legitimizing as a metaphysics of morals a work which involves empirical elements as *The Metaphysics of Morals* does: a metaphysics of morals cannot omit principles for applying universal moral principles; to apply universal moral principles to human nature, which we can cognize only empirically, a metaphysics of morals cannot avoid all empirical cognition; the required empirical cognition is quite limited (i.e., limited to only that which is needed for generating a system of duties for human beings as such); applying universal moral principles to human beings as such neither detracts from their pure, *a priori* source, nor entails modifying them in light of human nature.

Thus, in *The Metaphysics of Morals*, Kant still considers a metaphysics of morals to be a system of *a priori* cognition of freedom and its laws. Now, however, he presents the application of pure, *a priori* principles and concepts to human nature as an indispensable aspect of a metaphysics of morals. Insofar as empirical cognition of human beings is necessary for this application, it is a legitimate part of a metaphysics of morals.[6]

The Metaphysics of Morals is, then, less pure than Kant's earlier, more foundational works, the *Groundwork* and *Critique of Practical Reason*. Its project differs from theirs, and builds upon them. The *Groundwork* seeks to establish the supreme principle of morality, a pure, *a priori* principle. The *Critique of Practical Reason* aims to prove the reality of pure practical reason, that is, to show that pure reason is sufficient to determine the will. *The Metaphysics of Morals* derives from the pure, *a priori* moral principle, the supreme principle of morality, the complete system of duties of human beings as such. Yet Kant's articulation of this system leaves open most questions of the application of these principles to human beings in specific conditions, situations, or relationships (see 6:469; cf. 205f.). Furthermore, *The Metaphysics of Morals* relegates to moral anthropology other indispensable yet impure aspects of practical philosophy:

> The counterpart of a metaphysics of morals, the other member of the division of practical philosophy as a whole, would be moral anthropology, which, however, would deal only with the subjective conditions in human nature that hinder people or help them in *fulfilling* the laws of a metaphysics of morals. It would deal with the development, spreading, and strengthening of moral principles ... and with other similar teachings and precepts based on experience. (6:217)

---

[6] See Mary J. Gregor, *Laws of Freedom: A Study of Kant's Method of Applying the Categorical Imperative in the Metaphysik der Sitten* (Oxford: Basil Blackwell, 1963), chapter 1, especially 11–17.

This account of moral anthropology in the "Introduction to the Metaphysics of Morals" attributes to it a narrower scope than earlier accounts of practical or moral anthropology do. Kant's earlier accounts subsume under the heading of moral or practical anthropology all application of moral principles to human beings – including the application to human beings as such that Kant eventually came to regard as proper to *The Metaphysics of Morals* (see 29:599; cf. 4:388f.).[7]

In sum, moral philosophy that is pure in the strictest sense is necessary for and prior to all other practical philosophy. It does not, however, exhaust the sphere of practical philosophy. Most fundamentally, we must recognize the moral law in its strictness and purity, and its relation to our will's autonomy. Kant's *Groundwork* and second *Critique* speak to these foundational issues. We need also, however, to ascertain the duties to which the moral law binds us as human beings. This task pertains to *The Metaphysics of Morals*, and requires some empirical knowledge of human beings in general. Finally, we should seek to fulfill our duties, and to facilitate the fulfillment of duties by others. For this, a far richer appreciation of human life and social conditions – and thus further empirical knowledge of human beings – is needed.[8]

The Value of *The Metaphysics of Morals*

As the preceding indicates, *The Metaphysics of Morals* makes a distinctive contribution to Kant's moral philosophy. Ignoring it can lead to significant misunderstandings. H.J. Paton puts the point forcefully: "Without a study of this work we are in danger of misunderstanding, not only the methods by which Kant sought to apply his formal principles, but even the nature of the principles themselves and their bearing upon human freedom."[9]

Kant's purer works of moral philosophy, the *Groundwork* and *Critique of Practical Reason*, often strike readers as cold and abstract. Some readers get the impression that Kant's ethics is antagonistic to feelings such as love and sympathy, denying them any positive moral role. From the *Groundwork* in particular, one might infer that the moral life is joyless; that moral goodness invariably requires opposition to inclinations, feelings, and desires; and that acting rightly requires constantly testing one's maxims to see whether they can be universalized.

---

[7] See Allen W. Wood, "The Final Form of Kant's Practical Philosophy," in Mark Timmons (ed.), *Kant's Metaphysics of Morals: Interpretive Essays* (Oxford University Press, 2002), 1–21, especially 3f.

[8] See *Anthropology from a Pragmatic Point of View* [1798] Robert B. Louden (trans., ed.), with Introduction by Manfred Kuehn (Cambridge University Press, 2006). Student transcriptions of Kant's anthropology lectures are available in English in *Lectures on Anthropology*, edited by Allen W. Wood and Robert B. Louden (Cambridge University Press, 2012).

[9] H.J. Paton, Foreword to Gregor, *Laws of Freedom*, ix–x, ix.

The Metaphysics of Morals corrects these misconceptions, and thus facilitates a more accurate understanding of Kant's practical thought. It tells us not simply what morality requires of rational beings as such, but what it requires of rational beings like us, with human bodies and psychologies. The *Doctrine of Right* considers human beings as persons who occupy space and who can come into conflict with one another as they pursue their ends.[10] The *Doctrine of Virtue* discusses love and sympathy positively, both as maxims and as feelings (see 6:456f.). Moral goodness emerges in *The Metaphysics of Morals* as involving not only a good will, but virtue, a human being's cultivated moral strength, developed through struggle against vice (see 6:405–9). Particular virtues (such as love of honor) and vices (such as ingratitude) are enumerated. Kant's moral psychology is developed considerably, so that his account of acting from duty becomes more complicated, but also richer.[11] Kant's account of the faculty of desire makes clear that acting morally involves desire and feeling as well as cognition (see 6:211–14). *The Metaphysics of Morals* presents duties within a structured taxonomy, constituting a system. Kant's accounts of these duties, the various types of duties, their relations, and their grounding, reveal as mistaken the notions, which many readers take from the second section of the *Groundwork*, that each agent must ferret out her duties by testing the various maxims of actions that appeal to her, and that duties are isolated requirements generated as the results of such tests.[12]

The Metaphysics of Morals not only builds on earlier published works of moral philosophy, but also synthesizes and reworks ideas from decades of lecturing on natural right (*Naturrecht*) and ethics. It brings together, as the *Doctrine of Right* (*Rechtslehre*) and the *Doctrine of Virtue* (*Tugendlehre*), Kant's mature political and ethical thought. Although he experimented with other taxonomies of duties, Kant gives us, in *The Metaphysics of Morals*, his official presentation of the complete system of duties of human beings as such.[13] Thus, it offers Kant's considered views on the relation of the realms of right and virtue to each other, the fundamental principles of each sphere, the nature of our various duties, and essential features of the moral life for human beings.

The Metaphysics of Morals contains discussions which elucidate crucial elements of Kant's moral philosophy. Many of these are found in the "Introduction to the Metaphysics of Morals." Kant explicates the faculty of

---

[10] See Arthur Ripstein, *Force and Freedom: Kant's Legal and Political Philosophy* (Harvard University Press, 2009), 12, 370–3.

[11] See 6:399–403. See also Paul Guyer, "Moral Feelings in the *Metaphysics of Morals*," in Denis (ed.), *Kant's Metaphysics of Morals*, 130–51.

[12] See Wood, "The Final Form," 4f.; but cf. 6:225, 376.

[13] The *Groundwork* taxonomy is a placeholder; see 4:421n. Compare the taxonomy Kant presents in *The Metaphysics of Morals* with that of his 1793/4 lectures on the metaphysics of morals (e.g., 27:578–86).

desire and its relation to moral laws and analyzes concepts such as obligation and duty (see 6:222f.). Crucially, Kant illuminates autonomy as a property of the will (*Wille*) by distinguishing between two aspects (or functions or moments) of will, legislative will (also called "*Wille*") and choice (*Willkür*): "Laws proceed from the will, maxims from choice" (6:226). Autonomy of will (in the broad sense) consists in the legislation of will (in the narrow sense) to choice. Further, Kant here clarifies his conception of freedom of choice: "freedom can never be located in a rational subject's being able to choose in opposition to his (lawgiving) reason.... Only freedom in relation to the internal lawgiving of reason is really an ability; the possibility of deviating from it is an inability" (6:226f.).

Criticisms and Challenges

Notwithstanding my preceding claims about its value, *The Metaphysics of Morals* has faced harsh criticism, and poses some problems for readers.

One thing that may puzzle readers, and which some commentators have objected to, is an apparently poor fit between *The Metaphysics of Morals* and Kant's critical philosophy. As already noted, Kant's thinking about what a metaphysics of morals should be, and in what sense it would be pure philosophy, evolved over the course of his career. The resulting work is less pure than readers of the *Critique of Pure Reason, Groundwork*, or *Critique of Practical Reason* might have expected. Moreover, recognition of significant, substantive overlap between *The Metaphysics of Morals* and Kant's lectures from the mid-1770s onward has generated doubts about whether or to what degree *The Metaphysics of Morals* genuinely belongs to Kant's critical philosophy.[14]

Some serious problems are posed by the editing of the text, especially the *Doctrine of Right*. Many difficulties spring from the apparent reordering of paragraphs and sections of the *Rechtslehre* after the manuscript left Kant's hands. There is disagreement about what went wrong and how best to reconstruct the text.[15] Though far less problematic than the *Doctrine of Right*, the *Doctrine of Virtue* also has instances of questionable organization. It has been suggested, for example, that the casuistical questions concerning servility should have been inserted before (rather than after) §12, since the account of the duty regarding humanity in our own person in §12 seems to go

---

[14] See Kuehn, "Kant's *Metaphysics of Morals*," 10, especially n.5, and 17–21.

[15] See Translator's Note on the Text; see also Bernd Ludwig, *Kants Rechtslehre*, volume 2 of *Kant-Forschungen* (Hamburg: Felix Meiner, 1988, second edition 2005), especially Part I; and his *Einleitung* in *Metaphysische Anfangsgründe der Rechtslehre*, Ludwig (ed.) (Hamburg: Felix Meiner, 1986, 1998, 2009).

beyond the duty not to be servile and to pertain to the general duty to oneself as a moral being only (see 6:436f.).[16]

These textual issues certainly pose challenges for readers. They may also raise or intensify doubts about the value of the work. Critics of *The Metaphysics of Morals* have long seized upon problems of textual organization and continuity, apparently pre-critical qualities of the work, and Kant's advancing age, to question Kant's abilities at the time of his writing of *The Metaphysics of Morals*, and thus to question its reliability as a representation of his mature moral thought.[17]

A different way in which the text of *The Metaphysics of Morals* challenges contemporary readers, especially those relatively new to eighteenth-century philosophy, is that it rarely makes explicit where or how Kant is responding to or relying on the work of other philosophers. In this respect, *The Metaphysics of Morals* contrasts with Kant's lectures on ethics and natural right. In those lectures, Kant is using a textbook written by someone else, typically following the order of the headings in the texts, and sometimes explicitly endorsing, rejecting, or amending claims made in them. The *Doctrine of Right* reflects the influence of Gottfried Achenwall (1719–1777), on whose *Prolegomena Iuris Naturalis* and *Ius Naturae* Kant lectured, through not only the topics Kant discusses, but also the terminology he employs. Kant often develops his own positions by criticizing Achenwall's, only rarely attributing to Achenwall the positions or arguments to which he is responding.[18] In the *Doctrine of Virtue*, "Doctrine of the Elements of Ethics", much of the content – e.g., what the duties are, and how Kant characterizes them – resembles his accounts of these duties in his lectures on ethics, lectures which used Alexander Baumgarten's (1714–1762) *Initia philosophiae practicae primae* (19:7–91) and *Ethica Philosophica* (27:737–1028) as texts.[19] Because *The Metaphysics of Morals* does not make explicit Kant's engagement with Baumgarten, it is difficult for a contemporary reader to know where and

---

[16] See Stefano Bacin, "The Perfect Duty to Oneself Merely as a Moral Being," in Andreas Trampota, Oliver Sensen, and Jens Timmermann (eds.), *Kant's Tugendlehre: A Comprehensive Commentary* (Walter de Gruyter, 2013), 245–68, 247 n.7. See also Dieter Schönecker, "Duties to Others from Love," op cit., 309–41, especially 333 n.52; and Bacin and Schönecker, "Zwei Konjekturvorschläge zur 'Tugendlehre,' §9," *Kant-Studien* 101 (2010): 247–52.

[17] See (e.g.) Arthur Schopenhauer, "Prize Essay on the Basis of Morals" [1840], in Christopher Janaway (trans., ed.), *Two Fundamental Problems of Ethics*, (Cambridge University Press, 2009), 113–258, especially 125; and *The World as Will and Representation*, Volume I [1818], Judith Norman, Alistair Welchman, and Christopher Janaway (trans., ed.) (Cambridge University Press, 2010), especially 558f.

[18] See B. Sharon Byrd and Joachim Hruschka, *Kant's Doctrine of Right: A Commentary* (Cambridge University Press, 2010), 15–20, and Kuehn, "Kant's *Metaphysics of Morals*," 19–20.

[19] See Kuehn, "Kant's *Metaphysics of Morals*," 17–21.

how Kant is responding to Baumgarten, and to what extent Kant is being innovative.[20]

Some challenges for readers reflect challenges for translators. There are terms that are difficult to translate from the German of Kant's day to the English of today, or that are ambiguous, technical, or philosophically contentious. "*Recht*", for instance, presents a range of problems. As Mary Gregor discusses in her Translator's Note on the Text, "*Recht*" (like the Latin "*ius*", which it translates) can refer to more than one thing – e.g., to a moral power for putting others under obligation, an objectively correct set of relations, or a system of laws – and it is not always clear from the context which Kant has in mind.[21] Even where the context indicates which sense of "*Recht*" Kant intends, it is not always obvious which English word best captures it. For instance, when Kant has in mind a sphere or system, it might be that none of "law", "justice", or "right" is perfect. (I have maintained Gregor's use of "right" in such contexts.)

Finally, readers face interpretive questions about even fundamental aspects of the text – such as about whether and how the universal principle of right is grounded in the moral law, or whether all duties enumerated within the *Tugendlehre* are duties of virtue (see "Kant's System of Duties: Questions," below). This is not special to *The Metaphysics of Morals*, of course. Questions about how best to understand Kant's *Groundwork* account of the formulations of the categorical imperative have occupied commentators since 1785. Still, interpretive debates about *The Metaphysics of Morals* are deep and intense, possibly exacerbated by some of what has already been noted. Moreover, it is relatively recently that *The Metaphysics of Morals* has received significant attention from Anglophone Kant scholars and moral and political philosophers. For that reason, many interpretive debates, even about basic issues, such as the moral status of right, feel fresh and heated in ways that, say, arguments about the moral worth of a good will do not.

Kant's System of Duties: An Overview

Kant presents the metaphysics of morals as a system of duties, which falls into two parts, both of which are also systems of duties.[22] Every duty is either a duty of right or a duty of virtue (see 6:239). The duties belonging to the

---

[20] See Stefano Bacin, "Kant's Lectures on Ethics and Baumgarten's Moral Philosophy," in Lara Denis and Oliver Sensen (eds.), *Kant's Lectures on Ethics: A Critical Guide* (Cambridge University Press, 2015), 15–33.

[21] For valuable background on evolving notions of *ius*, see Brian Tierney, *The Idea of Natural Rights: Studies in Natural Rights, Natural Law, and Church Law* 1150–1625 (Grand Rapids, MI: William B. Eerdmans Publishing Company, 1997).

[22] See Guyer, *Kant's System of Nature and Freedom* (Oxford: Clarendon Press, 2005), 243–74.

Doctrine of Right – the system of juridically legislated duties or duties of right – appear to be grounded in the universal principle of right: "Any action is right if it can coexist with everyone's freedom in accordance with a universal law, or if on its maxim the freedom of choice of each can coexist with everyone's freedom in accordance with a universal law" (6:230). Correlatively, the duties belonging to the *Doctrine of Virtue* – the system of ethically legislated duties or duties of virtue – appear to be grounded in the supreme principle of the doctrine of virtue: "act in accordance with a maxim of *ends* that it can be a universal law for everyone to have" (6:395). These principles, it seems, are themselves grounded in the supreme principle of the doctrine of morals: "act on a maxim which can also hold as a universal law" (6:226). Kant's articulation of the supreme principle of the doctrine of morals is nearly identical with his proximate statement of the categorical imperative: "act upon a maxim that can also hold as a universal law" (6:225).[23] So it appears that Kant's entire system of duties is grounded in the categorical imperative.

The main division of *The Metaphysics of Morals* is between the *Doctrine of Right* (*Rechtslehre*) and the *Doctrine of Virtue* (*Tugendlehre*). Kant explains this distinction in several ways at different junctures. Roughly, the *Doctrine of Right* concerns that which is just in external conduct and relations among human beings, whereas the *Doctrine of Virtue* concerns that which is morally good in a human being's attitudes, ends, and maxims. The sphere of right is that of external freedom; that of virtue (ethics), inner freedom. In the "Introduction to the Metaphysics of Morals," Kant explains the division of the two parts of a metaphysics of morals by reference to the kind of lawgiving involved in each (cf. 6:239, 379). The *Doctrine of Right* concerns duties of right, which can be prescribed through juridical legislation. The duties enumerated in the *Doctrine of Virtue*, duties of virtue, are prescribed only through ethical legislation. Both types of lawgiving involve a law, which represents an action as a duty, and an incentive for compliance with the law (i.e., for fulfillment of the duty) (see 6:218). Only ethical lawgiving, however, makes duty the incentive (see 6:219). There is an asymmetry between the spheres of ethics and right: all duties of right are "indirectly ethical" in that our own reason compels our compliance with them, yet no duties of virtue are as such subject to juridical enforcement (see 6:219–21; cf. 383).

The Doctrine of Right

Kant defines the doctrine of right as "the sum of those laws for which an external lawing is possible" (6:229). Right is "the sum of the conditions under which the

---

[23] In German, the categorical imperative is stated as: "*handle nach einer Maxime, welche zugleich als ein allgemeines Gesetz gelten kann!*" (6:225). The supreme principle of the doctrine of morals reads: "*handle nach einer Maxime, die zugleich als allgemeines Gesetz gelten kann*" (6:226).

choice of one can be united with the choice of another in accordance with a universal law of freedom" (6:230). The universal principle of right (see 6:230) is not an imperative but a criterion of right: it states the conditions under which an action is right. Kant supplies a corresponding imperative, the universal law of right: "so act externally that the free use of your choice can coexist with the freedom of everyone in accordance with a universal law" (6:231). Although Kant says that this law "lays an obligation on me," he emphasizes that this law does not require that I should fulfill this obligation from duty; right is no less satisfied if I act from self-interest or if others coerce my compliance. Indeed, if an action infringes on external freedom in accordance with universal laws, external coercion opposing that infringement is right: "there is connected with right by the principle of contradiction an authorization to coerce someone who infringes upon it" (6:232).[24]

Kant divides rights in two ways: as "systematic *doctrines*," the division is between natural right and positive right; as moral capacities (faculties or powers), the division is between innate and acquired right (see 6:237). Kant analyzes innate right in terms of the right to freedom and a set of authorizations that follow from it.[25] "*Freedom* (independence from being constrained by another's choice), insofar as it can coexist with the freedom of every other in accordance with a universal law, is the only original right belonging to every human being by virtue of his humanity" (6:237). By "humanity," Kant means the human being's supersensible capacity for freedom, "his personality independent of physical attributes (*homo noumenon*)" (6:239).[26] From freedom follows innate equality, being one's own master, being beyond reproach, and being able to engage with others however one wishes provided that one does not infringe on their rights. The right to freedom and the authorizations which follow from it constitute the sphere of innate right (that which is internally mine or yours). Part I of the *Rechtslehre*, "Private Right," concerns acquired right (that which is externally mine or yours). The sphere of innate right concerns those rights which everyone has prior to performing any legally relevant action, whereas the sphere of acquired right concerns rights which depend on the performance of a legally relevant action (such as signing a contract). Kant contrasts private right with civil or public right (see 6:242), the subject of Part II of the *Rechtslehre*.[27] Public right specifies the powers a state must have in order to secure for its citizens what is mine or yours (both internally and externally).

---

[24] See Allen W. Wood, "Punishment, Retribution, and the Coercive Enforcement of Right," in Denis (ed.), *Kant's Metaphysics of Morals*, 111–29, especially 116–20.

[25] See Höffe, "Kant's Innate Right," in Denis (ed.), *Kant's Metaphysics of Morals*, 71–92.

[26] See Byrd and Hruschka, *Kant's Doctrine of Right*, 279–93.

[27] The basic division between private and public right stretches back to Roman law, as does the inclusion of property, contract, and status within private right. See Justinian, *Institutes*, I.1.1.4.

Private right addresses interactions among individual persons. All such interactions must be consistent with the innate right to freedom. Kant divides private right into property right (concerning rights to things) (see 6:260–70), contract right (concerning rights against persons) (see 6:271–6),[28] and domestic right (concerning "rights to persons akin to rights to things") (see 6:276ff.); within the last category are marriage right (see 6:277–80), parental right (see 6:280–2), and right of the head of household (see 6:282–4).

Kant transitions from private right to public right by arguing that the rights previously enumerated can be neither determinate, nor conclusive, nor secure except within a system of public justice: "A rightful condition is that relation of human beings among one another that contains the conditions under which alone everyone is able to *enjoy* his rights, and the formal condition under which this is possible in accordance with the idea of a will giving laws for everyone is called public justice" (6:305f.).[29] The postulate of public right states: "when you cannot avoid living side by side with all others, you ought to leave the state of nature and proceed with them into a rightful condition" (6:307).

Public right encompasses the right of state, the right of nations, and cosmopolitan right. In "The Right of a State," Kant defines public right as "the sum of the laws which need to be promulgated generally in order to bring about a rightful condition," and so also as "a system of laws for a people, that is, for a multitude of human beings, or for a multitude of peoples, which, because they affect one another, need a rightful condition under a will uniting them, a *constitution* ... so that they may enjoy what is laid down as right" (6:311). A state is "the whole of individuals in a rightful condition, in relation to its own members" (6:311), "a union of multiple human beings under laws of right" (6:313). The powers of the state are divided among three branches of government: legislative, executive, and judicial (see 6:313–18). Among the more intensely debated aspects of this part of the *Doctrine of Right* are Kant's denial of a right to revolution (see 6:321–3), his claim that the state may collect taxes for support of the poor and orphaned (see 6:325f.), and his insistence on the death penalty for murderers (see 6:334–7).[30]

"The Right of Nations" concerns rights of nations in relation to one another, including rights to go to war, rights during war, and rights after

---

[28] For an analysis of the "dogmatic division of all rights that can be acquired by contract" (6:284–6), see Byrd and Hruschka, *Kant's Doctrine of Right*, 71–92, especially, 80–90.

[29] See Ripstein, *Force and Freedom*, 145–81.

[30] On revolution, see Ripstein, *Force and Freedom*, 336–43. On welfare rights, see Allen W. Wood, *The Free Development of Each: Studies on Freedom, Right, and Ethics in Classical German Philosophy* (Oxford University Press, 2014), 83–9. The section on punishment includes a dense, knotty discussion of whether the death penalty is warranted and necessary for unmarried women who kill their infants (6:335–7). On this, see Jennifer K. Uleman, "On Kant, Infanticide, and Finding Oneself in a State of Nature," *Zeitschrift für philosophische Forschung* 54 (2) (2000): 173–95.

war (see 6:343–51). Regarding the last of these, Kant advocates the establishment of a voluntary coalition of states to preserve peace among nations (see 6:350f.).

"Cosmopolitan Right" concerns international commerce and the rights of individuals as "citizens of the world" to travel the earth and attempt to establish a global community (see 6:352f.).[31] Kant concludes the *Rechtslehre* with a discussion of perpetual peace as the highest political good, and "the entire final end of the doctrine of right within the limits of mere reason" (6:355).[32]

The Doctrine of Virtue

Kant identifies virtue with moral strength, self-constraint, and inner freedom (see 6:380, 383f., 394–7). The doctrine of virtue is constituted by those duties which can be legislated only ethically (internally) (see 6:379); performance of ethical duties can be compelled only though inner moral self-constraint (see 6:379f.). While juridical legislation pertains directly to actions, ethical legislation pertains directly to maxims of actions; that is, ethical duties are of "wide" rather than "narrow" obligation (6:389f.). The supreme principle of the doctrine of virtue is, "act in accordance with a maxim of *ends* that it can be a universal law for everyone to have" (6:395). Kant divides the *Tugendlehre* into the "Doctrine of the Elements of Ethics," which enumerates duties of virtue, and the much shorter "Doctrine of the Methods of Ethics," which concerns the teaching of ethics and practice of virtue. The "Doctrine of the Elements of Ethics" divides duties of virtue into duties to oneself (Part I) and duties to others (Part II).[33]

Kant opens his discussion of duties to oneself by presenting and resolving an apparent antinomy concerning the concept of such duties: their very concept is self-contradictory if the "I" who obligates is conceived of as identical with the "I" who is obligated (see 6:417). This worry has implications beyond duties to oneself, Kant notes, since all ethical obligation involves self-constraint (see 6:417f.). Kant's solution is to deny that we take the obligating and obligated

---

[31] There has recently been great interest in Kant's cosmopolitanism. See (e.g.) Pauline Kleingeld, *Kant and Cosmopolitanism: The Philosophical Ideal of World Citizenship* (Cambridge University Press, 2011).

[32] Cf. *Toward Perpetual Peace* [1795], in Gregor (ed.), *Practical Philosophy*, 311–51.

[33] This two-part division is a departure from the three-part division – duties to God, duties to self, and duties to others – common to natural law theories (and others) of the early modern era. See, e.g., Pufendorf, *On the Duty of Man and Citizen* [1673], James Tully (ed.), Michael Silverthorne (trans.) (Cambridge University Press, 1991) especially I.3.13, 37f. Cf. Baumgarten, *Ethica*, Part I, Chapter I. Kant denies the possibility of duties to God (see 6:241, 442–4, 486–91).

"I" as identical: the human being is thought of in two different senses, and thus no contradiction arises.[34]

Next, Kant explains his division of duties to oneself into perfect and imperfect duties, and into duties to oneself as an animal and moral being and duties to oneself as a moral being only. Perfect duties are formal, negative duties, proscribing conduct "contrary to the **end** of [our] nature" (6:419). Imperfect duties are material, positive duties, prescribing the promotion of an end: our perfection. Kant associates the perfect duties with "moral **health**" and the imperfect duties with "moral *prosperity*" (6:419).

Perfect duties to oneself as an animal and moral being are duties not to act on the vicious maxims of self-disembodiment (by killing or mutilating oneself),[35] sexual self-defilement (especially through "unnatural" sex[36]), and self-stupefication (through gluttony and drunkenness) (see 6:421–8). In acting on these maxims, we act against ourselves through misuse of our animal nature.

Perfect duties to oneself as a moral being only prohibit acting on the vicious maxims of lying, avarice, and servility (see 6:428–37). These maxims are, by their very form, antagonistic to our inner freedom and innate dignity.[37] Kant identifies love of honor as the virtue opposed to the vices of lying, avarice, and servility (see 6:420).

Kant discusses conscience under the heading of "the human being's duty to himself as his own innate judge" (6:437–41). Distinct from this is the duty of self-knowledge, which Kant calls "the *first command* of all duties to oneself" (6:441f.), and which involves honest, impartial scrutiny of the purity of one's moral disposition and moral worth.

According to Kant, we do not have duties to non-human animals, inanimate objects in nature, or God; we can have duties only to persons who are given as objects of experience. Still, we have duties – which are duties to ourselves – not to be wantonly destructive toward what is beautiful in nature

---

[34] The text is notoriously cryptic at this point. Kant distinguishes between the human being viewed as a sensible being (*homo phenomenon*) and viewed as a free, intelligible being (*homo noumenon*). Commentators disagree, however, about how that distinction contributes to the solution, and what precisely the solution is. For discussion of the philosophical and interpretive difficulties in this passage, see Andrews Reath, "Duties to Oneself and Self-Legislation," in Timmons (ed.), *Kant's Metaphysics of Morals*, 349–70. For a thorough interpretation of this segment of the text, see Jens Timmermann, "Duties to Oneself as Such," in Trampota, et al. (eds.) *Kant's Tugendlehre*, 207–19. Other, briefer accounts of Kant's solution can be found in Allen W. Wood, *Kantian Ethics* (Cambridge University Press, 2008), 172; and Byrd and Hruschka, *Kant's Doctrine of Right*, 287n.56. Pertinent passages from Kant's lecture transcriptions include 27:510, 579, 593.

[35] See Yvonne Unna, "Kant's Answers to the Casuistical Questions Concerning Self-Disembodiment," *Kant-Studien* 94 (2003): 454–73.

[36] See Lara Denis, "Kant on the Wrongness of 'Unnatural' Sex," *History of Philosophy Quarterly*, 16 (2) (1999): 225–48.

[37] See Oliver Sensen, *Kant on Human Dignity* (Berlin: Walter de Gruyter, 2011), especially, 191–7.

or cruel to animals,[38] and to recognize all our duties as divine commands (see 6:442–4).

Imperfect duties to oneself promote the obligatory end of one's own perfection (see 6:444–7). Kant divides this duty into the promotion of one's natural perfection and moral perfection. Regarding moral perfection, Kant distinguishes between our striving for holiness and our striving for perfection.

Kant divides duties of virtue to others into duties of love, which are imperfect, and duties of respect, which are perfect (see 6:448–52). Duties of love directly promote others' happiness as an end, through the virtues of beneficence, gratitude, and sympathy; they are opposed by vices of envy, ingratitude, and malice (see 6:452–61). Duties of respect concern the practical respect owed to others because of their humanity. Duties of respect oppose the vices of arrogance, defamation, and ridicule (see 6:462–8). Additionally, Kant discusses duties to others in light of their particular condition, circumstance, or status (6:468f.); the duty of friendship (6:469ff.); and the virtues of social intercourse (6:473f.).[39]

Kant's System of Duties: Questions

There is much that is unclear about how Kant's system of duties is structured and how precisely Kant himself views it as a system. One set of questions concerns Kant's *Doctrine of Right*; another concerns his *Doctrine of Virtue*. My aim is not to argue for positions on these issues, or even to present the debates in full. Rather, I intend to alert readers to these topics of controversy, raise some relevant considerations, and point them toward further reading.

The Moral Status of the System of Right

It is not entirely clear on what basis the system of right is part of the metaphysics of morals. Some have argued that the system of right does not properly belong to the metaphysics of morals at all.[40] It is uncontroversial that the duties constituting the system of right are part of the metaphysics of morals as indirectly ethical duties (see 6:219–21). Considered simply as juridical duties, however, there are doubts.[41]

---

[38] See Patrick Kain, "Duties Regarding Animals," in Denis (ed.), *Kant's Metaphysics of Morals*, 211–33.

[39] On the last, see Patrick Frierson, "The Moral Importance of Politeness in Kant's Anthropology," *Kantian Review* 9 (2005): 105–27.

[40] See Marcus Willaschek, "Why the Doctrine of Right Does Not Belong in the *Metaphysics of Morals*," *Jahrbuch für Recht und Ethik* 5 (1997): 205–27.

[41] Note that "strict right" includes no duties or obligations, but only rights as authorizations to coerce (see 6:232f.; cf. 239). See Marcus Willaschek, "Which Imperatives for Right?: On the Non-Prescriptive Character of Juridical Laws in Kant's *Metaphysics of Morals*," in Timmons (ed.) *Kant's Metaphysics of Morals*, 65–87, especially 79–82.

One target of concern regarding the moral status of right is Kant's characterization of the legislation definitive of the sphere of right. Kant characterizes the duties belonging to the *Rechtslehre* as those that can be externally legislated (see 6:218–21). Both inner (ethical) and external (juridical) legislation present an action as objectively necessary (a duty) and an incentive for its performance. Ethical legislation makes the idea of duty the incentive. By contrast, juridical lawgiving, "admits an incentive other than the idea of duty," an incentive which "must be drawn from pathological determining grounds of choice," specifically "from aversions" (6:219). "External constraint" (coercion) is the incentive juridical legislation connects with its duties (6:220).[42] The external legislation of juridical laws apparently disqualifies them as moral laws, for Kant presents autonomy as the basis of morality,[43] and moral laws as self-legislated. In the *Groundwork*, Kant depicts the human being as "subject *only to laws given by himself*" (4:432; see also 431) and defines morality as "the relation of actions to the autonomy of the will" (4:439). In the second *Critique*, Kant states: "*Autonomy* of the will is the sole principle of all moral laws and of duties in keeping with them" (5:33). Moreover, juridical legislation appears not to generate categorical imperatives, the sort of imperative Kant associates with morality (see 4:416).[44] Categorical imperatives demand obedience immediately and unconditionally, simply for their own sake (see 4:413f.; 6:222). Juridical laws require only external compliance – "legality", not "morality", of action (6:219). It seems, then, that juridical laws do not give rise to corresponding categorical imperatives and so are not moral laws.

We should perhaps hesitate to dismiss juridical legislation as non-moral based on claims about morality and autonomy most closely associated with the *Groundwork*. By the time he wrote *The Metaphysics of Morals*, Kant's views might have evolved; or the nature of the later work might have led Kant to present his views in a more nuanced way. It might be, for instance, that in *The Metaphysics of Morals* autonomy encompasses not only individual self-legislation but also a kind of collective self-legislation, that of "the united will of the people" (6:313f.; see also 223, 263).[45] If so, then insofar as juridical legislation is an expression of the latter, it is an expression of autonomy. Alternatively, it might be that *The Metaphysics of Morals* identifies autonomy specifically with *inner* freedom, and so as the ground of ethics, but identifies

---

[42] To clarify: juridical legislation does not prescribe this – or any – incentive for the agent to act on. See Willaschek, "Why the Doctrine of Right," 211–19.

[43] See Katrin Flikschuh, "Justice without Virtue," in Denis (ed.), *Kant's Metaphysics of Morals*, 51–70, 55f.

[44] See Willaschek, "Which Imperatives for Right?", 67–73.

[45] Juridical lawgiving will seem more or less at odds with autonomy depending on how we understand autonomy. See Flikschuh, "Justice without Virtue," 58f. Also, see Oliver Sensen (ed.), *Kant on Moral Autonomy* (Cambridge University Press, 2013), several chapters of which seek to illuminate Kant's distinctive conception of autonomy.

freedom more broadly construed as the ground of morals. Both juridical and ethical laws are laws of freedom, and thus moral laws (6:214), but juridical laws are laws of *outer* freedom.[46]

Another locus of doubt about the moral status of right is the relation between the universal principle of right to the moral law and categorical imperative. The non-imperatival quality of the universal principle of right precludes it from being a categorical imperative. Some commentators hold, however, that it is derived from the categorical imperative.[47] Others regard it as morally grounded in some other way – for instance, "derived from the concept of freedom as the fundamental principle of morality."[48] Unlike the universal principle of right, the universal law of right is an imperative. Yet some commentators take Kant's description of it as "a postulate that is incapable of further proof" (6:231) to indicate its (and the universal principle of right's) independence of the moral law or categorical imperative.[49] Furthermore, it has been suggested that the universal principle of right is analytic, rendering otiose any derivation from the moral law, which is synthetic.[50] Debates about these matters hinge partly on questions about Kant's conceptions of analytic judgments, postulates, deductions, and the categorical imperative.[51]

I will not pursue these debates further.[52] I will suggest, however, that how we answer questions about the moral status of right is largely determined by how we understand Kant's mature view of morality. If we hold Kant to the standard of the *Groundwork*, we might equate the moral with the ethical. If we do that, then we will either reject right as non-moral, or embrace it as moral only by seeing it as dependent on ethics. Alternatively, if we defer to *The Metaphysics of Morals* as the most mature, developed form of Kant's moral thought, we may be able to understand right as both independent of ethics and yet nevertheless an essential part of the metaphysics of morals. In other words: how one answers the question about the moral status of right depends in large part on how one understands Kant's mature conception of the nature and domain of morality – and on whether one takes *The Metaphysics of Morals* to be the authoritative expression of it.

---

[46] See Flikschuh, "Justice without Virtue," 57–69.

[47] See Allen D. Rosen, *Kant's Theory of Justice* (Ithaca, NY: Cornell University Press), 54f.

[48] See Guyer, "Kant's Deductions of the Principles of Right," in Timmons (ed.), *Kant's Metaphysics of Morals*, 23–64, 26 n.7.

[49] See Willaschek, "Why the Doctrine of Right," 220f., 223f.

[50] See Wood, "The Final Form," 7. Kant contrasts the "supreme principle[s]" of the doctrines of right and virtue as (respectively) analytic and synthetic, providing a deduction only for the latter (6:396). It appears, however, that Kant ascribes analyticity simply to the relation between right and the authorization to coerce, not to the universal principle or law of right.

[51] Regarding the first three, see Guyer, "Kant's Deduction."

[52] In addition to previously cited works, two important recent treatments of these issues are Arthur Ripstein, *Force and Freedom*, 11–13, 355–88, and Allen W. Wood, *The Free Development of Each*, 70–83.

Defining Duties of Virtue

There is no doubt that the duties enumerated in the *Doctrine of Virtue* are moral duties, or that the system of these duties is proper to the metaphysics of morals. There is, however, uncertainty about precisely how Kant conceives of a duty of virtue, and whether all duties enumerated within the *Tugendlehre* are, strictly speaking, duties of virtue.

A general question is how to understand and reconcile Kant's dual criteria for duties of virtue.[53] Kant provides a formal criterion, according to which external legislation, obligation, and coercion of these duties is impossible. Kant characterizes duties of virtue as duties which cannot be externally legislated or coercively compelled; they are subject only to ethical legislation, internal lawgiving, and self-constraint (see 6:218–21, 383). Kant also provides a material criterion, according to which they are duties to have certain ends – in particular, one's own perfection and the happiness of others (see 6:394f., 385–8, 398).[54]

A more specific, derivative question about the domain of duties of virtue is how, if at all, perfect duties to oneself and duties of respect for others are duties of virtue. Kant asserts that duties to oneself belong to ethics, that is, to the doctrine of virtue (see 6:220), and that all duties to oneself are duties of virtue (see 6:419). Kant also identifies duties of respect for others as duties of virtue (see 6:419, 448, 462). Yet perfect duties to oneself and duties of respect for others appear straightforwardly as duties of virtue only on the first (formal) criterion, not the second (material) criterion.

The impossibility of external legislation, obligation, and coercion would appear to be sufficient to distinguish the duties belonging to the *Tugendlehre* from those in the *Rechtslehre* (see 6:220, 379, 383). Given Kant's identification of virtue with moral self-constraint, it makes sense to call *all* directly ethical duties "duties of virtue" (6:381). Yet Kant does not simply allege a conjunction of their formal and material qualities, as he might seem to do when he says, "in the imperative that prescribes a duty of virtue there is added not only the concept of self-constraint but that of an *end*" (6:396). Rather, he posits an explanatory relation between the material and formal aspects of these duties. He says, for example, that ethics extends the concept of duty beyond right – interpersonal compatibility of external freedom – "through *ends* being laid down" (6:396; see also 382, 389). He suggests that it is because duties of virtue require having ends that they are subject to self-constraint only: "That ethics contains duties that one cannot be constrained by others (by natural means) to fulfill *follows merely from its being a doctrine of ends*, since *coercion* to ends (to have them) is self-contradictory" (6:381, first emphasis mine; see also 6:239). No one can be coerced to

---

[53] See Guyer, *Kant on Freedom, Law, and Happiness* (Cambridge University Press, 2000), 311–23.

[54] Barbara Herman develops a compelling account of the role and importance of obligatory ends in *Moral Literacy* (Cambridge, MA: Harvard University Press, 2007), 203–75.

have an end, whereas one can be coerced to perform or omit an external action: "determination to an end is the only determination of choice the very concept of which excludes the possibility of constraint through natural means by the choice of another" (6:381). Furthermore, Kant explains the wide obligation of duties of virtue in terms of ethical law's pertaining to maxims of action rather than directly to actions themselves, and asserts, "[o]nly *the concept of an end that is also a duty* ... establishes a law for maxims of actions" (6:389, my emphasis). Ethical legislation lays down ends for us to adopt, and to which our choice of more particular maxims, ends, and actions must conform. The ends we ought to have, and the obligations to them and their maxims, are "duties of virtue" (see 6:354, 6:385f., 391–93, 395). Finally, Kant explains the latitude of duties of virtue by their material quality: "the law cannot specify precisely in what way one is to act and how much one is to do by the action for an end that is also a duty" (6:390).

One may, however, doubt that Kant holds that all duties that are immune from coercion are duties to have certain ends, let alone that they are immune from coercion because they are duties to have certain ends. For Kant claims that the only duties for which coercion is morally possible are those concerning the use of external freedom in relation to others (see 6:230–3, 383; 27:584). Perfect duties to oneself are not like this: their violation does not as such infringe on the rightful external freedom of others; enforcing them could not be justified as hindering a hindrance to freedom in the relevant sense. Yet these duties are not obviously grounded in an obligatory end. Indeed, in Kant's 1793/4 lectures on the metaphysics of morals, he analyzes perfect duties to oneself as duties grounded directly in the right of humanity in our own person (see 27:587). Thus, at least in these lectures, Kant explicitly recognizes that duties might be morally immune from coercion yet not be duties to have an end (see 27:581f.).[55]

Still, if we accept that within *The Metaphysics of Morals* duties of virtue are immediately connected with ends, we may wonder *which* ends are duties of virtue, and whether *all* duties enumerated in the *Tugendlehre* can be construed as such. I here focus on the question of which morally necessary end corresponds to perfect duties to oneself in such a way as to make them duties of virtue. I suggest three possibilities.

The first is humanity in our own person, which Kant identifies with the freedom in virtue of which one is a moral being and the idea (or ideal) of oneself as a free, moral being (see 5:86–8; 6:418, 420, 429, 435f.; 27:579, 593, 609f.).[56] Two principles suggest that this is the end in question: more obviously and

---

[55] Admittedly, however, Kant did not, in these lectures, consider perfect duties to oneself duties of virtue, but rather inner duties of right (27:585). See Denis, "Freedom, Primacy, and Perfect Duties to Oneself," in Denis (ed.), *Kant's Metaphysics of Morals*, 170–91, especially 178–80.

[56] Cf. 4:428f., 447f.; 6:404f., 480.

directly, Kant's formula of humanity, "*So act that you use humanity, whether in your own person or in the person of any other, always at the same time as an end, never merely as a means*" (4:429); more proximately, the supreme principle of the doctrine of virtue, "act in accordance with a maxim of *ends* that it can be a universal law for everyone to have" (6:395). Kant elaborates on the latter: "In accordance with this principle, the human being is an end for himself as well as for others, and it is not enough that he is not authorized to use either himself or others merely as means (since he could then still be indifferent to them); it is in itself his duty to make the human being as such his end" (6:395; cf. 410). If we take "the human being as such" to refer to the human being in idea, that is, as a free, moral being (see 6:464),[57] we may regard the humanity in our own person as an end that this principle requires us to have, and indeed as the end to which perfect duties to oneself, as duties of virtue, immediately correspond. This reading appears consistent with Kant's *Doctrine of Virtue* exposition of perfect duties to oneself, which frequently refers to the dignity (or degradation) of humanity in our own person (see 6:420, 424, 429, 435f.; cf. 462). Furthermore, if we take the supreme principle of the doctrine of virtue as setting forth humanity in our own person as the end corresponding to perfect duties to oneself, we may be able to see this principle as grounding all duties within the *Doctrine of Virtue*, not only imperfect ones.[58] It would enhance the systematicity of the *Doctrine of Virtue* if all duties contained in it were grounded, as duties of virtue, in the supreme principle of the doctrine of virtue.

One might object to attributing this role to the supreme principle of the doctrine of virtue by claiming that if humanity in our own person is the end corresponding to perfect duties to oneself, then the formula of humanity is sufficient for grounding these duties, and the supreme principle of the doctrine of virtue is superfluous for this purpose.[59] In response, one might argue that the latter principle appears more specific, internal, and positive than the former. It is not humanity in general, but specifically humanity as embodied or realized by human beings that the supreme principle of the doctrine of virtue sets forth as an end. Moreover, it is not sufficient for compliance with the supreme principle of the doctrine of virtue that, coincidentally, one does not use humanity in one's own person as a mere means, or degrade or destroy it. We must make it one of

---

[57] Cf. Kant's gloss of "a state as such" as "*the state in idea*" at 6:313. At 6:435, Kant identifies the human being not simply as a person, but as "a person who has duties his own reason lays upon him"; see also 6:379f., 425, 438.

[58] We will be able to, provided that this principle credibly grounds also duties of respect for others.

[59] Many commentators regard the formula of humanity as the principle grounding perfect duties to oneself in *The Metaphysics of Morals*. See, e.g., Wood, "The Final Form," 12f.; Houston Smit and Mark Timmons, "Kant's Grounding Project in the *Metaphysics of Morals*," in Timmons and Sorin Baiasu (eds.), *Kantian Practical Justification: Interpretive Essays* (Oxford University Press, 2013), 229–68; and Denis, "Kant's Ethics and Duties to Oneself," *Pacific Philosophical Quarterly* 78 (1997): 321–48.

our ends, taking it as a source of reasons for action and omission, choosing and acting *for the sake of* humanity in our own person. Finally, the supreme principle of the doctrine of virtue sets forth humanity in our own person not simply as a limiting condition on our pursuit of other ends (cf. 4:428, 430f., 438), but as an idea to realize.[60] Even if these responses are adequate, however, both of our other candidate ends can also be seen as obligatory in light of the supreme principle of the doctrine of virtue and the obligation following from it to make the human being as such one's end.

The second end in relation to which we might understand perfect duties to oneself is the complex of moral self-preservation and moral health.[61] This interpretation is suggested when Kant introduces these duties as ones that "*forbid* a human being to act against the **end** of his nature and so have to do merely with his *moral self-preservation*"; they "belong to the moral **health** ... of a human being as object of both his outer senses and his inner sense, to the *preservation* of his nature in its perfection (as *receptivity*)" (6:419). Kant explicitly states that even though these are duties "of omission" they "belong to [virtue] as duties of virtue" (ibid.). On this reading, perfect duties to oneself are duties concerning the preservation and protection of essential conditions of human agency. They require our rejection of vices antagonistic to self-respect, other moral endowments constituting subjective conditions of receptiveness to concepts of duty, the proper functioning of our animal nature as a basis for moral agency, or our "*prerogative*" as a moral being (6:420). These ends are more specific than humanity in our own person; they illuminate the nature of these duties as duties to oneself in particular; and they suit the limiting quality of the duties.

The third candidate is one's own perfection. We could regard perfect duties to oneself as duties not to undermine the basic conditions of rational human agency without which perfection would be impossible, or as duties to oppose vices incompatible with having, or detrimental to promoting, our own perfection (because of their antagonism toward the essential conditions of our moral agency). The passages quoted above in relation to moral health and moral self-preservation support this interpretation as well. For if we adopt our own perfection as an end, we commit ourselves to preserving the aspects of our agency upon which that perfection must be built – e.g., the capacities that must be cultivated.

---

[60] Cf. Thomas E. Hill, Jr., "Imperfect Duties to Oneself," in Tampota et al. (eds.), *Kant's Tugendlehre*, 293–308, especially 295f.

[61] I interpret Kant's *Tugendlehre* treatment of perfect duties to oneself this way in Denis, "Freedom, Primacy, and Perfect Duties to Oneself," especially 176–8. See also Donald Wilson, "Middle Theory, Inner Freedom, and Moral Health," *History of Philosophy Quarterly* 24 (4) (2007): 393–413.

An advantage of the third interpretation is that it puts perfect duties to oneself in direct relation to the end Kant repeatedly identifies as *the* self-regarding obligatory end. Also, there is no question that this is an end to be promoted, which seems to be the kind of end Kant generally has in mind here (see 6:381, 384f.). Perhaps what is most compelling about this interpretation is its fit with Kant's *Tugendlehre* account of our perfection as an obligatory end.[62] The relevant notion of perfection is "qualitative" or "formal" perfection. This "concept belonging to *teleology* ... is taken to mean the harmony of a thing's properties with an *end*" and concerns the "totality of what belongs to a thing" (6:386). Thus, one can conceive of all of a human being's capacities as implicated or comprehended in his perfection. So understood, Kant's notion of perfection seems sufficiently broad to encompass the perfection of our nature as it is, which we must preserve, as well as the perfection we are to bring to it through active cultivation (see 6:419).[63] This continuity between the aims of perfect and imperfect duties to oneself, with both relating to one's own perfection, is further indicated in the Collins lecture transcriptions, where Kant portrays duties to oneself generally as requiring us to act so that any use of our freedom or powers is consistent with the greatest use of them (see 27:345-7).

---

[62] See Trampota, "The Concept and Necessity of an End in Ethics," in Trampota et al. (eds.), *Kant's Tugendlehre*, 139–57, 153–5.

[63] Gregor takes the end corresponding to perfect duties to oneself to be "the integrity of humanity in our person" (or "our moral integrity"), which she equates with "moral self-preservation, health, or *esse*," and which she understands as "the negative and formal aspect of moral perfection" (*Laws of Freedom*, 113–27, especially 125–7). Gregor regards perfect duties to oneself as duties of virtue only "in a wide sense," not "in the full sense" (*Laws of Freedom*, 126f.).

Chronology

Further reading

The standard German edition of *The Metaphysics of Morals*, on which Gregor's translation here is primarily based, is that of the Academy Edition [*Akademie-Ausgabe*] of Kant's collected writings: Immanuel Kant, *Die Metaphysik der Sitten*, ed. Paul Natorp, *Kants gesammelte Schriften*, Ausgabe der Königlich Preußischen Akademie der Wissenschaften, volume 6, 203–494 (Berlin: Walter de Gruyter, 1907; reprinted 1968). It is available free online within *Das Bonner Kant-Korpus* (University of Bonn) https://korpora.zim.uni-duis burg-essen.de/Kant/ (accessed January 1 2017). *Die Metaphysik der Sitten* was first published in 1797 (Königsberg: Friedrich Nicolovius). The Academy Edition text incorporates additions Kant made to its first part, the *Rechtslehre*, for the 1798 edition. Translations of Kant's works commonly include volume and page numbers of the Academy Edition. References to the Academy Edition often use "AA" for *Akademie-Ausgabe*.

An important alternative German edition of the first part of *The Metaphysics of Morals* is Bernd Ludwig, *Metaphysische Anfangsgründe der Rechtslehre* for *Philosophische Bibliothek* (Hamburg: Meiner, 1986, subsequent editions 1998, 2009). It arranges the text as Ludwig believes Kant intended, correcting what Ludwig takes to be errors in the published version. (The Translator's Note on the Text provides further information about Ludwig's edition of the *Rechtslehre*.)

The English translation of *The Metaphysics of Morals* standardly used by philosophers is Mary Gregor's in *Practical Philosophy*, within the Cambridge Edition of the Works of Immanuel Kant, Allen W. Wood and Paul Guyer, series editors (Cambridge University Press, 1996). Also frequently used are the versions of Gregor's translation published within Cambridge Texts in German Philosophy (1991) and Cambridge Texts in the History of Philosophy (CTHP) (first edition, 1996). The 1991 version of Gregor's translation follows the organization of the Academy Edition more closely than do her subsequently published ones.

Translations of the two parts of *The Metaphysics of Morals* sometimes appear separately. John Ladd's translation of the *Rechtslehre* appears in *The Metaphysical Elements of Justice: Part I of the Metaphysics of Morals* (Indianapolis: Bobbs-Merrill, 1965); a revised version is available from Hackett Publishing Group (second edition, Indianapolis: Hackett, 1999). A translation of the *Tugendlehre* by James W. Ellington is available as *The Metaphysical Principles of Virtue: Part II of the Metaphysics of Morals* (Indianapolis: Bobbs-Merrill, 1964); it is reprinted in *Ethical Philosophy* (Indianapolis: Hackett, 1983, second edition 1995). Ellington's translation relies primarily on the second edition (1803) of the *Tugendlehre*.

Mary J. Gregor, *Laws of Freedom* (Oxford: Blackwell, 1963) is an essential single-author commentary on *The Metaphysics of Morals* as a whole. Two recent anthologies that probe historical, textual, and philosophical questions pertaining to the complete work are: Mark Timmons (ed.), *Kant's Metaphysics of Morals: Interpretive Essays* (Oxford University Press, 2002); and Lara Denis (ed.), *Kant's Metaphysics of Morals: A Critical Guide* (Cambridge University Press, 2010).

The *Rechtslehre* and the *Tugendlehre* have also received extensive individual attention. In *Kants Rechtslehre, Kant-Forschungen*, volume 2 (Hamburg: Meiner, 1988, second edition 2005), Bernd Ludwig analyzes the arguments of the *Rechtslehre*, critiques its organization as published, and explains his own reconstruction of the text; Ludwig's critique and reconstruction have been influential. B. Sharon Byrd and Joachim Hruschka, *Kant's Doctrine of Right: A Commentary* (Cambridge University Press, 2010) is a detailed, scholarly, and rigorous commentary on the *Rechtslehre*. Arthur Ripstein's *Force and Freedom* (Harvard University Press, 2009) provides a compelling interpretation and defense of Kant's legal and political thought in the *Rechtslehre*. Katrin Flikschuh, *Kant and Modern Political Philosophy* (Cambridge University Press, 2000) clarifies what is distinctive about Kant's political philosophy, particularly in contrast with contemporary liberalism. *Kant and Law*, Byrd and Hruschka (eds.) (Burlington, VT: Ashgate, 2006) collects nineteen articles on Kant's theory of right by diverse contributors, covering the nature of right, private right, public right, punishment, the right of nations, and cosmopolitan right.

The *Doctrine of Virtue* receives intensive examination in Andreas Trampota, Oliver Sensen, and Jens Timmermann (eds.), *Kant's Tugendlehre: A Comprehensive Commentary* (Berlin: de Gruyter, 2013), with contributions by eighteen philosophers from Britain, Germany, Italy, and the United States. Anne Margaret Baxley, *Kant's Theory of Virtue: The Value of Autocracy* (Cambridge University Press, 2010) develops an insightful, appealing interpretation of Kant's theory of virtue. Recent collections exploring Kant's theory of virtue include Monika Betzler (ed.),

Kant's Ethics of Virtue (Berlin: de Gruyter, 2008) and Lawrence Jost and Julian Wuerth (eds.), *Perfecting Virtue: New Essays in Kantian Ethics and Virtue Ethics* (Cambridge University Press, 2011). The imperfect duty to promote one's own natural perfection is the subject of Robert N. Johnson, *Self-Improvement* (Oxford University Press, 2011).

Kant's *Metaphysics of Morals* is best understood in the context of his entire corpus. Most obviously relevant are Kant's foundational published works in practical philosophy, *Groundwork of the Metaphysics of Morals* [1785] (AA 4) and the *Critique of Practical Reason* [1788] (AA 5). Authoritative translations appear in *Practical Philosophy*, Mary J. Gregor (trans., ed.) (Cambridge University Press, 1996). Jens Timmermann has revised Gregor's translation of the *Groundwork* for *Groundwork of the Metaphysics of Morals: A German-English Edition* (Cambridge University Press, 2011) and the second CTHP edition (Cambridge University Press, 2012). Essential to understanding Kant's critical project in philosophy, and so all of his mature work, is the *Critique of Pure Reason* [1781/1787] (A-edition, AA 4 / B-edition, AA 3). Two respected English translations are those by Norman Kemp Smith (London: Macmillan, 1929) and by Paul Guyer and Allen W. Wood (Cambridge University Press, 1998).

The *Critique of the Power of Judgment* [1790] (AA 5) (in English, ed. Paul Guyer, trans. Paul Guyer and Eric Matthews [Cambridge University Press, 2000]) fleshes out Kant's practical philosophy in important ways. *Religion within the Boundaries of Mere Reason* [1793] (AA 6) is illuminating regarding Kant's theories of virtue, human nature, and, as is the third *Critique*, the highest good. *Anthropology from a Pragmatic Point of View* [1798] (AA 7) complements Kant's purer moral philosophy. Translations of *Religion* and *Anthropology* are available within both the Cambridge Edition and CTHP series.

Several short works of political philosophy that supplement or clarify positions and arguments of the *Rechtslehre* are: "An Answer to the Question: What is Enlightenment?" [1784] (AA 8); "On the Common Saying: That May be Correct in Theory, But It Is of No Use in Practice" [1793] (AA 8); and *Toward Perpetual Peace* [1795] (AA 8). Translations appear in Mary Gregor, *Practical Philosophy* (Cambridge University Press, 1996).

Four sets of student transcriptions from Kant's lectures on moral philosophy from the 1760s to the 1790s (AA 27, 29) appear in whole or part, in English, in *Lectures on Ethics*, ed. Peter Heath and J.B. Schneewind, trans. Peter Heath (Cambridge University Press, 1997). Most of Kant's surviving preparatory drafts of the *Rechtslehre* (AA 23), all of the Feyerabend lecture transcriptions on natural right from 1786 (AA 27), and Kant's own notes for his course on natural right (AA 19) are translated by Frederick Rauscher and Kenneth Westphal in *Lectures and Drafts on Political Philosophy* (Cambridge University

Press, 2016). Selections of Kant's reflections on moral philosophy (AA 19) are translated by Rauscher in *Notes and Fragments*, ed. Paul Guyer (Cambridge University Press, 2005).

Within the vast secondary literature on Kant's practical philosophy, some works especially worthwhile for readers of the *The Metaphysics of Morals* are the following. Allen W. Wood, *Kant's Ethical Thought* (Cambridge University Press, 1999) ranges from Kant's foundational ethical theory, through his practical anthropology and philosophy of history, to his mature moral philosophy. Henry Allison, *Kant's Theory of Freedom* (Cambridge University Press, 1990) analyzes Kant's arguments concerning freedom, the justification of morality, moral agency, autonomy, will, choice, character, virtue, holiness, and radical evil. Also ambitious is Roger J. Sullivan, *Immanuel Kant's Moral Theory* (Cambridge University Press, 1989). Robert B. Louden, *Kant's Impure Ethics* (Oxford University Press, 2000) explores the impact of Kant's philosophies of human nature, religion, history, art, and education on his moral thought. Patrick Frierson, *Kant's Empirical Psychology* (Cambridge University Press, 2014) analyzes Kant's empirical psychology, distinguishing it from his transcendental philosophy and pragmatic anthropology. Patrick Kain, "Kant's Defense of Human Moral Status," *Journal of the History of Philosophy* 47 (1) (2009): 59–102 draws on Kant's theories of biology and psychology to elucidate his view of human moral standing.

Works notable for blending insightful textual interpretation with practical application of Kantian moral principles include Barbara Herman, *The Practice of Moral Judgment* (Harvard University Press, 1993) and *Moral Literacy* (Harvard University Press, 2007); Allen W. Wood, *Kantian Ethics* (Cambridge University Press, 2008); Onora O'Neill, *Constructions of Reason* (Cambridge University Press, 1989); and Thomas E. Hill, Jr., *Virtue, Rules, and Justice* (Oxford University Press, 2012). Topics with which they grapple include character, moral education, aid, violence, punishment, sex, lies, and social justice.

Among works valuable particularly for readers new to Kant's practical philosophy are these. Paul Guyer, *Kant* (New York: Routledge, 2006, second edition 2014) and Allen W. Wood, *Kant* (Oxford: Blackwell, 2005) are comprehensive introductions to Kant's philosophy. Jennifer K. Uleman, *An Introduction to Kant's Moral Philosophy* (Cambridge University Press, 2010) and Roger J. Sullivan, *An Introduction to Kant's Ethics* (Cambridge University Press, 1994) focus on Kant's moral thought. Perhaps the best brief introduction to Kant's moral philosophy is J.B. Schneewind, "Autonomy, Obligation, and Virtue: An Overview of Kant's Moral Philosophy," in *The Cambridge Companion to Kant*, ed. Paul Guyer (Cambridge University Press, 1992). The first part of Patrick R. Frierson, *What is the Human Being?* (New York: Routledge, 2013) explains Kant's faculty psychology and much else about Kant's account of human agency. An excellent short introduction to Kant's theory of right and related interpretive debates is Helga Varden, "Immanuel Kant – Justice as Freedom," in Guttorm Fløistad (ed.), *Philosophy of Justice* (Dordrecht: Springer, 2015), 213–37.

Works that illuminate the development of Kant's moral thought include: Manfred Kuehn, *Kant: A Biography* (Cambridge University Press, 2001); Lewis White Beck, *Early German Philosophy: Kant and His Predecessors* (Cambridge University Press, 1969); Clemens Schwaiger, "The Theory of Obligation in Wolff, Baumgarten, and the Early Kant," in *Kant's Moral and Legal Philosophy*, ed. Karl Ameriks and Otfried Höffe, trans. Nicholas Walker (Cambridge University Press, 2009), 58–73; and *Kant's Lectures on Ethics: A Critical Guide*, ed. Lara Denis and Oliver Sensen (Cambridge University Press, 2015). For broader historical context, J.B. Schneewind, *The Invention of Autonomy* (Cambridge University Press, 1998) traces thought concerning morality and self-governance through the seventeenth- and eighteenth-centuries, presenting Kant's moral theory as its culmination.

Numerous reference works can deepen or broaden readers' understanding of Kant's moral philosophy. Of the online sources listed, most are free and regularly updated; all were accessed January 1 2017.

Das Bonner Kant-Korpus not only contains, but also allows electronic searching through, volumes 1–23 of the Academy Edition of Kant's collected writings; see https://korpora.zim.uni-duisburg-essen.de/Kant/.

Kant lexicons explain terms Kant uses and indicate where he uses them. Rudolf Eisler, *Kant-Lexikon: Nachschlagewerk zu Kants sämtlichen Schriften, Briefen und handschriftlichen Nachlaß* (Hildesheim, Germany: Olms, 1994), originally published in 1930 (Berlin: Mittler), is available online www.textlog.de/rudolf-eisler.html; it is in German. Two new lexicons are in progress. From Cambridge University Press, in English: *The Cambridge Kant Lexicon*, edited by Julian Wuerth; from de Gruyter, in German: *Kant-Lexikon*, edited by Marcus Willaschek, Jürgen Stolzenberg, Georg Mohr, and Stefano Bacin.

Readers grappling with Kant's texts in German can benefit from period-appropriate dictionaries. Both Johann Christoph Adelung's *Grammatisch-kritisches Wörterbuch der Hochdeutschen Mundart* and Jacob and Wilhelm Grimm's *Deutsches Wörterbuch* are available online, thanks to the Trier Center for Digital Humanities. See *Wörterbuchnetz* http://woerterbuch netz.de/.

The Stanford Encyclopedia of Philosophy https://plato.stanford.edu features many entries on Kant, and several on his ethical or political thought.

Two useful bibliographies are Jörg Schrott (ed.), *Literatur zu Kants Ethik* www.ethikseite.de/bib/bkant.pdf, which lists sources dating from 1786 to the present, and Lara Denis, "Immanuel Kant: Ethics," in *Oxford Bibliographies in*

Philosophy, ed. Duncan Pritchard (New York: Oxford University Press, 2013) www.oxfordbibliographies.com/view/document/obo-9780195396577/obo-9780195396577-0225.xml, which provides annotated entries on Kant's ethical works and relevant secondary sources.

One the most informative online Kant resources is *Kant in the Classroom*, edited by Steve Naragon http://users.manchester.edu/FacStaff/SSNaragon/Kant/.

Translator's note on the text

The Edition

The two parts of *The Metaphysics of Morals* were first published separately, the *Doctrine of Right* probably in January 1797 and the *Doctrine of Virtue* in August of the same year. In the edition of 1798, Kant's revisions to the text were apparently limited to adding a parenthetical explanation of his term *Läsion* (AA 249) and an appendix in reply to Friedrich Bouterwek's review of the *Doctrine of Right* published on 18 February 1797. A more extensively revised edition was published in 1803, during Kant's lifetime but without his cooperation.

The present translation is based on the text of *The Metaphysics of Morals* edited by Paul Natorp in volume 6 (1907) of the Prussian Academy of the Sciences edition of Kant's works.[1] Natorp's decision not to use the "improved" edition of 1803 is based on his conviction that such alterations in the *Doctrine of Virtue* as are improvements do not justify the use of a text in the production of which Kant was not involved. I have followed Natorp in relegating to notes any substantive emendations that clarify the text. I have also made use of his notes in identifying authors whose works Kant cites.

---

[1] LD: Here referred to as "the Academy Edition" or abbreviated as "AA" for *Akademie-Ausgabe*. The organization of this translation departs from the Academy Edition in some respects. Notably, Gregor incorporates changes numbered below as (2) and (6) from Ludwig's reconstruction of the *Doctrine of Right*. In addition, she follows the 1803 edition of *The Metaphysics of Morals* in presenting "On the Idea of Virtue in General" as §XIV of the Preface to the *Doctrine of Virtue* and numbering subsequent sections XV-XIX, whereas AA leaves that part of the text without a section number and numbers subsequent sections XIV-XVIII. The Cambridge Edition translation of *The Metaphysics of Morals* includes the previously mentioned changes to the *Doctrine of Right* but not to the *Doctrine of Virtue*. Gregor's 1991 translation of *The Metaphysics of Morals* for the Cambridge Texts in German Philosophy series makes none of these changes to the AA structure.

It has long been recognized that the text of *The Doctrine of Right* is corrupt to the extent that paragraphs 4–8 in §6 do not belong there. On the history of this discovery, see editorial note 22 at 6:250. Bernd Ludwig, in his *Philosophische Bibliothek* edition of the *Rechtslehre* (Hamburg, Meiner, 1986, with subsequent editions 1998, 2009), proceeded on the hypothesis that this corruption of the text could have been far more extensive than this passage and could account for the obscurity of the work elsewhere. More specifically, he suggested that the copyist misunderstood Kant's directions about deletions and insertions in the text, which had been put together from various manuscripts, and that Kant, who was by then working on the *Tugendlehre*, was unwilling to interrupt his work by reviewing the completed manuscript. Hence the manuscript delivered to the printer was not at all the text that Kant had in mind. As for Kant's failure to take notice of the published text, Ludwig cites Kant's general lack of interest in his completed works unless the occasion arose for examining them, and the cursory response to Bouterwek's question about *lädieren*.[2]

However, Ludwig maintained that Kant's original text can be reconstructed on the basis of evidence within the published text itself, such as explicit assertions about its structure, implicit assertions about the sequence of particular passages, and indirect indications derived from general rules of exposition, such as defining a term before applying it. Ludwig gives a detailed account of his thesis in the introduction to his edition of the *Rechtslehre* and in Part I of its companion volume *Kants Rechtslehre*, vol. 2 in Reinhard Brandt and Werner Stark (eds.), *Kant Forschungen* (Hamburg: Felix Meiner, 1988, second edition 2005). His reconstruction of a part of the text is discussed in "'The Right of State' in Immanuel Kant's *Doctrine of Right*," *Journal of the History of Philosophy* 28(3)(1990): 403–15.

A list of the major changes his edition made in the text is as follows:

(1) The "Table of the Division of the Doctrine of Right" (AA 210) is moved from the end of the Preface to the end of the "Introduction to the Doctrine of Right."

(2) The Sections of the "Introduction to the Metaphysics of Morals" are reordered II, I, IV, III.

(3) In the Section "*Philosophia Practica Universalis*," paragraph 14, followed by paragraph 16, is inserted after paragraph 8 and the block of paragraphs 9–13 and 15 is moved to follow paragraph 23.

(4) The "Division of the Metaphysics of Morals" (AA 239ff.) is removed from the "Introduction to the Doctrine of Right" and inserted in "On the Division of a Metaphysics of Morals," after AA 221. The final paragraph (AA 242) remains in the "Introduction to the Doctrine of Right," after the table inserted according to (1).

---

[2] In AA, spelled "*lädiren*". See AA 20:445–53.

(5) A title page, "Part I: Metaphysical First Principles of the Doctrine of Right," is inserted before the "Introduction to the Doctrine of Right."

(6) §2 is inserted in place of paragraphs 4–8 in §6. Paragraphs 4–8 are deleted.

(7) §3 is deleted.

(8) §10, paragraph 4 is moved to §17 (which has become §16) as its third paragraph. Paragraph 5 is deleted.

(9) §15 is deleted.

(10) The "Remark" (AA 270) is moved to §11, as its conclusion.

(11) §31, "Dogmatic Division of All Rights That Can Be Acquired by Contract," is inserted as a new §21a at the end of Section II, "On Contract Right" (AA 276).

(12) A title page, "The Doctrine of Right, Part II: Public Right" is inserted after §40 (AA 306).

(13) The order of §§43 and 44 is reversed. The heading "Public Right, Section I: the Right of a State" is moved to AA 313, preceding §45, so that §§43 and 44 are included in the twelve paragraphs forming the "Transition from What is Mine or Yours in a State of Nature to What is Mine or Yours in a Rightful Condition Generally."

(14) §§45–9, 51, and 52, are reordered 45, 48, 46, 49, 47, 51, 52. §50 is made a new "Remark," F, and "Remarks" A–F are put at the end of "The Right of a State." The Academy Edition §47 (AA 315–16) is made a new §50.

As for the format of this translation, there are three types of footnotes. Kant's notes are indicated by asterisks. My notes having to do with matters of translation are indicated by letters[3]; I have translated only those Latin words or passages which are not mere repetitions of the German or which are identifiable quotations.[4] Editorial notes are indicated by arabic numerals. The pagination of the Academy Edition of *The Metaphysics of Morals* is given in the margins of the present translation. All references to Kant's works are to the Academy Edition, which most translators of his works provide, so references to his other writings can be readily identified in the various translations available.

The present translation is, essentially, the translation published in 1991 in the Cambridge Texts in German Philosophy series modified with a view to the

---

[3] LD: To facilitate reference to the Academy Edition of *The Metaphysics of Morals*, the translation notes to this edition present the cited German words inflected and spelled as they are in AA. So, for example, the silent "h" appears in "*beurtheilen*", "*Eigenthum*", "*Noth*", and "*That*"; "c" appears instead of "z" in "*Princip*" and instead of "k" in "*Act*" and "*Affecten*"; "-irt" rather than "-iert" ends "*lädirt*"; "s" and "ß" sometimes appear where one familiar with contemporary German would expect the other (e.g., in "*blos*" and "*Bedürfniß*"); and the dative "e" appears in "*von einem Zwecke*" (6:382).

[4] LD: Kant sometimes inflects Latin words according to their role in his German sentences. Those inflections remain here. Kant's quotations from Latin verse (and the like) are sometimes inexact.

format of the Cambridge Texts in the History of Philosophy series. I am deeply indebted to Lewis White Beck, Douglas P. Dryer, and Raymond Geuss who read earlier versions of this translation and offered numerous very helpful suggestions. I have incorporated much of their advice in the present translation.[5]

The Terminology of the *Rechtslehre*

The most serious problem of translation in *The Metaphysics of Morals* is the term *Recht*. Like the Latin *ius*, it has multiple meanings. Kant's predecessors distinguished four senses of *ius* or *Ius*. As referring to an action, *ius* is derived from *iustum* or *non iniustum* and means that the action is not contrary to justice (*iustitia*) taken in a strict and narrow sense, which was then specified as not depriving someone of what is his (*suum*). Second, it refers to the body of laws concerned with such actions, as distinguished from a law (*lex*) or laws of whatever kind, e.g., "the law of love" as distinguished from justice. Third, it means a quality of a person, a "faculty" (*facultas*) by which he can have or do something without injustice, that is, in such a way that his action will be *iustum* or in accord with *Ius*. Finally, it means what has been decided by a court in cases of conflict about *ius* in the first three senses.

The German language can eliminate one of these four meanings; it has the word *Rechtens* for what has been decided by a court. For the rest, *Recht* can mean a system of what Kant calls external laws, such laws as can be given by someone other than the reason of those subject to them. As an adjective *recht* characterizes actions that conform with external laws; strictly speaking, such actions should be called *gerecht*, but when it is clear that the context of the discussion is *Recht* in the sense just specified Kant often uses *recht* instead. Finally, *Recht* can mean "a right." In addition, Kant uses a number of compound words (such as *Rechtspflicht* and *Rechtsgesetz*) and a number of adjectives derived from *Recht* (such as *rechtlich* and *rechtmäßig*).

A translator faces several problems, most notably, how to translate *Recht* itself in the sense of a system of external laws and how to distinguish this from the other substantive use of *Recht*, "a right." Two possibilities were considered and rejected. First, *Recht* as a system of laws could have been translated as "law." For Kant, there are two systems of laws, one comprising the subject matter of *Rechtslehre* and the other that of *Tugendlehre*. In order to distinguish the two systems, the first could have been capitalized, as is done in referring to a "Law faculty" or a "Law school." A number of considerations argued against this translation. I shall mention two. First, the only word available for *ein Recht* is "a right," and Kant, as might be expected, is not content to leave the various senses

⁵ LD: Gregor had added: "However, I am solely responsible for whatever errors remain." That is not true with respect to this edition: I made the final revisions and review.

of *ius* merely associated by their common reference to one member of a division of laws. He argues, instead, for a conceptual connection of *das Recht* and *ein Recht*, which will determine the way in which "a right" will be used in the text. Not only does "Law" obscure the conceptual tie, by way of *recht*, between the two substantive senses of *Recht*; it is not always clear in which sense *Recht* is being used (on some occasions the indefinite article or the plural form points to "a right" or "rights," but this guidepost is often missing and sometimes misleading). Second, if *Recht* were translated as Law, the adjectives derived from it would appropriately be translated as "legal," obscuring the distinction between a state of nature and civil society and Kant's argument for the moral necessity of living in a civil society.

A second possible translation of *Recht*, "justice," was also considered and rejected. In addition to the problem involved in Law, "justice" suggests "fairness in the distribution of goods." Kant does use *Gerechtigkeit* (justice) and *austheilende Gerechtigkeit* (distributive justice), but the *Rechtslehre* is not a treatise on "social justice." Even if this connotation could be avoided, Kant's use of *Gerechtigkeit* would, it seems, make it implausible to distinguish "natural justice" from "legal justice."

Unfortunately, the English language has no word for *das Recht*, and a translator is naturally reluctant to introduce one. However, the considerations discussed in the preceding paragraphs seemed to warrant the use of "right" for a system of external laws. When it is impossible to maintain in English Kant's distinction between a body of laws and the rights people have in accordance with such laws, a note indicates the translation's deviation from the text.

What Kant specifies as the subject matter of *Rechtslehre* determines the translation of a number of common words whose meaning would otherwise be indeterminate. The most important of these are discussed in notes as the word appears. As Kant's terminology about rights comes into play, the reader may find that a number of words and phrases used metaphorically throughout his practical and even his theoretical writings are here assigned their literal meaning. This is, perhaps, to be expected in a philosophical system concerned with determining boundaries which are not to be encroached upon.

The
METAPHYSICS OF MORALS
by
Immanuel Kant

Part I
Metaphysical First Principles
of the
DOCTRINE OF RIGHT

Preface [6:205]

The critique of *practical* reason was to be followed by a system, the metaphysics of **morals**, which falls into metaphysical first principles of the *doctrine of right*[a] and metaphysical first principles of the *doctrine of virtue*. (This is the counterpart of the metaphysical first principles of *natural science*, already published.)[1] The Introduction that follows presents and, to some degree, makes intuitive the form which the system will take in both these parts.

For the **doctrine of right**, the first part of the doctrine of morals, there is required a system derived from reason which could be called the *metaphysics of right*. But since the concept of right is a pure concept that still looks to practice (application to cases that come up in experience), a *metaphysical system* of right would also have to take account, in its divisions, of the empirical variety of such cases, in order to make its division complete (as is essential in constructing a system of reason). But *what is empirical* cannot be divided completely, and if this is attempted (at least to approximate to it), empirical concepts cannot be brought into the system as integral parts of it but can be used only as examples in remarks. So the only appropriate title for the first part of *The Metaphysics of Morals* will be *Metaphysical First Principles of the Doctrine of Right*; for in the application of these principles to cases the system itself cannot be expected, but only approximation to it. Accordingly, it will be dealt with as in the (earlier) *Metaphysical First Principles of Natural Science*: namely, that right which belongs to the system outlined *a priori* will go into the text, while rights taken from particular cases of experience will be put into remarks, which will sometimes be extensive; for otherwise it would [6:206] be hard to distinguish what is metaphysics here from what is empirical application of rights.[b]

Philosophic treatises are often charged with being obscure, indeed deliberately unclear, in order to affect an illusion of deep insight. I cannot better anticipate or forestall this charge than by readily complying with a duty that Mr. Garve, a philosopher in the true sense of the word, lays down for all writers, but especially for philosophic writers. My only reservation is imposed by the nature of the science that is to be corrected and extended.

---

[a] On the word "right" [*Recht*], see Translator's Note on the Text. As for "doctrine," Kant concludes his Preface to the *Critique of the Power of Judgment* by noting that this critique concludes the critical part of his enterprise and that he will now proceed to the doctrinal [*doctrinal*] part, i.e., to the application of the principles established in the first two critiques in a metaphysics of nature and a metaphysics of morals (5:170). Cf. *Groundwork of the Metaphysics of Morals* 4:387.

[b] *Rechtspraxis*

[1] *Metaphysische Anfangsgründe der Naturwissenschaft* (1786), in AA 4. (LD: It is titled *Metaphysical Foundations of Natural Science* within the Cambridge Texts in the History of Philosophy.)

This wise man rightly requires (in his work entitled *Vermischte Aufsätze*, pages 352 ff.)² that every philosophic teaching be capable of being made *popular* (that is, of being made sufficiently clear to the senses to be communicated to everyone) if the teacher is not to be suspected of being muddled in his own concepts. I gladly admit this with the exception only of the systematic critique of the faculty of reason[c] itself, along with all that can be established only by means of it; for this has to do with the distinction of the sensible in our cognition from that which is supersensible but yet belongs to reason. This can never become popular – no formal metaphysics can – although its results can be made quite illuminating for the healthy reason (of an unwitting metaphysician). Popularity (common language) is out of the question here; on the contrary, scholastic *precision*[d] must be insisted upon, even if this is censured as hairsplitting (since it is the *language of the schools*); for only by this means can precipitate reason be brought to understand itself, before making its dogmatic assertions.

But if *pedants* presume to address the public (from pulpits or in popular writings) in technical terms that belong only in the schools, the critical philosopher is no more responsible for that than the grammarian is for the folly of those who quibble over words (*logodaedalus*). Here ridicule can touch only the man, not the science.

It sounds arrogant, conceited, the belittling of those who have not yet renounced their old system to assert that before the coming of the critical [6:207] philosophy there was as yet no philosophy at all. – In order to decide about this apparent presumption, it need but be asked *whether there could really be more than one philosophy.* Not only have there been different ways of philosophizing and of going back to the first principles of reason in order to base a system, more or less successfully, upon them, but there had to be many experiments of this kind, each of which made its contribution to present-day philosophy. Yet since, considered objectively, there can be only one human reason, there cannot be many philosophies; in other words, there can be only one true system of

---

[c] *Vernunftvermögens.* In such compounds as *Vernunftvermögen, Erkenntnisvermögen, Begehrungsvermögen,* and so forth, *Vermögen* is translated as "faculty." In the present introductory material, a note indicates where the word *Vermögen* by itself has been translated as "capacity" or "ability." Within the two parts of the *The Metaphysics of Morals,* where a right as well as a virtue is a *Vermögen,* the standard translation of *Vermögen* is "capacity" or "ability." In a different but related sense, usually made clear by the context, *Vermögen* is translated by "wealth" (or "resources" or "means").

[d] *Pünktlichkeit*

[2] Christian Garve (1742–1798) was Professor of Philosophy at Leipzig. Part I of Kant's essay "On the Common Saying: That May Be Correct in Theory, But It Is of No Use in Practice" (*Berlinische Monatsschrift,* September 1793), which deals with the relation of theory to practice in moral philosophy in general, is a reply to some objections raised by Garve in his *Versuche über verschiedene Gegenstände aus der Moral und Literatur* (Breslau: William Gottfried Korn, 1792). Kant's reference to Garve in the present context is topical, since in his *Vermischte Aufsätze* (Breslau: William Gottfried Korn, 1796) Garve complains about the mischief that "various authors of the Kantian school" (though not Kant himself) have been making in popular philosophy.

4

philosophy from principles, in however many different and even conflicting ways one has philosophized about one and the same proposition. So the *moralist* rightly says that there is only one virtue and one doctrine of virtue, that is, a single system that connects all duties of virtue by one principle; the *chemist*, that there is only one chemistry (Lavoisier's);[3] the *teacher of medicine*, that there is only one principle for systematically classifying diseases (Brown's).[4] Although the *new system* excludes all the others, it does not detract from the merits of earlier moralists, chemists, and teachers of medicine, since without their discoveries and even their unsuccessful attempts we should not have attained that unity of the true principle which unifies the whole of philosophy into one system. – So anyone who announces a system of philosophy as his own work says in effect that before this philosophy there was none at all. For if he were willing to admit that there had been another (and a true) one, there would then be two different and true philosophies on the same subject, which is self-contradictory. – If, therefore, the critical philosophy calls itself a philosophy before which there had as yet been no philosophy at all, it does no more than has been done, will be done, and indeed must be done by anyone who draws up a philosophy on his own plan.

The charge that one thing which essentially distinguishes the critical philosophy is not original to it but was perhaps borrowed from another philosophy (or from mathematics) would be *less* important but not altogether negligible. A reviewer in Tübingen[5] claims to have discovered that the definition of philosophy which the author of the *Critique of Pure Reason* gives out as his own, not inconsiderable, discovery had been put forth many years earlier by someone else in almost the same words.[*] I leave it to anyone to judge[e] whether the words   [6:208]

---

[*] *Porro de actuali constructione hic non quaeritur, cum ne possint quidem sensibiles figurae ad rigorem definitionum effingi; sed requiritur cognitio eorum, quibus absolvitur formatio, quae intellectualis quaedam constructio est.* C.A. Hausen, *Elem. Mathes.* (1734), *Pars* I, 86.A. [Moreover, what is in question here is not an actual construction, since sensible figures cannot be devised in accordance

[e] *beurtheilen* LD: Throughout, Gregor regularly translates this word as "appraise" as well as "judge" (and handles variants accordingly). I have flagged some of her other translations of it.

[3] Antoine Laurent Lavoisier (1743–1794), whose discovery of the role of oxygen in combustion and influence in establishing the nomenclature of chemistry earned him the title of principal architect of the new science of chemistry.

[4] On the system of the controversial Scots physician John Brown (1735–1788), see Mary Gregor's introduction to the translation of Kant's *Rektoratsrede*, "On Philosophers' Medicine of the Body," in Lewis W. Beck (ed.), *Kant's Latin Writings* (New York and Berne: Peter Lang, 1986; rev. edn, 1992).

[5] According to Paul Natorp, editor of the Academy Edition (5:505–7), the reviewer from Tübingen was probably Johann Friedrich Flatt, to whom Kant refers in his Preface to the *Critique of Practical Reason* (5:8n.). In reviewing a mathematical dissertation by J.C. Yelin, Flatt remarked that, since everything must now be expressed in Kantian language, the author calls the construction of a quantity *eine Darstellung durch reine Anschauung* ["an exhibition by pure intuition"], and went on to use the text Kant cites from Hausen as proof that only the terminology, not the concept, is new. As might be expected, Kant was annoyed with Flatt's recurrent theme that his cardinal distinctions had already been made in substance by other writers. Compare Kant's reply (1790), to a similar charge by Johann August Eberhard, *On a Recent Discovery According to which Any New Critique of Pure Reason Has Been Made Superfluous by an Earlier One* (8:187–251).

intellectualis quaedam constructio could have yielded the thought of *the presentation of a given concept in an a priori intuition*, which at once completely distinguishes philosophy from mathematics. I am sure that Hausen[6] himself would not have allowed his words to be interpreted in this way; for the possibility of an *a priori* intuition, and that space is an *a priori* intuition and not (as Wolff explains it)[7] a juxtaposition of a variety of items outside one another given merely to empirical intuition (perception), would already have frightened him off, since he would have felt that this was getting him entangled in far-reaching philosophic investigations. To this acute mathematician the presentation made *as it were by means of the understanding* meant nothing more than an (empirical) *drawing* of a *line* corresponding to a concept, in which attention is paid only to the rule and abstraction is made from unavoidable deviations in carrying it out, as can also be perceived in equalities constructed in geometry.

As far as the spirit of the critical philosophy is concerned, the *least* important consideration is the mischief that certain imitators of it have made by using some of its terms, which in the *Critique of Pure Reason* itself cannot well be replaced by more customary words, outside the *Critique* in public exchange of thoughts. This certainly deserves to be condemned, although in condemning it Mr. Nicolai[8] reserves judgment as to whether such terms can be entirely dispensed with in their own proper field, as though they were used everywhere merely to hide poverty of thought. – Meanwhile it is more amusing to laugh at an *unpopular pedant* than at an *uncritical ignoramus* (for, in fact, a metaphysician who clings obstinately to his own system, heedless of any critique, can be classed as an uncritical ignoramus, even though he willfully[f] *ignores* what he does not want to let spread since it does not belong to his older school of thought). But if it is true, [6:209] as Shaftesbury asserts,[9] that a doctrine's ability to withstand *ridicule* is not a bad touchstone of its truth (especially in the case of a practical doctrine), then the critical philosophy's turn must finally come to laugh *last* and so laugh *best* when

---

with the strictness of a definition; what is required is, rather, cognition of what goes to make up the figure, and this is, as it were, a construction made by the intellect.]

[f] *willkürlich*

[6] Christian August Hausen (1693–1745) was Professor of Mathematics at Leipzig. His *Elementa matheseos* was published in Leipzig in 1734.

[7] See Christian Wolff, *Ontology* §588 (Frankfurt and Leipzig, 1730).

[8] See Walter Strauss, *Friedrich Nicolai und die kritische Philosophie: ein Beitrag zur Geschichte der Aufklärung* (Stuttgart: Kohlhammer, 1927). In 1796 Nicolai, in his *Beschreibung einer Reise durch Deutschland und die Schweiz im Jahre 1781* (12 vols., Berlin and Stettin, 1783–1796), ridiculed the use to which Schiller and his followers had put Kantian terminology. Despite Kant's warning that this criticism should not be extended to the critical philosophy itself, Nicolai did just that with his publication of *Leben und Meinungen Sempronius Gundiberts* (Berlin and Stettin, 1798), which called forth Kant's *Über die Buchmacherei: Zwei Briefe an Herrn Friedrich Nicolai* (8:431–8).

[9] Anthony Ashley Cooper, third Earl of Shaftesbury (1651–1713). The reference is to his *Characteristics of Men, Manners, Opinion, Times*, Treatise II, "*Sensus communis*, an Essay on the Freedom of Wit and Humour" (1709), Section I: "Truth ... may bear all Lights: and one of those principal Lights ... is Ridicule itself. ... So much, at least, is allow'd by All, who at any time appeal to this Criterion...".

it sees the systems of those who have talked big for such a long time collapse like houses of cards one after another and their adherents scatter, a fate they cannot avoid.

Toward the end of the book I have worked with less precision^g over certain sections than might be expected in comparison with the earlier ones, partly because it seems to me that they can be easily inferred from the earlier ones and partly, too, because the later sections (dealing with public right) are currently subject to so much discussion, and still so important, that they can well justify postponing a decisive judgment for some time.

I hope to have the *Metaphysical First Principles of the Doctrine of Virtue* ready shortly.[10]

---

[g] *mit minderer Ausführlichkeit.* LD: The above translation replaces "less thoroughly" from the previous edition. Cf. Mary Gregor and Jens Timmermann (eds.) *Groundwork of the Metaphysics of Morals: A German-English Edition* (Cambridge University Press, 2011), 162.

[10] That the *Doctrine of Right* was written and published before the *Doctrine of Virtue* accounts for the title page (6:203) and table of contents (6:210) in the Academy Edition.

Part I
Private Right with Regard to External Objects
(the Sum of Laws That Do Not Need to be Promulgated)

Chapter I
How to *Have* Something External as One's Own

Chapter II
How to *Acquire* Something External

Division of External Acquisition

Section I
On Property Right

Section II
On Contract Right

Section III
On Rights to Persons Akin to Rights to Things

Episodic Section
On Ideal Acquisition

Chapter III
On Acquisition That Is Dependent Subjectively upon the Decision of a Public
Court of Justice

Part II
Public Right
(The Sum of Laws that Need to be Promulgated)

Chapter I
The Right of a State

Chapter II
The Right of Nations

Chapter III
Cosmopolitan Right

Introduction
to the Metaphysics of Morals

I[a]

On the Idea of and the Necessity for a Metaphysics of Morals

It has been shown elsewhere that for natural science, which has to do with objects of outer sense, one must have *a priori* principles and that it is possible, indeed necessary, to prefix a system of these principles, called a metaphysical science of nature, to natural science applied to particular experiences, that is, to physics. Such principles must be derived from *a priori* grounds if they are to hold as universal in the strict sense. But physics (at least when it is a question of keeping its propositions free from error) can accept many principles as universal on the evidence of experience. So Newton assumed on the basis of experience the principle of the equality of action and reaction in the action of bodies upon one another, yet extended it to all material nature. Chemists go still further and base their most universal laws of the combination and separation of substances[b] by their own forces entirely on experience, and yet so trust to the universality and necessity of those laws that they have no fear of discovering an error in experiments made with them.

But it is different with moral laws. They hold as laws only insofar as they can be *seen* to have an *a priori* basis and to be necessary. Indeed, concepts and judgments about ourselves and our deeds and omissions signify nothing moral if what they contain can be learned merely from experience. And should anyone let himself be led astray into making something from that source into a moral principle, he would run the risk of the grossest and most pernicious errors.

If the doctrine of morals were merely the doctrine of happiness it would be absurd to seek *a priori* principles for it. For however plausible it may sound to say that reason, even before experience, could see the means for achieving a lasting enjoyment of the true joys of life, yet everything that is taught *a priori* on this subject is either tautological or assumed without any basis. Only experience can teach what brings us joy. Only the natural drives for food, sex, rest, and movement, and (as our natural predispositions develop) for honor, for enlarging our cognition, and so forth, can tell each of us, and each only in his particular way, in what he will *find* those joys; and, in the same way, only experience can teach him the means by which to *seek* them. All apparently *a priori* reasoning about this comes down to nothing but experience raised by induction to generality, a generality (*secundum principia generalia, non universalia*) still so tenuous that everyone must be allowed countless exceptions in order to adapt his choice[c] of a way of life to his particular

---

[a] The following section is numbered II in AA. See Translator's Note on the Text.
[b] *Materien*   [c] *Wahl*

inclinations and his susceptibility to satisfaction and still, in the end, to become prudent only from his own or others' misfortunes.

But it is different with the teachings of morality.[d] They command for everyone, without taking account of his inclinations, merely because and insofar as he is free and has practical reason. He does not derive instruction in its laws from observing himself and his animal nature or from perceiving the ways of the world, what happens and how human beings behave (although the German word *Sitten*, like the Latin *mores*, means only manners and customs). Instead, reason commands how human beings are to act even though no example of this could be found, and it takes no account of the advantages we can thereby gain, which only experience could teach us. For although reason allows us to seek our advantage in every way possible to us and can even promise us, on the testimony of experience, that it will probably be more to our advantage on the whole to obey its commands than to transgress them, especially if obedience is accompanied with prudence, still the authority of its precepts[e] *as commands* is not based on these considerations. Instead it uses them (as counsels) only as a counterweight against inducements to the contrary, to offset in advance the error of biased scales in practical appraisal, and only then to insure that the weight of a pure practical reason's *a priori* grounds will turn the scales in favor of the authority of its precepts.

If, therefore, a system of *a priori* cognition from concepts alone is called *metaphysics*, a practical philosophy, which has not nature but freedom of choice for its object, will presuppose and require a metaphysics of morals, that is, it is itself a *duty* to *have* such a metaphysics, and every human being also has it within himself, though in general only in an obscure way; for without *a priori* principles how could he believe that he has a giving of universal law within himself? But just as there must be principles in a metaphysics of nature for applying those highest universal principles of a nature in general to objects of experience, [6:217] a metaphysics of morals cannot dispense with principles of application, and we shall often have to take as our object the particular *nature* of human beings, which is cognized only by experience, in order to *show* in it what can be inferred from universal moral principles. But this will in no way detract from the purity of these principles or cast doubt on their *a priori* source. – This is to say, in effect,

---

[d] *mit den Lehren der Sittlichkeit.* In 6:219 Kant distinguishes between the legality of an action and its *Moralität* (*Sittlichkeit*); drawing the same distinction in 6:225 he uses *Sittlichkeit* (*moralitas*). In the present context, however, it would seem that he continues to discuss what he has been calling *Sittenlehre*, i.e., the "doctrine of morals" or of duties generally. In 6:239 he refers to the metaphysics of morals in both its parts as *Sittenlehre* (*Moral*).

[e] *Vorschriften* LD: In this edition, Gregor usually translates *Vorschrift* as "precept". I flag where she translates it otherwise. The revised edition of the *Groundwork of the Metaphysics of Morals* for CTHP (Mary Gregor and Jens Timmermann [eds.], [Cambridge University Press, 2012]), translates it as "prescription"; see Gregor and Timmermann (eds.), *Groundwork of the Metaphysics of Morals: A German-English Edition*, xiii.

that a metaphysics of morals cannot be based upon anthropology but can still be applied to it.

The counterpart of a metaphysics of morals, the other member of the division of practical philosophy as a whole, would be moral anthropology, which, however, would deal only with the subjective conditions in human nature that hinder people or help them in *fulfilling* the laws[f] of a metaphysics of morals. It would deal with the development, spreading, and strengthening of moral principles (in education in schools and in popular instruction), and with other similar teachings and precepts based on experience. It cannot be dispensed with, but it must not precede a metaphysics of morals or be mixed with it; for one would then run the risk of bringing forth false or at least indulgent moral laws, which would misrepresent as unattainable what has only not been attained just because the law has not been seen and presented in its purity (in which its strength consists) or because spurious or impure incentives[g] were used for what is itself in conformity with duty and good. This would leave no certain moral principles, either to guide judgment or to discipline the mind in observance of duty, the precepts of which[h] must be given *a priori* by pure reason alone.[i]

As for the higher division under which the division just mentioned falls, namely that of philosophy into theoretical and practical philosophy, I have already explained myself elsewhere (in the *Critique of Judgment*),[11] and I have explained that practical philosophy can be none other than moral wisdom. Anything that is practical and possible in accordance with laws of nature (the distinctive concern of art)[j] depends for its precepts entirely upon the theory of nature: only what is practical in accordance with laws of freedom can have principles that are independent of any theory; for there is no theory of what goes beyond the properties of nature. Hence philosophy can understand by its practical part (as compared with its theoretical part) no *technically practical* doctrine but only a *morally practical* doctrine; and if the proficiency of choice in accordance with laws of freedom, in contrast to laws of nature, is also to be

[6:218]

---

[f] *der Ausführung der Gesetze.* LD: or, with John Ladd, "the execution of the laws." (All references to Ladd are from *The Metaphysical Elements of Justice* [Indianapolis: Bobbs-Merrill, 1965].)

[g] *Triebfedern.* LD: Although "incentive" is now the standard English translation of *Triebfeder*, it might be misleading. *Triebfeder* generally refers to a source of action internal to the agent, not to an external lure or inducement. "Spring" (or "spring of action") is an alternative translation; cf. T.K. Abbott, *Fundamental Principles of the Metaphysics of Morals* (Upper Saddle River, NJ: Prentice Hall, 1949), 44 (4:427). For further discussion, see Stephen Engstrom, "The *Triebfeder* of Pure Practical Reason," in Andrews Reath and Jens Timmermann (eds.), *Kant's Critique of Practical Reason: A Critical Guide* (Cambridge University Press, 2010), 90–118, 91–3.

[h] *deren Vorschrift.* LD: Or perhaps, "the prescription of which."

[i] *schlechterdings nur durch reine Vernunft a priori gegeben werden muß*

[j] *Kunst.* In the *Groundwork of the Metaphysics of Morals* (4:415), Kant called such precepts those of "skill" [*Geschicklichkeit*].

[11] LD: *Kritik der Urtheilskraft* (1790, 1793), in AA 5. (It is titled *Critique of the Power of Judgment* within the Cambridge Edition.)

called *art* here, by this would have to be understood a kind of art that makes possible a system of freedom like a system of nature, truly a divine art were we in a position also to carry out fully, by means of it, what reason prescribes and to put the idea of it into effect.

[6:211]

II[k]
On the Relation of the Faculties of the Human Mind to Moral Laws

The *faculty of desire* is the faculty to be by means of one's representations the cause of the objects of these representations. The faculty of a being to act in accordance with its representations is called *life*.

First, pleasure or *displeasure*, susceptibility to which is called *feeling*[l], is always connected with desire[m] or aversion; but the converse does not always hold, since there can be a pleasure that is not connected with any desire for an object but is already connected with a mere representation that one forms of an object (regardless of whether the object of the representation exists or not). *Second,* pleasure or displeasure in an object of desire does not always precede the desire and need not always be regarded as the cause of the desire but can also be regarded as the effect of it.

The capacity[n] for having pleasure or displeasure in a representation is called *feeling* because both of them involve what is *merely subjective* in the relation of our representation and contain no relation at all to an object for possible [6:212] cognition of it[*] (or even cognition of our condition). While even sensations, apart from the quality (of, e.g., red, sweet, and so forth) they have because of the nature of the subject, are still referred to an object as elements in our cognition of it, pleasure or displeasure (in what is red or sweet) expresses nothing at all in the object but simply a relation to the subject. For this very reason pleasure and

---

[*] One can characterize sensibility as the subjective aspect of our representations in general; for it is the understanding that first refers representations to an object, i.e., only it *thinks* something by means of them. What is subjective in our representations may be such that it can also be referred to an object for cognition of it (either in terms of its form, in which case it is called pure intuition, or in terms of its matter, in which case it is called sensation); in this case sensibility, as susceptibility to such a representation, is *sense*. Or else what is subjective in our representations cannot become *an element in our cognition* because it involves *only* a relation of the representation to the *subject* and nothing that can be used for cognition of an object; and then susceptibility to the representation is called *feeling*, which is the effect of a representation (that may be either sensible or intellectual) upon a subject and belongs to sensibility, even though the representation itself may belong to the understanding or to reason.

[k] This section is numbered I in AA.
[l] *Gefühl.* LD: Gregor sometimes also translates *Empfindung* as "feeling," though she typically, as in Kant's note below, translates it as "sensation." Hereafter, where "feeling" translates *Empfindung* rather than *Gefühl*, I flag it.
[m] *Begehren*   [n] *Fähigkeit*

displeasure cannot be explained more clearly in themselves; instead, one can only specify what results they have in certain circumstances, so as to make them recognizable in practice.

That pleasure which is necessarily connected with desire (for an object whose representation affects feeling in this way) can be called *practical pleasure*, whether it is the cause or the effect of the desire. On the other hand, that pleasure which is not necessarily connected with desire for an object, and so is not at bottom a pleasure in the existence of the object of a representation but is attached only to the representation by itself, can be called merely contemplative pleasure or *inactive delight*. We call feeling of the latter kind of pleasure *taste*. Practical philosophy, accordingly, speaks of contemplative pleasure only *in passing*, not as if the concept *belonged within* it. As for practical pleasure, that determination of the faculty of desire which is caused and therefore necessarily *preceded* by such pleasure is called *desire*[o] in the narrow sense; habitual desire[p] is called *inclination*; and a connection of pleasure with the faculty of desire that the understanding judges to hold as a general rule (though only for the subject) is called an *interest*. So if a pleasure necessarily precedes a desire, the practical pleasure must be called an interest of inclination. But if a pleasure can only follow upon an antecedent determination of the faculty of desire it is an intellectual pleasure, and the interest in the object must be called an interest of reason; for if the interest were based on the senses and not on pure rational principles alone, sensation would then have to have pleasure connected with it and in this way be [6:213] able to determine the faculty of desire. Although where a merely pure interest of reason must be assumed no interest of inclination can be substituted for it, yet in order to conform to ordinary speech we can speak of an inclination for what can be an object only of an intellectual pleasure as a habitual desire from a pure interest of reason; but an inclination of this sort would not be the cause but rather the effect of this pure interest of reason, and we could call it a *sense-free inclination* (*propensio intellectualis*).

Concupiscence (lusting after something) must also be distinguished from desire itself, as a stimulus to determining desire. Concupiscence is always a sensible modification of the mind but one that has not yet become an act of the faculty of desire.

The faculty of desire in accordance with concepts, insofar as the ground determining it to action lies within itself and not in its object, is called a faculty to *do or to refrain from doing as one pleases.*[q] Insofar as it is joined with one's consciousness of the ability[r] to bring about its object by one's action it is called *choice*;[s] if it is not joined with this consciousness its act is called a *wish*.

[o] *Begierde*. Although it would be appropriate to translate *Begierde* by a word other than "desire," which has been used for *Begehren* and in *Begehrungsvermögen*, it is difficult to find a suitable word that has not been preempted. However, *Begierde*, as distinguished from *Neigung* ["inclination"], does not figure prominently in the present work.

[p] *Begierde* [q] *nach Belieben* [r] *des Vermögens* [s] *Willkür*

The faculty of desire whose inner determining ground, hence even what pleases it,[t] lies within the subject's reason is called the *will*.[u] The will is therefore the faculty of desire considered not so much in relation to action (as choice is) but rather in relation to the ground determining choice to action. The will itself, strictly speaking, has no determining ground; insofar as it can determine choice, it is instead practical reason itself.

Insofar as reason can determine the faculty of desire as such, not only *choice* but also mere *wish* can be included under the will. That choice which can be determined by *pure reason* is called free choice. That which can be determined only by *inclination* (sensible impulse, *stimulus*) would be animal choice (*arbitrium brutum*). Human choice, however, is a choice that can indeed be *affected* but not *determined* by impulses, and is therefore of itself (apart from an acquired proficiency[v] of reason) not pure but can still be determined to actions by pure will. *Freedom* of choice is this independence from being *determined* by sensible impulses; this is the negative concept of freedom. The positive concept of [6:214] freedom is that of the ability[w] of pure reason to be of itself practical. But this is not possible except by the subjection of the maxim of every action to the condition of its qualifying as universal law. For as pure reason applied to choice irrespective of its objects, it does not have within it the matter of the law; so, as a faculty of principles (here practical principles, hence a lawgiving faculty), there is nothing it can make the supreme law and determining ground of choice except the form, the fitness of maxims of choice to be universal law. And since the maxims of human beings, being based on subjective causes, do not of themselves conform with those objective principles, reason can prescribe this law only as an imperative that commands or prohibits absolutely.

In contrast to laws of nature, these laws of freedom are called *moral* laws. As directed merely to external actions and their conformity to law they are called *juridical* laws; but if they also require that they (the laws) themselves be the determining grounds of actions, they are *ethical* laws, and then one says that conformity with juridical laws is the *legality* of an action and conformity with ethical laws is its *morality*. The freedom to which the former laws refer can be only freedom in the *external* use of choice, but the freedom to which the latter refer is freedom in both the external and the internal use of choice, insofar as it is determined by laws of reason. In theoretical philosophy it is said that only objects of outer sense are in space, whereas objects of outer as well as of inner sense are in time, since the representations of both are still representations, and as such belong together to inner sense. So too, whether freedom in the external or in the internal use of choice is considered, its laws, as pure practical laws of reason for free choice generally, must also be internal determining grounds of choice, although they should not always be considered in this respect.

---

[t] *selbst das Belieben*   [u] *Wille*   [v] *Fertigkeit*   [w] *Vermögen*

III[x]

Preliminary Concepts[y] of the Metaphysics of Morals (*Philosophia practica universalis*)

The concept of *freedom* is a pure rational concept, which for this very reason is transcendent for theoretical philosophy, that is, it is a concept such that no instance corresponding to it can be given in any possible experience, and of an object of which we cannot obtain any theoretical cognition: the concept of freedom cannot hold as a constitutive but solely as a regulative and, indeed, merely negative principle of speculative reason.[12] But in reason's practical use the concept of freedom proves its reality by practical principles, which are laws of a causality of pure reason for determining choice independently of any empirical conditions (of sensibility generally) and prove a pure will in us, in which moral concepts and laws have their source.

On this concept of freedom, which is positive (from a practical point of view), are based unconditional practical laws, which are called *moral*. For us, whose choice is sensibly affected and so does not of itself conform to the pure will but often opposes it, moral laws are *imperatives* (commands or prohibitions) and indeed categorical (unconditional) imperatives. As such they are distinguished from technical imperatives (precepts of art), which always command only conditionally. By categorical imperatives certain actions are *permitted* or *forbidden*, that is, morally possible or impossible, while some of them or their opposites are morally necessary, that is, obligatory. For those actions, then, there arises the concept of a duty, observance or transgression of which is indeed connected with a pleasure or displeasure of a distinctive kind (moral *feeling*), although in practical laws of reason we take no account of these feelings (since they have nothing to do with the *basis* of practical laws but only with the subjective *effect* in the mind when our choice is determined by them, which can differ from one subject to another [without objectively, i.e., in the judgment of reason, at all adding to or detracting from the validity or influence of these laws]).

The following concepts are common to both parts of *The Metaphysics of Morals.* [6:222]

Obligation is the necessity of a free action under a categorical imperative of reason.

An imperative is a practical rule by which an action in itself contingent is *made* necessary. An imperative differs from a practical law in that a law indeed represents an action as necessary but takes no account of whether this action already inheres by an *inner* necessity in the acting subject (as in a holy being) or whether it is contingent (as in the human being); for where the former is the case there is no imperative. Hence an imperative is a rule the representation of

---

[x] This section is numbered IV in AA.   [y] *Vorbegriffe*

[12] LD: Cf. *Critique of Pure Reason* A 508/B 536; *Critique of Practical Reason* 5:48f.

which *makes* necessary an action that is subjectively contingent and thus represents the subject as one that must be *constrained* (necessitated)[z] to conform with the rule. – A categorical (unconditional) imperative is one that represents an action as objectively necessary and makes it necessary not indirectly, through the representation of some *end* that can be attained by the action, but through the mere representation of this action itself (its form), and hence directly. No other practical doctrine can furnish instances of such imperatives than that which prescribes obligation (the doctrine of morals). All other imperatives are *technical* and are, one and all, conditional. The ground of the possibility of categorical imperatives is this: that they refer to no other property of choice (by which some purpose[a] can be ascribed to it) than simply to its *freedom*.

That action is *permitted* (*licitum*) which is not contrary to obligation; and this freedom, which is not limited by any opposing imperative, is called an authorization (*facultas moralis*). Hence it is obvious what is meant by *forbidden* (*illicitum*).

Duty is that action to which someone is bound. It is therefore the matter of obligation, and there can be one and the same duty (as to the action) although we can be bound to it in different ways.

[6:223] A categorical imperative, because it asserts an obligation with respect to certain actions, is a morally practical *law*. But since obligation involves not merely practical necessity (such as a law in general asserts) but also *necessitation*, a categorical imperative is a law that either commands or prohibits, depending upon whether it represents as a duty the commission or omission of an action. An action that is neither commanded nor prohibited is merely *permitted*, since there is no law limiting one's freedom (one's authorization) with regard to it and so too no duty. Such an action is called morally indifferent (*indifferens, adiaphoron, res merae facultatis*). The question can be raised whether there are such actions and, if there are, whether there must be permissive laws (*lex permissiva*), in addition to laws that command (*lex praeceptiva, lex mandati*) and laws that prohibit (*lex prohibitiva, lex vetiti*), in order to account for someone's being free to do or not to do something as he pleases. If so, the authorization would not always have to do with an indifferent action (*adiaphoron*); for, considering the action in terms of moral laws, no special law would be required for it.[13]

An action is called a *deed* insofar as it comes under obligatory laws and hence insofar as the subject, in doing it, is considered in terms of the freedom of his

---

[z] *genöthigt* (*necessitirt*). Kant repeatedly gives *Zwang* ["constraint"] and *Nöthigung* ["necessitation"] as synonyms. Although *Nöthigung* is perhaps his favored term, I have often translated *Nöthigung* by the more common English word "constraint."

[a] *Abischt*

[13] On permissive laws see *Toward Perpetual Peace*, 8:347n and 373n.

choice. By such an action the agent is regarded as the *author* of its effect, and this, together with the action itself, can be *imputed* to him, if one is previously acquainted with the law by virtue of which an obligation rests on these.[b]

A *person* is a subject whose actions can be *imputed* to him. *Moral* personality is therefore nothing other than the freedom of a rational being under moral laws (whereas psychological personality is merely the ability[c] to be conscious of one's identity in different conditions of one's existence). From this it follows that a person is subject to no other laws than those he gives to himself (either alone or at least along with others).

A *thing* is that[d] to which nothing can be imputed. Any object of free choice which itself lacks freedom is therefore called a thing (*res corporalis*).

A deed is *right* or *wrong* (*rectum aut minus rectum*)[e] in general insofar as it conforms with duty or is contrary to it (*factum licitum aut illicitum*);[f] the duty itself, in terms of its content or origin, may be of any kind. A deed contrary to duty is called a *transgression* (*reatus*).   [6:224]

An *unintentional* transgression which can still be imputed to the agent is called a mere *fault* (*culpa*). An *intentional* transgression (i.e., one accompanied by consciousness of its being a transgression) is called a *crime* (*dolus*). What is right in accordance with external laws is called *just* (*iustum*); what is not, *unjust* (*iniustum*).[g]

A *conflict of duties* (*collisio officiorum s. obligationum*)[h] would be a relation between them in which one of them would cancel the other (wholly or in part). – But since duty and obligation are concepts that express the objective practical *necessity* of certain actions and two rules opposed to each other cannot be necessary at the same time, if it is a duty to act in accordance with one rule, to act in accordance with the opposite rule is not a duty but even contrary to duty; so a *collision of duties* and obligations is inconceivable (*obligationes non colliduntur*).[i] However, a subject may have, in a rule he prescribes to himself, two *grounds* of obligation[j] (*rationes obligandi*), one or the other of which is not sufficient to put him under obligation (*rationes obligandi non obligantes*), so that one of them is not a duty. – When two such grounds conflict with each other, practical philosophy says, not that the stronger obligation takes precedence

---

[b] *wenn man ... auf ihnen*. LD: Both Ladd and James Ellington here have "if he ... rests on him." (All references to Ellington are to *The Metaphysical Principles of Virtue* [Indianapolis: Bobbs-Merrill, 1964].)
[c] *Vermögen*
[d] *Sache ist ein Ding*. LD: or perhaps, "a thing is an entity". See Gregor and Timmermann (eds.), *Groundwork of the Metaphysics of Morals* (CTHP revised edition), 41n (4:428).
[e] right or less right   [f] licit or illicit act   [g] *gerecht ... ungerecht*
[h] collision of duties or obligations   [i] obligations do not conflict
[j] *zur Verpflichtung nicht zureichend ist*. Although Kant apparently uses both *Verbindlichkeit* and *Verpflichtung* for "obligation," the latter seems at times to have the sense of "put under obligation" and to be closely related to *verbinden*, which I often translate as "to bind."

(*fortior obligatio vincit*),[k] but that the stronger *ground of obligation* prevails[l] (*fortior obligandi ratio vincit*).[m]

Obligatory laws for which there can be an external lawgiving are called *external* laws (*leges externae*) in general. Those among them that can be recognized as obligatory *a priori* by reason even without external lawgiving are indeed external but *natural* laws, whereas those that do not bind without actual external lawgiving (and so without it would not be laws) are called *positive* laws. One can therefore conceive of external lawgiving which would contain only positive laws; but then a natural law would still have to precede it, which would establish the authority of the lawgiver (i.e., his authorization to bind others by his mere choice).

[6:225] A principle that makes certain actions duties is a practical law. A rule that the agent himself makes his principle on subjective grounds is called his *maxim*; hence different agents can have very different maxims with regard to the same law.

The categorical imperative, which as such only affirms what obligation is, is: act upon a maxim that can also hold as a universal law. – You must therefore first consider your actions in terms of their subjective principles; but you can know whether this principle also holds objectively only in this way: that when your reason subjects it to the test of conceiving yourself as also giving universal law through it, it qualifies for such a giving of universal law.

The simplicity of this law in comparison with the great and various consequences that can be drawn from it must seem astonishing at first, as must also its authority to command without appearing to carry any incentive with it. But in wondering at an ability[n] of our reason to determine choice by the mere idea that a maxim qualifies for the *universality* of a practical law, one learns that just these practical (moral) laws first make known a property of choice, namely its freedom, which speculative reason would never have arrived at, either on *a priori* grounds or through any experience whatever, and which, once reason has arrived at it, could in no way be shown theoretically to be possible, although these practical laws show incontestably that our choice has this property. It then seems less strange to find that these laws, like mathematical postulates, are *incapable of being proved* and yet *apodictic*, but at the same time to see a whole field of practical cognition open up before one, where reason in its theoretical use, with the same idea of freedom or with any other of its ideas of the supersensible, must find everything closed tight against it. – The conformity of an action with the law of duty is its *legality* (*legalitas*); the

---

[k] the stronger obligation wins
[l] *die Oberhand behalte . . . behält den Platz.* LD: Or, "retains the upper hand . . . retains the field," as in Timmermann, "Kantian Dilemmas? Moral Conflict in Kant's Ethical Theory," *Archiv für Geschichte der Philosophie* 95 (1) (2013):36–64, 51.
[m] the stronger ground of obligation wins   [n] *Vermögen*

conformity of the maxim of an action with a law is the *morality* (*moralitas*) of the action. A *maxim* is a *subjective* principle of action, a principle which the subject himself makes his rule (how he wills to act). A principle of duty, on the other hand, is a principle that reason prescribes to him absolutely and so objectively (how he *ought* to act).

The supreme principle of the doctrine of morals is, therefore: act on a maxim $\quad$ [6:226] which can also hold as a universal law. – Any maxim that does not so qualify is contrary to morals.

Laws proceed from the will, maxims from choice. In the human being° the latter is a free choice; the will, which is directed to nothing beyond the law itself, cannot be called either free or unfree, since it is not directed to actions but immediately to giving laws for the maxims of actions (and is, therefore, practical reason itself). Hence the will directs with absolute necessity and is itself *subject to* no necessitation. Only *choice* can therefore be called *free*.

But freedom of choice cannot be defined – as some have tried to define it – as the ability to make a choice^p for or against the law (*libertas indifferentiae*),^q even though choice as a *phenomenon* provides frequent examples of this in experience. For we know freedom (as it first becomes manifest to us through the moral law) only as a *negative* property in us, namely that of not being *necessitated* to act through any sensible determining grounds. But we cannot present *theoretically* freedom as a *noumenon*, that is, freedom regarded as the ability^r of the human being merely as an intelligence, and show how it can *exercise constraint* upon his sensible choice; we cannot therefore present freedom as a positive property. But we can indeed see that, although experience shows that the human being as a *sensible being* is able to choose^s *in opposition to* as well as *in conformity with* the law, his freedom as an *intelligible being* cannot be *defined* ^t by this, since appearances cannot make any supersensible object (such as free choice) understandable. We can also see that freedom can never be located in a rational subject's being able to choose in opposition to his (lawgiving)

° *im Menschen*. LD: This replaces "in man" from the previous edition; similar replacements have been made throughout.
^p *das Vermögen der Wahl* $\quad$ ^q liberty of indifference $\quad$ ^r *Vermögen*
^s *ein Vermögen zeigt . . . zu wählen*
^t As Kant notes in the *Critique of Pure Reason* A 730/B 758, the German language has only one word, *Erklärung*, to express "exposition," "explication," "declaration," and "definition." Despite the strictures he places upon "definition," he adds that "we need not be so stringent in our requirements as altogether to refuse to philosophic expositions [*Erklärungen*] the honorable title, definition." At the conclusion of the present paragraph he gives *definitio hybrida* as equivalent to *Bastarderklärung*. See also his use of *Definition* and *Erklärung* (or *definieren* and *erklären* in, e.g., 6:248f., 260, and 286f. Both in the *Doctrine of Right* and in the *Doctrine of Virtue*, where Kant is discussing the *Erklärung* of the concept of virtue, I have used "define" and "definition," indicating the German word in notes.

reason, even though experience proves often enough that this happens (though we still cannot comprehend how this is possible). – For it is one thing to accept a proposition (on the basis of experience) and another thing to make it the *expository principle*[u] (of the concept of free choice) and the universal feature for distinguishing it (from *arbitrio bruto s. servo*);[v] for the first does not maintain that the feature belongs *necessarily* to the concept, but the second requires this. – Only freedom in relation to the internal lawgiving of reason is really an ability;[w] the possibility of deviating from it is an inability. How can the former be defined[x] by the latter? It would be a definition that added to the practical concept the *exercise* of it, as this is taught by experience, a *hybrid definition* (*definitio hybrida*) that puts the concept in a false light.

[6:227]

A (morally practical) *law* is a proposition that contains a categorical imperative (a command). One who commands (*imperans*) through a law is the lawgiver (*legislator*). He is the author (*autor*) of the obligation in accordance with the law, but not always the author of the law. In the latter case the law would be a positive (contingent) and chosen[y] law. A law that binds us *a priori* and unconditionally by our own reason can also be expressed as proceeding from the will of a supreme lawgiver, that is, one who has only rights and no duties (hence from the divine will); but this signifies only the idea of a moral being whose will is a law for everyone, without his being thought of as the author of the law.

Imputation (*imputatio*) in the moral sense[14] is the *judgment* by which someone is regarded as the author (*causa libera*)[z] of an action, which is then called a *deed* (*factum*) and stands under laws. If the judgment also carries with it the rightful consequences of this deed, it is an imputation having rightful force (*imputatio iudiciaria s. valida*);[a] otherwise it is merely an imputation *appraising* the deed (*imputatio diiudicatoria*)[b] – The (natural or moral) person that is authorized to impute with rightful force is called a *judge*[c] or a court (*iudex s. forum*).

If someone does *more in* the way of duty than he can be constrained[d] by law to do, what he does is *meritorious* (*meritum*); if what he does is just exactly what the law *requires*, he does *what is owed*[e] (*debitum*); finally, if what he does is *less* than the law requires, it is morally *culpable*[f] (*demeritum*). The *rightful* effect of what is culpable is *punishment* (*poena*); that of a meritorious deed is *reward* (*praemium*)

[6:228] (assuming that the reward, promised in the law, was the motive to it); conduct in

---

[u] *Erklärungsprincip*   [v] animal or enslaved power of choice   [w] *Vermögen*
[x] *aus ... erklärt werden*   [y] *willkürlich*   [z] free cause   [a] judiciary or valid imputation
[b] judging imputation   [c] *Richter*   [d] *gezwungen werden kann*   [e] *Schuldigkeit*
[f] *Verschuldung*
[14] Cf. Kant's discussion, in the *Doctrine of Virtue*, of conscience (6:400f.) and of one's duty to oneself as judge of oneself (6:437–40).

keeping with what is owed has no rightful effect at all. – Kindly *recompense*[g] (*remuneratio s. respensio benefica*) stands in no *rightful relation*[h] to a deed.

The good or bad results of an action that is owed, like the results of omitting a meritorious action, cannot be imputed to the subject (*modus imputationis tollens*).[i]

The good results of a meritorious action, like the bad results of a wrongful[j] action, can be imputed to the subject (*modus imputationis ponens*).[k]

Subjectively, the degree to which an action *can be imputed* (*imputabilitas*) has to be assessed by the magnitude of the obstacles that had to be overcome. – The greater the natural obstacles (of sensibility) and the less the moral obstacle (of duty), so much the more merit is to be accounted for a *good deed*, as when, for example, at considerable self-sacrifice I rescue a complete stranger from great distress.

On the other hand, the less the natural obstacles and the greater the obstacle from grounds of duty, so much the more is a transgression to be imputed (as culpable). – Hence the state of mind of the subject, whether he committed the deed in a state of agitation or with cool deliberation, makes a difference in imputation, which has results.

IV[l]

[6:218]

On the Division of a Metaphysics of Morals[*]

In all lawgiving (whether it prescribes internal or external actions, and whether it prescribes them *a priori* by reason alone or by the choice of another) there are two elements: **first**, a *law*, which represents an action that is to be done as *objectively* necessary, that is, which makes the action a duty; and **second**, an incentive, which connects a ground for determining choice to this action *subjectively* with the representation of the law. Hence the second element is this: that the law makes duty the incentive. By the first the action is represented as a duty, and this is a merely theoretical cognition of a possible determination of choice, that is, of practical rules. By the second the obligation so to act is connected in the subject with a ground for determining choice generally.

---

[*] A *deduction* of the division of a system, i.e., a proof that it is both complete and *continuous* – that is, that a transition from the concept divided to the members of the division takes place without a leap (*divisio per saltum*) in the entire series of subdivisions – is one of the most difficult conditions which the architect of a system has to fulfill. Even what the *highest divided concept* would be, the divisions of which are *right* and *wrong* (*aut fas aut nefas*), calls for reflection. This concept is the *act of free choice* in general. Teachers of ontology similarly begin with the concepts of *something* and *nothing*, without being aware that these are already members of a division for which the concept divided is missing. This concept can be only that of an *object* in general.

[g] *gütige Vergeltung*   [h] *Rechtsverhältniß*   [i] by way of taking away imputation
[j] *unrechtmäßigen*   [k] by way of adding imputation   [l] This section is numbered III in AA.

All lawgiving can therefore be distinguished with respect to the incentive (even if it agrees with another kind with respect to the action that it makes [6:219] a duty, e.g., these actions might in all cases be external). That lawgiving which makes an action a duty and also makes this duty the incentive is *ethical*. But that lawgiving which does not include the incentive of duty in the law and so admits an incentive other than the idea of duty itself is *juridical*. It is clear that in the latter case this incentive which is something other than the idea of duty must be drawn from *pathological* determining grounds of choice[m], inclinations and aversions, and among these, from aversions; for it is a lawgiving, which constrains, not an allurement, which invites.

The mere conformity or nonconformity of an action with law, irrespective of the incentive to it, is called its *legality* (lawfulness); but that conformity in which the idea of duty arising from the law is also the incentive to the action is called its *morality*.

Duties in accordance with rightful[n] lawgiving can be only external duties, since this lawgiving does not require that the idea of this duty, which is internal, itself be the determining ground of the agent's choice; and since it still needs an incentive suited to the law, it can connect only external incentives with it. On the other hand, ethical lawgiving, while it also makes internal actions duties, does not exclude external actions but applies to everything that is a duty in general. But just because ethical lawgiving includes within its law the internal incentive to action (the idea of duty), and this feature must not be present in external lawgiving, ethical lawgiving cannot be external (not even the external lawgiving of a divine will), although it does take up duties which rest on another, namely an external, lawgiving by making them, *as duties*, incentives in its lawgiving.

It can be seen from this that all duties, just because they are duties, belong to ethics; but it does not follow that the *lawgiving* for them is always contained in ethics: for many of them it is outside ethics. Thus ethics commands that I still fulfill a contract I have entered into, even though the other party could not coerce[o] me to do so; but it takes the law (*pacta sunt servanda*) and the duty corresponding to it from the doctrine of right, as [6:220] already given there. Accordingly the giving of the law that promises agreed

---

[m] *von den pathologischen Bestimmungsgründen der Willkür*. LD: *pathologisch* conveys dependence on sensibility.

[n] *rechtlichen*. The term *rechtlich* is introduced here as, apparently, synonymous with "juridical" [*juridisch*].

[o] *zwingen*. Kant uses *Zwang* (and *zwingen*) for both the constraint exercised upon one's choice by one's own will, through the thought of duty, and the constraint exercised by another's choice, through one's aversions. When *Zwang* (or *zwingen*) occurs in the context of right and without the modifier *äußere* (external), it is translated as "coercion" (or "to coerce"). *Äußere Zwang* is translated as "external constraint." If there is room for doubt regarding the context, the word is given in a note. See also 6:222 note z.

to must be kept lies not in ethics but in *Ius*. All that ethics teaches is that if the incentive which juridical lawgiving connects with that duty, namely external constraint, were absent, the idea of duty by itself would be sufficient as an incentive. For if this were not the case, and if the lawgiving itself were not juridical so that the duty arising from it was not really a duty of right (as distinguished from a duty of virtue), then faithful performance (in keeping with promises made in a contract) would be put in the same class with actions of benevolence and the obligation to them, and this must not happen. It is no duty of virtue to keep one's promises but a duty of right, to the performance of which one can be coerced. But it is still a virtuous action (a proof of virtue) to do it even where no coercion may be *applied*.^P The doctrine of right and the doctrine of virtue are therefore distinguished not so much by their different duties as by the difference in their lawgiving, which connects one incentive or the other with the law.

Ethical lawgiving (even if the duties might be external) is that which *can* not be external; juridical lawgiving is that which can also be external. So it is an external duty to keep a promise made in a contract; but the command to do this merely because it is a duty, without regard for any other incentive, belongs to *internal* lawgiving alone. So the obligation is assigned to ethics not because the duty is of a particular kind (a particular kind of action to which one is bound) – for there are external duties in ethics as well as in right – but rather because the lawgiving in this case is an internal one and can have no external lawgiver. For the same reason duties of benevolence, even though they are external duties (obligations to external actions), are still assigned to ethics because their lawgiving can be only internal. – Ethics has its special duties as well (e.g., duties to oneself), but it also has duties in common with right; what it does not have in common with right is only the kind of *obligation*. For what is distinctive about ethical lawgiving is that one is to perform actions just because they are duties and to make the principle of duty itself, wherever the duty comes from, the sufficient incentive for choice. So while there are many *directly ethical* duties, internal lawgiving makes the [6:221] rest of them, one and all, indirectly ethical.

---

^P *besorgt werden darf*

Introduction
to the Doctrine of Right

§A
What the Doctrine of Right Is

The sum of those laws for which an external lawgiving is possible is called the *doctrine of right* (*ius*). If there has actually been such lawgiving, it is the doctrine of *positive right*, and one versed in this, a jurist (*iurisconsultus*), is said to be *experienced in the law* (*iurisperitus*) when he not only knows external laws but also knows them externally, that is, in their application to cases that come up in experience. Such knowledge can also be called *legal expertise* (*iurisprudentia*), but without both together it remains mere *juridical science* (*iurisscientia*). The last title belongs to *systematic* knowledge of the doctrine of natural right (*ius naturae*), although one versed in this must supply the immutable principles for any giving of positive law.

§B
What Is Right?

Like the much-cited query "what is truth?" put to the logician, the question "what is right?" might well embarrass the *jurist* if he does not want to lapse into a tautology or, instead of giving a universal solution, refer to what the laws in some country at some time prescribe. He can indeed state what is laid down as right[a] (*quid sit iuris*), that is, what the laws in a certain place and at a certain time say or have said. But whether what these laws prescribed is also right, and what the universal criterion is by which one could recognize right as well as wrong [6:230] (*iustum et iniustum*),[b] this would remain hidden from him unless he leaves those empirical principles behind for a while and seeks the sources of such judgments in reason alone, so as to establish the basis for any possible giving of positive laws (although positive laws can serve as excellent guides to this). Like the wooden head in Phaedrus's fable, a merely empirical doctrine of right is a head that may be beautiful but unfortunately it has no brain.

---

[a] *Was Rechtens sei.* According to 23:262, what is laid down as right (*Rechtens, iuris est*) is what is right or wrong in accordance with positive laws.

[b] In 6:223f. Kant used *gerecht* and *ungerecht*, *iustum* and *iniustum*, for what is right or wrong in accordance with external laws, and *recht* and *unrecht* for what is right or wrong generally. Within the *Doctrine of Right* he uses simply *recht* and *unrecht*, although the context makes it clear that only external laws are under consideration. In the present passage the Academy Edition capitalizes the words, as *Recht* and *Unrecht*.

The concept of right, insofar as it is related to an obligation corresponding to it (i.e., the moral concept of right), has to do, *first*, only with the external and indeed practical relation of one person to another, insofar as their actions, as deeds,[c] can have (direct or indirect) influence on each other. But, *second*, it does not signify the relation of one's choice to the mere *wish* (hence also to the mere need) of the other, as in actions of beneficence or callousness, but only a relation to the other's *choice*. *Third*, in this reciprocal relation of choice no account at all is taken of the *matter* of choice, that is, of the end each has in mind with the object he wants; it is not asked, for example, whether someone who buys goods from me for his own commercial use will gain by the transaction or not. All that is in question is the *form* in the relation of choice on the part of both, insofar as choice is regarded merely as *free*, and whether the action of one can be united with the freedom of the other in accordance with a universal law.

Right is therefore the sum of the conditions under which the choice of one can be united with the choice of another in accordance with a universal law of freedom.

§C
The Universal Principle of Right[d]

"Any action is *right* if it can coexist with everyone's freedom in accordance with a universal law, or if on its maxim the freedom of choice of each can coexist with everyone's freedom in accordance with a universal law."

If then my action or my condition[e] generally can coexist with the freedom of everyone in accordance with a universal law, whoever hinders me in it does me wrong;[f] for this hindrance (resistance) cannot coexist with freedom in accordance with a universal law.   [6:231]

It also follows from this that it cannot be required that this principle of all maxims be itself in turn my maxim, that is, it cannot be required that *I make it the maxim* of my action; for anyone can be free so long as I do not impair his freedom by my *external action*, even though I am quite indifferent to his freedom or would like in my heart to infringe upon it. That I make it my maxim to act rightly is a demand that ethics makes on me.

---

[c] *als Facta*, perhaps "as facts." In 6:227 *factum* was given as the parenthetical equivalent of *That* or "deed." In some passages, it is unclear whether *That* is to be taken as "fact" or as "deed" or as both. See 6:231, note i.

[d] *Allgemeines Princip des Rechts*

[e] *Zustand.* Throughout the *Doctrine of Right*, *Zustand* is translated as "condition" except (1) where the familiar term "state of nature" is called for, and (2) where it seems to require the translation "status," in Kant's discussion of rights to persons akin to rights to things. In the *Doctrine of Virtue*, where there is no occasion for mistaking "state" for *Staat*, "state" and "condition" are used interchangeably. In the few texts in which "condition" in the sense of *Zustand* and of *Bedingung* might be confused, the German word is provided in a note.

[f] *thut der mir Unrecht*

Thus the universal law of right,[g] so act externally that the free use of your choice can coexist with the freedom of everyone in accordance with a universal law, is indeed a law that lays an obligation on me, but it does not at all expect, far less demand, that I *myself should* limit my freedom to those conditions[h] just for the sake of this obligation; instead, reason says only that freedom *is* limited to those conditions in conformity with the idea of it and that it may also be actively[i] limited by others; and it says this as a postulate that is incapable of further proof. – When one's aim is not to teach virtue but only to set forth what is *right*, one may not and should not represent that law of right as itself the incentive to action.

§D
Right Is Connected with an Authorization to Use Coercion

Resistance that counteracts the hindering of an effect promotes this effect and is consistent with it. Now whatever is wrong is a hindrance to freedom in accordance with universal laws. But coercion is a hindrance or resistance to freedom. Therefore, if a certain use of freedom is itself a hindrance to freedom in accordance with universal laws (i.e., wrong), coercion that is opposed to this (as a *hindering* of a *hindrance to freedom*) is consistent with freedom in accordance with universal laws, that is, it is right. Hence there is connected with right by the principle of contradiction an authorization to coerce someone who infringes upon it.

[6:232]

§E
A Strict Right Can Also Be Represented as the Possibility of a Fully Reciprocal Use of Coercion That Is Consistent with Everyone's Freedom in Accordance with Universal Laws

This proposition says, in effect, that right should not be conceived as made up of two elements, namely an obligation in accordance with a law and an authorization of him who by his choice puts another under obligation to coerce him to fulfill it. Instead, one can locate the concept of right directly in the possibility of connecting universal reciprocal coercion with the freedom of everyone. That is to say, just as right generally has as its object only what is external in actions, so strict right, namely that which is not mingled with anything ethical, requires only external grounds for determining choice; for only then is it pure and not mixed with any precepts of virtue. Only a completely external right can therefore be called *strict* (right in the narrow sense). This is indeed based on everyone's consciousness of obligation in

---

[g] *das allgemeine Rechtsgesetz*　　[h] *Bedingungen*　　[i] *thätlich*, perhaps "in fact"

28

accordance with a law; but if it is to remain pure, this consciousness may not and cannot be appealed to as an incentive to determine his choice in accordance with this law. Strict right rests instead on the principle of its being possible to use external constraint that can coexist with the freedom of everyone in accordance with universal laws. – Thus when it is said that a creditor has a right to require his debtor to pay his debt, this does not mean that he can remind the debtor that his reason itself puts him under obligation to perform this; it means, instead, that coercion which constrains everyone to pay his debts can coexist with the freedom of everyone, including that of debtors, in accordance with a universal external law. Right and authorization to use coercion therefore mean one and the same thing.

The law of a reciprocal coercion necessarily in accord with the freedom of everyone under the principle of universal freedom is, as it were, the *construction* of that concept, that is, the presentation of it in pure intuition *a priori*, by analogy with presenting the possibility of bodies moving freely under the law of the *equality of action* and *reaction*. In pure mathematics we [6:233] cannot derive the properties of its objects immediately from concepts but can discover them only by constructing concepts. Similarly, it is not so much the *concept* of right as rather a fully reciprocal and equal coercion brought under a universal law and consistent with it, that makes the presentation of that concept possible. Moreover, just as a purely formal concept of pure mathematics (e.g., of geometry) underlies this dynamical concept, reason has taken care to furnish the understanding as far as possible with *a priori* intuitions for constructing the concept of right. – A right line (*rectum*), one that is straight, is opposed to one that is *curved* on the one hand and to one that is *oblique* on the other hand. As opposed to one that is curved, straightness is that *inner property* of a line such that there is only *one* line between two given points. As opposed to one that is oblique, straightness is that *position* of a *line* towards another intersecting or touching it such that there can be only *one* line (the perpendicular) which does not incline more to one side than to the other and which divides the space on both sides equally. Analogously to this, the doctrine of right wants to be sure that *what belongs* to each[j] has been determined (with mathematical exactitude). Such exactitude cannot be expected in the *doctrine of virtue*, which cannot refuse some room for exceptions (*latitudinem*). – But without making incursions into the province of ethics, one finds two cases that lay claim to a decision about rights although no one can be found to decide them, and that belong as it were within the *intermundia* of Epicurus. – We must first separate these two cases from the doctrine of right proper, to which we are about to proceed, so that their

---

[j] *das Seine.* This term, which subsequently comes to the foreground, is often translated as "what is his," "an object that is his," "one's belongings," "what belongs to him." Similar expressions are used for *das Meine* and *das Deine.*

wavering principles will not affect the firm basic principles of the doctrine of right.

Appendix to the Introduction to the Doctrine of Right
On Ambiguous[k] Right (*Ius aequivocum*)

[6:234] An authorization to use coercion is connected with any right in the *narrow* sense (*ius strictum*). But people also think of a right in a *wider* sense (*ius latum*), in which there is no law by which an authorization to use coercion can be determined. – There are two such true or alleged rights, *equity* and the *right of necessity*. The first admits a right without coercion, the second, coercion without a right. It can easily be seen that this ambiguity really arises from the fact that there are cases in which a right is in question but for which no judge can be appointed to render a decision.

I
Equity (Aequitas)

Equity (considered objectively) is in no way a basis for merely calling upon another to fulfill an ethical duty (to be benevolent and kind). One who demands something on this basis stands instead upon his *right*, except that he does not have the conditions that a judge needs in order to determine by how much or in what way his claim could be satisfied.[15] Suppose that the terms on which a trading company was formed were that the partners should share equally in the profits, but that one partner nevertheless *did* more than the others and so *lost* more when the company met with reverses. *By equity* he can demand more from the company than merely an equal share with the others. In accordance with proper (strict) right, however, his demand would be refused; for if one thinks of a judge in this case, he would have no definite particulars (*data*) to enable him to decide how much is due by the contract. Or suppose that a domestic servant is paid his wages at the end of a year in money that has depreciated in the interval, so that he cannot buy with it what he could have bought with it when he concluded the contract. The servant cannot appeal to his right to be compensated when he gets the same amount of money but it is of unequal value. He can appeal only on grounds of equity (a mute divinity who cannot be heard); for nothing was specified about this in the contract, and a judge cannot pronounce in accordance with indefinite conditions.

It also follows from this that a *court of equity* (in a conflict with others about their rights) involves a contradiction. Only where the judge's own rights are

---

[k] or "equivocal", *zweideutigen*
[15] Cf. 6:296–300

concerned, and he can dispose of the case for his own person, may and should he   [6:235]
listen to equity, as, for example, when the crown itself bears the damages that
others have incurred in its service and for which they petition it to indemnify
them, even though it could reject their claim by strict right on the pretext that
they undertook this service at their own risk.

The *motto* (*dictum*) of *equity* is, "the strictest right is the greatest wrong"
(*summum ius summa iniuria*). But this ill cannot be remedied by way of what is
laid down as right, even though it concerns a claim to a right; for this claim
belongs only to the *court of conscience* (*forum poli*) whereas every question of what
is laid down as right must be brought before *civil right* (*forum soli*).[1]

II
The Right of Necessity[m][16] *(Ius necessitatis)*

This alleged right is supposed to be an authorization to take the life of another
who is doing nothing to harm me, when I am in danger of losing my own life. It is
evident that were there such a right the doctrine of right would have to be in
contradiction with itself. For the issue here is not that of a *wrongful*[n] assailant
upon my life whom I forestall by depriving him of his life (*ius inculpatae tutelae*),[o]
in which case a recommendation[p] to show moderation (*moderamen*) belongs not
to right but only to ethics. It is instead a matter of violence being permitted
against someone who has used no violence against me.

It is clear that this assertion is not to be understood objectively, in terms of
what a law prescribes, but only subjectively, as the verdict[q] that would be given
by a court. In other words, there can be no *penal law* that would assign the death
penalty to someone in a shipwreck who, in order to save his own life, shoves
another, whose life is equally in danger, off a plank on which he had saved
himself. For the punishment threatened by the law could not be greater than the
loss of his own life. A penal law of this sort could not have the effect intended,
since a threat of an ill that is still *uncertain* (death by a judicial verdict) cannot
outweigh the fear of an ill that is *certain* (drowning). Hence the deed of saving
one's life by violence is not to be judged *inculpable* (*inculpabile*) but only   [6:236]
unpunishable (*impunibile*), and by a strange confusion jurists take this *subjective*
impunity to be *objective* impunity (conformity with law).

---

[1] court of heaven ... court of earth (LD: translations added to this edition; cf. Ladd.)
[m] *Das Nothrecht*   [n] *ungerechten*   [o] right to blameless (self-)defense
[p] *Anempfehlung*
[q] *die Sentenz*, perhaps "the sentence." Throughout *The Metaphysics of Morals*, Kant seems to draw
     no clear or consistent distinction between a "sentence" and a "verdict" or "decision" of a court.
     LD: Gregor uses "verdict" to translate several German words (including *Ausspruch, Spruch,
     Rechtsspruch, Sentenz*, and *Urtheil*), and does not reserve it for reference to the decision of a jury.
[16] For further discussion of "the right of necessity," see "Theory and Practice," 8:300n.

The motto of the right of necessity says: "Necessity[r] has no law" (*necessitas non habet legem*). Yet there could be no necessity that would make what is wrong conform with law.

One sees that in both appraisals of what is right (in terms of a right of equity and a right of necessity) the *ambiguity* (*aequivocatio*) arises from confusing the objective with the subjective basis of exercising the right (before reason and before a court). What someone by himself recognizes on good grounds as right will not be confirmed by a court, and what he must judge to be of itself wrong is treated with indulgence by a court; for the concept of right, in these two cases, is not taken in the same sense.

Division of the Doctrine of Right

A
General Divison of Duties of Right

One can follow Ulpian[17] in making this division if a sense is ascribed to his formulae which he may not have thought distinctly in them but which can be explicated[s] from them or put into them. They are the following:

1) *Be an honorable human being* (*honeste vive*). *Rightful honor*[t] (*honestas iuridica*) consists in asserting one's worth as a human being in relation to others, a duty expressed by the saying, "Do not make youself a mere means for others but be at the same time an end for them." This duty will be explained later as obligation from the *right* of humanity in our own person (*Lex iusti*).[18]

2) *Do not wrong anyone* (*neminem laede*) even if, to avoid doing so, you should have to stop associating with others and shun all society (*Lex iuridica*).

---

[r] *Noth*

[s] *entwickeln.* In the context of organisms generally, and more specifically with reference to the human being's talents and capacities, *entwickeln* is translated as "to develop." However, in the context of analytic and synthetic propositions, see the Jäsche *Logik* (9:111, *Anmerkung* 1), where it is said that in an implicitly identical proposition (as distinguished from a tautology), a predicate that lies *unentwickelt* (*implicite*) in the concept of the subject is made clear by means of *Entwickelung* (*explicatio*). (LD: This note was imported from the Cambridge Edition of the *Groundwork*; Gregor's first edition refers to the text.)

[t] *Sei ein rechtlicher Mensch ... Die rechtliche Ehrbarkeit*

[17] LD: Roman jurist Domitius Ulpianus (d. 228)

[18] On the basis of the concluding sentence of §A and the diagram on 6:240, one would expect this explanation within the *Doctrine of Virtue*'s discussion of perfect duties to oneself. No such explanation is provided, although the virtue contrary to at least some of the vices discussed there is called, in 6:420, *Ehrliebe* (*honestas interna, iustum sui aestimium*). See also the use of *Ehrlichkeit* with regard to lying, 6:429. What all these terms have in common is the practical affirmation of one's dignity as a person. Their source may well be the Stoic *honestum*. There are occasional references to "the *right* of humanity in one's own person" in AA 23, e.g., 276, 390; see also 27:593, 603f. Within the *Doctrine of Right*, however, "the right of humanity" seems to be a limiting condition on the rights of others.

3) If you cannot help associating with others) *enter* into a society with them in which each can keep what is his (*suum cuique tribue*). – If this last formula were translated "Give to each what is *his*," what it says would be absurd, since one cannot give anyone something he already has. In order to make sense it would have to read: "*Enter* a condition in which what belongs to each can be secured to him against everyone else" (*Lex iustitiae*). [6:237]

So the above three classical formulae serve also as principles for dividing the system of duties of right into *internal* duties, *external* duties, and duties that involve the derivation of the latter from the principle of the former by subsumption.

B
General Division of Rights

1) As systematic *doctrines*, rights are divided into *natural right*, which rests only on *a priori* principles, and *positive* (statutory) *right*,[u] which proceeds from the will of a legislator.

2) The highest division of rights, as (moral) *capacities*[v] for putting others under obligations[w] (i.e., as a lawful basis, *titulum*, for doing so), is the division into *innate* and *acquired* right. An innate right is that which belongs to everyone by nature, independently of any act that would establish a right;[x] an acquired right is that for which such an act is required.

---

[u] emphasis added to "right"   [v] *Vermögen*[19]   [w] *zu verpflichten*

[x] *von allem rechtlichen Act.* In 23:262, Kant defines a rightful action (*eine rechtliche Handlung, actus iuridicus*) as "someone's action from which a right of his arises." This involves complications. Strictly speaking, an *Act*, translated as "act," is not the same as an "action," *Handlung*, although actions are necessary but not sufficient conditions for acquiring rights; and a rightful act can also be one by which someone gives up a right (6:300). In any case, this translation is too narrow to cover all the contexts in which Kant uses *rechtliche Act*. In the following paragraph, it seems to mean, more generally, an act affecting rights. On the translation of *rechtlich*, see Translator's Note on the Text.

[19] A right, as a *Vermögen*, might be called a "faculty" in an unusual sense. Kant's predecessors in the natural right tradition, most notably Hugo Grotius, had conceptually distinguished but sometimes verbally conflated *potestas* and *facultas*. A moral power is one's title to do what is not unjust. In accordance with the law of nature, every human being has his original *suum*, which includes his life, limbs, and liberty. Since it is right for him to use and to consume what he needs, and wrong for anyone to interfere with him, he has moral power to use force in defense of what is originally his. But a right in the derivative sense of a moral faculty involves an extension of one's *suum* and has to be acquired. Because all human beings are equal with respect to the original *suum*, it is necessary that others transfer to him, by express or at least tacit consent, a part of what is theirs, i.e., control over their actions and, indirectly, over things (*De Iure Belli ac Pacis Libri Tres* I.1.x.7 and I.11.i.5). In view of Kant's distinction between Grotius's historical "primitive community" and his own rational "*original* community" (6:251, 258), he may be rejecting Grotius's distinction between *potestas* and *facultas* in favor of his own distinction between innate and acquired rights. However, the relation is too tenuous to warrant translating *Vermögen* in the sense of a right as "faculty." On Kant's distinction between authorization to do something (*facultas moralis generatim*) and authorization to use coercion (*facultas iuridica*), see 6:383.

What is innately mine or yours can also be called what is *internally* mine or yours (*meum vel tuum internum*); for what is externally mine or yours must always be acquired.

There is Only One Innate Right

Freedom (independence from being constrained by another's choice), insofar as it can coexist with the freedom of every other in accordance with a universal law, is the only original right belonging to every human being by virtue of his humanity. – This principle of innate freedom already involves the following authorizations, which are not really distinct from it (as if they were members of the division of some higher concept of a right): innate *equality*, that is, independence from being bound by others to more than one can in turn bind [6:238] them; hence a human being's quality of being *his own master* (*sui iuris*), as well as being a human being *beyond reproach* (*iusti*), since before he performs any act affecting rights[y] he has done no wrong to anyone; and finally, his being authorized to do to others anything that does not in itself diminish what is theirs, so long as they do not want to accept it – such things as merely communicating his thoughts to them, telling or promising them something, whether what he says is true and sincere or untrue and insincere (*veriloquium aut falsiloquium*); for it is entirely up to them whether they want to believe him or not.[*]

The aim in introducing such a division within the system of natural right (insofar as it is concerned with innate right) is that when a dispute arises about an acquired right and the question comes up, on whom does the burden of proof (*onus probandi*) fall, either about a controversial fact or, if this is settled, about a controversial right, someone who refuses to accept this obligation can appeal methodically to his innate right to freedom (which is now specified in its various relations), as if he were appealing to various bases for rights.

---

[*] Telling an untruth intentionally, even though merely frivolously, is usually called a *lie* (*mendacium*) because it can also harm someone, at least to the extent that if he ingenuously repeats it others ridicule him as gullible. The only kind of untruth we want to call a lie, in the sense bearing upon rights [*Im rechtlichen Sinne*], is one that directly infringes upon another's right, e.g., the false allegation that a contract has been concluded with someone, made in order to deprive him of what is his (*falsiloquium dolosum*).[z] And this distinction between closely related concepts is not without basis; for when someone merely says what he thinks, another always remains free to take it as he pleases. But a rumor, having some basis, that this is a human being whose talk cannot be believed comes so close to the reproach of calling him a liar that the borderline separating what belongs to *Ius* from what must be assigned to ethics can only be drawn in just this way.

[y] *rechtlichen Act*   [z] deceitful falsehood

With regard to what is innately, hence internally, mine or yours, there are not several *rights*; there is only *one* right. Since this highest division consists of two members very unequal in content, it can be put in the prolegomena and the division of the doctrine of right can refer only to what is externally mine or yours.

Division of the Metaphysics of Morals as a Whole   [6:239]
I

All duties are either *duties of right* (*officia iuris*), that is, duties for which external lawgiving is possible, or *duties of virtue* (*officia virtutis s. ethica*),[a] for which external lawgiving is not possible. – Duties of virtue cannot be subject to external lawgiving simply because they have to do with an *end* which (or the having of which) is also a duty. No external lawgiving can bring about someone's setting an end for himself (because this is an internal act of the mind), although it may prescribe external actions that lead to an end without the subject making it his end.

But why is the doctrine of morals usually called (especially by Cicero) a doctrine of *duties* and not also a doctrine of *rights*, even though rights have reference to duties? – The reason is that we know our own freedom (from which all moral laws, and so all rights as well as duties proceed) only through the *moral imperative*, which is a proposition commanding duty, from which the capacity for putting others under obligation,[b] that is, the concept of a right, can afterwards be explicated.[c]

II

In the doctrine of duties a human being can and should be represented in terms of his capacity for freedom, which is wholly supersensible, and so too merely in terms of his *humanity*, his personality independent of physical attributes (*homo noumenon*), as distinguished from the same subject represented as affected by physical attributes, a *human being* (*homo phaenomenon*). Accordingly right and end, related in turn to duty in this twofold property, yield the following division:

---

[a] duties of virtue or ethics   [b] *Vermögen, andere zu verpflichten*   [c] *entwickelt*

DIVISION
in Accordance with the Objective Relation of Law to Duty

Perfect Duty

	Perfect Duty		
Duty to Oneself	1. The right of humanity in our own person 3. The end of humanity in our own person	(of right) Duty (of virtue)	2. The right of human beings 4. The end of human beings	Duty to Others

Imperfect Duty

[6:241] *III*

The subjects between whom a relation of right to duty can be thought of (whether admissibly or not) stand related to each other in different ways, and so a division can also be made from this point of view.

DIVISION
in Accordance with the Relation of the Subject Imposing Obligation to the
Subject Put Under Obligation

1. The relation in terms of rights of human beings toward beings that have neither rights nor duties.	2. The relation in terms of rights of human beings toward beings that have rights as well as duties.
Vacat[d] For these are beings lacking reason, which can neither bind us nor by which we can be bound.	*Adest* For this is a relation of human beings to human beings.
3. The relation in terms of rights of human beings toward beings that have only duties but no rights.	4. The relation in terms of rights of human beings toward a being that has only rights but no duties (God).

---

[d] *Vacat* might be rendered "has no members," *Adest* "has members".

<table>
<tr><td>*Vacat*</td><td>*Vacat*</td></tr>
</table>

Vacat	*Vacat*
For these would be human beings without personality (serfs, slaves).	At least in philosophy, since such a being is not an object of possible experience.

So only in Number 2 is there found a *real* relation between right and duty. The reason that it is not to be found in Number 4 is that this would be a *transcendent* duty, that is, a duty for which no corresponding external subject imposing the obligation can *be given*, so that the relation here is only *ideal* from a theoretical point of view, that is, a relation to a thought-entity.[c] We ourselves *make* the concept of this being, but this concept is not altogether *empty*; instead it is fruitful in reference to ourselves and to maxims of internal morality, and so for an internal practical purpose, inasmuch as our entire *immanent* duty (that which can be fulfilled) lies only in this relation that can merely be thought of. [6:242]

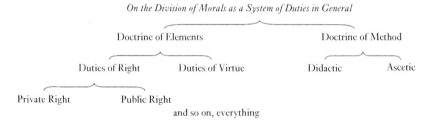

On the Division of Morals as a System of Duties in General

that involves not only the contents of a scientific doctrine of morals but also its architectonic form, once its metaphysical first principles have traced out completely the universal principles for it.

* * *

The highest division of natural right cannot be the division (sometimes made) into *natural* and *social* right; it must instead be the division into natural and *civil* right, the former of which is called *private right* and the latter *public right*. For a *state of nature* is not opposed to a social but to a civil condition, since there can certainly be society in a state of nature, but not *civil* society (which secures what is mine or yours by public laws). This is why right in a state of nature is called private right.

[c] *einem Gedankendinge*

37

The Doctrine of Right

Part I
PRIVATE RIGHT

The Universal Doctrine of Right
Part I
PRIVATE RIGHT
Concerning What is Externally Mine or Yours[a] in General

Chapter I

How to *Have*[b] Something External as One's Own

§1

That is *rightfully mine* (*meum iuris*) with which I am so connected that another's use of it without my consent would wrong me. The subjective condition of any possible use is *possession*.

But something *external* would be mine only if I may assume that I could be wronged by another's use of a thing *even though I am not in possession of it.* – So it would be self-contradictory to say that I have something external as my own if the concept of possession could not have different meanings, namely *sensible* possession and *intelligible* possession, and by the former could be understood *physical* possession but by the latter a *merely rightful* possession of the same object.

But the expression "an object is *external to me*" can mean either that it is an object merely *distinct* from me (the subject) or else that it is also to be found in *another location* (*positus*) in space or time. Only if it is taken in the first sense can possession be thought of as rational possession; if taken in the second sense it would have to be called empirical possession. – *Intelligible* possession (if this is [6:246] possible) is possession of an object *without holding it* (*detentio*).

§3[c]

Whoever wants to assert that he has a thing as his own must be in possession of an object, since otherwise he could not be wronged[d] by another's use of it without his consent. For if something outside this object which is not connected with it by rights affects it, it would not be able to affect himself (the subject) and do him any wrong.

---

[a] In the translation of the phrase *Mein und Dein (meum et tuum)*, "and" has been changed to "or."
[b] emphasis added, to match 6:210
[c] §2 is omitted here but replaces a portion of the text of §6. See Translator's Note on the Text.
[d] *lädirt.* In 6:249 Kant gives *Abbruch an meiner Freiheit* . . . as a parenthetical explanation of *Läsion.*

§4
Exposition of the Concept of External Objects That Are Yours or Mine

There can be only *three* external objects of my choice: 1) a (corporeal) *thing* external to me; 2) another's *choice* to perform a specific deed (*praestatio*); 3) another's *status*^e in relation to me. These are objects of my choice in terms of the categories of *substance, causality,* and *community* between myself and external objects in accordance with laws of freedom.

a) I cannot call an object in *space* (a corporeal thing) mine unless, *even though I am not in physical possession of it*, I can still assert that I am actually in some other (hence not physical) possession of it. – So I shall not call an apple mine because I have it in my hand (possess it physically), but only if I can say that I possess it even though I have put it down, no matter where. In the same way, I shall not be able to say that the land on which I have lain down is mine because I am on it, but only if I can assert that it still remains in my possession even though I have left the place. For [6:248] someone who tried in the first case (of empirical possession) to wrest the apple from my hand or to drag me away from my resting place would indeed wrong me with regard to what is *internally* mine (freedom); but he would not wrong me with regard to what is externally mine unless I could assert that I am in possession of the object even without holding it. I could not then call these objects (the apple and the resting place) mine.

b) I cannot call the *performance* of something by another's choice mine if all I can say is that it came into my possession *at the same time* that he promised it (*pactum re initum*),^f but only if I can assert that I am in possession of the other's choice (to determine him to perform it) even though the time for his performing it is still to come. The other's promise is therefore included in my belongings and goods (*obligatio activa*), and I can count it as mine not merely if (as in the first case) I already have *what was promised* in my possession, but even though I do not possess it yet. So I must be able to think that I am in possession of this object independently of being limited by temporal conditions, and so independently of empirical possession.

---

^e *Zustand*
^f having undertaken a compact regarding a thing. LD: Ladd has, "a pact begun through the thing pacted"; B. Sharon Byrd and Joachim Hruschka, "a contract closed with regard to an object [of choice]" (*Kant's Doctrine of Right: A Commentary* [Cambridge University Press, 2010], 233 n.6).

c) I cannot call a *wife*, a *child*, a *servant*, or, in general, another person mine because I am now in charge of them as members of my household or have them within my restraining walls and in my control and possession, but only if, although they have withdrawn from such constraint and I do not possess them (empirically), I can still say that I possess them merely by my will, hence *merely rightfully*, as long as they exist somewhere or at some time. Only if and insofar as I can assert this are they included in my belongings.

§5
Definition of the Concept of External Objects That Are Mine or Yours

The *nominal definition*[g] of what is externally mine – that which suffices only to *distinguish* the object from all others and arises from a complete and determinate *exposition* of the concept – would be: that outside me is externally mine which it would be a wrong[h] (an infringement upon my   [6:249] freedom which can coexist with the freedom of everyone in accordance with a universal law) to prevent me from using as I please. – But the *real definition*[i] of this concept – that which also suffices for the *deduction* of it (cognition of the possibility of the object) – goes like this: something external is mine if I would be wronged by being disturbed in my use of it *even though I am not in possession of it* (not holding the object). – I must be in some sort of possession of an external object if it is to be called *mine*, for otherwise someone who affected this object against my will would not also affect me and so would not wrong me. So, in consequence of §4, *intelligible possession* (*possessio noumenon*) must be assumed to be possible if something external is to be mine or yours. Empirical possession (holding) is then only possession in *appearance* (*possessio phaenomenon*), although the *object* itself that I possess is not here treated, as it was in the Transcendental Analytic[20], as an appearance but as a thing in itself; for there reason was concerned with theoretical cognition of the nature of things and how far it could extend, but here it is concerned with the practical determination of choice in accordance with laws of *freedom*, whether the object can be cognized through the senses or through the pure understanding alone, and *right* is a pure practical *rational concept* of choice under laws of freedom.

For the same reason, it is not appropriate to speak of possessing a right to this or that object but rather of possessing it *merely rightfully*; for a right is already an

[g] *Namenerklärung*   [h] *Läsion*   [i] *Sacherklärung*
[20] LD: of the *Critique of Pure Reason*

intellectual possession of an object and it would make no sense to speak of possessing a possession.

§6
Deduction of the Concept of Merely Rightful Possession of an External Object (*possessio noumenon*)

The question: how is it possible for *something external to be mine or yours?* resolves itself into the question: how is *merely rightful* (intelligible) *possession* possible? and this, in turn, into the third question: how is a *synthetic a priori* proposition about right possible?

All propositions about right[j] are *a priori* propositions, since they are laws of reason (*dictamina rationis*). An *a priori* proposition about right with regard to [6:250] *empirical possession* is *analytic*, for it says nothing more than what follows from empirical possession in accordance with the principle of contradiction, namely, that if I am holding a thing (and so physically connected with it), someone who affects it without my consent (e.g., snatches an apple from my hand) affects and diminishes what is internally mine (my freedom), so that his maxim is in direct contradiction with the axiom of right.[21] So the proposition about empirical possession in conformity with rights does not go beyond the right of a person with regard to himself.

On the other hand, a proposition about the possibility of possessing a thing *external to myself*, which puts aside any conditions of empirical possession in space and time (and hence presupposes the possibility of *possessio noumenon*), goes beyond those limiting conditions; and since it affirms possession of something even without holding it, as necessary for the concept of something external that is mine or yours, it is *synthetic*. Reason has then the task of showing how such a proposition, which goes beyond the concept of empirical possession, is possible *a priori*.[22]

---

[j] *Rechtssätze*

[21] In his essay "On a Supposed Right to Lie from Philanthropy," Kant says that a metaphysics of right requires "1) an axiom, that is, an apodictically certain proposition that issues immediately from the definition of external right (consistency of the freedom of each with the freedom of everyone in accordance with a universal law..." (8:349). He goes on to add that it requires "2) a postulate (of external public law)...".

[22] It is generally agreed that the five paragraphs in note k, which were originally printed here and appear here in the Academy Edition, do not belong here. On the history of this discovery, see Thomas Mautner, "Kant's Metaphysics of Morals: A Note on the Text," *Kant-Studien*, 72 (1981): 396–9. For further discussion of the state of the text, see Translator's Note on the Text. According to Ludwig's reconstruction of the text, §2 should be inserted in place of these five paragraphs, as has been done in this edition.

Postulate of Practical Reason with Regard to Rights[kl]   [6:246]

It is possible for me to have any external object of my choice as mine, that is, a maxim by which, if it were to become a law, an object of choice would *in itself* (objectively) have to *belong to no one* (*res nullius*) is contrary to rights.[m]

For an object of my choice is something that I have the *physical* power to use. If it were nevertheless absolutely not within my *rightful* power to make use of it, that is, if the use of it could not coexist with the freedom of everyone in accordance with

---

[k] The next three paragraphs in the body of text, originally numbered §2, and appearing as §2 in the Academy Edition, replace the following five-paragraph passage, which appears in the Academy Edition on 250f. in §6:

In this way, for example, taking possession of a separate piece of land is an act of private choice, without being *unsanctioned*.[a] The possessor bases his act on an innate *possession in common*[b] of the surface of the earth and on a general will corresponding *a priori* to it, which permits *private possession* on it (otherwise, unoccupied things would in themselves and in accordance with a law be made things that belong to no one). By being the first to take possession he originally acquires a definite piece of land[c] and resists with right (*iure*) anyone else who would prevent him from making private use of it. Yet since he is in a state of nature, he cannot do so by legal proceedings[d] (*de iure*) because there does not exist any public law in this state.

Even if a piece of land were considered or declared to be *free*, that is, open to anyone's use, one could still not say that it is free by nature or *originally* free, prior to any act establishing a right; for that would again be a relation to things, namely to the land, which would refuse possession of itself to anyone; instead one would say that this land is free because of a prohibition on everyone to make use of it, and for this, possession of it in common is required, which cannot take place without a contract. But land that can be free only in this way must really be in the possession of all those (joined together) who forbid or suspend one another's use of it.

[6:251] This *original* community of land, and with it of things upon it (*communio fundi originaria*), is an idea that has objective (rightfully practical) reality. This kind of community must be sharply distinguished from a *primitive community* (*communio primaeva*), which is a fiction;[23] for a primitive community would have to be one that was *instituted* and arose from a contract by which everyone gave up private possessions and, by uniting his possessions with those of everyone else, transformed them into a collective possession;[e] and history would have to give us proof of such a contract. But it is contradictory to claim that such a procedure is an *original* taking possession and that each human being could and should have based his separate possession upon it.

Residing[f] on land (*sedes*) is to be distinguished from being in possession (*possessio*) of it, and *settling* or making a settlement[g] (*incolatus*), which is a lasting private possession of a place dependent upon the presence of the subject on it, is to be distinguished from taking possession of land with the intention of some day acquiring it. I am not talking here about settling as a second act to establish a right, which can either follow upon taking possession or not take place at all; for settling of this kind would not be original possession but would be possession derived from others' consent.

Merely physical possession of land (holding it) is already a right to a thing, though certainly not of itself sufficient for regarding it as mine. Relative to others, since (as far as one knows) it is first possession, it is consistent with the principle of outer freedom and is also involved in original *possession in common*, which provides *a priori* the basis on which any private possession is possible. Accordingly, to interfere with the use of a piece of land by the first occupant of it is to wrong him. Taking first possession has therefore a rightful basis (*titulus possessionis*), which is original possession in common; and the saying "Happy are those who are in possession" (*beati possidentes*), because none is bound to certify his possession, is a basic principle of natural right, which lays down taking first possession as a rightful basis for acquisition on which every first possessor can rely.

[23] Although Kant does not mention Hugo Grotius by name, he is presumably thinking here, as in 6:258, of Grotius's theory (adopted by others in the natural right tradition) of how people moved from a primitive common possession of goods, in which each could rightly use what he needed, to the institution of private property. See *De Iure Belli ac Pacis Libri Tres* ii.1–2.

a universal law (would be wrong), then freedom would be depriving itself of the use of its choice with regard to an object of choice, by putting *usable* objects beyond any possibility of being *used*; in other words, it would annihilate them in a practical respect and make them into *res nullius*, even if in the use of things choice were formally consistent with everyone's outer freedom in accordance with universal laws.[n] – But since pure practical reason lays down only formal laws as the basis for using choice and thus abstracts from its matter, that is, from other properties of the object *provided only that it is an object of choice*, it can contain no absolute prohibition against using such an object, since this would be a contradiction of outer freedom with itself. – But an object of my *choice* is that which I have the physical capacity[o] to use as I please, that whose use lies within my power[p] (*potentia*). This must be distinguished from having the same object under my control[q] (*in potestatem meam redactum*), which presupposes not merely a *capacity* but also an *act* of choice. But in order to *think of* something simply as an object of my choice it is sufficient for me to be conscious of having it within my power. – It is therefore an *a priori* presupposition of practical reason to regard and treat any object of my choice as something which could objectively be mine or yours.

[6:247]   This postulate can be called a permissive law (*lex permissiva*) of practical reason, which gives us an authorization that could not be got from mere concepts of right as such, namely to put all others under an obligation, which they would not otherwise have, to refrain from using certain objects of our choice because we have been the first to take them into our possession. Reason wills that this hold as a principle, and it does this as *practical* reason, which extends itself *a priori* by this postulate of reason.

[6:251]   In an *a priori theoretical* principle, namely, an *a priori* intuition would have to
[6:252]   underlie the given concept (as was established in the *Critique of Pure Reason*); and so something would have to be *added to* the concept of possession of an object. But with this practical principle the opposite procedure is followed and all conditions of intuition which establish empirical possession must be *removed* (disregarded), in order to *extend* the concept of possession beyond empirical possession and to be able to say: it is possible for any external object of my choice

<hr>

[a] *ohne doch eigenmächtig zu sein*   [b] *Gemeinbesitze*   [c] *bestimmten Boden*
[d] *von rechtswegen*   [e] *Gesammtbesitz*   [f] *Sitz*   [g] *Niederlassung, Ansiedelung*
[l] *Rechtliches Postulat.* On the translation of *rechtlich*, see Translator's Note on the Text.
[m] *rechtswidrig.* On the translation of *rechtswidrig* and its opposite, *rechtmäßig*, see Translator's Note on the Text.
[n] *obgleich die Willkür formaliter ... zusammenstimmte.* LD: I have followed Byrd in replacing Gregor's "even though ... choice was formally consistent..." with the subjunctive "even if ... choice were formally consistent ...". See "Intelligible Possession of Objects of Choice," in Lara Denis (ed.) *Kant's Metaphysics of Morals: A Critical Guide* (Cambridge University Press, 2010), 93–110, 99f.
[o] *Vermögen*   [p] *in meiner Macht*   [q] *in meiner Gewalt*

to be reckoned as rightfully mine if I have control of it (and only in so far as I have control of it) without being in possession of it.

The possibility of this kind of possession, and so the deduction of the concept of nonempirical possession, is based on the postulate of practical reason with regard to rights: "that it is a duty of right to act towards others so that what is external (usable) could also become someone's," together with the exposition of the concept of an external object that belongs to someone, since that concept rests simply on that of *nonphysical* possession. There is, however, no way of proving of itself the possibility of nonphysical possession or of having any insight into it (just because it is a rational concept for which no corresponding intuition can be given); its possibility is instead an immediate consequence of the postulate referred to. For if it is necessary to act in accordance with that principle of right, its intelligible condition (a merely rightful possession) must then also be possible. – No one need be surprised that *theoretical* principles about external objects that are mine or yours get lost in the intelligible and represent no extension of cognition, since no theoretical deduction can be given for the possibility of the concept of freedom on which they are based. It can only be inferred from the practical law of reason (the categorical imperative) as a fact of reason.[24]

§7
Application to Objects of Experience of the Principle That It Is Possible for Something External to Be Mine or Yours

The concept of merely rightful possession is not an empirical concept (dependent upon conditions of space and time) and yet it has practical reality, that is, it must be applicable to objects of experience, cognition of which is dependent upon those conditions. – The way to proceed with the concept of a right with respect to such objects, so that they can be external objects which are mine or yours, is the following. Since the concept of a right is simply a rational concept, it cannot be applied *directly* to objects of experience and to the concept of empirical *possession*, but must first be applied to the understanding's pure concept of *possession* in general. So the concept to which the concept of a right is directly applied is not that of *holding* (*detentio*), which is an empirical way of thinking of possession, but rather the concept of *having*,[25] in which abstraction is made from all spatial and temporal conditions and the object is thought of only as *under my control* (*in potestate mea positum esse*). So too the expression *external* does not mean existing in a *place other* than where I am, or that my decision and acceptance are occurring at a different time from the making of the offer; it means only an object *distinct* from me. Now, practical reason requires me, by its law of right, to apply mine or yours

[6:253]

---

[24] LD: See the *Critique of Practical Reason*, 5:31
[25] In 23:325, Kant points out that in the critical philosophy "having" (*habere*) is a predicable, or derivative concept, of the category of causality.

to objects not in accordance with sensible conditions but in abstraction from them, since it has to do with a determination of choice in accordance with laws of freedom, and it also requires me to think of possession of them in this way, since only a *concept of the understanding* can be subsumed under concepts of right. I shall therefore say that I possess a field even though it is in a place quite different from where I actually am. For we are speaking here only of an intellectual relation to an object, insofar as I have it *under my control* (the understanding's concept of possession independent of spatial determinations), and the object is *mine* because my will to use it as I please does not conflict with the law of outer freedom. Here practical reason requires us to think of possession *apart from* possession of this object of my choice in appearance (holding it), to think of it not in terms of empirical concepts but of concepts of the understanding, those that can contain *a priori* conditions of empirical concepts. Upon this is based the validity of such a concept of possession (*possessio noumenon*), as a *giving of law* that holds for everyone; for such lawgiving is involved in the expression "this external object is *mine*," since by it an obligation is laid upon all others, which they would not otherwise have, to refrain from using the object.

[6:254]   So the way to have something external as what is mine consists in a merely rightful connection of the subject's will with that object in accordance with the concept of intelligible possession, independently of any relation to it in space and time. – It is not because I occupy a place on the earth with my body that this place is something external which is mine (for that concerns only my outer *freedom*, hence only possession of myself, not a thing external to me, so that it is only an internal right). It is mine if I still possess it even though I have left it for another place; only then is my external right involved. And anyone who wants to make my continuous occupation of this place by my person the condition of my having it as mine must either assert that it is not at all possible to have something external as mine (and this conflicts with the postulate §2[r]) or else require that in order to have it as mine I be in two places at once. Since this amounts to saying that I am to be in a place and also not be in it, he contradicts himself.

This can also be applied to the case of my having accepted a promise. For my having and possession in what was promised is not annulled by the promisor's saying at one time "this thing is to be yours" and then at a later time saying of the same thing "I now will that it not be yours." For in such intellectual relations it is as if the promisor had said, without any time between the two declarations of his will, "this is to be yours" and also "this is not to be yours," which is self-contradictory.

The same holds of the concept of rightful possession of a person, as included in the subject's belongings (his wife, child, servant). This domestic community and the possession of their respective status vis-à-vis one another by all its members is not annulled by their being authorized to separate from one another and go to

[r] LD: In this edition, the postulate presented as §2 originally (and in AA) has been placed within §6.

48

different *places*; for what connects them is a relation *in terms of rights*, and what is externally mine or yours here is based, as in the preceding cases, entirely on the assumption that purely rational possession without holding each other is possible.

Rightfully practical reason is forced into a critique of itself in the concept of something external which is mine or yours, and this by an antinomy of propositions concerning the possibility of such a concept; that is, only by an unavoidable dialectic in which both thesis and antithesis make equal claims   [6:255] to the validity of two conditions that are inconsistent with each other is reason forced, even in its practical use (having to do with rights), to make a distinction between possession as appearance and possession that is thinkable merely by the understanding.

The *thesis* says: *It is possible* to have something external as mine even though I am not in possession of it.

The *antithesis* says: *It is not possible* to have something external as mine unless I am in possession of it.

Solution: Both propositions are true, the first if I understand, by the word "possession", empirical possession (*possessio phaenomenon*), the second if I understand by it purely intelligible possession (*possessio noumenon*). – But we cannot see how intelligible possession is possible and so how it is possible for something external to be mine or yours, but must infer it from the postulate of practical reason. With regard to this postulate it is particularly noteworthy that practical reason *extends* itself without intuitions and without even needing any that are *a priori*, merely by *leaving out* empirical conditions, as it is justified in doing by the law of freedom. In this way it can lay down *synthetic a priori* propositions about right, the proof of which (as will soon be shown) can afterwards be adduced, in a practical respect, in an analytic way.

§8

It Is Possible to Have Something External as One's Own Only in a Rightful Condition, under an Authority Giving Laws Publicly, That Is, in a Civil Condition

When I declare (by word or deed), I will that something external is to be mine, I thereby declare that everyone else is under obligation to refrain from using that object of my choice, an obligation no one would have were it not for this act of mine to establish a right. This claim involves, however, acknowledging that I in turn am under obligation to every other to refrain from using what is externally his; for the obligation here arises from a universal rule having to do with external rightful relations. I am therefore not under obligation to leave external objects belonging to others untouched unless everyone else provides me assurance that he will behave in accordance with the same principle with regard to what is mine. This assurance   [6:256] does not require a special act to establish a right, but is already contained in the concept of an obligation corresponding to an external right, since the universality, and with it the reciprocity, of obligation arises from a universal rule. – Now, a unilateral will cannot serve as a coercive law for everyone with regard to possession that is external and therefore contingent, since that would infringe upon freedom in accordance with universal laws. So it is only a will putting everyone under obligation, hence only a collective general (common) and powerful will, that can provide everyone this assurance. – But the condition of being under a general external (i.e., public) lawgiving accompanied with power is the civil condition. So only in a civil condition can something external be mine or yours.

Corollary: If it must be possible, in terms of rights, to have an external object as one's own, the subject must also be permitted to constrain everyone else with whom he comes into conflict about whether an external object is his or another's to enter along with him into a civil constitution.

§9
In a State of Nature Something External Can Actually Be Mine or Yours but Only *Provisionally*

When people are under a civil constitution, the statutory laws obtaining in this condition cannot infringe upon *natural right* (i.e., that right which can be derived from *a priori* principles for a civil constitution); and so the rightful principle "whoever acts on a maxim by which it becomes impossible to have an object of my choice as mine wrongs me," remain in force. For a civil constitution is just the rightful condition, by which what belongs to each is only secured, but not actually settled and determined.[s] – Any guarantee, then, already presupposes what belongs to someone (to whom it secures it). Prior to a civil constitution (or in *abstraction* from it), external objects that are mine or yours must therefore be assumed to be possible, and with them a right to constrain everyone with whom we could have any dealings to enter with us into a constitution in which external objects can be [6:257] secured as mine or yours. – Possession in anticipation of and preparation for the civil condition, which can be based only on a law of a common will, possession which therefore accords with the *possibility* of such a condition, is *provisionally rightful* possession, whereas possession found in an *actual* civil condition would be *conclusive* possession. – Prior to entering such a condition, a subject who is ready for it resists with right those who are not willing to submit to it and who want to interfere with his present possession; for the will of all others except for himself, which proposes to put him under obligation to give up a certain possession, is merely *unilateral*, and hence has as little lawful force in denying him possession as he has in asserting it (since this can be found only in a general will), whereas he at least has the advantage of being compatible with the introduction and establishment

---

[s] *eigentlich aber nicht ausgemacht und bestimmt wird*

of a civil condition. – In summary, the way to have something external as one's own *in a state of nature* is physical possession which has in its favor the rightful *presumption* that it will be made into rightful possession through being united with the will of all in a public lawgiving, and in anticipation of this holds *comparatively* as rightful possession.

In accordance with the formula *Happy is he who is in possession* (*beati possidentes*), this prerogative of right arising from empirical possession does not consist in its being unnecessary for the possessor, since he is presumed to be an *honest man*, to furnish proof that his possession is in conformity with right (for this holds only in disputes about rights). This prerogative arises, instead, from the capacity[t] anyone has, by the postulate of practical reason, to have an external object of his choice as his own. Consequently, any holding of an external object is a condition whose conformity with right is based on that postulate by a previous act of will; and so long as this condition does not conflict with another's earlier possession of the same object he is provisionally justified, in accordance with the law of outer freedom, in preventing anyone who does not want to enter with him into a condition of public lawful freedom from usurping the use of that object, in order to put to his own use, in conformity with the postulate of reason, a thing that would otherwise be annihilated practically.

[t] *Vermögen*

CHAPTER II

How to *Acquire*[a] Something External

§10

General Principle of External Acquisition

I acquire something when I bring it about (*efficio*) that it becomes *mine*. – Something external is originally mine which is mine without any act that establishes a right to it. But that acquisition is original which is not derived from what is another's.

Nothing external is originally mine, but it can indeed be acquired originally, that is, without being derived from what is another's. – A condition of community (*communio*) of what is mine and yours can never be thought to be original but must be acquired (by an act that establishes an external right), although possession of an external object can originally be only possession in common. Even if one thinks (problematically) of an *original* community (*communio mei et tui originaria*), it must still be distinguished from a *primitive* community (*communio primaeva*), which is supposed to have been instituted in the earliest *time* of relations of rights among human beings and cannot be based, like the former, on principles but only on history. Although primitive, it would always have to be thought to be acquired and derived (*communio derivativa*).

The principle of external acquisition is as follows: that is mine which I bring under my *control* (in accordance with the law of outer *freedom*); which, as an object of my choice, is something that I have the capacity to use (in accordance with the postulate of practical reason); and which, finally, I *will* to be mine (in conformity with the idea of a possible united *will*).

The aspects[b] (*attendenda*) of *original* acquisition are therefore: 1.) *Apprehension* of an object that belongs to no one; otherwise it would conflict with another's freedom in accordance with universal laws. This *apprehension* is taking possession of an object of choice in space and time, so that the possession in which I put myself is *possessio phaenomenon*. 2.) *Giving a sign* (*declaratio*) of my possession of this object [6:259] and of my act of choice to exclude everyone else from it. 3.) *Appropriation* (*appropriatio*) as the act of a general will (in idea) giving an external law through which everyone is bound to agree with my choice. – The validity of this last aspect of acquisition, on which rests the conclusion "this external object is *mine*," that is, the conclusion that my possession holds as possession *merely by right* (*possessio noumenon*), is based on this: since all these acts *have to do with a right* and so proceed from practical reason, in the question of what is laid down as right abstraction can be made from the empirical conditions of possession, so that the conclusion, "the external object is mine," is correctly drawn from sensible to intelligible possession.

---

[a] emphasis added, to match 6:210   [b] *Momente*

Original acquisition of an external object of choice is called *taking control*^c of it (*occupatio*), and only corporeal things (substances) can be acquired originally. When it takes place, what it requires as the condition of empirical possession is priority in time to anyone else who wants to take control of the object (*qui prior tempore potior iure*).^d As original, it is only the result of a *unilateral* choice, for if it required a bilateral choice the acquisition would be derived from the contract of two (or more) persons and so from what is another's. – It is not easy to see how an act of choice of that kind could establish what belongs to someone. – However, if an acquisition is *first* it is not therefore *original*. For the acquisition of a public rightful condition by the union of the will of all for giving universal law would be an acquisition such that none could precede it, yet it would be derived from the particular wills of each and would be *omnilateral*, whereas original acquisition can proceed only from a unilateral will.

Division of the Acquisition of Something External That Is Mine or Yours

1. In terms of the *matter* (the object), I acquire either a corporeal *thing* (substance), or another's *performance* (causality), or another *person* himself, that is, the status of that person, in so far as I get a right to make arrangements about him^e (deal with him).

2. In terms of the *form* (the kind of acquisition), it is either a *right to a thing*^f (*ius reale*), or a *right against a person*^g (*ius personale*), or a *right to a person akin to a right to a thing*^h (*ius realiter personale*), that is, possession (though not use) of another person as a thing.   [6:260]

3. In terms of the *basis* of the acquisition *in right*ⁱ (*titulus*), something external is acquired through the act of a *unilateral, bilateral,* or *omnilateral* choice (*facto, pacto, lege*). Although this is not, strictly speaking, a special member of the division of rights, it is still an aspect of the way acquisition is carried out.

---

^c *Bemächtigung.* In the case of land, "occupying it" would be the appropriate translation. However, Kant also uses *Bemächtigung* in the context of rights to things generally and of rights against persons akin to rights to things.

^d who is first in time has the stronger right

^e *über denselben zu verfügen.* The phrase *über . . . verfügen* is followed by (*disponiren*) in 6:330; it is also used (inflected) in 6:313. *Verfügung* is used in 6:314.

^f *Sachenrecht*   ^g *persönliches Recht*   ^h *dinglich–persönliches Recht*   ⁱ *Rechtsgrunde*

Section I
On Property Right[j]

§11
What Is a Right to a Thing?[k]

The usual exposition of a *right to a thing* (*ius reale, ius in re*), that "it is a right *against every possessor of it*," is a correct nominal definition. – But what is it that enables me to recover an external object from anyone who is holding it and to constrain him (*per vindicationem*) to put me in possession of it again? Could this external rightful relation of my choice be a *direct* relation to a corporeal thing? Someone who thinks that his right is a direct relation to things rather than to persons would have to think (though only obscurely) that since there corresponds to a right on one side a duty on the other, an external thing always remains *under obligation* to the first possessor even though it has left his hands; that, because it is already under obligation to him, it rejects anyone else who pretends to be the possessor of it. So he would think of my right as if it were a *guardian spirit* accompanying the thing, always pointing me out to whoever else wanted to take possession of it and protecting it against any incursions by them. It is therefore absurd to think of an obligation of a person to things or the reverse, even though it may be permissible, if need be, to make this rightful relation perceptible by picturing it and expressing it in this way.

So the real definition would have to go like this: *a right to a thing* is a right to [6:261] the private use of a thing of which I am in (original or instituted) possession in common[l] with all others. For this possession in common is the only condition under which it is possible for me to exclude every other possessor from the private use of a thing (*ius contra quemlibet huius rei possessorem*)[m] since, unless such a possession in common is assumed, it is inconceivable how I, who am not in possession of the thing, could still be wronged by others who are in possession of it and are using it. – By my unilateral choice I cannot bind another to refrain from using a thing, an obligation he would not otherwise have; hence I can do this only through the united choice of all who possess it in common. Otherwise I would have to think of a right to a thing as if the thing had an obligation to me, from which my right against every other possessor of it is then derived; and this is an absurd way of representing it.

By the term "property right" (*ius reale*) should be understood not only a right to a thing (*ius in re*) but also the *sum* of all the laws having to do with things being mine or yours. – But it is clear that someone who was all alone on the earth could

---

[j] *Sachenrecht.* Kant introduces the term "property" (*Eigenthum, dominium*), a full right to a thing, in his concluding remark to this section, 6:270.

[k] *Sachenrecht* [l] *Gesammtbesitze* [m] right against whoever is possessor of the thing

really neither have nor acquire any external thing as his own, since there is no relation whatever of obligation between him, as a person, and any other external object, as a thing. Hence, speaking strictly and literally, there is also no (direct) right to a thing. What is called a right to a thing is only that right someone has against a person who is in possession of it in common[n] with all others (in the civil condition).

§12
First Acquisition of a Thing Can Be Only Acquisition of Land

Land (understood as all habitable ground) is to be regarded as the *substance* with respect to whatever is movable upon it, while the existence of the latter is to be regarded only as *inherence*. Just as in a theoretical sense accidents cannot exist apart from a substance, so in a practical sense no one can have what is movable on a piece of land as his own unless he is assumed to be already in rightful possession of the land.

For suppose that the land belonged to no one: I could then remove every [6:262] movable thing on it from its place and take it for myself until they were all gone, without thereby infringing upon the freedom of anyone else who is not now holding it; but whatever can be destroyed, a tree, a house, and so forth, is movable (at least in terms of its matter), and if a thing that cannot be moved without destroying its form is called *immovable*, then by what is mine or yours with regard to that is understood not its substance but what adheres to it, which is not the thing itself.

§13
Any Piece of Land[o] Can Be Acquired Originally, and the Possibility of Such Acquisition Is Based on the Original Community[p] of Land in General

The first proposition rests on the postulate of practical reason (§2).[q] The proof of the second proposition is as follows.

All human beings are originally (i.e., prior to any act of choice that establishes a right) in a possession of land that is in conformity with right, that is, they have a right to be wherever nature or chance (apart from their will) has placed them. This kind of possession (*possessio*) – which is to be distinguished from residence (*sedes*), a chosen and therefore an acquired *lasting* possession – is a possession *in*

---

[n] *im gemeinsamen Besitz*   [o] *Ein jeder Boden*   [p] *Gemeinschaft*
[q] LD: In this edition, the postulate presented as §2 originally (and in AA) has been placed within §6.

common[r] because the spherical surface of the earth unites all the places on its surface; for if its surface were an unbounded plane, human beings could be so dispersed on it that they would not come into any community with one another, and community would not then be a necessary result of their existence on the earth. – The possession by all human beings on the earth which precedes any acts of theirs that would establish rights (as constituted by nature itself) is an *original possession in common*[s] (*communio possessionis originaria*), the concept of which is not empirical and dependent upon temporal conditions, like that of a supposed *primitive possession in common* (*communio primaeva*), which can never be proved. Original possession in common is, rather, a practical rational concept which contains *a priori* the principle in accordance with which alone human beings can use a place on the earth in accordance with principles of right.

[6:263]

§14
In Original Acquisition, the Act Required to Establish a Right Is Taking Control (*occupatio*)

The only condition under which *taking possession* (*apprehensio*), beginning to hold (*possessionis physicae*) a corporeal thing in space, conforms with the law of everyone's outer freedom (hence *a priori*) is that of *priority* in time, that is, only in so far as it is the *first* taking possession (*prior apprehensio*), which is an act of choice. But the will that a thing (and so too a specific, separate place[t] on the earth) is to be mine, that is, appropriation of it (*appropriatio*), in original acquisition can be only *unilateral* (*voluntas unilateralis s. propria*).[u] Acquisition of an external object of choice by a unilateral will is *taking control* of it. So original acquisition of an external object, and hence too of a specific and separate piece of land, can take place only through taking control of it (*occupatio*).

No insight can be had into the possibility of acquiring in this way, nor can it be demonstrated by reasons;[v] its possibility is instead an immediate consequence of the postulate of practical reason. But the aforesaid will can justify an external acquisition only insofar as it is included in a will that is united *a priori* (i.e., only through the union of the choice of all who can come into practical relations with one another) and that commands absolutely. For a unilateral will (and a bilateral but still *particular* will is also unilateral) cannot put everyone under an obligation that is in itself contingent; this requires a will that is *omnilateral*, that is united not contingently but *a priori* and therefore necessarily, and because of this is the only will that is lawgiving. For only in accordance with this principle of the will is it possible for the free choice of each to accord with the freedom of all, and

---

[r] *ein gemeinsamer Besitz* [s] *Gesammtbesitz* [t] *bestimmter abgetheilter*
[u] unilateral or proper will [v] *durch Gründe darthun*

therefore possible for there to be any right, and so too possible for any external object to be mine or yours.

§15 [6:264]
Something Can Be Acquired *Conclusively* Only in a Civil Constitution; in a State of Nature It Can Also Be Acquired, but Only *Provisionally*

A civil constitution, though its realization is subjectively contingent, is still objectively necessary, that is, necessary as a duty. With regard to such a constitution and its establishment there is therefore a real law of natural right[w] to which any external acquisition is subject.

The *empirical title* of acquisition was taking physical possession (*apprehensio physica*), based on the original community of land. Since there is only possession in *appearance* to put under possession in accordance with rational concepts of right, a title to take intellectual possession (setting aside all empirical conditions of space and time) must correspond to this empirical title of acquisition. This intellectual title is the basis of the proposition: "What I bring under my control in accordance with laws of outer freedom and will to become mine becomes mine."

But the *rational title* of acquisition can lie only in the idea of a will of all united *a priori* (necessarily to be united), which is here tacitly assumed as a necessary condition (*conditio sine qua non*); for a unilateral will cannot put others under an obligation they would not otherwise have. – But the condition in which the will of all is actually united for giving law is the civil condition. Therefore something external can be *originally* acquired only in conformity with the idea of a civil condition, that is, with a view to it and to its being brought about, but prior to its realization (for otherwise acquisition would be derived). Hence *original* acquisition can be only *provisional*. – *Conclusive* acquisition takes place only in the civil condition.

Still, that provisional acquisition is true acquisition; for, by the postulate of practical reason with regard to rights, the possibility of acquiring something external in whatever condition human beings may live together (and so also in a state of nature) is a principle of private right, in accordance with which each is justified in using that coercion which is necessary if human beings are to leave the state of nature and enter the civil condition, which can alone make any acquisition conclusive.

The question arises, how far does authorization to take possession of a piece [6:265] of land extend? As far as the capacity[x] for controlling it extends, that is, as far as whoever wants to appropriate it can defend it – as if the land were to say, if you cannot protect me you cannot command me. This is how the dispute over

---

[w] *wirkliches Rechtsgesetz der Natur*   [x] *Vermögen*

whether the sea is *free* or *closed* also has to be decided; for example, as far as a cannon shot can reach no one may fish, haul up amber from the ocean floor, and so forth, along the coast of a territory that already belongs to a certain state. – Moreover, in order to acquire land is it necessary to develop it (build on it, cultivate it, drain it, and so on)? No. For since these forms (of specification) are only accidents, they make no object of direct possession and can belong to what the subject possesses only insofar as the substance is already recognized as his. When first acquisition is in question, developing land is nothing more than an external sign of taking possession, for which many other signs that cost less effort can be substituted. – Furthermore, may one party interfere with another in its *act* of taking possession, so that neither enjoys the right of priority and the land remains always free, belonging to no one? Not *entirely*; since one party can prevent another from taking possession only by being on adjacent land, where it itself can be prevented from being, *absolute* hindrance would be a contradiction. But *with respect to* a certain piece of land (lying between the two), leaving it unused, as *neutral* territory to separate the two parties, would still be consistent with the right of taking control. In that case, however, this land really belongs to both in common^y and is not something *belonging to no one* (*res nullius*), just because it is *used* by both to keep them apart. – Again, can anyone have a thing as his own on land no part of which belongs to someone? Yes, as in Mongolia where, since all the land belongs to the people, the use of it belongs to each individual, so that anyone can leave his pack lying on it or recover possession of his horse if it runs away, since it is his. On the other hand, it is only by means of a *contract* that anyone can have a movable thing as his on land that belongs to another. – Finally, can two neighboring peoples (or families) resist each other in adopting a certain use of land, for example, can a hunting people resist a pasturing people or a farming people, or the latter resist a people that wants to plant orchards, and so forth? Certainly, since as long as they keep within their boundaries the way they want to *live* on their land is up to their own discretion (*res merae facultatis*).

[6:266]

Lastly, it can still be asked whether, when neither nature nor chance but just our own will brings us into the neighborhood of a people that holds out no prospect of a civil union with it, we should not be authorized to found colonies, by force if need be, in order to establish a civil union with them and bring these human beings (savages) into a rightful condition (as with the American Indians, the Hottentots, and the inhabitants of New Holland); or (which is not much better), to found colonies by fraudulent purchase of their land, and so become owners of their land, making use of our superiority without regard for their first possession. Should we not be authorized to do

^{y} *gemeinschaftlich*

58

this, especially since nature itself (which abhors a vacuum) seems to demand it, and great expanses of land in other parts of the world, which are now splendidly populated, would have otherwise remained uninhabited by civilized people or, indeed, would have to remain forever uninhabited, so that the end of creation would have been frustrated? But it is easy to see through this veil of injustice (Jesuitism), which would sanction any means to good ends. Such a way of acquiring land is therefore to be repudiated.

The indeterminacy, with respect to quantity as well as quality, of the external object that can be acquired makes this problem (of the sole, original external acquisition) the hardest of all to solve. Still, there must be some original acquisition or other of what is external, since not all acquisition can be derived. So this problem cannot be abandoned as insoluble and intrinsically impossible. But even if it is solved through the original contract, such acquisition will always remain only provisional unless this contract extends to the entire human race.

§16

Exposition of the Concept of Original Acquisition of Land

[6:267]

All human beings are originally in *common possession*[z] of the land of the entire earth (*communio fundi originaria*) and each has by nature the *will* to use it (*lex iusti*) which, because the choice of one is unavoidably opposed by nature to that of another, would do away with any use of it if this will did not also contain the principle for choice by which a *particular possession* for each on the common land could be determined (*lex iuridica*). But the law which is to determine for each what land is mine or yours[a] will be in accordance with the axiom of outer freedom only if it proceeds from a will that is united *originally* and *a priori* (that presupposes no rightful act[b] for its union). Hence it proceeds only from a will in the civil condition (*lex iustitiae distributivae*), which alone determines what is *right*, what is *rightful*, and what is *laid down as right*.[c] – But in the former condition, that is, before the establishment of the civil condition but with a view to it, that is, *provisionally*, it is a *duty* to proceed in accordance with the principle of external acquisition. Accordingly, there is also a rightful *capacity*[d] of the will to bind everyone to recognize the act of taking possession and of appropriation as valid, even though it is only unilateral. Therefore provisional acquisition of land, together with all its rightful consequences, is possible.

Provisional acquisition, however, needs and gains the *favor*[e] of a law (*lex permissiva*) for determining the limits of possible rightful possession. Since this acquisition precedes a rightful condition and, as only leading to it, is not yet

---

[z] *Gesammt–Besitz*   [a] *das austheilende Gesetz des Mein und Dein eines jeden am Boden*
[b] *rechtlichen Act*. See 6:237, note x.   [c] *was recht, was rechtlich und was Rechtens ist*
[d] *rechtliches Vermögen*   [e] *Gunst*

conclusive, this favor does not extend beyond the point at which *others* (participants) consent to its establishment. But if they are opposed to entering it (the civil condition), and as long as their opposition lasts, this favor carries with it all the effects of acquisition in conformity with right, since leaving the state of nature is based upon duty.

§17
Deduction of the Concept of Original Acquisition

We have found the *title* of acquisition in an original community of land, and therefore of external possession subject to spatial conditions. We have found the *manner of acquisition* in the empirical conditions of taking possession (*apprehensio*), joined with the will to have the external object as one's own. Now we still need to explicate[f] from principles of pure practical reason with regard to rights *acquisition* itself, that is, the external mine or yours, which follows from the two elements given; that is, we need to explicate intelligible possession (*possessio noumenon*) of an object from what is contained in the concept of it.

The *concept belonging to right*[g] of what is *externally* mine or yours, so far as this is a *substance*, cannot mean, as far as the term *external to me* is concerned, in another *place* than where I am, for it is a rational concept; instead, since only a pure concept of the understanding can be subsumed under a rational concept, the term can mean merely something *distinct* from me. And this rational concept cannot signify the concept of empirical possession (a continual taking possession, as it were), but only that of *having an external object under my control* (the connection of the object with me insofar as this is the subjective condition of its being possible for me to use it), which is a pure concept of the understanding. Now, if these sensible conditions of possession, as a relation of a person to *objects* that have no obligation, are left out or disregarded (abstracted from), possession is nothing other than a relation of a person to persons, all of whom are *bound*, with regard to the use of the thing, by the *will* of the first person, insofar as his will conforms with the axiom of outer freedom, with the *postulate* of his capacity to use external objects of choice, and with the *lawgiving* of the will of all[h] thought as united *a priori*. This, then, is *intelligible possession* of a thing, that is, possession by mere right, even though the object (the thing I possess) is a sensible object.

The first working, enclosing, or, in general, *transforming* of a piece of land can furnish no title of acquisition to it; that is, possession of an accident can provide no basis for rightful possession of the substance. What is mine or yours must instead be derived from ownership[i] of the substance in accordance with this rule (*accessorium sequitur suum principale*),[j] and whoever expends his

[f] *entwickeln*   [g] *Rechtsbegriff*   [h] *allgemeinen Gesetzgebung*   [i] *Eigenthum*
[j] accessory [possession] following on this principle

labor on land that was not already his has lost his pains and toil to who was first. This is so clear of itself that it is hard to assign any other cause for that opinion, which is so old and still so widespread, than the tacit prevalent deception of personifying things and of thinking of a right to things as being a right *directly* against them, as if someone could, by the work he expends upon them, put things under an obligation to serve him and no one else; for otherwise people would probably not have passed so lightly over the question that naturally arises (already noted above), "How is a right to a thing possible?" For a right against every possessor of a thing means only an authorization on the part of someone's particular choice to use an object, insofar as this authorization can be thought as contained in a synthetic general will and as in accord with the law of this will.

As for corporeal things on land that is already mine, if they do not otherwise belong to another they belong *to me* without my needing a particular act establishing a right in order to make them mine (not *facto* but *lege*), for they can be regarded as accidents inhering in the substance (*iure rei meae*)[k]. Anything else that is so connected with a thing of mine that another cannot separate it from what is mine without changing this also belongs to me (e.g., gold plating, mixing some stuff belonging to me with other materials, alluvium, or, also, a change in a riverbed adjoining my land and the resulting extension of my land, and so forth). Whether land that extends beyond dry land can be acquired – that is, whether a tract of the ocean floor can be acquired (the right to fish off my shore, to bring up amber, and so forth) – must be decided[l] in accordance with the same principles. My *possession* extends as far as I have the mechanical ability,[m] from where I *reside*, to secure my land against encroachment by others (e.g., as far as cannon reach from the shore), and up to this limit the sea is closed (*mare clausum*). But since it is not possible to *reside* on the high seas themselves, possession also cannot extend to them and the open seas are free (*mare liberum*). But the owner of a shore cannot include, in his right to acquire, what is unintentionally *washed up on shore*, whether human beings or things belonging to them, since this is not wronging him (not a deed at all), and though a thing has been cast up on land which belongs to someone, it cannot be treated as a *res nullius*.[n] On the other hand, a river can be originally acquired by someone who is in possession of both banks, as far as his possession of the banks extends; he can acquire the river just as he can acquire any dry land subject to the conditions mentioned above.

[6:270]

* * *

---

[k] my right in the thing   [l] *muß ... beurtheilt werden*   [m] *Vermögen*
[n] thing belonging to no one

An external object which in terms of its substance belongs to someone is his *property* (*dominium*), in which all rights in this thing inhere (as accidents of a substance) and which the owner (*dominus*) can, accordingly, dispose of as he pleases (*ius disponendi de re sua*).[o] But from this it follows that an object of this sort can be only a corporeal thing (to which one has no obligation). So someone can be his own master (*sui iuris*) but cannot be the owner *of himself* (*sui dominus*) (cannot dispose of himself as he pleases) – still less can he dispose of others as he pleases – since he is accountable to the humanity in his own person. This is not, however, the proper place to discuss this point, which has to do with the right of humanity, not that of human beings. It is mentioned only incidentally, for a better understanding of what was discussed a little earlier. – Furthermore, there can be two complete owners of one and the same thing, without its being both mine and yours in common; they may only be possessors in common of what *belongs to only one of them as his*. This happens when one of the so-called joint owners (*condomini*) has only full possession without use, while the other has all the use of the thing along with possession of it. So the one who has full possession without use (*dominus directus*)[p] only restricts the other (*dominus utilis*)[q] to some continual performance without thereby limiting his use of the thing.

[6:271]

Section II
On Contract Right[r]

§18

My possession of another's choice, in the sense of my capacity[s] to determine it by my own choice to a certain deed in accordance with laws of freedom (what is externally mine or yours with respect to the causality of another), is *a* right (of which I can have several against the same person or against others); but there is only a single sum (system) of laws, *contract right*, in accordance with which I can be in this sort of possession.

A right against a person can never be acquired originally and on one's own initiative[t] (for then it would not conform to the principle of the consistency of my choice with the freedom of everyone, and would therefore be wrong). So too, I cannot acquire a right against another through a deed of his that is *contrary to right* (*facto iniusto alterius*);[u] for even if he has wronged me and I have a right to demand compensation from him, by this I will still only preserve what is mine undiminished but will not acquire more than what I previously had.

[o] right to dispose of the thing which is his
[p] direct owner
[q] owner of the use
[r] *Vom persönlichen Recht*
[s] *Vermögen*
[t] *eigenmächtig*
[u] act unjustly to another

Acquisition through another's deed to which I determine him in accordance with laws of right is, accordingly, always derived from what is his; and this derivation, as an act that establishes a right, cannot take place through a *negative* act of the other, namely his *abandoning* or *renouncing* what is his (*per derelictionem aut renunciationem*); for by such an act this would only cease to belong to one or the other, but nothing would be acquired. This derivation can take place only by *transferring* (*translatio*), which is possible only through a common will by means of which the object is always under the control of one or the other, since as one gives up his share in this common undertaking^v the object becomes the other's through his acceptance of it (and so by a positive act of choice). – Transfer of the *property* of one to another is *alienation*. An act of the united choice of two persons by which anything at all that belongs to one passes to the other is a *contract*.

§19

For every contract there are two *preparatory* and two *constitutive* rightful acts of choice. The first two (of *negotiating*) are *offering* (*oblatio*) and *assent* (*approbatio*) to it; the two others (of *concluding*) are *promise* (*promissum*) and *acceptance* (*acceptatio*). – For an offering cannot be called a promise apart from a preliminary judgment that what is offered (*oblatum*) would be *acceptable* to the promisee. This is indicated by the first two declarations, but by them alone nothing is as yet acquired.

But what belongs to the promisor does not pass to the promisee (as acceptant) by the *separate* will of either but only by the *united will* of both, and consequently only insofar as both wills are declared *simultaneously*. But this cannot take place by empirical acts of declaration, which must necessarily *follow* each other in time and are never simultaneous. For if I have promised and the other now wants to accept, I can still during the interval (however short it may be) regret having promised, since I am still free before he accepts; and because of this the one who accepts it, for his part, can consider himself as not bound to his counter-declaration after the promise. – The external formalities (*solennia*) in concluding a contract (shaking hands or breaking a straw, *stipula*, held by both persons), and all the confirmations back and forth of the declarations they have made, manifest the perplexity of the contracting parties as to how and in what way they are going to represent their declarations as existing *simultaneously*, at the same moment, although they can only be successive. They still do not succeed in this since their acts can only follow each other in time, so that when one act *is* the other is either *not yet* or is *no longer*.

---

^v *Gemeinschaft*

Only a transcendental deduction of the concept of acquisition by contract can remove all these difficulties. It is true that in an external relation of *rights* my taking possession of another's choice (and his taking possession of mine in turn), as the basis for determining it to a deed, is first thought of empirically, by means of a declaration and counter-declaration of the choice of each in time; this is the sensible condition of taking possession, in which both acts required for establishing the right can only follow one upon another. Since, [6:273] however, that relation (as a rightful relation) is purely intellectual, that possession is represented through the will, which is a rational capacity^w for giving laws, as intelligible possession (*possessio noumenon*) in abstraction from those empirical conditions, as what is mine or yours. Here both acts, promise and acceptance, are represented not as following one upon another but (as if it were *pactum re initum*) as proceeding from a single *common* will (this is expressed by the word *simultaneously*); and the object (*promissum*) is represented, by omitting empirical conditions, as acquired in accordance with a principle of pure practical reason.

That this is the true and the only possible deduction of the concept of acquisition by contract is sufficiently confirmed by the painstaking but always futile efforts of those who investigate rights (e.g., Moses Mendelssohn in his *Jerusalem*) [26] to produce a proof of its possibility. – The question was, *why ought* I to keep my promise? for *that I ought* to keep it everyone readily grasps. But it is absolutely impossible to furnish a proof of this categorical imperative, just as it is impossible for a geometer to prove by means of inferences based on reason alone^x that in order to make a triangle he must take three lines (an analytic proposition), two of which together must be greater than the third (a synthetic proposition, but both propositions are *a priori*). That I ought to keep my promise is a postulate of pure reason (pure as abstracting from all sensible conditions of space and time in what concerns the concept of right). The theory that it is possible to abstract from those conditions without giving up possession of the promise is itself the deduction of the concept of acquisition by contract, just as was the case in the preceding section for the theory of acquisition of external things by taking control of them.

---

^w *Vernunftvermögen*   ^x *Vernunftschlüsse*, which could also be translated "syllogisms"

[26] Mendelssohn, *Gesammelte Schriften* (Hildesheim: H. A. Gerstenberg, 1972), 255–362. Kant is probably referring to Mendelssohn's view that "a contract is nothing other than one party's relinquishing his right and the other party's accepting it" (279). By this, the first party's "perfect right" to something he does not need for his preservation (his right to use coercion) becomes an "imperfect right" (a right to request or petition). The terminology of "perfect" and "imperfect" rights seems to have originated with Samuel Pufendorf, as an emendation of Grotius's distinction between "faculties" and "aptitudes." Although Kant rejects the distinction, in the *Doctrine of Virtue* he uses the language of what is "owed" or "due" with regard to duties of respect.

§20

By a contract I acquire something external. But what is it that I acquire? Since it is only the causality of another's choice with respect to a performance he has promised me, what I acquire directly by a contract is not an external thing but rather his deed, by which that thing is brought under my control so that I make it mine. – By a contract I therefore acquire another's promise (not what he promised), and yet something is added to my external belongings; I have become *enriched*[y] (*locupletior*)[z] by acquiring an active obligation on the freedom and means[a] of the other. – This *right* of mine is, however, only a right *against a person*, namely a right against a *specific* physical person, and indeed a right to act upon his causality (his choice) to *perform* something for me; it is not a *right to a thing*, a right against that *moral person* which is nothing other than the idea of the *choice of all united a priori*, by which alone I can acquire *a right against every possessor of the thing*, which is what constitutes any right to a thing.

Transfer by contract of what is mine takes place in accordance with the law of continuity (*lex continui*), that is, possession of the object is not interrupted for a moment during this act; for otherwise I would acquire, in this condition, an object as something that has no possessor (*res vacua*), hence would acquire it originally, and this contradicts the concept of contract. – Because of this continuity, however, that which transfers what is mine to the other is not one of the two separate wills (*promittentis et acceptantis*),[b] but their united will. So the transfer does not take place in such a way that the promisor first abandons (*derelinquit*) his possession for the other's advantage, or renounces (*renunciat*) his right, and the other immediately takes it up, or the reverse. Transfer is therefore an act in which an object belongs, for a moment, to both together, just as when a stone that has been thrown reaches the apex of its parabolic path it can be regarded as, for just a moment, simultaneously rising and falling, and so first passing from its rising motion to its falling.

§21

In a contract by which a thing is acquired, it is not acquired by *acceptance* (*acceptatio*) of the promise, but only by *delivery* (*traditio*) of what was promised. For any promise has to do with a *performance*, and if what is promised is a thing, the performance can be discharged only by an act in which the promisor puts the promisee in possession of the thing, that is, delivers it to him. So before the thing is delivered and received, the performance has not yet taken place: the thing has not yet passed from one to the other and so has not been acquired by the promisee. Hence the right that arises from a contract is only a right against a person, and becomes a right to a *thing* only by delivery of the thing.

[6:274]

[6:275]

---

[y] *vermögender*   [z] richer   [a] *Vermögen*   [b] promising and accepting

A contract that is immediately followed by delivery (*pactum re initum*) excludes any interval between its being concluded and its being discharged and requires no further separate act by which what belongs to one is transferred to the other. But if a (definite or indefinite) time for delivering the thing is allowed between the conclusion and the discharge of the contract, the question arises whether the thing already belongs to the acceptor by the contract, prior to its being delivered, and his right is a right to the thing, or whether a separate contract having to do only with its being delivered must be added, so that the right acquired by mere acceptance is only a right against a person and becomes a right to a thing only by its being delivered. – That the latter is really the case is clear from the following.

If I conclude a contract about a thing that I want to acquire, for example, a horse, and at the same time put it in my stable or otherwise in my physical possession, it is then mine (*vi pacti re initi*),^c and my right is a *right to the thing*. But if I leave it in the seller's hands, without making any separate arrangements with him as to who is to be in physical possession of the thing (*holding* it) before I take possession of it (*apprehensio*), and so before the change of possession, then this horse is not yet mine, and what I have acquired is only a right against a specific person, namely the seller, *to put me in possession* (*poscendi traditionem*), which is the subjective condition of its being possible for me to use it as I please. My right is only a right against a person, to require of the seller *performance* (*praestatio*) of his promise to put me in possession of the thing. Now if a contract does not include delivery *at the same time* (as *pactum re initum*), so that some time elapses between its being concluded and my taking possession of what I am acquiring, during this time I cannot gain possession without exercising a separate act to establish that right, namely a *possessory act* (*actum possessorium*), which constitutes a separate contract. This contract consists in my saying that I shall send for the thing (the horse) and the seller's agreeing to it. For it is not a matter of course that the seller will take charge, at his own risk, of something for another's use; this instead requires a separate contract, by which the one who is alienating a thing still remains its owner *for a specified time* (and must bear any risk that might affect it). Only if the one who is acquiring the thing delays beyond this time can the seller regard him as its owner and the thing as delivered to him. Before this possessory act all that has been acquired through the contract is therefore a right against a person, and the promisee can acquire an external thing only by its being delivered.

[6:276]

---

^c by force of starting the contract regarding a thing. LD: Or "by force of a *pactum re initum*"; see 6:248 note f.

Section III
On Rights to Persons Akin to Rights to Things[d]
§22

This right is that of possession of an external object *as a thing* and use of it *as a person*. – What is mine or yours in terms of this right is what is mine or yours *domestically*, and the relation of persons in the domestic condition is that of a community of free beings who form a society of members of a whole called a *household* (of persons standing in *community* with one another) by their affecting one another in accordance with the principle of outer freedom (*causality*). – Acquisition of this status, and within it, therefore takes place neither by a deed on one's own initiative (*facto*) nor by a contract (*pacto*) alone but by law (*lege*); for, since this kind of right is neither a right to a thing nor merely a right against a person but also possession of a person, it must be a right lying beyond any rights to things and any rights against persons. That is to say, it must be the right of humanity in our own person, from which there follows a natural permissive law, by the favor of which this sort of acquisition is possible for us.

§23

[6:277]

In terms of the object, acquisition in accordance with this principle is of three kinds: a *man* acquires a *wife*;[e] a *couple* acquires *children*; and a *family* acquires *servants*. – Whatever is acquired in this way is also inalienable and the right of possessors of these objects is the *most personal* of all rights.

On the Right of Domestic Society
Title I
Marriage Right
§24

Sexual union (*commercium sexuale*) is the reciprocal use that one human being makes of the sexual organs and capacities of another (*usus membrorum et facultatum sexualium alterius*). This is either a *natural* use (by which procreation of a being of the same kind is possible) or an *unnatural* use, and unnatural use takes place either with a person of the same sex or with an animal of a nonhuman species. Since such transgressions of laws, called unnatural (*crimina carnis contra*

---

[d] *Von dem auf dingliche Art persönlichen Recht.* As in Sections I and II, the heading here suggests "the sum of laws" having to do with such possession. However, this third member of the division of rights is an innovation on Kant's part, and there is no English term for it corresponding to "property" and "contract." At the beginning and at the end of Section III, accordingly, I have sometimes used "rights" in contexts that would call for "right."

[e] *Weib*

naturam)^f or also unmentionable vices, do wrong to humanity in our own person, there are no limitations or exceptions whatsoever that can save them from being repudiated completely.

Natural sexual union takes place either in accordance with mere animal *nature* (*vaga libido, venus volgivaga, fornicatio*)^g or in accordance with *law*. – Sexual union in accordance with law is *marriage* (*matrimonium*), that is, the union of two persons of different sexes for lifelong possession of each other's sexual attributes. – The end of begetting and bringing up children may be an end of nature, for which it implanted the inclinations of the sexes for each other; but it is not requisite for human beings who marry to make this their end in order for their union to be compatible with rights, for otherwise marriage would be dissolved when procreation ceases.

Even if it is supposed that their end is the pleasure of using each other's sexual attributes, the marriage contract is not up to their discretion but is a contract that [6:278] is necessary by the law of humanity, that is, if a man and a woman want to enjoy each other's sexual attributes they *must* necessarily marry, and this is necessary in accordance with pure reason's laws of right.

§25

For the natural use that one sex makes of the other's sexual organs is *enjoyment*, for which one gives itself up to the other. In this act a human being makes himself into a thing, which conflicts with the right of humanity in his own person. There is only one condition under which this is possible: that while one person is acquired by the other *as if it were a thing*, the one who is acquired acquires the other in turn; for in this way each reclaims itself and restores its personality. But acquiring a member of a human being is at the same time acquiring the whole person, since a person is an absolute unity. Hence it is not only admissible for the sexes to surrender and to accept each other for enjoyment under the condition of marriage, but it is possible for them to do so *only* under this condition. That this *right against a person* is also *akin to a right to a thing* rests on the fact that if one of the partners in a marriage has left or given itself into someone else's possession, the other partner is justified, always and without question, in bringing its partner back under its control, just as it is justified in retrieving a thing.

§26

For the same reasons, the relation of the partners in a marriage is a relation of *equality* of possession, equality both in their possession of each other as persons

---

^f carnal crimes against nature
^g illicit sexual love, illicit sexual desire of the masses, fornication

(hence only in *monogamy*, since in polygamy the person who surrenders herself gains only a part of the man who gets her completely, and therefore makes herself into a mere thing), and also equality in their possession of material goods. As for these, the partners are still authorized to forgo the use of a part, though only by a separate contract.

For this reason it follows that neither concubinage nor hiring a person for enjoyment on one occasion (*pactum fornicationis*)[h] is a contract that could hold in right. As for the latter, everyone will admit that a person who has concluded such a contract could not rightfully be held to the fulfillment of her promise if she regrets it. So, with regard to the former, a contract to be a *concubine* (as *pactum turpe*)[i] also comes to nothing; for this would be a contract to *let* and *hire* (*locatio-conductio*) a member for another's use, in which, because of the inseparable unity of members in a person, she would be surrendering herself as a thing to the other's choice. Accordingly, either party can cancel the contract with the other as soon as it pleases without the other having grounds for complaining about any infringement of its rights. – The same considerations also hold for a morganatic marriage, which takes advantage of the inequality of estate of the two parties to give one of them domination over the other; for in fact morganatic marriage is not different, in terms of natural rights only, from concubinage and is no true marriage. – If the question is therefore posed, whether it is also in conflict with the equality of the partners for the law to say of the husband's relation to the wife, he is to be your master (he is the party to direct,[j] she to obey): this cannot be regarded as conflicting with the natural equality of a couple if this dominance is based only on the natural superiority of the husband to the wife in his capacity to promote the common interest of the household, and the right to direct that is based on this can be derived from the very duty of unity and equality with respect to the *end*.

[6:279]

§27

A marriage contract is *consummated* only *by conjugal sexual intercourse* (*copula carnalis*). A contract made between two persons of opposite sex, either with a tacit understanding to refrain from sexual intercourse or with awareness that one or both are incapable of it, is a *simulated contract*, which institutes no marriage and can also be dissolved by either of them who pleases. But if incapacity appears only afterwards, that right cannot be forfeited through this accident for which no one is at fault.

Acquisition of a wife or of a husband therefore takes place neither *facto* (by intercourse) without a contract preceding it nor *pacto* (by a mere marriage

[6:280]

---

[h] pact of fornication   [i] wrongful pact   [j] *er der befehlende ... Theil*

contract without intercourse following it) but only *lege*, that is, as the rightful consequence of the obligation not to engage in sexual union except through *possession* of each other's person, which is realized only through the use of their sexual attributes by each other.

On the Right of Domestic Society
Title II
Parental Right
§28

Just as there arose from one's duty to oneself, that is, to the humanity in one's own person, a right (*ius personale*) of both sexes to acquire each other as persons *in the manner of things* by marriage, so there follows from *procreation* in this community a duty to preserve and care for its *offspring*; that is, children, as persons, have by their procreation an original innate (not acquired) right to the care of their parents until they are able to look after themselves, and they have this right directly by law (*lege*), that is, without any special act being required to establish this right.

For the offspring is a *person*, and it is impossible to form a concept of the production of a being endowed with freedom through a physical operation.[*] [6:281] So from a *practical point of view* it is a quite correct and even necessary idea to regard the act of procreation as one by which we have brought a person into the world without his consent and on our own initiative, for which deed the parents incur an obligation to make the child content with his condition so far as they can. – They cannot destroy their child as if he were something they had *made* (since a being endowed with freedom cannot be a product of this kind) or as if he were their property, nor can they even just abandon him to chance, since they

---

[*] No concept can be formed of how it is possible for *God to create* free beings, for it seems as if all their future actions would have to be predetermined by that first act, included in the chain of natural necessity and therefore not free. But that such beings (we human beings) are still free the categorical imperative proves for morally practical purposes, as through an authoritative decision of reason without its being able to make this relation of cause to effect comprehensible for theoretical purposes, since both are supersensible. – All that one can require of reason here would be merely to prove that there is no contradiction in the concept of a *creation of free beings*, and it can do this if it shows that the contradiction arises only if, [6:281] along with the category of causality, the *temporal condition*, which cannot be avoided in relation to sensible objects (namely, that the ground of an effect precedes it), is also introduced in the relation of supersensible beings. As for the supersensible, if the causal concept is to obtain objective reality for theoretical purposes, the temporal condition would have to be introduced here too. But the contradiction vanishes if the pure category (without a schema put under it) is used in the concept of creation with a morally practical and therefore non-sensible intent.

If the philosophic jurist reflects on the difficulty of the problem to be resolved and the necessity of solving it to satisfy principles of right in this matter, he will not hold this investigation, all the way back to the first elements of transcendental philosophy in a metaphysics of morals, to be unnecessary pondering that gets lost in pointless obscurity.

have brought not merely a worldly being but a citizen of the world into a condition which cannot now be indifferent to them even just according to concepts of right.

§29

From this duty there must necessarily also arise the right of parents to *manage* and develop the child, as long as he has not yet mastered the use of his members or of his understanding: the right not only to feed and care for him but to educate him, to develop him both *pragmatically*, so that in the future he can look after himself and make his way in life, and *morally*, since otherwise the fault for having neglected him would fall on the parents. They have the right to do all this until the time of his emancipation (*emancipatio*), when they renounce their parental right to direct him as well as any claim to be compensated for their support and pains up till now. After they have completed his education, the only obligation (to his parents) with which they can charge him is a mere duty of virtue, namely the duty of gratitude.

From a child's personality it also follows that the right of parents is not just [6:282] a right to a thing, since a child can never be considered as the property of his parents, so that their right is not alienable (*ius personalissimum*).^{k} But this right is also not just a right against a person, since a child still belongs to his parents as what is theirs (is still in their *possession* like a thing and can be brought back even against his will into his parents' possession from another's possession). It is, instead, a right to a person *akin to a right to a thing*.

From this it is evident that, in the doctrine of right, there must necessarily be added to the headings rights to things and rights against persons the heading *rights to persons akin to rights to things*; the division made up till now has not been complete. For when we speak of the rights of parents to children as part of their household, we are referring not merely to the children's duty to return when they have run away but to the parents' being justified in taking control of them and impounding them as things (like domestic animals that have gone astray).

On the Right of Domestic Society
Title III
Right of a Head of the Household^l
§30

The children of a household, who together with their parents formed a *family*, reach their *majority* (*maiorennes*) without any contract to withdraw from their

---

^{k} most personal right ^{l} *Das Hausherren-Recht*

former dependence, merely by attaining the ability to support themselves (which happens partly as a natural coming of age in the general course of nature, partly in keeping with their particular natural qualities). In other words, they become their own masters (*sui iuris*) and acquire this right without any special act to establish it and so merely by law (*lege*). – Just as they are not in debt to their parents for their education, so the parents are released in the same way from their obligation to their children, and both children and parents acquire or reacquire their natural freedom. The domestic society that was necessary in accordance with law is now dissolved.

[6:283] Both parties can now maintain what is actually the same household but with a different form of obligation, namely, as the connection of the head of the household with servants (male or female servants of the house). What they maintain is the same domestic society but it is now a society *under the head of the household* (*societas herilis*),[m] formed by a contract through which the head of the household establishes a domestic society with the children who have now attained their majority or, if the family has no children, with other free persons (members of the household). This would be a society of unequals (one party *being in command* or being its head, the other *obeying*, i.e., serving) (*imperantis et subiecti domestici*)[n].

Servants are included in what belongs to the head of a household, and, as far as the form (the *way of his being in possession*)[o] is concerned, they are his by a right that is like a right to a thing; for if they run away from him he can bring them back in his control by his unilateral choice. But as far as the matter is concerned, that is, what *use* he can make of these members of his household, he can never behave as if he owned them (*dominus servi*); for it is only by a contract that he has brought them under his control, and a contract by which one party would completely renounce its freedom for the other's advantage would be self-contradictory, that is, null and void, since by it one party would cease to be a person and so would have no duty to keep the contract but would recognize only force. (The right of ownership with regard to someone who has forfeited his personality by a crime is not under consideration here.)

The contract of the head of a household with servants can therefore not be such that his *use* of them would amount to *using them up*; and it is not for him alone to judge about this, but also for the servants (who, accordingly, can never be serfs); so the contract cannot be concluded for life but at most only for an unspecified time, within which one party may give the other notice. But children (even those of someone who has become a slave through his crime) are at all times free. For everyone is born free, since he has not yet committed a crime; and the cost of educating him until he comes of age cannot be accounted against him

---

[m] household society   [n] domestic ruler and subject   [o] *Besitzstand.* See 6:306.

as a debt that he has to pay off. For the slave would have to educate his children if he could, without charging them with the cost of their education, and if he cannot the obligation devolves on his possessor.

* * *

So we see here again, as in the two preceding headings, that there is a right to persons akin to a right to things (of the head of the house over servants); for he can fetch servants back and demand them from anyone in possession of them, as what is externally his, even before the reasons that may have led them to run away and their rights have been investigated.

Dogmatic Division of All Rights That Can Be Acquired by Contract
§31

A metaphysical doctrine of right can be required to enumerate *a priori* the members of a division (*divisio logica*) in a complete and determinate way, and to establish thereby a true *system* of them. Instead of providing a system, any *empirical division* is merely *fragmentary* (*partitio*), and leaves it uncertain whether there are not additional members that would be needed to fill out the entire sphere of the concept divided. – A division in accordance with an *a priori* principle (in contrast with empirical divisions) can be called *dogmatic*.

Every contract consists in itself, that is, considered *objectively*, of two acts that establish a right, a promise and its acceptance. Acquisition through acceptance is not a *part* of a contract (unless the contract is a *pactum re initum*, which requires delivery) but the rightfully necessary *result* of it. – But considered *subjectively* – that is, as to whether this rationally necessary result (the *acquisition* that *ought* to occur) will actually *result* (be the *natural* result) – accepting the promise still gives me no *guarantee* that it will actually result. Since this guarantee belongs externally to the modality of a contract, namely *certainty* of acquisition by means of a contract, it is an additional factor serving to complete the means for achieving the acquisition that is the purpose of a contract. – For this, three persons are involved: a *promisor*, an *acceptor*, and a *guarantor*. The acceptor, indeed, gains nothing more with regard to the object by means of the guarantor and his separate contract with the promisor, but he still gains the means of coercion for obtaining what is his.

In accordance with these principles of logical (rational) division there are, strictly speaking, only three simple and *pure* kinds of contract. There are innumerable mixed and empirical kinds of contract, which add, to the principles of what is mine or yours in accordance only with laws of reason, statutory and conventional ones; but they lie beyond the sphere of the metaphysical doctrine of right, which is all that should be considered here.

Every contract has for its purpose either A. *unilateral* acquisition (a gratuitous contract) or B. acquisition *by both parties* (an onerous contract), or no acquisition but only C. *guaranteeing what belongs to someone* (this contract can be gratuitous on one side but can still be onerous on the other side).

A. A *gratuitous* contract (*pactum gratuitum*) is:

    a) *Keeping goods* on trust (*depositum*).

    b) *Lending* a thing (*commodatum*).

    c) *Making a gift* (*donatio*).

B. *Onerous* contracts.

  I. *A contract to alienate something* (*permutatio late sic dicta*).[p]

    a) *Barter* (*permutatio stricte sic dicta*).[q] Goods for goods.

    b) *Buying and selling* (*emtio venditio*). Goods for money.

    c) *Loan for consumption* (*mutuum*). Lending a thing on the condition of its being returned only in kind (e.g., grain for grain, or money for money).

  II. *A contract to let and hire* (*locatio conductio*).

    α. *Lending a thing of mine* to another for his use (*locatio rei*). Insofar as the contract is onerous, a *payment of interest* may also be added (*pactum usurarium*) if *repayment* can be made only in kind.

    β. A contract of *letting of work* on hire (*locatio operae*), that is, granting another the use of my powers for a specified price (*merces*). By this *contract* the worker is hired help (*mercennarius*).

    γ. A *contract empowering an agent* (*mandatum*). Carrying on another's affairs in his place and *in his name*. If someone carries on another's affairs in place of him but not also in his name, this is called *carrying on his affairs* without being *commissioned* to do so (*gestio negotii*); but when this is done in the other's name we speak of a *mandate*. As a contract of hiring this is an onerous contract (*mandatum onerosum*).

C. *Contracts providing security* (*cautio*).

    a) A joint *giving and taking of a pledge* (*pignus*).

    b) *Assuming liability* for another's promise (*fideiussio*).

    c) *Personally vouching for a person's performance* of something (*praestatio obsidis*).

[6:286]

---

[p] changing (ownership) broadly speaking   [q] changing (ownership) narrowly speaking

In this table of all the ways of *transferring* (*translatio*) what belongs to one to another are to be found concepts of objects or instruments of transfer which [seem]ʳ to be entirely empirical and, even in terms of their possibility, have no proper place in a *metaphysical* doctrine of right, in which division must be made in accordance with *a priori* principles, abstracting from the matter that is exchanged (which could be conventional) and considering only the form. Such, for example, is the concept of *money*, in contrast to all other alienable things, namely *goods*, under the heading of *buying and selling*, as well as the concept of a *book*. – But it will be shown that the concept of money, as the greatest and most useful means human beings have for *exchange* of things, called *buying and selling* (commerce), and so too the concept of a book, as the greatest means for exchanging thoughts, can still be resolved into pure intellectual relations. So the table of pure contracts need not be made impure by anything empirical mixed into it.

I
What Is Money?

Money is a thing that can be *used* only by being *alienated*. This is a good *nominal definition*ˢ of it (as given by Achenwall);²⁷ that is to say, it is sufficient for distinguishing this kind of object of choice from any other, though it tells us nothing about the possibility of such a thing. Still, from the nominal definition one can see this much: *first*, that the alienation of money in exchange is intended not as a gift but for *reciprocal* acquisition (by a *pactum onerosum*); and *second*, that money *represents* all goods, since it is conceived as a universally accepted mere *means* of commerce (within a nation), having no value in itself, as opposed to things which are *goods* (i.e., which have value in themselves and are related to the [6:287] particular needs of one or another in the nation).

A bushel of grain has the greatest direct value as a means for satisfying human needs. It can be used as fodder for animals, which nourish us, transport us, and work in place of us; by means of it, furthermore, the human population is increased and preserved, and in turn not only raises these natural products again but also helps to satisfy our needs with the products of art, by building houses, making clothes, providing the enjoyments we seek and, in general, all the conveniences that form the goods of industry.ᵗ By contrast, the value of money is only indirect. One cannot enjoy money itself or make immediate use

---

ʳ The structure of the sentence, *welche ganz empirisch zu sein und ... nicht Platz haben,* seems to require this addition.
ˢ *Namenerklärung*   ᵗ *Industrie*
²⁷ Gottfried Achenwall's *Ius Naturae* (5th edn, Gottingen, 1763) was one of the texts Kant used for the course on natural right that he gave at least twelve times during his teaching career. Achenwall's text, with Kant's comments on it, is included in AA 19:325–442.

of it in any way. Yet it is still a means which, among all things, has the greatest usefulness.

On this basis a preliminary *real definition* of money can be given: it is the universal *means by which human beings exchange their industriousness*[u] *with one another*. Thus a nation's wealth, insofar as it is acquired by means of money, is really only the sum of the industry with which human beings pay one another and which is represented by the money in circulation within it.

The thing to be called money must, therefore, have cost as much *industry* to produce or to obtain from other human beings as the *industry* by which those goods (natural or artificial products) are acquired for which that industry is exchanged. For if it were easier to procure the stuff called money than goods, more money would then come into the market than goods for sale; and since the seller would have to have expended more industry for his goods than the buyer, who got the money more readily, industry in producing goods, and therefore trade in general, would diminish and be curtailed, along with the productive industry[v] which results in the nation's wealth. – Hence bank notes and promissory notes cannot be regarded as money, though they can substitute for it temporarily; for they cost almost no industry to produce and their value is based solely on the opinion that they will continue as before to be convertible into *hard cash*; but if it is eventually discovered that there is not enough [6:288] hard cash for which they can be readily and securely exchanged, this opinion suddenly collapses and makes failure of payment inevitable. – So the productive industry of those who work the gold and silver mines in Peru or New Mexico, especially in view of the industry vainly expended in searches for deposits that are so often unsuccessful, is apparently still greater than that expended on the manufacture of goods in Europe; and this excess of industry would be discontinued from not being paid, letting those countries soon sink into poverty, if the Europeans did not increase their industry proportionately through being stimulated by those very materials, so that the luxuries they offer constantly stimulate in others a desire for mining. In this way industry always keeps pace with industry.[w]

But how is it possible that what were at first only goods finally became money? This would happen if a powerful, opulent *ruler* who at first used a material for the adornment and splendour of his attendants (his court) came to levy taxes on his subjects in this material (as goods) (e.g., gold, silver, copper, or a kind of beautiful seashell, *cowries*; or as in the Congo a kind of matting called *makutes*, in Senegal iron ingots, or on the Coast of Guinea even black slaves), and in turn

---

[u] *Fleiß*. In view of what Kant regards as his direct quotation from Adam Smith (6:289), one would expect him to use *Arbeit*, "labour," rather than *Fleiß*, "industriousness" or "diligence." However, in "translating" Smith's sentence into German Kant uses *Fleiß*. In the remainder of this passage "industry" is used in the sense of "industriousness."

[v] *Erwerbfleiß* [w] *so daß immer Fleiß gegen Fleiß in Concurrenz kommen.*

paid with this same material those his demand moved to industry in procuring it, in accordance with exchange regulations with them and among them (on a market or exchange). – In this way only (so it seems to me) could a certain merchandise have become a lawful means of exchange of the industry of subjects with one another, and thereby also become the wealth of the nation, that is, *money*.

The intellectual concept under which the empirical concept of money falls is therefore the concept of a thing which, in the circulation of possessions (*permutatio publica*), determines the *price* of all other things (goods), among which even the sciences belong, insofar as they would not otherwise be taught to others. The amount of money in a nation therefore constitutes its wealth (*opulentia*). For the price (*pretium*) of a thing is the judgment of the public about its *value* (*valor*) in proportion to that which serves as the universal means to represent reciprocal exchange of *industry* (its circulation). – Accordingly, where there is a great deal of trade, neither *gold* nor copper is regarded as strictly money but only as merchandise, since there is too little gold and too much copper for them to be easily put into circulation and yet available in sufficiently small parts, as is necessary for the exchange of merchandise, or a mass of it, in the smallest purchase. *Silver* (more or less alloyed with copper) is, accordingly, taken as the proper material for money and the measure for reckoning prices in the great trade of the world; other metals (even more so, nonmetallic materials) can be found as money only in a nation where there is little trade. – But when the first two metals are not only weighed but also stamped, that is, provided with a sign indicating how much they are to be worth, they are lawful money, that is, *coinage*.

[6:289]

"Money is therefore" (according to Adam Smith) "that material thing the alienation of which is the means and at the same time the measure of the industry by which human beings and nations carry on trade with one another."[28] – This definition[x] brings the empirical concept of money to an intellectual concept by looking only to the *form* of what each party provides in return for the other in onerous contracts (and abstracting from their matter), thereby bringing it to the concept of right in the exchange of what is mine or yours generally (*commutatio late sic dicta*),[y] so as to present the table above as a dogmatic division *a priori*, which is appropriate to the metaphysics of right as a system.

---

[x] *Erklärung*   [y] exchange broadly speaking

[28] Adam Smith says merely: "It is in this manner that money has become in all civilized nations the universal *instrument* of commerce, by the intervention of which goods of all kinds are bought and sold, or exchanged for one another," *The Wealth of Nations*, Bk. I, ch. 4 (Middlesex and New York: Penguin Books, 1970), 131. He does, however, develop in ch. 5 the notion that labor determines the value of all goods.

II
What Is a Book?

A book is a writing (it does not matter, here, whether it is written in hand or set in type, whether it has few or many pages), which represents a discourse that someone delivers to the public by visible linguistic signs. – One who *speaks* to the public in his own name is called the *author* (*autor*). One who, through a writing, discourses publicly in another's (the author's) name is a *publisher*. When a publisher does this with the author's permission, he is the legitimate publisher; but if he does it without the author's permission, he is an illegitimate publisher, that is, an *unauthorized publisher*.[z] The sum of all the reproductions of the original writing (the copies) is an *edition*.

Unauthorized Publishing of Books[a] Is Forbidden as a Matter of Right[b]

A *writing* is not an immediate sign of a *concept* (as is, for example, an etching which represents a certain person in a *portrait*, or a work in plaster that is a *bust*). It is rather a *discourse* to the public; that is, the author *speaks* publicly through the publisher. – But the *publisher* speaks (through his foreman, *operarius*, the printer), not in his own name (for he would then pass himself off as the author), but in the name of the author; and so he is entitled to do this only when the author *gives him a mandate* (*mandatum*). – Now it is true that an unauthorized publisher also speaks, by an edition on his own initiative,[c] in the name of the author, but he does so without having been given a mandate by the author (*gerit se mandatarium absque mandato*).[d] He therefore commits the crime of stealing the profits from the publisher who was appointed by the author (who is therefore the only legitimate one), profits the legitimate publisher could and would have derived from the use of his right (*furtum usus*). So *unauthorized publishing of books is forbidden as a matter of right*.

Why does unauthorized publishing, which strikes one even at first glance as unjust, still have an appearance of being rightful? Because *on the one hand* a book is a corporeal *artifact* (*opus mechanicum*)[e] that can be reproduced (by someone in legitimate possession of a copy of it), so that there is a *right to a thing* with regard

[6:290]

---

[z] *Nachdrucker*

[a] Or "publishing books without having been empowered by the author." To translate *Büchernachdruck* as "literary piracy" would seem inconsistent with the "appearance of being rightful" which Kant says it has. The language used here is similar to that of his essay "*Von der Unrechtmäßigkeit des Büchernachdrucks*," ["On the Wrongfulness of Unauthorized Publication of Books"] *Berliner Monatsschrift* (May 1785) (AA 8:77–87).

[b] *von rechtswegen verboten*. The term *von rechtswegen* was used earlier (6:250), apparently in the sense of "by legal proceedings."

[c] *durch seinen eigenmächtigen Verlag*   [d] acts as if he has a mandate without having a mandate

[e] mechanical work

to it. *On the other hand* a book is also a mere *discourse* of the publisher to the public, which the publisher may not repeat publicly without having a mandate from the author to do so (*praestatio operae*), and this is a *right against a person*. The error consists in mistaking one of these rights for the other.

* * *

There is another case, under contracts to let and hire (B, ii, (α)), in which the confusion of a right against a person with a right to a thing is material for disputes, that of *renting to a tenant* (*ius incolatus*). – The question arises, whether an owner who has leased his house (or land) to someone and sells it to someone else before the lease expires is bound to attach to the contract of sale the condition that the lease is to continue, or whether one can say that purchase breaks a lease (though notice is to be given the lessee, the time being determined by custom). – On the first alternative the house actually had an *encumbrance* (*onus*) on it, a right to this thing that the lessee had acquired in it (the house). [6:291] This can indeed take place (by entering this encumbrance in the land register, as included in the contract to lease); but then this would not be a mere contract to lease, but one to which another contract had had to be added (one to which few landlords would agree). So the saying "Purchase breaks a lease" is valid, that is, a full right to a thing (property) outweighs any right against a person that cannot exist together with it. But it is still left open for the lessee to complain, on the basis of his right against a person, that he is to be compensated for any damages arising from the breaking of the contract.

Episodic Section
On *Ideal Acquisition* of an External Object of Choice

§32

I call acquisition *ideal* if it involves no causality in time and is therefore based on a mere *idea* of pure reason. It is nonetheless *true*, not imaginary, acquisition, and the only reason I do not call it real is that the act of acquiring is not empirical, since the subject acquires from another who either *does not yet* exist (only the possibility that he may exist is admitted) or who has *ceased to exist*, or when the subject *no longer exists*, so that coming into possession is merely a practical idea of reason. – There are three kinds of such acquisition: 1) by *prolonged possession*, 2) by *inheritance*, and 3) by *merit surviving death* (*meritum immortale*), that is, the claim to a good reputation after death. All three can, indeed, take effect only in a public rightful condition, but they are not *based* only on its constitution and the chosen^f statutes in it: they are also conceivable *a priori* in the state of nature and

---

^f *willkürlichen*

must be conceived as prior to such statutes, in order that laws in the civil constitution may afterwards be adapted to them (*sunt iuris naturae*).

I
Acquisition by Prolonged Possession[g][29]
§33

I acquire another's property merely by *long possession of it* (*usucapio*), not because [6:292] I may legitimately *presume* that he consents to my acquiring it (*per consensum praesumtum*), nor because I can assume that, since he does not contradict me, he *has given it up* (*rem derelictam*), but because, even if there should be someone who was the true owner and as such laid claim to it (a claimant), I may still *exclude* him merely by virtue of my long possession, ignore his existence up to now, and carry on as if he existed up to the time of my possession only as a thought-entity, even if I should later learn of his reality as well as that of his claim. – Although this way of acquiring is called acquisition by *prescription*[h] (*per praescriptionem*), this is not altogether correct, since exclusion of claims is to be regarded only as a result of acquisition: acquisition must have come first. – It has now to be proved that it is possible to acquire something in this way.

Someone who does not exercise a continuous *possessory act* (*actus possessorius*) with regard to an external thing, as something that is his, is rightly regarded as someone who does not exist at all (as its possessor). For he cannot complain of being wronged as long as he does nothing to justify his title of possessor; and even if later on, when another has already taken possession of it, he declares himself its possessor, all he is saying is that he was once its owner, not that he still is and that his possession has remained uninterrupted without a continuous rightful act. – Hence if someone does not use a thing for a long time, only a rightful possessory act, and indeed one that is continuously maintained and documented, can guarantee that it is his.

For suppose that failure to perform this possessory act did not result in another's being able to base a firm right (*possessio irrefragabilis*) on his lawful

---

[g] *Ersitzung.* See note 29.   [h] or "superannuation of claims," *Verjährung*

[29] The distinction between "long possession" or "usucaption" (*Ersitzung, usucapio*) and "super-annuation of claims" or "prescription" (*Verjährung, praescriptio*) discussed here has a long history. In Roman law, acquiring ownership (*dominium*) of a thing by *usucapio* was originally available only under the *ius civile*, for Roman citizens, and *praescriptio* had to be devised as an analogous procedure for provincials or foreigners. It did not confer ownership but enabled the possessor to bar a claimant's right of action against him if he could show that he had been possessor in good faith for the prescribed period of time. But before the code of Justinian, prescription had come to extinguish the claimant's title instead of merely barring his action; and when Justinian abolished the distinction between Italian and provincial land (which had belonged to the Roman people or to the Emperor), prescription by thirty years' possession gave ownership to a possessor in good faith, even if the thing had originally been stolen. See R. W. Leage, *Roman Private Law* (London: Macmillan and Co., Ltd, 1930), 159–71.

possession in good faith (*possessio bonae fidei*) and to regard himself as having acquired the thing that is in his possession. Then no acquisition at all would be conclusive (guaranteed); all acquisition would be only provisional (up to the present), since investigation of the past cannot reach all the way back to the first possessor and his act of acquisition. – The presumption on which prolonged possession (*usucapio*) is based is therefore not merely in *conformity with right* (permitted, *iusta*) as a *conjecture* but is also in accord with rights (*praesumtio iuris et de iure*) as an assumption in terms of coercive laws (*suppositio legalis*). Whoever fails to document his possessory act has lost his claim to the present possessor, and the length of time during which he failed to do it (which cannot and need not be specified) is put forward only to support the certainty of his omission. That a hitherto unknown possessor could always get something back (recover it) when his possessory act has been interrupted (even through no fault of his own) contradicts the above postulate of practical reason with regard to rights (*dominia rerum incerta facere*).[i]   [6:293]

If he is a member of a commonwealth, that is, lives in the civil condition, the state (representing him) can indeed preserve his possession for him, although it was interrupted as private possession, and a present possessor need not prove his title of acquisition by tracing it back to the first possessor or basing it on prolonged possession. In the state of nature, however, prolonged possession is in conformity with right not, strictly speaking, for acquiring a thing but for maintaining possession of it without an act establishing the right; and this immunity from claims is also usually called acquisition. – Prescription[j] of an earlier possessor therefore belongs to natural right (*est iuris naturae*).

II
Inheritance (*Acquisitio haereditatis*)
§34

Inheritance is transfer (*translatio*) of the belongings and goods of someone who is dying to a survivor by agreement of the wills of both. – Acquisition by the *heir* (*haeredis instituti*) and leaving by the *testator* (*testatoris*), that is, this change of belongings, takes place in one moment, namely the moment at which the testator ceases to exist (*articulo mortis*). It is therefore not, strictly speaking, a transfer (*translatio*) in the empirical sense, since this assumes two acts following each other, namely the acts by which one person first leaves his possessions and the other then comes into them. Instead it is an ideal acquisition. – Now inheritance in the state of nature cannot be conceived of without a *last will* (*dispositio ultimae voluntatis*). Whether this is a *contract of inheritance*

---

[i] to act on uncertain ownerships of things   [j] *Präscription*

(*pactum successorium*) or a *unilateral disposition to the heir* (*testamentum*) amounts to the question, whether and how it is possible for belongings to pass from one to the other precisely at the moment at which the subject ceases [6:294] to exist. The question of how it is possible to acquire by inheritance must accordingly be investigated apart from the many ways in which it can be carried out (which are found only in a commonwealth).

"It is possible to acquire something through disposition to the heir." For the testator, Caius, promises and in his last will declares to Titius, who knows nothing of this promise, that upon his death his belongings are to pass to Titius. As long as he lives, Caius therefore remains sole owner of his belongings. Now it is true that by a unilateral will alone nothing can pass to the other person; for this there is required, besides the promise, acceptance (*acceptatio*) by the other party and a simultaneous will (*voluntas simultanea*), which is still lacking here; for, as long as Caius is alive, Titius cannot explicitly accept, so as to acquire by his acceptance, since Caius has promised only on the occasion of his death (otherwise the property would for a moment be common property, and this is not the testator's will). – Titius, however, still tacitly acquires a proprietary right[k] to the legacy as a right to a thing: namely, he has the exclusive right to accept it (*ius in re iacente*), so that the legacy at the moment of death is called *haereditas iacens*. Now, since every human being would necessarily accept such a right (since he can always gain but never lose by it), and so accepts tacitly, and since Titius, after Caius' death, is in this situation, he can acquire the bequest by acceptance of the promise, and the bequest has not become altogether ownerless (*res nullius*) in the meantime but only *vacant* (*res vacua*). For Titius alone has the right to make the choice as to whether or not he wants to make the belongings left to him his own.

Accordingly, testaments are also valid in accordance with mere natural right (*sunt iuris naturae*). This assertion, however, is to be taken as meaning that testaments are fit for and worth being introduced and sanctioned in the civil condition (if this makes its appearance some day). For only the civil condition (the general will in it) confirms possession of a legacy while it hovers between acceptance and rejection and strictly speaking belongs to no one.

---

[k] *eigenthümliches Recht*

III
Leaving Behind a Good Reputation after One's Death
(*Bona fama defuncti*)
§35

It would be absurd to think that someone who has died can still possess something after his death (and so when he no longer exists), if what he left behind were a thing. But a *good reputation* is an innate external belonging, though an ideal one only, which clings to the subject as a person, a being of such a nature that I can and must abstract from whether he ceases to be entirely at his death or whether he survives as a person; for in the context of his rights in relation to others, I actually regard every person simply in terms of his humanity, hence as *homo noumenon*. So any attempt to stain someone's reputation by falsehood after his death is suspect, because it is at least ungenerous to spread reproaches against one who is absent and cannot defend himself, unless one is quite certain of them. Nevertheless, a well-founded accusation against him is still in order (so that the principle *de mortuis nihil nisi bene*[1] is incorrect).

For someone to acquire by an irreproachable life and the death that ends it a (negatively) good name, which continues to be his when he no longer exists as *homo phaenomenon;* for those who survive him (relatives or strangers) to be also authorized by right to defend him (for unproved charges are dangerous to them as well, since they could get similar treatment when they die); for someone to be able to acquire such a right is, I say, a phenomenon as strange as it is undeniable, a phenomenon of reason giving law *a priori* which extends its commands and prohibitions even beyond the limits of life. – If anyone spreads it abroad that someone who has died committed a crime which in his lifetime would have made him dishonorable or only contemptible, whoever can produce proof that this charge is an intentional untruth and a lie can then publicly declare the one who spread the evil gossip a calumniator and so take away his honor. He could not do this unless he could rightly assume that the deceased was wronged by it, even though he is dead, and that this defense brings him satisfaction even though he no longer exists.[*] An apologist need not prove his authorization to play the role

[6:296]

---

[*] But one is not to draw from this any visionary conclusions about presentiments of a future life or about unseen relations to disembodied souls. For what is under discussion here does not go beyond the purely moral and rightful relations to be found among human beings during life as well. These are relations in which human beings stand as intelligible beings, insofar as one *logically puts aside*, that is, *abstracts from*, everything physical (i.e., everything belonging to their existence in space and time); but one does not remove them from this nature of theirs and let them become spirits, in which condition they would feel the injury of those who slander them. – Someone who, a hundred years from now, falsely repeats something evil about me injures me right now; for in a relation purely of rights, which is entirely intellectual, abstraction is made from any physical conditions (of time), and whoever robs me of my honor (a slanderer) is just as punishable as if he had done it

[1] speak nothing but good about the dead

of apologist for the dead, for every human being inevitably arrogates this to himself as belonging not merely to duty of virtue (duty regarded ethically) but to the right of humanity as such; and the stain on the deceased need not have been prejudicial to anyone in particular, such as his friends and relatives, to justify such censure. – It is therefore indisputable that there is a basis for such an ideal acquisition and for someone's right after his death against those who survive him, even though no deduction of its possibility can be given.

during my lifetime – punishable, however, not by a criminal court but only by public opinion, which, in accordance with the right of retribution, inflicts on him the same loss of the honor he diminished in another. – Even a *plagiarism* that a writer perpetrates on a dead person, though it does not indeed stain the dead person's honor but only steals a part of it from him, is still avenged with right, as having wronged him (robbed the human being).[m]

[m] *als Läsion desselben* (*Menschenraub*) LD: *Menschenraub* can be translated as "kidnapping" or "abduction."

Chapter III

On Acquisition That Is Dependent Subjectively upon the Decision of a Public Court of Justice

§36

If by natural right is understood only non-statutory right, hence simply right that can be cognized *a priori* by everyone's reason, natural right will include not only the *justice* that holds among persons in their exchanges with one another (*iustitia commutativa*) but also distributive justice (*iustitia distributiva*), insofar as it can be cognized *a priori* in accordance with the principle of distributive justice how its decisions[a] (*sententia*) would have to be reached. [6:297]

The moral person that administers justice is a *court* (*forum*) and its administration of justice is a *judgment*[b] (*iudicium*). All this is here thought out *a priori* only in accordance with conditions of right, without taking account of how such a constitution is to be actually set up and organized (*statutes*, hence empirical principles, belong to an actual constitution).

So the question here is not merely what is *right in itself*, that is, how every human being has to judge about it on his own, but what is right before a court, that is, what is laid down as right. And here there are *four* cases in which two different and opposing judgments can result and persist side by side, because they are made from two different points of view, both of which are true: one in accordance with private right, the other in accordance with the idea of public right. These cases are: 1) A *contract to make a gift* (*pactum donationis*). 2) A *contract to lend a thing* (*commodatum*). 3) *Recovering* something (*vindicatio*). 4) *Taking an oath* (*iuramentum*).

It is a common fault (*vitium subreptionis*) of experts on right to *misrepresent*, as if it were also the objective principle of what is right in itself, that rightful principle which a court is authorized and indeed bound to adopt for its own use (hence for a subjective purpose) in order to pronounce and judge[c] what belongs to each as his right, although the latter is very different from the former. – It is therefore of no slight importance to recognize this specific distinction and to draw attention to it.

A
On a Contract to Make a Gift
§37

In accordance with *private right*, this contract (*donatio*), by which I *alienate without remuneration* (*gratis*) what is mine, a thing of mine (or my right), involves a relation of myself, the donor (*donans*), to another, the recipient (*donatarius*), by [6:298]

---

[a] *Spruch*   [b] *Gericht*. LD: Ladd here has "trial."   [c] *zu sprechen und zu richten*

which what is mine passes to the recipient by his acceptance of it (*donum*). – But it is not to be presumed that I intend by this contract to be coerced to keep my promise and so also to give up my *freedom* gratuitously and, as it were, to throw myself away (*nemo suum iactare praesumitur*).[d] Yet this is what would happen in accordance with right in the civil condition, where the one who is to receive my gift can *coerce* me to carry out my promise. So, if the matter were to come before a court, that is, in accordance with public right, it would either have to be presumed that the donor consented to this coercion, which is absurd, or else the court in its judgment (verdict) simply takes no account of whether the donor did or did not want to reserve his freedom to go back on his promise, but takes account only of what is certain, namely, the promise and the promisee's acceptance of it. So even if, as can well be supposed, the promisor thought that he could not be bound to keep his promise should he regret having made it before it is time to fulfill it, the court assumes that he would have had to make this reservation expressly, and that if he did not he could be coerced to fulfill his promise. The court adopts this principle because otherwise its verdict on rights would be made infinitely more difficult or even impossible.

B
On a Contract to Lend a Thing
§38

In this contract (*commodatum*) by which I permit someone to use without compensation something of mine, if the parties to the contract agree that *this very same thing* is to be brought under my control again, the borrower (*commodatarius*) cannot presume that the thing's owner (*commodans*) also assumes every risk (*casus*) of possible loss of the thing, or of what makes it useful, that might arise from its having been put into the borrower's possession. For it is not a matter of course that the owner, in addition to granting the borrower the use of his thing (such loss to himself as is inseparable from parting with it), has also

[6:299] issued the borrower a *guarantee* against any damage that could arise from his having let it out of his custody. A separate contract would have to be made about that. So the question can only be: on which of the two, the lender or the borrower, is it incumbent to attach expressly to a contract to lend the condition about assuming the risk for possible damage to the thing? or, if no such condition is attached, who can be *presumed* to have *agreed* to guarantee the lender's property (by the return of it, or its equivalent, to him)? Not the lender, for it cannot be presumed that he has gratuitously agreed to more than the mere use of the thing (that is, that he has also undertaken to guarantee the property). It is,

---

[d] no one is presumed to throw away what is his

rather, the borrower, because in taking on this guarantee he performs nothing more than is already contained in the contract.

Suppose, for example, that having been caught in the rain I go into a house and ask to borrow a coat, which is then, say, permanently stained when someone carelessly pours discoloring material from a window, or is stolen from me when I go into another house and take it off. Everyone would find it absurd to say that I need do nothing more than return the coat as it is, or that I have only to report that the theft occurred and that it was at most a matter of courtesy for me to commiserate with the owner over his loss, since he could demand nothing on the basis of his right. – But no one would think it absurd if, in requesting to use something, I also ask its owner beforehand to take on himself the risk of any mischance that might happen to it while it is in my hands, because I am poor and unable to compensate him for the loss. No one will find this superfluous and ridiculous, except, perhaps, when the lender is known to be a rich and considerate man, since it would then be almost insulting him not to presume that he would generously remit my debt in this case.

* * *

Now if (as the nature of a contract to lend involves) nothing is stipulated in it about a possible mischance (*casus*) that might affect the thing, so that agreement about this can only be presumed, a contract to lend is an uncertain contract (*pactum incertum*) with regard to what is mine and what is yours by it. Consequently, the judgment about this, that is, the decision as to who must bear the misfortune, cannot be made from the conditions of the contract itself; it can be decided only as it would be decided *before a court*, which always considers only what is certain in the case (which is here the possession of the thing as property). So the judgment in the *state of nature*, that is, in terms of the intrinsic character of the matter, will go like this: the damage resulting from mischance to a thing loaned falls on the *borrower* (*casum sentit commodatarius*).[c] But in the *civil condition*, and so before a court, the verdict will come out: the damage falls on the *lender* (*casum sentit dominus*).[f] This verdict will indeed be given on different grounds from the decree of sound reason alone, since a public judge cannot get involved in presumptions as to what the one party or the other may have thought. He can consider only that whoever has not attached a separate contract stipulating that he is free from any damages to the thing lent must himself bear them. – Hence the difference between the judgment that a court must make and that which each is justified in making for himself by his private reason is a point that is by no means to be overlooked in amending judgments about rights.[g]

[6:300]

[c] the case is borne by the borrower [f] the case is borne by the lender
[g] *in Berichtigung der Rechtsurtheile*

C
On Recovery (Repossession) of Something Lost (*vindicatio*)
§39

It is clear from the foregoing that something of mine that continues to exist remains mine even though I am not continuously holding it; that it does not of itself cease to be mine apart from some act by which I give up my right to it (*derelictionis vel alienationis*);[h] and that I have a right to this thing (*ius reale*) and therefore a right against *whoever* holds it, not merely a right against a specific person (*ius personale*). But the question now is whether this right must also be regarded *by everyone else* as ownership that continues of itself, if I have *only not renounced* it, when the thing is in another's possession.

[6:301] Suppose that someone has lost a thing (*res amissa*) and that someone else takes it *in good faith* (*bona fide*), as a supposed find. Or suppose that I get a thing by its being formally alienated by someone possessing it who represents himself as its owner although he is not. Since I cannot acquire a thing from someone who *is not its owner* (*a non domino*), the question arises whether I am excluded by the real owner from any right to this thing and left with only a personal right against the illegitimate possessor. – The latter is obviously the case if acquisition is judged merely in accordance with the intrinsic grounds that justify it (in the state of nature), not in accordance with what is appropriate for a court.

It must be possible for whatever can be alienated to be acquired by someone or other. The legitimacy of acquisition, however, rests entirely on the form in accordance with which what is possessed by another is transferred to me and accepted by me, that is, on the formalities of the act of exchange (*commutatio*) between the possessor of the thing and the one acquiring it, by which a right is established; I may not ask how the possessor obtained possession of it, since this would already be an offense (*quilibet praesumitur bonus, donec etc.*).[i][30] Suppose, now, that it later turns out that the possessor was not the owner but that someone else was. I cannot then say that the owner could straightway take the thing from me (as he could from anyone else who might be holding it). For I have stolen nothing from him, but have, for example, bought a horse offered for sale in the public market in conformity with the law (*titulo emti venditi*). The title of acquisition on my part is indisputable since I (as buyer) am not bound or even authorized to search the other's (the seller's) title of possession – this

---

[h] abandonment or alienation

[i] everyone is presumed to be good until the contrary is proved. (LD: This translation slightly revises Gregor's from the previous edition. The Latin covered by the "*etc.*" is "*probetur contrarium*".)

[30] LD: On this and related rebuttable presumptions (e.g., at 6:307), see Byrd and Hruschka, "From the State of Nature to the Juridical State of States," *Law and Philosophy* 27 (6) (2008):599–641, 615–22.

investigation would go on to infinity in an ascending series. If the purchase is formally correct, I become not just the *putative* but the *true* owner of the horse.

But against this, the following argument arises with regard to rights. Any acquisition from one who is not the owner of a thing (*a non domino*) is null and void. I can derive no more from another than what he legitimately has. Even though, in buying a stolen horse for sale in the market, I proceed quite correctly as far as the form of acquisition (*modus acquirendi*) is concerned, my title of acquisition is still defective, since the horse did not belong to the one who actually sold it. I may well be its possessor *in good faith* (*possessor bonae fidei*), but I am still only its putative owner (*dominus putativus*) and the true owner has [6:302] a right to *recover* it (*rem suam vindicandi*).

If one asks what is to be laid down as right *in itself* (in the state of nature) in the acquisition of external things in accordance with principles of justice in human beings' exchanges with one another (*iustitia commutativa*), then one must answer as follows. If someone intends to acquire an external thing in this way, it is in fact necessary for him to investigate whether the thing he wants to acquire does not already belong to someone else; that is to say, even if he has strictly observed the formal conditions for deriving the thing from what belongs to another (has bought the horse on the market in the proper way), as long as he remains ignorant as to whether someone else (other than the seller) is the true owner of it, the most he could have acquired is only a *right against a person* with regard to the thing (*ius ad rem*), so that if someone comes forth who can document his previous ownership of it, nothing is left to the alleged new owner but to have legitimately enjoyed the use of it up to this moment as its possessor in good faith. – Since it is largely impossible to discover who was absolutely first (the original owner) in the series of putative owners deriving their right from each other, no trade in external things, no matter how well it may agree with the formal conditions of this kind of justice (*iustitia commutativa*), can guarantee a secure acquisition.

* * *

Here again reason giving laws with regard to rights comes forth with a principle of *distributive justice*, of adopting as its guiding rule for the legitimacy of possession, not the way it would be judged *in itself* by the private will of each (in the state of nature), but the way it would be judged before a *court* in a condition brought about by the united will of all (in a civil condition). In a civil condition, conformity with the formal conditions of acquisition, which of themselves establish only a right against a person, is postulated as an adequate substitute for the material grounds (which establish derivation from what belonged to a previous alleged owner); and what is *in itself* a right against a person, *when brought before a court*, holds as a right to a thing. A horse,

[6:303] for example, that someone puts up for sale in a public market regulated by police ordinances becomes my property if all the rules of buying and selling are strictly observed (but in such a way that the true owner retains the right to put forward a claim against the seller on the ground of his earlier, unforfeited possession of it); and what would otherwise be my right against a person is converted into a right to a thing, in accordance with which I can take (recover) it as mine wherever I find it, without having to get involved in how the seller obtained it.

So it is only for the sake of a court's verdict (*in favorem iustitiae distributivae*) that a right to a thing is taken and treated not *as it is in itself* (as a right against a person) but as it can be *most readily* and surely *judged* (as a right to a thing), and yet in accordance with a pure *a priori* principle. – On this principle various statutory laws (ordinances) are subsequently based, the primary purpose of which is to set up conditions under which alone a way of acquiring is to have rightful force, conditions *such that a judge* can assign to each what is his *most readily and with least hesitation*. For example, in the saying "Purchase breaks a lease," what is a right to a thing (the lease) in accordance with the nature of the contract, that is, in itself, holds as a mere right against a person; and conversely, as in the case discussed above, what is in itself only a right against a person holds as a right to a thing. In such cases the question is what principles a court in the civil condition should rely on in order to proceed most surely in its verdicts about the rights belonging to each.

D
On Acquiring Guarantees by Oath[31](*Cautio iuratoria*)
§40

No other reason could be given which could bind human beings as a matter of right[i] to *believe* and acknowledge that there are gods than that they could thereby swear an oath and be constrained to be truthful in what they say and faithful in keeping their promises by their fear of an all-seeing, almighty power whose vengeance they would have solemnly called down upon themselves in case their [6:304] declarations were false. That in requiring oaths one does not count on morality in these two respects but only on blind superstition is clear from this: that one does not expect any guarantee *merely* from their *solemn* declarations before

---

[i] *rechtlich*

[31] Kant seems to be thinking here of "the decisory oath," which would decide a fact at issue in a case. This was one of the devices of civil procedure designed to protect the judge from threats by the wealthy and the powerful. "The decisory oath worked in the following way: Party A could put Party B on his oath as to a fact at issue that was within Party B's knowledge. If Party B refused to swear, the fact was taken as conclusively proved against him. If Party B swore, the fact was taken as conclusively proved in his favor" (John Henry Merryman, *The Civil Law Tradition* [Stanford: Stanford University Press, 1969], 126).

a court in matters of rights, even though everyone clearly sees the duty to be truthful in a case having to do with what is most sacred of all among human beings (the right of human beings). So mere fairy tales are the incentive in taking oaths, as, for example, according to Marsden's testimony, the Rajangs, a pagan people of Sumatra, swear by the bones of their dead ancestors even though they do not believe that there is a life after death; or as the Negroes of Guinea take an oath on their *fetish*, such as a bird's feather, calling upon it to break their neck, and so forth. They believe that an invisible power, whether it has understanding or not, already has by its nature this magical power that will come into play by their invocations. – This sort of belief is called religion but should strictly be called superstition. It is, however, indispensable for the administration of justice since, without counting on it, a *court* would not be sufficiently in a position to ascertain facts kept secret and give the right verdict. A law binding a people to take oaths is therefore obviously laid down only on behalf of the judicial authority.

But now the question is, what basis is there for the obligation that someone before a court is supposed to have, to accept another's oath as a proof, valid for right, of the truth of his testimony, which puts an end to all dispute? That is to say, what binds me as a matter of right to believe that another (who swears an oath) has any religion, so as to make my rights dependent upon his oath? So too, can I be bound to take an oath? Both are wrong in themselves.

Yet with reference to a court, and so in the civil condition, if one admits that there is no other means than an oath for getting at the truth in certain cases, one must assume that everyone has a religion, so that it can be used as an expedient (*in casu necessitatis*) for the purpose of proceedings about rights *before a court*, which regards this spiritual coercion (*tortura spiritualis*) as a handy means, in keeping with the human propensity to superstition, for uncovering secrets and considers itself authorized to use it because of this. – But the legislative authority acts in a way that is fundamentally wrong in conferring authorization to do this on the judicial authority, since even in the civil condition coercion to take oaths [6:305] is contrary to human freedom, which must not be lost.

An oath of office is usually *promissory*, an oath, namely, that the official earnestly *resolves* to fulfill his post in conformity with his duties. If it were changed into an *assertoric* oath – if, that is, the official was bound, say at the end of a year (or more), to swear that he had faithfully fulfilled his office during that time – this would arouse his conscience more than an oath he takes as a promise; for having taken a promissory oath, he can always make the excuse to himself later on that with the best of intentions he did not foresee the difficulties which he experienced only later, during the administration of his office. Moreover, he would be more concerned about being accused of failing in his duty if an observer is going to look at the sum of his offenses than if they are merely censured one after the other (and the earlier ones have been forgotten). – But a court can certainly not demand swearing to a *belief* (*de credulitate*). For in the first place, it involves a self-contradiction; this thing intermediate between opinion and knowledge is the sort of thing that one can dare to bet on but certainly not to swear to. Second, a judge who requires swearing to a belief from a party in order to find out something relevant to his purpose, even if this purpose is the common good, commits a grave offense against the conscientiousness of the person taking the oath, partly by the thoughtlessness to which the oath misleads him and by which the judge defeats his own purpose, partly by the pangs of conscience a human being must feel, when he can find a certain matter very likely today, considered from a certain point of view, but quite unlikely tomorrow, when he considers it from a different point of view. A judge therefore wrongs one whom he constrains to take such an oath.

Transition from What Is Mine or Yours in a State of Nature to What Is Mine or Yours in a Rightful Condition Generally
§41

A rightful condition is that relation of human beings among one another that contains the conditions under which alone everyone is able to *enjoy* his rights, and the formal condition under which this is possible in accordance with the idea of a will giving laws for everyone[k] is called public justice. With reference to either the possibility or the actuality or the necessity of possession of objects (the matter of choice) in accordance with laws, public justice can be divided into *protective justice* (*iustitia tutatrix*), *justice in acquiring from one another* (*iustitia commutativa*), and *distributive justice* (*iustitia distributiva*). – In these the law says, *first*, merely what conduct is intrinsically *right*[l] in terms of its form (*lex iusti*); *second*, what [objects] are capable of being covered externally by law, in terms of their matter, that is, what way of being in possession is *rightful*[m] (*lex iuridica*); *third*, what is the decision of a court in a particular case in accordance with the given law under which it falls, that is, what is *laid down as right*[n] (*lex iustitiae*). Because of this a court is itself called the *justice* of a country, and whether such a thing exists or does not exist is the most important question that can be asked about any arrangements having to do with rights.

A condition that is not rightful, that is, a condition in which there is no distributive justice, is called a state of nature (*status naturalis*). What is opposed to a state of nature is not (as Achenwall thinks) a condition that is *social* and that could be called an artificial condition (*status artificialis*), but rather the *civil* condition (*status civilis*), that of a society subject to distributive justice. For in the state of nature, too, there can be societies compatible with rights (e.g., conjugal, paternal,

[6:306]

---

[k] *eines allgemein gesetzgebenden Willens*   [l] *recht*   [m] *dessen Besitzstand rechtlich ist*
[n] *Rechtens*

domestic societies in general, as well as many others); but no law, "You ought to enter this condition," holds *a priori* for these societies, whereas it can be said of a *rightful* condition that all human beings who could (even involuntarily)^o come into relations of rights with one another *ought* to enter this condition.

The first and second of these conditions can be called the condition of *private right*, whereas the third and last can be called the condition of *public right*. The latter contains no further or other duties of human beings among themselves than can be conceived in the former state; the matter of private right is the same in both. The laws of the condition of public right, accordingly, have to do only with the rightful form of their association (constitution), in view of which these laws must necessarily be conceived as public.

The *civil union* (*unio civilis*) cannot itself be called a *society*, for between the *commander*^{p} (*imperans*) and the *subject* (*subditus*) there is no partnership. They are not fellow-members: one is *subordinated to*, not *coordinated with* the other; and those who are coordinate with one another must for this very reason consider themselves equals since they are subject to common laws. The civil union *is* not so much a society but rather *makes* one.   [6:307]

§42

From private right in the state of nature there proceeds the postulate of public right: when you cannot avoid living side by side with all others,^{q} you ought to leave the state of nature and proceed with them into a rightful condition, that is, a condition of distributive justice. – The ground of this postulate can be explicated^r analytically from the concept of *right* in external relations, in contrast with *violence* (*violentia*).

No one is bound to refrain from encroaching on what another possesses if the other gives him no equal assurance that he will observe the same restraint towards him. No one, therefore, need wait until he has learned by bitter experience of the other's contrary disposition;^{s} for what should bind him to

---

^{o} *unwillkürlich*

^{p} *Befehlshaber*. Kant has not yet discussed the relation of the legislative, executive, and judicial authorities in a state. When he does so, in 6:316, the *(Ober)befehlshaber* is associated with the executive authority. Here, however, as in §47, Kant is apparently using the word simply in the sense of "a superior in general."

^{q} Grammatically, the relation of "with all others" to the rest of the sentence is ambiguous: the phrase could modify "proceed". My reasons for the above translation are, first, Kant's thesis of "original possession in common" of the earth's habitable surface by the whole human race and, second, the fact that the heading of §41 indicates that §42 is part of the transition from private right to the whole of public right. As Kant has said (6:266), until "the original contract" extends to the whole human race, acquisition will always remain provisional.

^{r} *entwickeln*

^{s} *Gesinnung*. LD: The translation of *Gesinnung* as "disposition" might suggest that it is a mere (possibly habitual) behavioral tendency; it is not. For Kant, *Gesinnungen* are closely connected with ways of thinking [*Denkungsarten*] and maxims. "Attitude" is an alternative translation of *Gesinnung*.

wait till he has suffered a loss before he becomes prudent, when he can quite well perceive within himself the inclination of human beings generally to lord it over others as their masters (not to respect the superiority of the rights of others when they feel superior to them in strength or cunning)? And is it not necessary to wait for actual hostility; one is authorized to use coercion against someone who already, by his nature, threatens him with coercion. (*Quilibet praesumitur malus, donec securitatem dederit oppositi.*)[t]

Given the intention to be and to remain in this state of externally lawless freedom, human beings do *one another* no wrong at all when they feud among themselves; for what holds for one holds also in turn for the other, as if by mutual consent (*uti partes de iure suo disponunt, ita ius est*).[u] But in general they do wrong in the highest degree[*] by willing to be and to remain in a condition that is [6:308] not rightful, that is, in which no one is assured of what is his against violence.

---

[*] This distinction between what is merely formally wrong and what is also materially wrong has many applications in the doctrine of right. An enemy who, instead of honorably carrying out his surrender agreement with the garrison of a besieged fortress, mistreats them as they march out or otherwise breaks the agreement, cannot [6:308] complain of being wronged if his opponent plays the same trick on him when he can. But in general they do wrong in the highest degree, because they take away any validity from the concept of right itself and hand everything over to savage violence, as if by law, and so subvert the right of human beings as such.

[r] Everyone is presumed to be bad until he has given security of the opposite. (LD: This translation replaces Gregor's from the previous edition. Cf. Ladd; and see Byrd and Hruschka, *Kant's Doctrine of Right*, 190 n.10.)

[u] however the parties dispose of their right, so right is. (LD: This translation replaces Gregor's from the previous edition; cf. Ladd.)

The Doctrine of Right

Part II
PUBLIC RIGHT

Public Right
Section I

The Right of a State
§43

The sum of the laws which need to be promulgated generally in order to bring about a rightful condition is *public right*. – Public right is therefore a system of laws for a people, that is, a multitude of human beings, or for a multitude of peoples, which, because they affect one another, need a rightful condition under a will uniting them, a *constitution* (*constitutio*), so that they may enjoy what is laid down as right. – This condition of the individuals within a people in relation to one another is called a *civil* condition (*status civilis*), and the whole of individuals in a rightful condition, in relation to its own members is called a *state* (*civitas*). Because of its form, by which all are united through their common interest in being in a rightful condition, a state is called a *commonwealth* (*res publica latius sic dicta*).[a] In relation to other peoples, however, a state is called simply a *power* (*potentia*) (hence the word *potentate*). Because the union of the members is (presumed to be) one they inherited, a state is also called a *nation* (*gens*). Hence, under the general concept of public right we are led to think not only of the right of a state but also of a *right of nations* (*ius gentium*).[b] Since the earth's surface is not unlimited but closed, the concepts of the right of a state and of a right of nations lead inevitably to the idea of a *right for all nations*[c] (*ius gentium*) or *cosmopolitan right* (*ius cosmopoliticum*). So if the principle of outer freedom limited by law is lacking in any one of these three possible forms of rightful condition, the framework of all the others is unavoidably undermined and must finally collapse.

§44

It is not experience from which we learn of human beings' maxim of violence and of their malevolent tendency to attack one another before external legislation[d] endowed with power appears. It is therefore not some fact that

---

[a] a republic in the broad sense

[b] The English terms "municipal law" and "international law" might be used here, if it were kept in mind that Kant's concern is only with *a priori* principles. However, given the meaning of *Recht* specified in 6:229, it seems preferable to continue using this term throughout for *das öffentliche Recht* or "public right."

[c] *eines Völkerstaatsrechts*. LD: or "a right for a state of nations," as in the Cambridge Edition.

[d] Although Kant continues to use *Gesetzgebung* and *Gesetzgeber*, which were translated in private right as "lawgiving" and "lawgiver," he is now discussing a condition in which there are positive laws. Hence "legislation" and "legislator" seem appropriate.

makes coercion through public law necessary. On the contrary, however well disposed and right-loving[c] human beings might be, it still lies *a priori* in the rational idea of such a condition (one that is not rightful) that before a public lawful condition is established individual human beings, peoples, and states can never be secure against violence from one another, since each has its own right to do *what seems right and good to it* and not to be dependent upon another's opinion about this. So, unless it wants to renounce any concepts of right, the first thing it has to resolve upon is the principle that it must leave the state of nature, in which each follows its own judgment, unite itself with all others (with which it cannot avoid interacting), subject itself to a public lawful external coercion, and so enter into a condition in which what is to be recognized as belonging to it is determined *by law* and is allotted to it by adequate *power* (not its own but an external power); that is, it ought above all else to enter a civil condition.

It is true that the state of nature need not, just because it is natural, be a state of *injustice* (*iniustus*), of dealing with one another only in terms of the degree of force each has. But it would still be a state *devoid of justice* (*status iustitia vacuus*), in which when rights are *in dispute* (*ius controversum*), there would be no judge competent to render a verdict having rightful force. Hence each may impel the other by force to leave this state and enter into a rightful condition; for although each can acquire something external by taking control of it or by contract in accordance with its *concepts of right*, this acquisition is still only *provisional* as long as it does not yet have the sanction of public law, since it is not determined by public (distributive) justice and secured by an authority putting this right into effect.

If no acquisition were cognized as rightful even in a provisional way prior to entering the civil condition, the civil condition itself would be impossible. For [6:313] in terms of their form, laws concerning what is mine or yours in the state of nature contain the same thing that they prescribe in the civil condition, insofar as the civil condition is thought of by pure rational concepts alone. The difference is only that the civil condition provides the conditions under which these laws are put into effect (in keeping with distributive justice). – So if external objects were not even *provisionally* mine or yours in the state of nature, there would also be no duties of right with regard to them and therefore no command to leave the state of nature.

---

[c] *rechtliebend*. LD: The current translation follows Helga Varden. As Varden explains, Gregor's translation in the previous edition, "law-abiding," does not so well capture the "subjective willingness to be rightful" conveyed by the original. See Varden, "Kant's Non-Voluntarist Conception of Political Obligations: Why Justice is Impossible in the State of Nature," *Kantian Review* 13 (2) (2008):1–45, 42n.61. Cf. Arthur Ripstein, *Force and Freedom: Kant's Legal and Political Philosophy* (Cambridge, MA: Harvard University Press, 2009), 3f. n.4.

§45

A *state* (*civitas*) is a union of a multitude of human beings under laws of right. Insofar as these are *a priori* necessary as laws, that is, insofar as they follow of themselves from concepts of external right as such (are not statutory), its form is the form of a state as such, that is, of *the state in idea*, as it ought to be in accordance with pure principles of right. This idea serves as a norm (*norma*) for every actual union into a commonwealth (hence serves as a norm for its internal constitution).[f]

Every state contains three authorities[g] within it, that is, the general united will consists of three persons (*trias politica*): the *sovereign authority* (sovereignty)[h] in the person of the legislator; the *executive authority* in the person of the ruler (in conformity to law); and the *judicial authority* (to award to each what is his in accordance with the law) in the person of the judge (*potestas legislatoria, rectoria et iudiciaria*). These are like the three propositions in a practical syllogism: the major premise, which contains the *law* of that will; the minor premise, which contains the *command* to behave in accordance with the law, that is, the principle of subsumption under the law; and the conclusion, which contains the *verdict* (sentence), what is laid down as right in the case at hand.

§46

The legislative authority can belong only to the united will of the people. For since all right is to proceed from it, it *can* not do anyone wrong by its law. Now when someone makes arrangements about *another*, it is always possible for him to do the other wrong; but he can never do wrong in what he decides upon with regard to himself (for *volenti non fit iniuria*).[i] Therefore only the concurring and united will [6:314] of all, insofar as each decides the same thing for all and all for each, and so only the general united will of the people, can be legislative.

The members of such a society who are united for giving law (*societas civilis*), that is, the members of a state, are called *citizens of a state* (*cives*). In terms of

---

[f] *also im Inneren*

[g] or "powers" [*Gewalten*]. In §43 and §44 Kant used *Macht* (*potentia*), which was translated as "power." He now begins to use *Gewalt* (*potestas*). But once he distinguishes the three "powers" or "authorities" within a state, it is only the executive authority that has "power" in one sense, i.e., it is the authority which exercises coercion.

[h] *Herrschergewalt (Souveränität)*. In this initial distinction of the three authorities within a state Kant specifies that "sovereignty" belongs to the legislative authority. Subsequently he introduces, without explanation, such a variety of terms that it is not always clear which of the three authorities is under discussion. I have used "sovereign," without noting the word used, only when Kant specifies *Souverän*. When "sovereign" is used for *Herrscher* or *Beherrscher*, a note is provided. Otherwise I have used the more general "head of state," except for passages which might indicate that one (physical) person has both legislative and executive authority.

[i] no wrong is done to someone who consents

rights, the attributes of a citizen, inseparable from his essence (as a citizen), are: lawful *freedom*, the attribute of obeying no other law than that to which he has given his consent; civil *equality*, that of not recognizing among the people any superior with the moral capacity[j] to bind him as a matter of right in a way that he could not in turn bind the other; and third,[k] the attribute of civil *independence*, of owing his existence and preservation to his own rights and powers as a member of the commonwealth, not to the choice of another among the people. From his independence follows his civil personality, his attribute of not needing to be represented by another where rights are concerned.

The only qualification for being a citizen is being fit to vote. But being fit to vote presupposes the independence of someone who, as one of the people, wants to be not just a part of the commonwealth but also a member of it, that is, a part of the commonwealth acting from his own choice in community with others. This quality of being independent, however, requires a distinction between *active* and *passive* citizens, though the concept of a passive citizen seems to contradict the concept of a citizen as such. – The following examples can serve to remove this difficulty: an apprentice in the service of a merchant or artisan; a domestic servant (as distinguished from a civil servant); a minor (*naturaliter vel civiliter*); all women and, in general, anyone whose preservation in existence (his being fed and protected) depends not on his management of his own business but on arrangements made by another (except the state). All these people lack civil personality and their existence is, as it were, only inherence. – The woodcutter I hire to work in my yard; the blacksmith in India, who goes into people's houses to work on iron with his hammer, anvil, and bellows, as compared with the European carpenter or blacksmith who can put the products of his work up as goods for sale to the public; the private tutor, as compared with the school teacher; the tenant farmer as compared with the leasehold farmer, and so forth; these are mere underlings[l] of the commonwealth because they have to be under the direction or protection of other individuals, and so do not possess civil independence.

[6:315]

This dependence upon the will of others and this inequality is, however, in no way opposed to their freedom and equality *as human beings*, who together make up a people; on the contrary, it is only in conformity with the conditions of freedom and equality that this people can become a state and enter into a civil constitution. But not all persons qualify with equal right to vote within this constitution, that is, to be citizens and not mere associates in the state. For from their being able to demand that all others treat them in accordance with the laws of natural freedom and equality as *passive* parts of the state, it does not follow that they also have the right to manage the state itself as *active* members

---

[j] *Vermögen*
[k] Presumably in this sequence Kant means the first feature is freedom, and the second is equality.
[l] *Handlanger*

of it, the right to organize it or to cooperate for introducing certain laws. It follows only that, whatever sort of positive laws the citizens might vote for, these laws must still not be contrary to the natural laws of freedom and of the equality of everyone in the people corresponding to this freedom, namely that anyone can work his way up from this passive condition to an active one.

§47

All those three authorities in a state are dignities,[m] and since they arise necessarily from the idea of a state as such, as essential for the establishment (constitution) of it, they are *civic dignities*. They comprise the relation of a *superior* over all (which, from the viewpoint of laws of freedom, can be none other than the united people itself) to the multitude of that people severally as *subjects*, that is, the relation of a *commander*[n] (*imperans*) to *those who obey* (*subditus*). – The act by which a people forms itself into a state is the *original contract*. Properly speaking, the original contract is only the idea of this act, in terms of which alone we can think of the legitimacy of a state. In accordance with the original contract, everyone (*omnes et singuli*) within a *people* gives up his external freedom in order to take it up again immediately as a member of a commonwealth, that is, of a people considered as a state (*universi*). And one cannot say: the human being in a state has sacrificed [6:316] a *part* of his innate outer freedom for the sake of an end, but rather, he has relinquished entirely his wild, lawless freedom in order to find his freedom as such undiminished, in a dependence upon laws, that is, in a rightful condition, since this dependence arises from his own lawgiving will.

§48

Accordingly, the three authorities in a state are, *first*, coordinate with one another (*potestates coordinatae*) as so many moral persons, that is, each complements the others to complete the constitution of a state (*complementum ad sufficientiam*).[o] But, *second*, they are also *subordinate* (*subordinatae*) to one another, so that one of them, in assisting another, cannot also usurp its function; instead, each has its own principle, that is, it indeed commands in its capacity[p] as a particular person, but still under the condition of the will of a superior. *Third*, through the union of both each subject is apportioned his rights.[32]

---

[m] *Würden*   [n] *Gebietenden*   [o] complement to sufficiency   [p] *Qualität*

[32] Natorp suggests that a fairly extensive portion of the text may be missing here, in which "first," "second," and "third" occurred twice, and the first occurrence of "third" got replaced by the second. In any case, the "third" point here seems to concern the relation of the judicial authority to the legislative and the executive authorities, not another relation parallel to coordination and subordination.

It can be said of these authorities, regarded in their dignity, that the will of the *legislator* (*legislatoris*) with regard to what is externally mine or yours is *irreproachable* (irreprehensible); that the executive power of the *supreme ruler* (*summi rectoris*) is *irresistible*; and that the verdict of the highest *judge* (*supremi iudicis*) is *irreversible* (cannot be appealed).

§49

The *ruler* of a state (*rex, princeps*) is that (moral or natural) person to whom the executive authority (*potestas executoria*) belongs. He is the *agent* of the state, who appoints the magistrates and prescribes to the people rules in accordance with which each of them can acquire something or preserve what is his in conformity with the law (through subsumption of a case under it). Regarded as a moral person, he is called the *directorate*, the government. His *directives* to the people, and to the magistrates and their superior (the minister) whom he charges with *administering the state* (*gubernatio*), are ordinances or *decrees* (not laws); for they are directed to decisions in particular cases and are given as subject to being changed. A *government* that was also legislative would have to [6:317] be called a *despotic* as opposed to a *patriotic* government; but by a patriotic government is understood not a *paternalistic* one (*regimen paternale*), which is the most despotic of all (since it treats citizens as children), but one *serving the native land* (*regimen civitatis et patriae*). In it the state (*civitas*) does treat its subjects as members of one family but it also treats them as citizens of the state, that is, in accordance with laws of their own independence: each is in possession of himself and is not dependent upon the absolute will of another alongside him or above him.

So a people's sovereign^q (legislator) cannot also be its *ruler*, since the ruler is subject to the law and so is put under obligation through the law by *another*, namely the sovereign.^r The sovereign can also take the ruler's authority away from him, depose him, or reform his administration. But it cannot *punish* him (and the saying common in England, that the king, i.e., the supreme executive authority, can do no wrong, means no more than this); for punishment is, again, an act of the executive authority, which has the supreme capacity to *exercise coercion* in conformity with the law, and it would be self-contradictory for him to be subject to coercion.

Finally, neither the head of state nor its ruler can *judge*^s, but can only appoint judges^t as magistrates. A people judges itself through those of its fellow citizens whom it designates as its representatives for this by a free choice and, indeed, designates especially for each act. For a verdict (a sentence) is an individual act of public justice (*iustitiae distributivae*) performed by an administrator of the state

---

^q *Beherrscher*   ^r *Souverän*   ^s *richten*   ^t *Richter* (a judge or court) upon a subject, that is, upon someone belonging to the people; and so this act is invested with no authority to assign (allot) to a subject what is his.ᵘ Since each individual among a people is only passive in this relationship (to the authorities), if either the legislative or the executive authority were to decide in a controversial case what belongs to him, it might do him a wrong, since it would not be the people itself doing this and pronouncing a verdict of *guilty* or *not guilty*ᵛ upon a fellow citizen. But once the facts in a lawsuit have been established, the court has judicial authority to apply the law, and to render to each what is his with the help of the executive authority. Hence only the *people* can give a judgment upon one of its members, although only indirectly, by means of representatives (the jury) whom it has delegated. – It would also be beneath the dignity of the head of state to play the judge, that is, to put himself in a position where he could do wrong and so have his decision appealed (*a rege male informato ad regem melius informandum*).ʷ   [6:318]

There are thus three distinct authorities (*potestas legislatoria, executoria, iudiciaria*) by which a state (*civitas*) has its autonomy, that is, by which it forms and preserves itself in accordance with laws of freedom. – A state's *well-being* consists in their being united (*salus reipublicae suprema lex est*).ˣ By the well-being of a state must not be understood the *welfare* of its citizens and their *happiness*; for happiness can perhaps come to them more easily and as they would like it to in a state of nature (as Rousseau asserts) or even under a despotic government. By the well-being of a state is understood, instead, that condition in which its constitution conforms most fully to principles of right; it is that condition which reason, *by a categorical imperative*, makes it obligatory for us to strive after.

General Remark
On the Effects with Regard to Rights That Follow from the Nature of the Civil Union
A

A people should not *inquire* with any practical aim in view into the origin of the supreme authority to which it is subject, that is, a subject *ought not to reason subtly* for the sake of actionʸ about the origin of this authority, as a right that can

---

ᵘ *mithin mit keiner Gewalt bekleidet ist, ihm das Seine zuzuerkennen (zu ertheilen)*. LD: Byrd and Hruschka dispute Gregor's translation, which inserts "this act", because they read it as denying to the administrator of the state a power they take it to have. See *Kant's Doctrine of Right*, 165f. n.87.

ᵛ *schuldig oder nichtschuldig*. LD: or perhaps "*liable* or *not liable*", for applicability to civil as well as criminal trials (see Byrd and Hruschka, *Kant's Doctrine of Right*, 165 n.86).

ʷ from a king badly instructed to a king to be better instructed

ˣ the well-being of the commonwealth is the supreme law. The saying seems to stem from Cicero, *De Legibus* III.iii.8: "*Salus populi suprema lex esto*."

ʸ *werkthätig vernünfteln*

still be called into question (*ius controversum*) with regard to the obedience he owes it. For, since a people must be regarded as already united under a general legislative will in order to judge with rightful force about the supreme authority[z] (*summum imperium*), it cannot and may not judge otherwise than as the present head of state (*summus imperans*) wills it to. – Whether a state began with an actual contract of submission (*pactum subiectionis civilis*) as a fact, or whether power came first and law arrived only afterwards, or even whether they should have followed in this order: for a people already subject to civil law these subtle reasonings are altogether pointless and, moreover, threaten a state with danger. If a subject, having pondered over the ultimate origin of the authority now [6:319] ruling,[a] wanted to resist this authority, he would be punished, got rid of, or expelled (as an outlaw, *exlex*) in accordance with the laws of this authority, that is, with every right. – A law that is so holy (inviolable) that it is already a crime even to call it in doubt *in a practical way*, and so to suspend its effect for a moment, is thought as if it must have arisen not from human beings but from some highest, flawless lawgiver; and that is what the saying "All authority is from God" means. This saying is not an assertion about the *historical basis* of the civil constitution; it instead sets forth an idea as a practical principle of reason: the principle that the presently existing legislative authority ought to be obeyed, whatever its origin.

Now, from this principle follows the proposition: the sovereign[b] has only rights against his subjects and no duties (that he can be coerced to fulfill).[c] – Moreover, even if the organ of the sovereign, the *ruler*, proceeds contrary to law, for example, if he goes against the law of equality in assigning the burdens of the state in matters of taxation, recruiting, and so forth, subjects may indeed oppose this injustice by *complaints* (*gravamina*) but not by resistance.

Indeed, even the constitution cannot contain any article that would make it possible for there to be some authority in a state to resist the supreme commander[d] in case he should violate the law of the constitution, and so to limit him.[33] For, someone who is to limit the authority in a state must have even more power[e] than he whom he limits, or at least as much power as he has; and, as a legitimate commander[f] who directs the subjects to resist, he must also be able to *protect* them and to render a judgment having rightful force in any case that comes up; consequently he has to be able to command resistance publicly. In that case, however, the supreme commander[g] in a state is not the supreme commander;

---

[z] *Staatsgewalt*   [a] *jetzt herrschenden*   [b] *Herrscher*   [c] *keine (Zwangs-) Pflichten*
[d] *obersten Befehlshaber*   [e] *Macht*   [f] *rechtmäßiger Gebieter*   [g] *oberste Befehlshaber*

[33] Although Kant goes on to call a "moderate" [*gemäßigte*] constitution *ein Unding* (an "absurdity" in the sense, apparently, of a logical impossibility), it would seem from 6:322 that the absurdity consists in supposing that a parliament representing the people can *actively* resist the highest executive authority. I take it that his references to a "moderate" (6:320) and to a "limited" [*eingeschränkte*] (6:322) constitution are both directed at the British Constitution. Cf. "Theory and Practice" 8:303.

instead, it is the one who can resist him, and this is self-contradictory. In that case the sovereign behaves through its minister as also the ruler and so as a despot; and the illusion that allows us to think of the people, through its deputies, as the limiting authority (though it has, properly speaking, only legislative authority) cannot conceal the despotism, so that it does not come to light from the measures the minister takes. The people, in being represented by its deputies (in parliament), has, in these guardians of its freedom and rights, people who have a lively interest in positions for themselves and their families, in the army, the navy, and the civil service, that depend on the minister, and who are always ready to play into the government's hands (instead of resisting its encroachments; besides, a public [6:320] declaration of resistance requires unanimity in a people which has been prepared in advance, and this cannot be permitted in time of peace). – Hence a so-called moderate constitution, as a constitution for the inner rights of a state, is an absurdity. Instead of belonging to right it is only a principle of prudence, not so much to make it more difficult for a powerful transgressor of the people's rights to exercise at will his influence^h upon the government as to disguise his influence under the illusion of an opposition permitted to the people.

Therefore a people cannot offer any resistance to the legislative head of a state which would be consistent with right, since a rightful condition is possible only by submission to its general legislative will. There is, therefore, no right to *sedition* (*seditio*), still less to *rebellion* (*rebellio*), and least of all is there a right against the head of a state as an individual person (the monarch), *to attack his person* or even his life (*monarchomachismus sub specie tyrannicidii*) on the pretext that he has abused his authority (*tyrannis*). – Any attempt whatsoever as this is *high treason* (*proditio eminens*), and whoever commits such treason must be punished by nothing less than death for attempting *to destroy his fatherland* (*parricida*). – – The reason a people has a duty to put up with even what is held to be an unbearable abuse of supreme authority is that its resistance to the highest legislation can never be regarded as other than contrary to law, and indeed as abolishing the entire legal constitution. For a people to be authorized to resist, there would have to be a public law permitting it to resist, that is, the highest legislation would have to contain a provision that it is not the highest and that makes the people, as subject, by one and the same judgment sovereign over him to whom it is subject. This is self-contradictory, and the contradiction is evident as soon as one asks who is to be the judge in this dispute between people and sovereign (for, considered in terms of rights, these are always two distinct moral persons). For it is then apparent that the people wants to be the judge in its own suit.[*]

---

[*] The *dethronement* of a monarch can still be thought of as if he had *voluntarily* laid aside the crown and abdicated his authority, [6:321] giving it back to the people, or as if, without any attack on the highest person, he had relinquished his authority and been reduced to the rank of a private person.

^h *seine willkürliche Einflüsse*

[6:321]   A change in a (defective) constitution, which may certainly be necessary at
[6:322]   times, can therefore be carried out only through *reform* by the sovereign itself,
but not by the people, and therefore not by *revolution*; and when such a change

Because of this the people who extorted this from him have at least the pretext of a *right of necessity* (*casus necessitatis*) in favor of its crime. But they never have the least right to punish him, the head of state, because of his previous administration, since everything he did, in his capacity as head of state, must be regarded as having been done in external conformity with rights, and he himself, as the source of the law, can do no wrong. Of all the atrocities involved in overthrowing a state by rebellion, the *assassination* of the monarch is not itself the worst, for we can still think of the people as doing it from fear that if he remained alive he could marshal his forces and inflict on them the punishment they deserve, so that their killing him would not be an enactment of punitive justice but merely a dictate of self-preservation. It is the formal *execution* of a monarch that strikes horror in a soul filled with the idea of human beings' rights, a horror that one feels repeatedly as soon as and as often as one thinks of such scenes as the fate of Charles I or Louis XVI. But how are we to explain this feeling, which is not aesthetic feeling (sympathy, an effect of imagination by which we put ourselves in the place of the sufferer) but moral feeling resulting from the complete over-turning of all concepts of rights? It is regarded as a crime that remains forever and can never be expiated (*crimen immortale, inexpiabile*), and it seems to be like what theologians call the sin that cannot be forgiven either in this world or the next. The explanation of this phenomenon in the human mind seems to arise from the following reflections upon itself, which throw light on the principles of political rights themselves.

    Any transgression of the law can and must be explained only as arising from a maxim of the criminal (to make such a crime his rule); for if we were to derive it from a sensible impulse, he would not be committing it as a *free* being and it could not be imputed to him. But how it is possible for the subject to form such a maxim contrary to the clear prohibition of lawgiving reason absolutely cannot be explained, since only what happens in accordance with the mechanism of nature is capable of being explained. Now the criminal can commit his misdeed either on a maxim he has taken as an objective rule (as holding universally) or only as an exception to the rule (exempting himself from it occasionally). In the *latter* case *he only deviates* from the law (though intentionally); he can at the same time detest his transgression and, without formally renouncing obedience to the law, only want to evade it. In the *first* case, however, he rejects the authority of the law itself, whose validity he still cannot deny before his own reason, and makes it his rule to act contrary to the law. His maxim is therefore opposed to the law not by way of *default* only (*negative*) but [6:322] by *rejecting* it (*contrarie*) or, as we put it, his maxim is *diametrically* opposed to the law, as contradictory to it (hostile to it, so to speak). As far as we can see, it is impossible for a human being to commit a crime of this kind, a formally evil (wholly pointless) crime; and yet it is not to be ignored in a system of morals (although it is only the idea of the most extreme evil).

    The reason for horror at the thought of the formal execution of a monarch *by his people* is therefore this: that while his *murder* is regarded as only an *exception* to the rule that the people makes its maxim, his *execution* must be regarded as a complete *overturning* of the principles of the relation between a sovereign and his people (in which the people, which owes its existence only to the sovereign's legislation, makes itself his master), so that violence is elevated above the most sacred rights brazenly and in accordance with principle. Like a chasm that irretrievably swallows everything, the execution of a monarch seems to be a crime from which the people cannot be absolved, for it is as if the state commits suicide. There is, accordingly, reason for assuming that the agreement to execute the monarch actually originates not from what is supposed to be a rightful principle but from fear of the state's vengeance upon the people if it revives at some future time, and that these formalities are undertaken only to give that deed the appearance of punishment, and so of a *rightful procedure* (such as murder would not be). But this disguising of the deed miscarries; such a presumption on the people's part is still worse than murder, since it involves a principle that would have to make it impossible to generate again a state that has been overthrown.

takes place this reform can affect only the *executive authority*, not the legislative. –
In what is called a limited constitution, the constitution contains a provision that
the people can legally *resist* the executive authority and its representative (the
minister) by means of its representatives (in parliament). Nevertheless, no active
resistance (by the people combining at will[i] to coerce the government to take
a certain course of action, and so itself performing an act of executive authority)
is permitted, but only *negative* resistance, that is, a *refusal* of the people (in
parliament) to accede to every demand the government puts forth as necessary
for administering the state. Indeed, if these demands were always complied with,
this would be a sure sign that the people are corrupt, that its representatives can
be bought, that the head of the government is ruling despotically through his
minister, and that the minister himself is betraying the people.

Moreover, once a revolution has succeeded and a new constitution has been
established, the lack of legitimacy with which it began and has been implemen-   [6:323]
ted cannot release the subjects from the obligation to comply with the new order
of things as good citizens, and they cannot refuse honest obedience to the
authority that now has the power. A dethroned monarch (who survives
the upheaval) cannot be held to account, still less be punished, for what he
previously carried out, provided he returns to the estate[j] of a citizen and prefers
peace for himself and the state to the risk of running away in order to engage in
the adventure of trying, as a claimant,[k] to get his throne back, whether by
covertly inciting a counter-revolution or by the assistance of other powers.
But if he prefers the latter course, his right to do so cannot be challenged
since the insurrection that dispossessed him was unjust. But do other powers
have the right to band together in an alliance on behalf of this deposed monarch,
merely so as not to let that crime perpetrated by the people go unavenged and
persist as a scandal for all states? Are they therefore authorized and called upon
to restore by force the old constitution in any other state where the presently
existing constitution has come about *by revolution?* These questions belong to
the right of nations.

B

Can the sovereign[l] be regarded as the supreme proprietor[m] (of the land), or must
he be regarded only as the one who has supreme command over the people by
law? Since the land is the ultimate condition that alone makes it possible to have
external things as one's own, and the first right that can be acquired is possession
and use of such things, all such rights must be derived from the sovereign as *lord
of the land*, or better, as the supreme proprietor of it (*dominus territorii*).

---

[i] *der willkürlichen Verbindung*   [j] *Stand*   [k] or "pretender," *Prätendent*
[l] *Beherrscher*   [m] or "supreme owner," *Obereigenthümer*

The people, the multitude of subjects, also belong to him (they are his people). But they belong to him not as if he owned them (by a right to things); they instead belong to him as their supreme commander[n] (by a right against persons). – This supreme proprietorship is, however, only an idea of the civil union that serves to represent in accordance with concepts of right the necessary union of the private property of everyone within the people under a general public possessor, so that determination of the particular property of each is in
[6:324] accordance with the necessary formal principle of *division* (*division of land*), instead of with principles of *aggregation* (which proceeds empirically from the parts to the whole). In accordance with concepts of right, the supreme proprietor cannot have any land at all as his private property (for otherwise he would make himself a private person). All land belongs only to the people (and indeed to the people taken distributively, not collectively), except in the case of a nomadic people under a sovereign,[o] with whom there is no private ownership of land. – The supreme commander[p] can therefore have no *domains*, that is, no estates for his private use (for maintaining his court). For if he did, it would then be up to his own discretion how far they should be extended, so that the state would run the risk of seeing all ownership of land in the hands of the government and all subjects as *serfs* (*glebae adscripti*), possessors only of what is the property of another, and therefore deprived of all freedom (*servi*). – One can say of the lord of the land that *he possesses nothing* (of his own) except himself; for if he had something of his own alongside others in the state, a dispute could arise between them and there would be no judge to settle it. But one can also say that *he possesses everything*, since he has the right of command over the people, to whom all external things belong (*divisim*) (the right to assign to each what is his).

From this it follows that within a state there can also be no corporation, estate, or order which, as owner of land, can pass it on in accordance with certain statutes to succeeding generations for their exclusive use (in perpetuity). The state can repeal such statutes at any time, provided it compensates those who are left. A *knightly order* (whether a corporation or merely a rank of individual persons who enjoy special honors) or a *clerical order*, called the church, can never acquire from those privileges with which they are favored ownership in land to pass on to their successors; they can acquire only use of it up to the present. The estates of a knightly order can be revoked without scruple (though under the condition mentioned above) if public opinion has ceased to favor *military honors* as a means for safeguarding the state against indifference in defending it. The holdings of the church can be similarly revoked if public opinion has ceased to want masses for souls, prayers, and a multitude of clerics appointed for this as the means for saving the people from eternal fire. Those
[6:325] affected by such reforms cannot complain of their property being taken from

---

[n] *Oberbefehlshaber*   [o] *nomadisch-beherrschtes*   [p] *Oberbefehlshaber*

them, since the reason for their possession hitherto lay only in the *people's opinion* and also had to hold as long as that lasted. But as soon as this opinion lapses, and even lapses only in the judgment of those who by their merit have the strongest claim to guide judgment, the supposed property has to cease, as if by an appeal of the people to the state (*a rege male informato ad regem melius informandum*).[q]

On this originally acquired ownership of land rests, again, the right of the supreme commander,[r] as supreme proprietor (lord of the land), to *tax* private owners of land, that is, to require payment of taxes on land, excise taxes, and import duties, or to require the performance of services (such as providing troops for military service). This must, however, be done in such a way that the people taxes itself, since the only way of proceeding in accordance with principles of right in this matter is for taxes to be levied by those deputized by the people, even in case of forced loans (deviating from previously existing law), which it is permissible to exact by the right of majesty when the state is in danger of dissolution.

On this supreme proprietorship also rests the right to administer the state's economy, finances, and police. Police provide for public *security, convenience*, and *decency*; for, the government's business of guiding the people by laws is made easier when the feeling for decency (*sensus decori*), as negative taste, is not deadened by what offends the moral sense, such as begging, uproar on the streets, stenches, and public prostitution (*venus volgivaga*).[s]

A third right also belongs to the state for its preservation, that of *inspection* (*ius inspectionis*), so that no association (of political or religious fanatics) that could affect the *public* well-being of society (*publicum*) remains concealed. Instead, no association can refuse to disclose its constitution when the police demand it. But the police are not authorized to search anyone's private residence except in a case of necessity, and in every particular case they must be warranted to do so by a higher authority.

C

To the supreme commander[t] there belongs *indirectly*, that is, insofar as he has taken over the duty of the people, the right to impose taxes on the people for its own preservation, such as taxes to support organizations providing for the *poor, foundling homes*, and *church organizations*, usually called charitable or pious institutions. [6:326]

The general will of the people has united itself into a society which is to maintain itself perpetually; and for this end it has submitted itself to the internal authority of the state in order to maintain those members of the society who are

---

[q] from a king badly informed to a king better informed   [r] *Oberbefehlshabers*
[s] illicit sexual love of the masses   [t] *Oberbefehlshaber*

unable to maintain themselves.^u For reasons of state the government is therefore authorized to constrain the wealthy^v to provide the means of sustenance to those who are unable to provide for even their most necessary natural needs. The wealthy have acquired an obligation to the commonwealth, since they owe their existence to an act of submitting to its protection and care, which they need in order to live; on this obligation the state now bases its right to contribute what is theirs to maintaining their fellow citizens. This can be done either by imposing a tax on the property or commerce of citizens, or by establishing funds and using the interest from them, not for the needs of the state (for it is rich), but for the needs of the people.^w It will do this by way of coercion (since we are speaking here only of the *right* of the state against the people), by public taxation, not merely by *voluntary* contributions, some of which are made for gain (such as lotteries, which produce more poor people and more danger to public property than there would otherwise be, and which should therefore not be permitted). The question arises whether the care of the poor should be provided for by *current contributions* – collected not by begging, which is closely akin to robbery, but by legal levies – so that each generation supports its own poor, or instead by *assets* gradually accumulated and by *pious* institutions generally (such as widows' homes, hospitals, and the like). – Only the first arrangement, which no one who has to live can withdraw from, can be considered in keeping with the right of a state; for even if current contributions increase with the number of the poor, this arrangement does not make poverty a means of acquisition for the lazy (as is to be feared of religious institutions), and so does not become an *unjust* burdening of the people by government.

As for maintaining those children abandoned because of poverty^x or shame, or indeed murdered because of this, the state has a right to charge the people with the duty of not knowingly letting them die, even though they are an unwelcome addition to the population.^y Whether this should be done by taxing elderly [6:327] unmarried people of both sexes generally (by which I mean *wealthy* unmarried people), since they are in part to blame for there being abandoned children, in order to establish foundling homes, or whether it can be done rightly in another way (but it would be hard to find another means for preventing this^z) is a problem which has not yet been solved in such a way that the solution offends against neither rights nor morality.

As for *churches* (as institutions for public *divine worship* on the part of the people, to whose opinion or conviction they owe their origin), they must be carefully distinguished from religion, which is an inner disposition lying wholly beyond the civil power's sphere of influence. Churches thus also become a true need of a state, the need for people to regard themselves as subjects also of

---

^u *die es selbst nicht vermögen*   ^v *die Vermögenden*   ^w *Volksbedürfnissen*   ^x *Noth*
^y or "to the wealth [resources] of the state," *des Staatsvermögens*
^z i.e. preventing knowingly letting unwanted children die

a supreme *invisible* power to which they must pay homage and which can often come into very unequal conflict with the civil power. So a state does have a right with regard to churches. It does not have the right to legislate the internal constitutions of churches or to organize them in accordance with its own views, in ways it deems advantageous to itself, that is, to prescribe to the people or command beliefs and forms of divine worship (*ritus*) (for this must be left entirely to the teachers and directors the people itself has chosen). A state has only a *negative* right to prevent public teachers from exercising an influence on the *visible* political commonwealth that might be prejudicial to public peace. Its right is therefore that of policing, of not letting a dispute arising within a church or among different churches endanger civil harmony. For the supreme authority to say that a church should have a certain belief, or to say which it should have or that it must maintain it unalterably and may not reform itself, are interferences by it which are *beneath its dignity*; for in doing this, as in meddling in the quarrels of the schools, it puts itself on a level of equality with its subjects (the monarch makes himself a priest), and they can straightway tell him that he understands nothing about it. The supreme authority especially has no right to prohibit internal reform of churches, for what the whole people cannot decide upon for itself the legislator also cannot decide for the people. But no people can decide [6:328] never to make further progress in its insight (enlightenment) regarding beliefs, and so never to reform its churches, since this would be opposed to the humanity in their own persons and so to the highest right of the people. So no supreme authority can decide on this for the people. – – But as for the expenses of maintaining churches: for the very same reason these cannot be charged to the state but must rather be charged to the part of the people who profess one or another belief, that is, only to the congregation.

D

The rights of the supreme commander[a] of a state also include: 1) the distribution of *offices*, which are salaried administrative positions; 2) the distribution of *dignities*, which are eminent estates without pay, based on honor alone, that is, a division of rank into the higher (destined to command) and the lower (which, though free and bound only by public law, is still destined to obey the former); and 3) besides these (relatively beneficient) rights, the *right to punish* as well.

With regard to civil offices, the question arises whether the sovereign, once having given someone an office, has a right to take it away as he pleases (if the official has not committed a crime). I say, no. For the head of state can never make a decision about a civil official which the united will of the people would

---

[a] *obersten Befehlshabers*

not make. Now the people (which has to bear the costs incurred from appointing an official) undoubtedly wants him to be competent for the position he is assigned to; and this he can be only after he has spent a sufficiently long time in preparation and training, time he could have spent in training for another position that would have supported him. If the head of state had this right, offices would be filled as a rule by people who had not acquired the skill requisite for them and the mature judgment achieved by practice, and this would be contrary to the intention of the state, which also requires that everyone be able to rise from lower to higher offices (which would otherwise fall into the hands of sheer incompetence). Hence civil officials must be able to count on lifelong support.

Among *dignities*, not just those attached to an office but also those which make its possessors members of a higher estate even without any special services on their part, is that of the *nobility*, which is distinct from the civil [6:329] estate of the people and is transmitted to male descendants and by them to a wife born as a commoner, though if a woman born into the nobility marries a commoner she does not pass this rank on to her husband but herself reverts to the mere civil rank (of the people). – – Now the question is whether the sovereign is entitled to establish a nobility, insofar as it is an estate intermediate between himself and the rest of the citizens that *can be inherited*. What this question comes down to is not whether it would be prudent for the sovereign to do this, with a view to his own or the people's advantage, but only whether it would be in accord with the rights of the people for it to have an estate of persons above it who, while themselves subjects, are still *born* rulers[b] (or at least privileged) with respect to the people. – – The answer to this question comes from the same principle as the reply to the preceding one: "What a people (the entire mass of subjects) cannot decide with regard to itself and its fellows, the sovereign can also not decide with regard to it." Now a *hereditary* nobility is a rank that precedes merit and also provides no basis to hope for merit, and is thus a thought-entity without any reality. For if an ancestor had merit he could still not bequeath it to his descendants: they must acquire it for themselves, since nature does not arrange things in such a way that talent and will, which make meritorious service to the state possible, are also *hereditary*. Since we cannot admit that any human being would throw away his freedom, it is impossible for the general will of the people to assent to such a groundless prerogative, and therefore for the sovereign to validate it. – – The anomaly of subjects who want to be more than citizens of the state, namely born officials (a born professor, perhaps) may have crept into the machinery of government from older times (feudalism, which was organized almost entirely for war). The only way the state can then

---

[b] *Befehlshaber*

gradually correct this mistake it has made, of conferring hereditary privileges contrary to right, is by letting them lapse and not filling vacancies in these positions. So it has a provisional right to let these titled positions of dignity continue until even in public opinion the division into sovereign, nobility, and commoners has been replaced by the only natural division into sovereign and people.

Certainly no human being in a state can be without any dignity, since he at least has the dignity of a citizen. The exception is someone who has lost it by his own *crime*, because of which, though he is kept alive, he is made a mere tool of another's choice (either of the state or of another citizen). Whoever is another's tool (which he can become only by a verdict and right)^c is a *bondsman*^d (*servus in sensu stricto*) and is the *property* (*dominium*) of another, who is accordingly not merely his *master* (*herus*) but also his *owner* (*dominus*) and can therefore alienate him as a thing, use him as he pleases (only not for shameful purposes), and *dispose of his powers*, though not of his life and members. No one can bind himself to this kind of dependence, by which he ceases to be a person, by a contract, since it is only as a person that he can make a contract. Now it might seem that someone could put himself under obligation to another person, by a contract to let and hire (*locatio conductio*), to perform services (in return for wages, board, or protection) that are permissible in terms of their quality but *indeterminate* in terms of their quantity, and that he thereby becomes just a subject (*subiectus*), not a bondsman (*servus*). But this is only a deceptive appearance. For if the master is authorized to use the powers of his subject as he pleases, he can also exhaust them until his subject dies or is driven to despair (as with the Negroes on the Sugar Islands); his subject will in fact have given himself away, as property, to his master, which is impossible. – Someone can therefore hire himself out only for work that is determined as to its kind and its amount, either as a day laborer or as a subject living on his master's property. In the latter case he can make a contract, for a time or indefinitely, to perform services by working on his master's land in exchange for the use of it instead of receiving wages as a day laborer, or to pay rent (a tax) specified by a lease in return for his own use of it, without thereby making himself a *serf* (*glebae adscriptus*), by which he would forfeit his personality. Even if he has become a *personal* subject by his crime, his subjection cannot be *inherited*, because he has incurred it only by his own guilt. Nor can a bondsman's offspring be claimed as a bondsman

[6:330]

---

c *Urtheil und Recht*

d *Leibeigener*, technically, "serf." In 6:241 Kant classed *Leibeigene* and *Sklaven* together: they would be "human beings without personality." In 6:324 he used *grunduntherthänig* (*glebae adscripti*) – as in the present passage he uses *Gutsunterthan* (*glebae adscriptus*) – and calls serfs *servi*. Here too he refers to a *Leibeigener* as *servus in sensu stricto* or simply *servus*. In 6:333, a criminal is said to have reduced himself to the status of a slave, *Sklavenstand*. I shall henceforth reserve "serf" for *Gutsunterthan* and "slave" for *Sklave* and use the more general "bondsman" for *Leibeigener*.

because he has given rise to the expense of being educated; for parents have an absolute natural duty to educate their children and, when the parents are in bondage, their masters take over this duty along with possession of their subjects.

E
On the Right to Punish and to Grant Clemency

I

The *right to punish* is the right a ruler has against a subject to inflict pain upon him because of his having committed a crime. The head of a state can therefore not be punished; one can only withdraw from his dominion. – A transgression of public law that makes someone who commits it unfit to be a citizen is called a *crime* (*crimen*) simply but is also called a public crime (*crimen publicum*);[34] so the first (private crime) is brought before a civil court, the latter before a criminal court. – *Embezzlement*, that is, misappropriation of money or goods entrusted for commerce, and fraud in buying and selling, when committed in such a way that the other could detect it,[e] are private crimes. On the other hand, counterfeiting money or bills of exchange, theft and robbery, and the like are public crimes, because they endanger the commonwealth and not just an individual person. – They can be divided into crimes arising from a *mean* character (*indolis abiectae*) and crimes arising from a *violent* character (*indolis violentae*).

Punishment by a court (*poena forensis*) – that is distinct from *natural punishment* (*poena naturalis*), in which vice punishes itself and which the legislator does not take into account – can never be inflicted merely as a means to promote some other good for the criminal himself or for civil society. It must always be inflicted upon him only *because he has committed a crime*. For a human being can never be treated merely as a means to the purposes of another or be put among the objects of rights to things: his innate personality protects him from this, even though he can be condemned to lose his civil personality. He must previously have been found *punishable* before any thought can be given to drawing from his punishment something of use for himself or his fellow citizens. The law of punishment is a categorical imperative, and woe to him who crawls through the windings of eudaemonism in order to discover something that releases the criminal from punishment or even reduces its amount by the advantage it promises, in [6:332] accordance with the pharisaical saying, "It is better for *one* human being to die than for an entire people to perish."[f] For if justice goes, there is no longer any

---

[e] *bei sehenden Augen des Anderen*   [f] John 11:50

[34] Natorp suggests that, here again, something is apparently missing from the text, regarding the first kind of crime.

value in human beings' living on the earth. – What, therefore, should one think of the proposal to preserve the life of a criminal sentenced to death if he agrees to let dangerous experiments be made on him and is lucky enough to survive them, so that in this way physicians learn something new of benefit to the commonwealth? A court would reject with contempt such a proposal from a medical college, for justice ceases to be justice if it can be bought for any price whatsoever.

But what kind and what amount of punishment is it that public justice makes its principle and measure? None other than the principle of equality (in the position of the needle on the scale of justice), to incline no more to one side than to the other. Accordingly, whatever undeserved evil you inflict upon another within the people, that you inflict upon yourself. If you insult him, you insult yourself; if you steal from him, you steal from yourself; if you strike him, you strike yourself; if you kill him, you kill yourself. But only the *law of retribution* (*ius talionis*) – it being understood, of course, that this is applied by a court (not by your private judgment) – can specify definitely the quality and the quantity of punishment; all other principles are fluctuating and unsuited for a sentence of pure and strict justice because extraneous considerations are mixed into them. – Now it would indeed seem that differences in social rank would not allow the principle of retribution, of like for like;[g] but even when this is not possible in terms of the letter, the principle can always remain valid in terms of its effect if account is taken of the sensibilities of the upper classes. – A fine, for example, imposed for a verbal injury has no relation to the offense, for someone wealthy might indeed allow himself to indulge in a verbal insult on some occasion; yet the outrage he has done to someone's love of honor can still be quite similar to the hurt done to his pride if he is constrained by judgment and right not only to apologize publicly to the one he has insulted but also to kiss his hand, for instance, even though he is of a lower class. Similarly, someone of high standing given to violence could be condemned not only to apologize for striking an innocent citizen socially inferior to himself but also to undergo a solitary confinement involving hardship; in addition to the discomfort he undergoes, the offender's vanity would be painfully affected, so that through his shame like would be fittingly repaid with like. – But what does it mean to say, "If you steal from someone, you steal from yourself?" Whoever steals makes the property of everyone else insecure and therefore deprives himself (by the principle of retribution) of security in any possible property. He has nothing and can also acquire nothing; but he still wants to live, and this is now possible only if others provide for him. But since the state will not provide for him free of charge, he must let it have his powers for any kind of work it pleases (in convict or prison labor) and is reduced to the status of a slave for a certain time, or permanently if

[6:333]

---

[g] *Gleiches mit Gleichem*

115

the state sees fit. – If, however, he has committed murder he must *die*. Here there is no substitute that will satisfy justice. There is no *similarity* between life, however wretched it may be, and death, hence no likeness between the crime and the retribution unless death is judicially carried out upon the wrongdoer, although it must still be freed from any mistreatment that could make the humanity in the person suffering it into something abominable. – Even if a civil society were to be dissolved by the consent of all its members (e.g., if a people inhabiting an island decided to separate and disperse throughout the world), the last murderer remaining in prison would first have to be executed, so that each has done to him what his deeds deserve and blood guilt does not cling to the people for not having insisted upon this punishment; for otherwise the people can be regarded as collaborators in this public violation of justice.

This fitting of punishment to the crime, which can occur only by a judge imposing the death sentence in accordance with the strict law of retribution, is shown by the fact that only by this is a sentence of death pronounced on every criminal in proportion to his *inner wickedness* (even when the crime is not murder but another crime against the state that can be paid for only by death). – Suppose that some (such as Balmerino[35] and others) who took part in the recent Scottish rebellion believed that by their uprising they were only performing a duty they owed the House of Stuart, while others on the contrary were out for their private interests; and suppose that the judgment pronounced by the highest court had been that each is free to make the choice between death and convict labor. I say that in this case the man of honor would choose

[6:334] death, and the scoundrel convict labor. This comes along with the nature of the human mind; for the man of honor is acquainted with something that he values even more highly than life, namely *honor*, while the scoundrel considers it better to live in shame than not to live at all (*animam praeferre pudori. Iuven.*).[h] Since the man of honor is undeniably less deserving of punishment than the other, both would be punished quite proportionately if all alike were sentenced to death; the man of honor would be punished mildly in terms of his sensibilities and the scoundrel severely in terms of his. On the other hand, if both were sentenced to convict labor the man of honor would be punished too severely and the other too mildly for his vile action. And so here too, when sentence is pronounced on a number of criminals united in a plot, the best equalizer before public justice is *death*. – Moreover, one has never heard of anyone who was sentenced to death for murder complaining that he was dealt with too severely and therefore wronged; everyone would laugh in his face if he

---

[h] preferring a life of shame. Juvenal (*Satires*, III.viii.83).

[35] Arthur Elphinstone, 6th Baron Balmerino, who took part in the attempt of 1745–1746 to put Prince Charles Edward Stuart on the British throne, was captured in the defeat of the Scots forces at Culloden and subsequently beheaded.

said this. – If his complaint were justified it would have to be assumed that even though no wrong is done to the criminal in accordance with the law, the legislative authority of the state is still not authorized to inflict this kind of punishment and that, if it does so, it would be in contradiction with itself.

Accordingly, every murderer – anyone who commits murder, orders it, or is an accomplice in it – must suffer death; this is what justice, as the idea of judicial authority, wills in accordance with universal laws that are grounded *a priori*. – If, however, the number of accomplices (*correi*) to such a deed is so great that the state, in order to have no such criminals in it, could soon find itself without subjects; and if the state still does not want to dissolve, that is, to pass over into the state of nature, which is far worse because there is no external justice at all in it (and if it especially does not want to dull the people's feeling by the spectacle of a slaughterhouse), then the sovereign must also have it in his power, in this case of necessity (*casus necessitatis*), to assume the role of judge (to represent him) and pronounce a judgment that decrees for the criminals a sentence other than capital punishment, such as deportation, which still preserves the population.[36] This cannot be done in accordance with public law but it can be done by an executive decree that is, by an act of the right of majesty which, as clemency, can always be exercised only in individual cases.

In opposition to this the Marchese Beccaria,[37] moved by overly compassionate feelings of an affected humanity[i] (*compassibilitas*), has put forward his assertion that any capital punishment is wrongful because it could not be contained in the original civil contract; for if it were, everyone in a people would have to have consented to lose his life in case he murdered someone else (in the people), whereas it is impossible for anyone to consent to this because no one can dispose of his own life. This is all sophistry and juristic trickery.

No one suffers punishment because he has willed *it* but because he has willed a *punishable action*; for it is no punishment if what is done to someone is what he wills, and it is impossible *to will* to be punished. – Saying that I will to be punished if I murder someone is saying nothing more than that I subject myself together with everyone else to the laws, which will naturally also be penal laws if there are any criminals among the people. As a co-legislator in dictating the *penal law*, I cannot possibly be the same person who, as a subject, is punished in accordance with the law; for as one who is punished, namely as a criminal,

[6:335]

---

[i] *affectirten Humanität*

[36] Kant is apparently referring to deportation to a province as distinguished from exile. See below, 6:338.

[37] Cesare Bonesana, Marchese Beccaria, whose influential *Dei delitti e della pene* (1764) argued for a reform of the harsh penal codes of the time. Kant's interest in Beccaria may well have arisen from Beccaria's reliance on a text from Rousseau's *Social Contract*, which had been published in 1762: "All laws must be regarded as if they proceeded from the unanimous will of the people."

I cannot possibly have a voice in legislation (the legislator is holy). Consequently, when I draw up a penal law against myself as a criminal, it is pure reason in me (*homo noumenon*), legislating with regard to rights, which subjects me, as someone capable of crime and so as another person (*homo phaenomenon*), to the penal law, together with all others in a civil union. In other words, it is not the people (each individual in it) that dictates capital punishment but rather the court (public justice), and so another than the criminal; and the social contract contains no promise to let oneself be punished and so to dispose of oneself and one's life. For, if the authorization to punish had to be based on the offender's *promise*, on his *willing* to let himself be punished, it would also have to be left to him to find himself punishable and the criminal would be his own judge. – The chief point of error (πρωτον ψευδος) in this sophistry consists in its confusing the criminal's own judgment (which must necessarily be ascribed to his *reason*) that he has to forfeit his life with a resolve on the part of his *will* to take his own life, and so in representing as united in one and the same person the judgment upon a right^j and the realization of that right.^k

[6:336]   There are, however, two crimes deserving of death, with regard to which it still remains doubtful whether *legislation* is also authorized to impose the death penalty. The feeling of honor leads to both, in one case the *honor of one's sex*, in the other *military honor*, and indeed true honor, which is incumbent as duty on each of these two classes of human beings. The one crime is a mother's *murder of her child* (*infanticidium maternale*); the other is *murdering a fellow soldier* (*commilitonicidium*) in a *duel*. – Legislation cannot remove the disgrace of an illegitimate birth any more than it can wipe away the stain of suspicion of cowardice from a subordinate officer who fails to respond to a humiliating affront with a force of his own rising above fear of death. So it seems that in these two cases human beings find themselves in the state of nature, and that these acts of *killing* (*homicidium*), which would then not even have to be called murder (*homicidium dolosum*), are certainly punishable but cannot be punished with death by the supreme power. A child that comes into the world apart from marriage is born outside the law (for the law is marriage) and therefore outside the protection of the law. It has, as it were, stolen into the commonwealth (like contraband merchandise), so that the commonwealth can ignore its existence (since it was not right^l that it should have come to exist in this way), and can therefore also ignore its annihilation; and no decree can remove the mother's shame when it becomes known that she gave birth without being married. – So too, when a junior officer is insulted he sees himself constrained by the public opinion of the other members of his estate to obtain satisfaction for himself and, as in the state of nature, *punishment* of the offender not by law, taking him before a court, but by a *duel*, in which he exposes himself to death in order to prove his military

^j   *Rechtsbeurtheilung*   ^k   *Rechtsvollziehung*   ^l   *billig* courage, upon which the honor of his estate essentially rests. Even if the duel should involve *killing* his opponent, the killing that occurs in this fight which takes place in public and with the consent of both parties, though reluctantly, cannot strictly be called murder (*homicidium dolosum*). – – What, now, is to be laid down as right in both cases (coming under criminal justice)? – Here penal justice finds itself very much in a quandary. Either it must declare by law that the concept of honor (which is here no illusion) counts for nothing and so punish with death, or else it must remove from the crime the capital punishment appropriate to it, and so be either cruel or indulgent. The knot can be undone in the following way: the categorical imperative of penal justice remains (unlawful killing of another must be punished by death); but the legislation itself (and consequently also the civil constitution), as long as it remains barbarous and undeveloped, is responsible for the discrepancy between the incentives of honor in the people (subjectively) and the measures that are (objectively) suitable for its purpose. So the public justice arising from the state becomes an *injustice* from the perspective of the justice arising from the people.

[6:337]

II

Of all the rights of a sovereign, the *right to grant clemency* to a criminal (*ius aggratiandi*), either by lessening or entirely remitting punishment, is the slipperiest one for him to exercise; for it must be exercised in such a way as to show the splendor of his majesty, although he is thereby doing injustice in the highest degree. – With regard to crimes of *subjects* against one another it is absolutely not for him to exercise it; for here failure to punish (*impunitas criminis*) is the greatest wrong against his subjects. He can make use of it, therefore, only in case of a wrong done *to himself* (*crimen laesae maiestatis*). But he cannot make use of it even then if his failure to punish could endanger the people's security. – This right is the only one that deserves to be called the right of majesty.

On the Relation with Regard to Rights of a Citizen to His Native Land and to Foreign Countries
§50

A *country* (*territorium*) whose inhabitants are citizens of it simply by its constitution, without their having to perform any special act to establish the right (and so are citizens by birth), is called their *native land*. A country of which they are not citizens apart from this condition is called a *foreign country*. If a foreign country forms part of a larger realm it is called a *province* (in the sense in which the Romans used this word), which must respect the land of the state that rules it as the *mother country* (*regio domina*); for a province is not an integral part of the realm (*imperii*), a place of *residence* for fellow citizens, but only a possession of it, a *secondary house*^m for them.

[6:338]   1) A *subject* (regarded also as a citizen) has the right to emigrate, for the state could not hold him back as its property. But he can take out of it with him only his movable belongings, not his fixed belongings, as he would be doing if he were authorized to sell the land he previously possessed and take with him the money he got for it.

2) The *lord of the land* has the right to encourage *immigration* and settling by foreigners (colonists), even though his native subjects might look askance at this, provided that their private ownership of land is not curtailed by it.

3) He also has the right to *banish* a subject to a province outside the country, where he will not enjoy any of the rights of a citizen, that is, to *deport* him, if he has committed a crime that makes it harmful to the state for his fellow citizens to associate with him.

4) He also has the right to *exile* him altogether (*ius exilii*), to send him out in to the wide world, that is, entirely outside his country (in Old German, this is called *Elend* [misery]). Since the lord of the land then withdraws all protection from him, this amounts to making him an outlaw within his boundaries.

§51

The three authorities in a state, which arise from the concept of a *commonwealth* as such (*res publica latius dicta*), are only the three relations of the united will of the people, which is derived *a priori* from reason. They are a pure idea of a head of state, which has objective practical reality. But this head of state (the sovereign) is only a *thought-entity* (to represent the entire people) as long as there is no physical person to represent the supreme authority in the state and to make this idea effective on the people's will. Now, the relation of this physical person to the people's will can be thought of in three different ways: either that *one* in the state has command over all; or that *several*, equal among themselves, are united in command over all the others; or that *all* together have command over each and so over themselves as well. In other words, the *form of a state* is either *autocratic, aristocratic*, or *democratic*. (The expression *monarchical*, in place [6:339]   of *autocratic*, is not suitable for the concept intended here; for a *monarch* is one who has the *highest* authority, whereas an *autocrat*, who *rules by himself*, has *all* the authority. The autocrat is the sovereign, whereas the monarch merely represents the sovereign.) – It is easy to see that the autocratic form of state is

---

^m *Unterhauses*. Some editors suggest that this is a typographical error for *Unterthans*, in which case the phrase would mean only that the mother country possesses the province as a subject. If *Unterhauses* is not an error, Kant may mean that the citizens of the mother country are not, by birth, citizens of the province of the ruling state. See 6:338 and 348. A province is a "foreign country" [*Ausland*], as far as the "mother country" or ruling state is concerned.

the *simplest*, namely the relation of one (the king) to the people, so that only one is legislator. The aristocratic form of state is already *composed* of two relations: the relation of the nobility (as legislator) to one another, to constitute the sovereign, and then the relation of this sovereign to the people. But the democratic form of state is the most composite of all, since it involves the following relations: first, it unites the will of all to form a people; then it unites the will of the citizens to form a commonwealth; then it sets this *sovereign*, which is itself the united will of the citizens, over the commonwealth.* It is true that, with regard to the administration of right within a state, the simplest form is also the best. With regard to right itself, however, this form of state is the most dangerous for a people, in view of how conducive it is to despotism. It is indeed the most reasonable maxim to simplify the mechanism of unifying a nation by coercive laws, that is, when all the members of the nation are passive and obey *one* who is over them; but in that case none who is a subject is also a *citizen of the state*. As for the consolation with which the people is supposed to be content – that monarchy (strictly speaking here, autocracy) is the best constitution *when the monarch is good* (i.e., when he not only intends what is good but also has insight into it) – this is one of those wise remarks that are tautologous. It says nothing more than that the best constitution is the one by which the administrator of the state is made into the best ruler, that is, that the best constitution is that which is best.

§52

It is *futile* to inquire into the *historical warrant*[n] of the mechanism of government, that is, one cannot reach back to the time at which civil society began (for savages draw up no record of their submission to law; besides, we can already gather from the nature of uncivilized human beings that they were originally subjected to it by force). But it is *punishable*[o] to undertake this inquiry with a view to possibly changing by force the constitution that now exists. For this transformation would have to take place by the people acting as a mob, not by legislation; but insurrection in a constitution that already exists overthrows all civil rightful relations and therefore all right, that is, it is not change in the civil constitution but dissolution of it. The transition to a better constitution is not then a metamorphosis but a palingenesis, which requires a new social contract on which the previous one (now annulled) has no effect. – But it must still be possible, if the existing constitution cannot well be reconciled with the idea of

[6:340]

---

* I shall not mention the adulterations of these forms that arise from invasion by powerful unauthorized people (*oligarchy* and *ochlocracy*), or the so-called mixed constitutions, since this would take us too far afield.

[n] *Geschichtsurkunde.* LD: or perhaps, as in the Cambridge Edition, "historical documentation"

[o] *sträflich.* LD: or perhaps, as the Cambridge Edition has it, "culpable"

the original contract, for the sovereign to change it, so as to allow to continue in existence that form which is essentially required for a people to constitute a state. Now this change cannot consist in a state's reorganizing itself from one of the three forms into another, as, for example, aristocrats agreeing to submit to autocracy or deciding to merge into a democracy, or the reverse, as if it rested on the sovereign's free choice[p] and discretion which kind of constitution it would subject the people to. For even if the sovereign decided to transform itself into a democracy, it could still do the people a wrong, since the people itself could abhor such a constitution and find one of the other forms more to its advantage.

The different forms of states are only the *letter* (*littera*) of the original legislation in the civil state, and they may therefore remain as long as they are taken, by old and long-standing custom (and so only subjectively), to belong necessarily to the machinery of the constitution. But the *spirit* of the original contract (*anima pacti originarii*) involves an obligation on the part of the constituting authority to make the *kind of government* suited to the idea of the original contract. Accordingly, even if this cannot be done all at once, it is under obligation to change the kind of government gradually and continually so that it harmonizes *in its effect* with the only constitution that accords with right, that of a pure republic, in such a way that the old (empirical) statutory forms, which served merely to bring about the *submission* of the people, are replaced by the original (rational) form, the only form which makes *freedom* the principle and indeed the condition for any exercise of *coercion*, as is required by a rightful constitution of a state in the strict sense of the word. Only it will finally lead to what is literally a state. – This is the only constitution of a state that lasts, the constitution in which *law* itself rules and depends on no particular person. It is the final end of all public right, the only condition in which each can be assigned *conclusively*[q] what is his; on the other hand, so long as those other forms of state are supposed to represent literally just so many different moral persons invested with supreme authority, no absolutely rightful condition of civil society can be acknowledged, but only *provisional* right within it.

[6:341]

Any true republic is and can only be a *system representing* the people, in order to protect its rights in its name, by all the citizens united and acting through their delegates (deputies). But as soon as a person who is head of state (whether it be a king, nobility, or the whole of the population, the democratic union) also lets itself be represented, then the united people does not merely *represent* the sovereign: it *is* the sovereign itself. For in it (the people) is originally found the supreme authority from which all rights of individuals as mere subjects (and

[p] *freien Wahl*

[q] *peremtorisch zugetheilt werden kann.* LD: Byrd and Hruschka advocate replacing "assigned" with "granted" here, because the "idea behind *zuteilen* is that you become able to exercise or enjoy the rights you have" (*Kant's Doctrine of Right*, 25f. n.5).

in any event as officials of the state) must be derived; and a republic, once established, no longer has to let the reins of government out of its hands and give them over again to those who previously held them and could again nullify all new institutions by their absolute choice.

A powerful ruler in our time[38] therefore made a very serious error in judgment when, to extricate himself from the embarrassment of large state debts, he left it to the people to take this burden on itself and distribute it as it saw fit; for then the legislative authority naturally came into the people's hands, not only with regard to the taxation of subjects but also with regard to the government, namely to prevent it from incurring new debts by extravagance or war. The consequence was that the monarch's sovereignty[r] wholly disappeared (it was not merely suspended) and passed to the people, to whose legislative will the belongings of every subject became subjected. Nor can it be said that in this case one must assume a tacit but still contractual promise of the National Assembly not to make itself the sovereign but only to [6:342] administer this business of the sovereign and, having attended to it, return the reins of government into the monarch's hands; for such a contract is in itself null and void. The right of supreme legislation in a commonwealth is not an alienable right but the most personal of all rights. Whoever has it can control the people only through the collective will of the people; he cannot control the collective will itself, which is the ultimate basis of any public contract. A contract that would impose obligation on the people to give back its authority would not be incumbent upon the people as the legislative power, yet would still be binding upon it; and this is a contradiction, in accordance with the saying "No one can serve two masters."[s]

---

[r] *Herrschergewalt*   [s] Matthew 6:24 and Luke 16:3

[38] In 1789 Louis XVI convoked the Estates General, which transformed itself into the National Assembly and then, as the Constituent Assembly, adopted a new constitution in 1791.

Public Right
Chapter II

The Right of Nations
§53

As natives of a country, those who constitute a nation can be looked upon analogously to descendants of the same *ancestors* (*congeniti*) even though they are not. Yet in an intellectual sense and from the perspective of rights, since they are born of the same mother (the republic) they constitute as it were one family (*gens, natio*), whose members (citizens of the state) are of equally high birth and do not mix with those who may live near them in a state of nature, whom they regard as inferior; the latter (savages), however, for their own part consider themselves superior because of the lawless freedom they have chosen, even though they do not constitute states but only tribes. The right of *states* in relation to one another (which in German is called, not quite correctly, the *right of nations*, but should instead be called the right of states, *ius publicum civitatum*) is what we have to consider under the title the right of nations. Here a state, as a moral person, is considered as living in relation to another state in the condition of natural freedom and therefore in a condition of constant war. The rights of states consist, therefore, partly of their right *to go to* war, partly of their right *in* war, and partly of their right to constrain each other to leave this condition of war and so form a constitution that will establish lasting peace, that is, its right *after* war. In this problem the only difference between the state of nature of individual human beings or of families (in relation to one another) and that of nations is that in the right of nations we have to take into consideration

not only the relation of one state toward another as a whole, but also the relation of individual persons of one state toward the individuals of another, as well as toward another state as a whole. But this difference from the rights of individuals in a state of nature makes it necessary to consider only such features as can be readily inferred from the concept of a state of nature.

§54

The elements of the right of nations are these: 1) states, considered in external relation to one another, are (like lawless savages) by nature in a non-rightful condition. 2) This non-rightful condition is a *condition* of war (of the right of the stronger), even if it is not a condition of actual war and actual attacks being constantly made (hostilities). Although no state is wronged by another in this condition (insofar as neither wants anything better), this condition is in itself still wrong in the highest degree, and states neighboring upon one another are under obligation to leave it. 3) A league of nations in accordance with the idea of an original social contract is necessary, not in order to meddle in one another's internal dissensions but to protect against attacks from without. 4) This alliance must, however, involve no sovereign authority (as in a civil constitution), but only an *association* (federation); it must be an alliance that can be renounced at any time and so must be renewed from time to time. This is a right *in subsidium* of another and original right, to avoid getting involved in a state of actual war among the other members (*foedus Amphictyonum*).[39]

§55

As regards the original right that free states in a state of nature have to go to war with one another (in order, perhaps, to establish a condition more closely approaching a rightful condition), the first question that arises is: what right has a state *against its own subjects* to use them for war against other states, to expend their goods and even their lives in it, or to put them at risk, in such a way that whether they shall go to war does not depend on their own judgment but they may be sent into it by the supreme command of the sovereign?

It might seem that this right can be easily proved, namely from the right to do what one wants with what belongs to one (one's property). Anyone has an incontestable property in anything the substance of which he has himself *made*. – What follows, then, is the deduction, as a mere jurist would draw it up.

[6:345]

There are various *natural products* in a country that must still be considered *artifacts* (*artefacta*) of the state as far as the *abundance* of natural products of a certain kind is concerned, since the country would not have yielded them in such abundance had there not been a state and an orderly, powerful government, but the inhabitants had been in a state of nature. – Whether from lack of food or from the presence of predatory animals in the country where I live, hens (the most useful kind of fowl), sheep, swine, cattle, and so forth would either not exist at all or at best would be scarce unless there were a government in this country, which secures the inhabitants in what they acquire and possess. – This holds true of the human population as well, which can only be small, as it is in the American wilderness, even if we attribute to these people the greatest industry (which they do not have). The inhabitants would be very scarce since they could not take their attendants and spread out on a land that is always in danger of being laid waste by human beings or by wild and predatory beasts. There would

---

[39] An amphictyonic league, in Greek history, was an association of neighboring states or tribes for the protection of and in the interests of a common religious center. When capitalized, the Amphictyonic League refers to the Delphic Amphictyony, formed to protect the temple of Apollo at Delphi and to direct the Pythian games.

therefore not be adequate sustenance for such a great abundance of human beings as now live in a country. – – Now just as we say that since vegetables (e.g., potatoes) and domestic animals are, as regards their abundance, a human *product*, which he can use, wear out, or destroy (kill), it seems we can also say that since most of his subjects are his own product, the supreme authority in a state, the sovereign, has the right to lead them into war as he would take them on a hunt, and into battles as on a pleasure trip.

While such an argument for this right (which may well be present obscurely in the monarch's mind) holds with regard to animals, which can be one's *property*, it simply cannot be applied to human beings, especially as citizens of a state. For they must always be regarded as co-legislating members of a state (not merely as means, but also as ends in themselves), and must therefore give their free assent, [6:346] through their representatives, not only to waging war in general but also to each particular declaration of war. Only under this limiting condition can a state direct them to serve in a way full of danger to them.

We shall therefore have to derive this right from the *duty* of the sovereign to the people (not the reverse); and for this to be the case the people will have to be regarded as having given its vote to go to war. In this capacity it is, although passive (letting itself be disposed of), also active and represents the sovereign itself.

§56

In the state of nature among states, the *right to go to war* (to engage in hostilities) is the way in which a state is permitted to prosecute its right against another state, namely by its own *force*, when it believes it has been wronged by the other state; for this cannot be done in the state of nature by a lawsuit (the only means by which disputes are settled in a rightful condition). – In addition to active violations (first aggression, which is not the same as first hostility) it may be *threatened*. This includes another state's being the first to undertake *preparations*, upon which is based the right of *prevention* (*ius praeventionis*), or even just the *menacing* increase in another state's *power* (by its acquisition of territory) (*potentia tremenda*).[a] This is a wrong to the lesser power merely by the *condition* of the *superior power*, before any deed on its part, and in the state of nature an attack by the lesser power is indeed legitimate.[40] Accordingly, this is also the basis of the right to a balance of power among all states that are contiguous and could act on one another.

As for *active violations* which give a *right to go to war*, these include *acts of retaliation* (*retorsio*), a state's taking it upon itself to obtain satisfaction for an offense committed against its people by the people of another state, instead of

---

[a] awesome power

[40] In *Toward Perpetual Peace*, however, Kant reaches the opposite conclusion by using his "principle of publicity" 8:384.

seeking compensation (by peaceful methods) from the other state. In terms of formalities, this resembles starting a war without first renouncing peace (without a *declaration of war*); for if one wants to find a right in a condition of war, something analogous to a contract must be assumed, namely, *acceptance* of the declaration of the other party that both want to seek their right in this way.

§57 [6:347]

The greatest difficulty in the right of nations has to do precisely with right during a war; it is difficult even to form a concept of this or to think of law in this lawless state without contradicting oneself (*inter arma silent leges*).[b] Right during a war would, then, have to be the waging of war in accordance with principles that always leave open the possibility of leaving the state of nature among states (in external relation to one another) and entering a rightful condition.

No war of independent states against each other can be a *punitive war* (*bellum punitivum*). For punishment occurs only in the relation of a superior (*imperantis*) to those subject to him (*subditum*), and states do not stand in that relation to each other. – Nor, again, can any war be either a *war of extermination* (*bellum internecinum*) or of *subjugation* (*bellum subiugatorium*), which would be the moral annihilation of a state (the people of which would either become merged in one mass with that of the conqueror or reduced to servitude).[c] The reason there cannot be a war of subjugation is not that this extreme measure a state might use to achieve a condition of peace would in itself contradict the right of a state; it is rather that the idea of the right of nations involves only the concept of an antagonism in accordance with principles of outer freedom by which each can preserve what belongs to it, but not a way of acquiring, by which one state's increase of power could threaten others.

A state against which war is being waged is permitted to use any means of defense except those that would make its subjects unfit to be citizens; for it would then also make itself unfit to qualify, in accordance with the rights of nations, as a person in the relation of states (as one who would enjoy the same rights as others). Means of defense that are not permitted include: using its own subjects as spies; using them or even foreigners as assassins or poisoners (among whom so-called snipers, who lie in wait to ambush individuals, might well be classed); or using them merely for spreading false reports – in a word, using such underhanded means as would destroy the trust requisite to establishing a lasting peace in the future.

[b] in time of war the laws are silent (Cicero, *Pro Milone*, IV.11). (LD: Kant's phrasing is common; the original is: "*Silent enim leges inter arma.*")
[c] *Knechtschaft*

[6:348] In war it is permissible to exact supplies and contributions from a defeated enemy, but not to plunder the people, that is, not to force individual persons to give up their belongings (for that would be robbery, since it was not the conquered people that waged the war; rather, the state under whose rule they lived waged the war *through the people*). Instead, receipts should be issued for everything requisitioned, so that in the peace that follows the burden imposed on the country or province can be divided proportionately.

§58

The right of a state *after a war*, that is, at the time of the peace treaty and with a view to its consequences, consists in this: the victor lays down the conditions on which it will come to an agreement with the vanquished and hold *negotiations* for concluding peace. The victor does not do this from any right he pretends to have because of the wrong his opponent is supposed to have done him; instead, he lets this question drop and relies on his own force. The victor can therefore not propose compensation for the costs of the war since he would then have to admit that his opponent had fought an unjust war. While he may well think of this argument he still cannot use it, since he would then be saying that he had been waging a punitive war and so, for his own part, committing an offense against the vanquished. Rights after a war also include a right to an exchange of prisoners (without ransom), without regard for their being equal in number.

A defeated state or its subjects do not lose their civil freedom through the conquest of their country, so that the state would be degraded to a colony and its subjects to bondage; for if they did the war would have been a *punitive war*, which is self-contradictory. – A *colony* or province is a people that indeed has its own constitution, its own legislation, and its own land, on which those who belong to another state are only foreigners even though this other state has supreme *executive* authority over the colony or province. – The state having that executive authority is called the *mother state*, and the daughter state, though ruled by it, still governs itself (by its own parliament, possibly with a viceroy presiding over it) (*civitas hybrida*).[d] This was the relation Athens had with respect to various islands and that Great Britain now has with regard to Ireland.

[6:349] Still less can *bondage* and its legitimacy be derived from a people's being overcome in war, since for this one would have to admit that a war could be punitive. Least of all can hereditary bondage be derived from it; hereditary bondage as such is absurd since guilt from someone's crime cannot be inherited.

[d] hybrid state

The concept of a peace treaty already contains the provision that an *amnesty* goes along with it.

§59

The right to peace is 1) the right to be at peace when there is a war in the vicinity, or the right to *neutrality*; 2) the right to be assured of the continuance of a peace that has been concluded, that is, the right to a *guarantee*; 3) the right to an *alliance* (confederation) of several states for their common *defense* against any external or internal attacks, but not a league for attacking others and adding to their own territory.

§60

There are no limits to the rights of a state against an *unjust enemy* (no limits with respect to quantity or degree, though there are limits with respect to quality); that is to say, an injured state may not use *any* means *whatever* but may use those means that are allowable to any degree that it is able to, in order to maintain what belongs to it. – But what is an *unjust enemy* in terms of the concepts of the right of nations, in which, as is the case in a state of nature generally, each state is judge in its own case? It is an enemy whose publicly expressed will (whether by word or deed) reveals a maxim by which, if it were made a universal rule, any condition of peace among nations would be impossible and, instead, a state of nature would be perpetuated. Violation of public contracts is an expression of this sort. Since this can be assumed to be a matter of concern to all nations whose freedom is threatened by it, they are called upon to unite against such misconduct in order to deprive the state of its power to do it. But they are not called upon *to divide its territory among themselves* and to make the state, as it were, disappear from the earth, since that would be an injustice against its people, which cannot lose its original right to unite itself into a commonwealth, though it can be made to adopt a new constitution that by its nature will be unfavorable to the inclination for war.

It is *redundant*, however, to speak of an unjust enemy in a state of nature; for a state of nature is itself a condition of injustice. A just enemy would be one that I would be doing wrong by resisting; but then he would also not be my enemy. [6:350]

§61

Since a state of nature among nations, like a state of nature among individual human beings, is a condition that one ought to leave in order to enter a lawful condition, before this happens any rights of nations, and anything external that is mine or yours which states can acquire or retain by war, are merely *provisional*.

Only in a universal *association of states* (analogous to that by which a people becomes a state) can rights come to hold *conclusively* and a true *condition of peace* come about. But if such a state made up of nations were to extend too far over vast regions, governing it and so too protecting each of its members would finally have to become impossible, while several such corporations would again bring on a state of war. So *perpetual peace*, the ultimate goal of the whole right of nations, is indeed an unachievable idea. Still, the political principles directed toward perpetual peace, of entering into such alliances of states, which serve for continual *approximation* to it, are not unachievable. Instead, since continual approximation to it is a task based on duty and therefore on the right of human beings and of states, this can certainly be achieved.

Such an *association* of several *states* to preserve peace can be called a *permanent congress of states*, which each neighboring state is at liberty to join. Something of this kind took place (at least as regards the formalities of the right of nations for the sake of keeping the peace) in the first half of the present century, in the assembly of the States General at the Hague. The ministers of most of the courts of Europe and even of the smallest republics lodged with it their complaints about attacks being made on one of them by another. In this way they thought of the whole of Europe as a single confederated state which they accepted as arbiter, so to speak, in their public disputes. But later, instead of this, the right of nations survived only in books; it disappeared from cabinets or else, after force had already been used, was relegated in the form of a deduction to the obscurity of archives.

[6:351]   By a *congress* is here understood only a voluntary[e] coalition of different states which can be *dissolved* at any time, not a federation (like that of the American states) which is based on a constitution and can therefore not be dissolved. – Only by such a congress can the idea of a public right of nations be realized, one to be established for deciding their disputes in a civil way, as if by a lawsuit, rather than in a barbaric way (the way of savages), namely by war.

[e] *willkürliche*

130

Public Right
Chapter III

Cosmopolitan Right[41]

§62

This rational idea of a *peaceful*, even if not friendly, thoroughgoing community of all nations on the earth that can come into relations affecting one another is not a philanthropic (ethical) principle but a principle *having to do with rights.* Nature has enclosed them all together within determinate limits (by the spherical shape of the place they live in, a *globus terraqueus*).[a] And since possession of the land, on which an inhabitant of the earth can live, can be thought only as possession of a part of a determinate whole, and so as possession of that to which each of them originally has a right, it follows that all nations stand *originally* in a community of land, though not of *rightful* community of possession (*communio*) and so of use of it, or of property in it; instead they stand in a community of possible physical *interaction* (*commercium*), that is, in a thoroughgoing relation of each to all the others of *offering to engage in commerce* with any other,[b] and each has a right to make this attempt without the other being authorized to behave toward it as an enemy because it has made this attempt. – This right, since it has to do with the possible union of all nations with a view to certain universal laws for their possible commerce, can be called *cosmopolitan right* (*ius cosmopoliticum*).

Although the seas might seem to remove nations from any community with one another, they are the arrangements of nature most favoring their commerce by means of navigation; and the more *coastlines* these nations have in the vicinity of one another (as in the Mediterranean), the more lively their commerce can be. However, visiting these coasts, and still more settling there to connect them with the mother country, provide the occasion for troubles and acts of violence in one place on our globe to be felt all over it. Yet this possible abuse cannot annul the right of citizens of the world *to try to* establish community with all and, to this end, to *visit* all

---

[a] globe of earth and water
[b] Kant moves between *Wechselwirkung*, i.e., interaction, intercourse, or "commerce" in a very general sense, and *Verkehr*, which he used in his discussion of contracts to signify exchange of property, "commerce" in a more specific sense.
[41] Part III of "Theory and Practice," directed against Moses Mendelssohn, is concerned with cosmopolitan right, as Part II, directed against Hobbes, is concerned with the right of a state. In *Toward Perpetual Peace*, 8:368, Kant maintains that "the spirit of commerce" is a driving force in human nature, and, since commerce and war are incompatible, one of the forces by which nature can be viewed as working toward peace.

regions of the earth. This is not, however, a right to *make a settlement* on the land of another nation (*ius incolatus*);[c] for this, a specific contract is required.

The question arises, however: in newly discovered lands, may a nation undertake to *settle* (*accolatus*)[d] and take possession in the neighborhood of a people that has already settled in the region, even without its consent? –

If the settlement is made so far from where that people resides that there is no encroachment on anyone's use of his land, the right to settle is not open to doubt. But if these peoples are shepherds or hunters (like the Hottentots, the Tungusi, or most of the American Indian nations) who depend for their sustenance on great open regions, this settlement may not take place by force but only by contract, and indeed by a contract that does not take advantage of the ignorance of those inhabitants with respect to ceding their lands. This is true despite the fact that sufficient specious reasons to justify the use of force are available: that it is to the world's advantage, partly because these crude peoples will become civilized (this is like the pretext by which even Büsching[42] tries to excuse the bloody introduction of Christianity into Germany), and partly because one's own country will be cleaned of corrupt human beings, and they or their descendants will, it is hoped, become better in another part of the world (such as New Holland). But all these supposedly good intentions cannot wash away the stain of injustice in the means used for them. – Someone may reply that such scruples about using force in the beginning, in order to establish a lawful condition, might well mean that the whole earth would still be in a lawless condition; but this consideration can no more annul that condition of right[e] than can the pretext of revolutionaries within a state, that when constitutions are bad it is up to the people to reshape them by force and to be unjust once and for all so that afterwards they can establish justice all the more securely and make it flourish.

[6:354]   * * *

---

[c] right to inhabit   [d] dwell near, as a neighbor   [e] *Rechtsbedingung*

[42] Anton Friedrich Büsching (1724–1793) was a well-known geographer and also a theologian.

Conclusion

If someone cannot prove that a thing is, he can try to prove that it is not. If (as often happens) he cannot succeed in either, he can still ask whether he has any *interest in assuming* one or the other (as an hypothesis), either from a theoretical or from a practical point of view. An assumption is adopted from a theoretical point of view in order merely to explain a certain phenomenon (such as, for astronomers, the retrograde motion and stationary state of the planets). An assumption is adopted from a practical point of view in order to achieve a certain end, which may be either a *pragmatic* (merely technical end)^f or a *moral* end, that is, an end such that the maxim of adopting it is itself a duty. – Now it is evident that what would be made our duty in this case is not the *assumption* (*suppositio*) that this end can be realized, which would be a judgment about it that is merely theoretical and, moreover, problematic; for there can be no obligation to do this (to believe something). What is incumbent upon us as a duty is rather to act in conformity with the idea of that end, even if there is not the slightest theoretical likelihood that it can be realized, as long as its impossibility cannot be demonstrated either.

Now morally practical reason pronounces in us its irresistible *veto: there is to be no war*, neither war between you and me in the state of nature nor war between us as states, which, although they are internally in a lawful condition, are still externally (in relation to one another) in a lawless condition; for war is not the way in which everyone should seek his rights. So the question is no longer whether perpetual peace is something real or a fiction, and whether we are not deceiving ourselves in our theoretical judgment when we assume that it is real. Instead, we must act as if it is something real, though perhaps it is not; we must work toward establishing perpetual peace and the kind of constitution that seems to us most conducive to it (say, a republicanism of all states, together and separately) in order to bring about perpetual peace and put an end to the heinous waging of war, to which as their chief aim all states without exception have hitherto directed their internal arrangements. And even if the complete realization of this objective always remains a pious wish, still we are certainly not deceiving ourselves in [6:355] adopting the maxim of working incessantly towards it. For this is our duty, and to admit that the moral law within us is itself deceptive would call forth in us the wish, which arouses our abhorrence, rather to be rid of all reason and to regard ourselves as thrown by one's principles into the same mechanism of nature as all the other species of animals.

It can be said that establishing universal and lasting peace constitutes not merely a part of the doctrine of right but rather the entire final end of the doctrine of right within the limits of reason alone; for the condition of peace is

---

^f *Kunstzweck*

the only condition in which what is mine and what is yours are secured under *laws* for a multitude of human beings living in proximity to one another and therefore under a constitution. But the rule for this constitution, as a norm for others, cannot be derived from the experience of those who have hitherto found it most to their advantage; it must, rather, be derived *a priori* by reason from the ideal of a rightful association of human beings under public laws as such. For all examples (which only illustrate but cannot prove anything) are treacherous, so that they certainly require a metaphysics. Even those who ridicule metaphysics admit its necessity, though carelessly, when they say for example, as they often do, "the best constitution is that in which power belongs not to human beings but to the laws." For what can be more metaphysically sublimated than this very idea, which even according to their own assertion has the most confirmed objective reality, as can also be easily shown in actually occurring cases? The attempt to realize this idea should not be made by way of revolution, by a leap, that is, by violent overthrow of an already existing defective constitution (for there would then be an intervening moment in which any rightful condition would be annihilated). But if it is attempted and carried out by gradual reform in accordance with firm principles, it can lead to continual approximation to the highest political good, perpetual peace.

Explanatory Remarks on the *Metaphysical First Principles of the Doctrine of Right*

I take the occasion for these remarks chiefly from the review of this book in the *Göttingen Journal* (No. 28, 18 Feb. 1797).[43] In this review the book was examined with insight and rigor, but also with appreciation and "the hope that those first principles will be a lasting gain for the science." I shall use this review as a guide for my criticism as well as for some elaboration of this system.

My astute critic takes exception to a definition at the very beginning of the *Introduction* to the *Doctrine of Right*.[a] What is meant by the *faculty of desire*? It is, the text says, the capacity[b] to be by means of one's representations the cause of the objects of these representations. – To this exposition he objects "that it comes to nothing as soon as one abstracts from the *external* conditions of the result of desire. – But the faculty of desire is something even for an idealist, even though the external world is nothing for him." *I reply*: but are there not also intense but still consciously futile longings (e.g., Would to God that man were still alive!), which are *devoid of any deed* but not *devoid of any result*, since they still work powerfully within the subject himself (make him ill), though not on external things? A desire, as a *striving (nisus)* to be a *cause* by means of one's representations, is still always causality, at least within the subject, even when he sees the inadequacy of his representations for the effect he envisages. – The misunderstanding here amounts to this: that since [6:357] consciousness of one's capacity *in general* is (in the case mentioned) also consciousness of one's *incapacity*[c] with respect to the external world, the definition is not applicable to an idealist. Since, however, all that is in question here is the relation of a cause (a representation) to an effect (a feeling) in general, the causality of a representation (whether the causality is external or internal) with regard to its object must unavoidably be thought in the concept of the faculty of desire.

I

Logical Preparation for a Recently Proposed Concept of a Right

If philosophers versed in right want to rise or venture all the way to metaphysical first principles of the doctrine of right (without which all their juridical science[d]

---

[a] LD: In this edition, the passage referred to here (6:211) is not at the very beginning of the Introduction to the *Doctrine of Right* (as in AA), but rather at the beginning of §II of that Introduction.

[b] *Vermögen*   [c] *seines Vermögens überhaupt . . . seines Unvermögens*

[d] *Rechtswissenschaft.* See 6:229, where Kant seemed to say that only systematic knowledge of natural right is a true science. When coupled with that passage, his use here of *erheben oder versteigen*, which I have translated as "rise or venture," might be a suggestion that some philosophic jurists have got out of their element in attempting to discuss the issues at hand.

[43] The appendix was added in the 1798 edition of the *Doctrine of Right* in reply to a review by Friedrich Bouterwek (reprinted in AA 20:445–53). Kant's quotations are not always accurate.

would be merely statutory), they cannot be indifferent to assurance of the completeness of their *division* of concepts of rights, since otherwise that science would not be a *rational system* but merely an aggregate hastily collected. – For the sake of the form of the system, the *topic* of principles must be complete, that is, the *place* for a concept (*locus communis*) must be indicated, the place that is left open for this concept by the synthetic form of the division. Afterwards one may also show that one or another concept which might be put in this place would be self-contradictory and falls from this place.

Up to now jurists have admitted two commonplaces: that of a right to *things* and that of a right against *persons*. By the mere form of joining these two concepts together into one, two more places are opened up for concepts, as members of an *a priori* division: that of a right to a thing akin to a right against a person and that of a right to a person akin to a right to a thing. It is therefore natural to ask whether we have to add some such new concept and whether we must come across it in the complete table of division, even if it is only problematic. There can be no doubt that this is the case. For a merely logical division (which abstracts from the content of cognition, from the object) is always a *dichotomy*, for example, any right is either a right to a thing or not a right to a thing. But the division in question here, namely [6:358] the metaphysical division, might also be a fourfold division; for besides the two simple members of the division, two further relations might have to be added, namely those of the conditions limiting a right, under which one right enters into combination with the other. This possibility requires further investigation. – The concept of a *right to a thing akin to a right against a person* drops out without further ado, since no right of a *thing* against a *person* is conceivable. Now the question is whether the reverse of this relation is just as inconceivable or whether this concept, namely that of a *right to a person akin to a right to a thing*, is a concept that not only contains no self-contradiction but also belongs necessarily (as given *a priori* in reason) to the concept of what is externally mine or yours, that of not *treating* persons in a similar way to *things* in all respects, but still of *possessing* them as things and dealing with them as things in many relations.

2
Justification of the Concept of a Right to a Person Akin to a Right to a Thing

Put briefly and well, the definition of a right to a person akin to a right to a thing is this: "It is the right of a human being to have a *person* other than himself as *his own*."* I take care to say "a *person*"; for while it is true that someone can have as

---

* I do not say here "to have a person as mine" (using the adjective), but "to have a person as *what is mine*," (*to meum*, using the substantive). For I can say "this is *my father*," and that signifies only my physical relation (of connection) to him in a general way, e.g., I *have* a father; but I cannot say "I have him as *what is mine*." However, if I say "my wife" this signifies a special, namely a rightful,

his own another *human being* who by his crime has forfeited his personality (become a bondsman), this right to a thing is not what is in question here.

We must now examine whether this concept, this "new phenomenon in the juristic sky," is a *stella mirabilis*[e] (a phenomenon never seen before, growing into a star of the first magnitude but gradually disappearing again, perhaps to return at some time) or merely a *shooting star*. [6:359]

3
Examples

To have something external as one's own means to possess it rightfully; but possessing something is the condition of its being possible to use it. If this condition is thought as merely physical, possession is called *holding*. – That I am legitimately holding something is not of itself sufficient for saying that the object is mine or for making it mine. But if I am authorized, for whatever reason, to insist upon holding an object that has escaped from my control or been torn from it, this concept of a right is a *sign* (as an effect is a sign of its cause) that I consider myself authorized to treat this object and to use it as *what is mine*, and consider myself as also in intelligible possession of it.

What is one's own here does not, indeed, mean what is one's own in the sense of property in the person of another (for a human being cannot have property in himself, much less in another person), but means what is one's own in the sense of usufruct (*ius utendi fruendi*),[f] to make direct use of a person *as of* a thing, as a means to my end, but still without infringing upon his personality.

But this end, as the condition under which such use is legitimate, must be morally necessary. A man cannot desire a woman in order to *enjoy* her as a thing, that is, in order to take immediate satisfaction in merely animal intercourse with her, nor can a woman give herself to him for this without both renouncing their personalities (in carnal or bestial cohabitation), that is, this can be done only under the condition of *marriage*. Since marriage is a reciprocal giving of one's very person into the possession of the other, it must *first* be concluded, so that neither is dehumanized through the bodily use that one makes of the other.

Apart from this condition carnal enjoyment is *cannibalistic* in principle (even if not always in its effect). Whether something is *consumed* by mouth and teeth, or whether the woman is consumed by pregnancy and the perhaps fatal delivery resulting from it, or the man by exhaustion of his sexual capacity from the woman's frequent demands upon it, the difference is merely in the manner of [6:360]

relation of the possessor to an object as a *thing* (even though the object is also a person). Possession (*physical* possession), however, is the condition of being able to *manage* (*manipulatio*) something as a thing, even if this must, in another respect, be treated at the same time as a person.

[e] wondrous star, or supernova   [f] right of the use of the fruits

enjoyment. In this sort of use by each of the sexual organs of the other, each is actually a *consumable* thing (*res fungibilis*)^g with respect to the other, so that if one were to make oneself such a thing by *contract*, the contract would be contrary to law (*pactum turpe*).^{h}

Similarly, a man and a woman cannot beget a child as their joint *work* (*res artificialis*) and without both of them incurring an obligation towards the child and towards each other to maintain it. This is, again, acquisition of a human being *as of* a thing, but only formally so (as befits a right to a person that is only akin to a right to a thing). Parents* have a right against every possessor (*ius in re*)^i of their child who has been removed from their control. Since they also have a right to constrain it to carry out and comply with any of their directions that are not contrary to a possible lawful freedom (*ius ad rem*),^{j} they also have a right against a person against the child.

Finally, when their duty to provide for their children comes to an end as they reach maturity, parents still have a right to use them as members of the household subject to their direction, for maintaining the household, until they leave. This is a duty of parents towards them which follows from the natural limitation of the parents' right. Up until this time children are indeed members of the household and belong to the *family*; but from now on they belong to the *service* of the family (*famulatus*), so that the head of the house cannot add them to what is his (as his domestics) except by contract. – In the same way, the head of a house can also make the service of those *outside the family* his own in terms of a right to them akin to a right to a thing and acquire them as domestics (*famulatus domesticus*) by a contract. Such a contract is not just a contract to *let and hire (locatio conductio operae)*,^{k} but a giving up of their persons into the possession of the head of the house, a lease (*locatio conductio personae*).^{l} What distinguishes such a contract from letting and hiring is that the servant agrees *to do whatever is permissible* for the welfare of the household, instead of being commissioned for a specifically determined job, whereas someone who is hired for a specific job (an artisan or day laborer) does not give himself up as part of the other's belongings and so is not a member of the household. – Since he is not in the rightful possession of another who puts him under obligation to perform certain services, even if he lives in the other's house (*inquilinus*) the head of the house cannot *take possession* of him as a thing (*via facti*); he must instead insist upon the laborer's doing what he promised in terms of a right against a person, as something he can command by rightful proceedings (*via iuris*). – – So much for the clarification

[6:361]

---

* In written German *Ältern* means *Seniores* and *Eltern* (used here) means *Parentes*. Although the two words cannot be distinguished in speech, they are very different in meaning.
^{g} a thing that can be consumed ^{h} wrongful compact ^{i} right in the thing
^{j} right to the thing ^{k} let and hire of a work ^{l} let and hire of a person

and defense of a strange type of right which has recently been added to the doctrine of natural law, although it has always been tacitly in use.

4
On Confusing a Right to a Thing with a Right Against a Person

I have also been censured for heterodoxy in natural private right for the proposition that *sale breaks a lease*. (*Doctrine of Right*, §31, [AA 6:]290).

It does seem at first glance to conflict with all rights arising from a contract that someone could give notice to someone leasing his house before the period of residence agreed upon is up and, so it seems, break his promise to the lessee, provided he grants him the time for vacating it that is customary by the civil laws where they live. – But if it can be proved that the lessee knew or must have known, when he contracted to lease it, that the promise made to him by the *lessor*, the owner, naturally (without its needing to be stated expressly in the contract) and therefore tacitly included the condition, *as long as the owner does not sell the house during this time* (or does not have to turn it over to his creditors if he should become bankrupt), then the lessor has not broken his promise, which was already a conditional one in terms of reason, and the lessee's right was not encroached upon if he was given notice before the lease expired.

For the right a lessee has by a contract to lease is a right *against a person*, to   [6:362]
something a certain person has to perform for another (*ius ad rem*); it is not a right against *every* possessor of a thing (*ius in re*), not a right to a *thing*.

A lessee could, indeed, secure himself in his *contract to lease* and procure a right to a thing as regards the house; he could, namely, have this right only to the lessor's house *registered* (entered in the land register), as attached to the land. Then he could not be turned out of his lease, before the time settled upon had expired, by the owner's giving notice or even by his death (his natural death or also his civil death, bankruptcy). If he does not do this, perhaps because he wanted to be free to conclude a lease on better terms elsewhere or because the owner did not want to encumber his house with such an *onus*, it may be concluded that, as regards the time for giving notice, each of the parties was aware that he had made a contract subject to the tacit condition that it could be dissolved if this became convenient (except for the period of grace for vacating, as determined by civil law). Certain rightful consequences of a *bare* contract to lease give further confirmation of one's authorization to break a lease by sale; for if a lessor dies, no obligation to continue the lease is ascribed to his heir, since this is an obligation only on the part of a certain person and ceases with his death (though the legal time for giving notice must still be taken into account in this case). Neither can the right of a lessee, as such, pass to his heir without a separate contract; nor, as long as both parties are alive, is a lessee authorized to sublet to anyone without an explicit agreement.

5

Further Discussion of the Concept of the Right to Punish

The mere idea of a civil constitution among *human beings* carries with it the concept of punitive justice belonging to the supreme authority. The only question is whether it is a matter of indifference to the legislator what kinds of punishment are adopted, as long as they are effective measures for eradicating crime (which violates the security a state gives each in his possession of what is his), or whether the legislator must also take into account respect for the humanity in the person of the wrongdoer (i.e., respect for the species) simply on grounds of right. I said that the *ius talionis*^m is by its form always the principle for the right to punish since it alone is the principle determining this idea *a priori* (not derived from experience of which measures would be most effective for eradicating crime).* – But what is to be done in the case of crimes that cannot be punished by a *return* for them because this would be either impossible or itself a punishable crime against *humanity* as such, for example, rape as well as pederasty or bestiality? The punishment for rape and pederasty is castration (like that of a white or black eunuch in a seraglio), that for bestiality, permanent expulsion from civil society, since the criminal has made himself unworthy of human society. – *Per quod quis peccat, per idem punitur et idem*^n – The crimes mentioned are called unnatural because they are perpetrated against humanity itself. To inflict *whatever* punishments *one chooses*^o for these crimes would be literally contrary to the concept of *punitive justice*. For the only time a criminal cannot complain that a wrong is done him is when he brings his misdeed^p back upon himself, and what is done to him in accordance with penal law is what he has perpetrated on others, if not in terms of its letter at least in terms of its spirit.

[6:363]

---

* In every punishment there is something that (rightly) offends the accused's feeling of honor, since it involves coercion that is unilateral only, so that his dignity as a citizen is suspended, at least in this particular case; for he is subjected to an external duty to which he, for his own part, may offer no resistance. A man of nobility or wealth who has to pay a fine feels the loss of his money less than the humiliation of having to submit to the will of an inferior. *Punitive justice* (*iustitia punitiva*) must be distinguished from *punitive prudence*, since the argument for the former is *moral*, in terms of being *punishable* (*quia peccatum est*) while that for the latter is *merely pragmatic* (*ne peccetur*) and based on experience of what is most effective in eradicating crime; and punitive justice has an entirely different *place* in the topic of concepts of right, [6: 364] *locus iusti*; its place is not that of the *conducibilis*, of what is *useful* for a certain purpose, nor that of the mere *honesti*, which must be sought in ethics.

^m right (or law) of retaliation
^n One who commits a sin is punished through it and in the same way.   ^o *Willkürlich Strafen*
^p *Übelthat*

6
On a Right from Prolonged Possession

"A right based on *prolonged possession* (*Usucapio*) should, according to pp. [AA 6:]291ff., be established by natural right. For unless one admits that an *ideal acquisition*, as it is here called, is established by possession in good faith, no acquisition at all would be conclusively secured. (Yet Mr. Kant himself admits only provisional acquisition in the state of nature, and because of this insists on the juristic necessity of a civil constitution. – – I assert that I am the *possessor* of something *in good faith*, however, only against someone who cannot prove that he was *possessor* of the same thing *in good faith* before me and has not ceased by his will to be its possessor.)" – – This is not the question here. The question is whether I can also *assert* that I am the owner even if someone should come forward claiming to be the *earlier* true owner of the thing, but where it was *absolutely* impossible to learn of his existence as its possessor and of his being in possession as its owner. This occurs if the claimant has not (whether by his own fault or not) given any publicly valid sign of his uninterrupted possession, for example, by recording it in the registry or by voting as undisputed owner in civil assemblies. [6:364]

For the question here is, who ought to prove his legitimate acquisition? This obligation (*onus probandi*)[q] cannot be imposed on the possessor, since he has been in possession of it as far back as his confirmed history reaches. In accordance with principles of right, the one who claims to be the earlier owner of the thing is cut completely out of the series of successive possessors by the interval during which he has given no civilly valid sign of his ownership. This failure to perform any public possessory act makes him a claimant without a title. (Against his claim it can be said here, as in theology, *conservatio est continua creatio*).[r] Even if a claimant who had not previously appeared should later come forward supplied with documents he found, there would be room for doubt, in his case again, whether a still earlier claimant could appear at some future time and base his claim on earlier possession. – Finally acquiring something by *prolonged possession* of it (*acquirere per usucapionem*)[s] does not depend at all on the *length of time* one has possessed it. For it is absurd to suppose that a wrong becomes a right because it has continued for a long time. Far from a right in a thing being based on use of it, *use* of it (however long) presupposes a right in it. Therefore *prolonged possession* (*usucapio*), regarded as acquisition of a thing by long use of it, is a self-contradictory concept. Prescription[t] as a means of conserving possession (*conservatio possessionis meae per praescriptionem*) is no [6:365]

---

[q] burden of proof   [r] conservation is *continuous* creation
[s] to acquire by *usucapio*, i.e. by prolonged possession
[t] or "superannuation of claims," *Verjährung der Ansprüche*

less self-contradictory, although it is a distinct concept as far as the argument for appropriation is concerned.[u] That is to say, a negative basis, that is, the entire *non-use* of one's right, not even that which is necessary to show oneself as possessor, is taken to be an *abandonment* of this right (*derelictio*), a rightful act, that is, the use of one's right against another, so as to acquire the object of the earlier possessor by excluding it (*per praescriptionem*) from his claim; and this involves a contradiction.

I therefore acquire without giving proof and without any act establishing my right. I have no need for proof; instead I acquire by law (*lege*). What follows? *Public* immunity from claims, that is, *security in my possession* by law, since I do not need to produce proof, and take my stand on my uninterrupted possession. But that any *acquisition* in a state of nature is only provisional has no bearing on the question of the security of *possession* of what is acquired, which must precede acquisition.

7
On Inheritance

As for the right of inheritance, this time the acuteness of the reviewer has failed to find him the nerve of the proof of my assertion. – I did not say (p. [AA 6:]294) that every human being necessarily accepts any *thing offered* him which he can only gain and not lose by accepting (for there are indeed no such things). I said, rather, that everyone always in fact accepts, unavoidably and tacitly but still validly, the *right to accept the offer* at the same moment, namely when the nature of the matter involves the absolute impossibility of the offer being retracted, the moment of the testator's death; for then the promisor cannot withdraw it and the promisee, without needing to do any act to establish the right, is at the same moment the accepter, not of the legacy [6:366] promised but of the right to accept or refuse it. When the will is opened he sees that he had already at that moment, before accepting the legacy, become richer than he was before, since he had acquired the exclusive *authorization to accept* and this is already an enriching circumstance. – Although a civil condition is presupposed in order for someone who no longer exists to make *something belong to another*, this transfer of possession by one who is dead does not alter the possibility of acquiring in accordance with universal principles of natural right, even though a civil constitution is the necessary basis for applying these principles to the case at hand. – That is to say, something left unconditionally to my free choice[v] to accept or refuse is called a *res iacens*.

---

[u] *Zueignung*. In 6:259 *Zueignung* (*appropriatio*) was said to be the third of the *Momente* (*attendenda*) in original acquisition. As Kant pointed out (6:291), ideal acquisition can take effect only in civil society. In the remainder of the paragraph the text seems to be corrupt.
[v] *freien Wahl*

If the owner of something offers it to me gratuitously (promises that it will be mine), for example, when he offers me a piece of furniture of the house I am about to move from, I have the exclusive right to accept his offer (*ius in re iacente*)[w] so long as he does not withdraw it (and if he dies in the meantime this is impossible), that is, I alone can accept it or refuse it as I please; and I do not get this exclusive right to make the choice through any special rightful act of declaring that I will to have this right. I acquire it without any such act (*lege*). – So I can indeed declare that I will *not to have the thing* (because accepting it might involve me in unpleasantness with others), but I cannot will to have the exclusive choice of *whether it is to belong to me or not*; for I have this right (to accept or refuse) immediately from the offer, without my declaring my acceptance of it, since if I could refuse even to have this choice I would be choosing not to choose, which is a contradiction. Now this right to choose passes to me at the moment of the testator's death, and by his testament (*institutio haeredis*) I acquire, not yet his belongings and goods, but nevertheless *merely rightful* (intelligible) possession of his belongings or a part of them, which I can now refuse to accept to the advantage of others. Consequently this possession is not interrupted for a moment; succession passes instead in a continuous series from the dying to the appointed heirs by their acceptance. The proposition *testamenta sunt iuris naturae*[x] is thus established beyond any doubt.

8
On the Right of a State with Regard to *Perpetual* Foundations for its Subjects

[6:367]

A *foundation* (*sanctio testamentaria beneficii perpetui*) is an institution that has been voluntarily established, and confirmed by a state, for the benefit of certain members of it who succeed one another until they have all died out. – It is called *perpetual* if the statute for maintaining it is bound up with the constitution of the state itself (for a state must be regarded as perpetual). Those who are to benefit from a foundation are either the *people* generally, or a part of them united by certain special principles, or a certain *estate*, or a *family* and its descendants continuing in perpetuity. An example of the first kind is a *hospital*; of the second, a *church*; of the third, an *order* (spiritual or secular); and of the fourth, an estate that is *entailed*.

It is said that such corporations and their *right* of succession cannot be annulled, since it became by a *bequest* the property of the heirs appointed, so that annulling such a constitution (*corpus mysticum*)[y] would amount to depriving someone of his belongings.

---

[w] right in a thing cast aside   [x] testaments are by right of nature   [y] mystical body

A

Those institutions for the benefit of the poor, invalids and the sick^z which have been set up at the expense of the state (foundations and hospitals) can certainly not be done away with. But if the intention of the testator's will rather than its letter is to have priority, circumstances can arise in time which make it advisable to nullify such a foundation at least in terms of its form. – So it has been found that the poor and the sick (except for patients in mental hospitals) are cared for better and more economically when they are helped with certain sums of money (proportioned to the needs of the time), with which they can board where they want, with relatives or acquaintances, than when – as in the hospital at Greenwich – they are provided splendid institutions, serviced by expensive personnel, which severely limit their freedom. – It cannot be said then that the state is depriving the people, which is entitled to the benefits of this foundation, of what is theirs; the state is instead promoting this by choosing wiser means for preserving it.

[6:368] *B*

The clergy which does not propagate itself carnally (the Catholic clergy) possesses, with the favor of the state, estates and the subjects attached to them. These belong to a spiritual state (called a church), to which the laity, for the salvation of their souls, have given themselves by their bequests as its property.^{a} And so the clergy, as a special estate, has possessions which can be bequeathed by law from one generation to the next, and which are adequately documented by papal bulls. – But may one assume that this relation to the laity can be directly taken from the clergy by the absolute power of the secular state? Would this not amount to depriving someone by force of what is his, as the unbelievers of the French republic are attempting to do?

The question here is whether the church can belong to the state or the state belong to the church; for two supreme authorities cannot without contradiction be subordinate one to the other. – It is evident that only the *first constitution* (*politico-hierarchica*) could subsist by itself, since every civil constitution is of *this* world because it is an earthly authority (of human beings) that, along with its results, can be confirmed in experience. Even if we concede to believers, whose *kingdom* is in heaven and the *other world*, a constitution relating to that world (*hierarchico-politica*), they must submit to the sufferings of this era under the

---

^{z} *Die wohlthätige Anstalt...*

^{a} *welchem die Weltliche durch Vermächtniß ... sich als ihr Eigenthum hingegeben haben*[44]

[44] In the context of the discussion, one would have expected Kant to say that laymen have given their estates and the feudal subjects attached to them to a church. So too, at the beginning of the next paragraph when Kant raises the quesiton of whether the church "can belong to" (*als das Seine angehören könne*) the state or the state to the church, the kind of right involved would seem to require a distinction between the estates of a church and a church as a body of believers (6:327).

higher authority of human beings of this world. – Hence only the first constitution is to be found.

Religion (in appearance), as belief in the dogmas of a church and in the power of priests, who are the aristocrats of such a constitution though it can also be monarchical (papal), can neither be imposed upon a people nor taken away from them by any civil authority; nor can a citizen be excluded from the service of the state and the advantages this brings him because his religion is different from that of the court (as Great Britain has done with the Irish nation).

In order to partake of the grace a church promises to show believers even after their death, certain devout and believing souls establish foundations in perpetuity, by which certain estates of theirs are to become the property of a church after their death; and the state may pledge itself to fealty to a church regarding this or that foundation, or indeed all of them,[b] so that these people may have the prayers, indulgences, and penances by which the servants of the church appointed for this (clergy) promise that they will fare well in the other world. But such a foundation, supposedly instituted in perpetuity, is not at all established in perpetuity; the state can cast off this burden a church has laid upon it when it wants to. – For a church itself is an institution built merely upon belief, so that when the illusion arising from this opinion disappears through popular enlightenment, the fearful authority of the clergy based on it also falls away and the state, with full right, takes control of the property the church has arrogated to itself, namely the land bestowed on it through bequests. However, the feudal tenants of the institution that hitherto existed have the right to demand compensation as long as they live. [6:369]

Even perpetual foundations for the poor, and educational institutions, cannot be founded in perpetuity and be a perpetual encumbrance on the land because they have a certain character specified by the founder in accordance with his ideas; instead the state must be free to adapt them to the needs of the time. – No one need be surprised that it becomes more and more difficult for this idea to be carried out in all its details (e.g., that poor students must supplement an inadequate educational fund beneficently established by singing for alms); for if the one who sets up the foundation is somewhat ambitious as well as good-natured, he does not want someone else to alter it in accordance with his concepts; he wants to be immortalized in it. That, however, does not change the nature of the matter itself and the right, indeed the duty, of a state to alter any foundation if it is opposed to the preservation of the state and its progress to the better. Such a foundation, therefore, can never be regarded as established in perpetuity.

---

[b] *an diesem oder jenem Theil, oder gar ganz.* Perhaps "in this or that respect, or indeed entirely." The remainder of the sentence is grammatically defective, and Natorp suggests that it may have been written in the margin for insertion earlier in the sentence, after "believing souls." In that case, it would be the intention of these souls, not of the state, to improve their lot in the next world.

C

The nobility of a country that is not under an aristocratic but a monarchical constitution is an institution that may be permitted for a certain period of time and may even be necessary by circumstances. But it cannot be asserted that this estate can be established in perpetuity, and that the head of a state should not be
[6:370] authorized to annul this preeminence of estate entirely, or that if he does this he has deprived his (noble) subjects of what was *theirs*, of what belonged to them by inheritance. A nobility is a temporary fraternity authorized by the state, which must go along with the circumstances of the time and not infringe upon the universal right of human beings which has been suspended for so long. – For the rank of nobleman in a state is not only dependent upon the constitution itself; it is only an accident of the constitution, which can exist only by inherence in a state (a nobleman as such is conceivable only in a state, not in the state of nature). Accordingly, when a state alters its constitution, someone who thereby loses his title and precedence cannot say that he was deprived of what was his, since he could call it his only under the condition that this form of state continued; but a state has the right to alter its form (e.g., to reform itself into a republic). – Orders and the privilege of bearing certain signs of them, therefore, give no *perpetual* right of possession.

D

Finally, as regards the *foundation of entailed estates*, in which someone possessed of goods arranges his inheritance so that the next of kin in the series of successive heirs should always be lord of the estate (by analogy with a state having a hereditary monarchy, where the *lord of the land* is determined in this way): not only can such a foundation be annulled at any time with the consent of all male relatives and need not last in perpetuity – as if the right of inheritance were attached to the land – and it cannot be said that letting an entailment terminate violates the foundation and the will of the original lord who established it, its founder; but a state also has a right and indeed a duty in this matter: as reasons for reforming itself gradually become apparent, not to let such a federative system of its subjects, as if they were viceroys (analogous to dynasties and satrapies), revive when it has once become extinct.

Conclusion

Finally, the reviewer has made the following remark about the ideas I presented under the heading of *public right*, with regard to which, as he
[6:371] says, space does not permit him to express himself: "So far as we know, no philosopher has yet admitted that most paradoxical of all paradoxical

propositions: the proposition that the mere *idea* of sovereignty should constrain me to obey as my lord whoever has set himself up as my lord, without my asking who has given him the right to command me. Is there to be no difference between saying that one ought to recognize sovereignty and supreme authority and saying that one ought to hold *a priori* as his lord this or that person, whose existence is not even given *a priori*?" – Now, granting the *paradox* here, I at least hope that, once the matter is considered more closely, I cannot be convicted of *heterodoxy*. I hope, rather, that my astute and careful reviewer, who criticizes with moderation (and who, despite the offense he takes, "regards these metaphysical first principles of a doctrine of right on the whole as a gain for the science") will not regret having taken them under his protection against the obstinate and superficial condemnation of others, at least as an attempt not unworthy of a second examination.

That one who finds himself in possession of supreme executive and legislative authority over a people must be obeyed; that obedience to him is so rightfully unconditional that even to *investigate* publicly the title by which he acquired his authority, and so to cast doubt upon it with a view to resisting him should this title be found deficient, is already punishable; that there is a categorical imperative, *Obey the authority who has power over you* (in whatever does not conflict with inner morality) – this is the offensive proposition called in question. – But what seems to shock the reviewer's reason is not only this principle, which makes an actual deed[c] (taking control) the condition and the basis for a right, but also that the *mere idea* of sovereignty over a people constrains me, as belonging to that people, to obey without previously investigating the right that is claimed (*Doctrine of Right* §49).

Every actual deed (fact) is an object in *appearance* (to the senses). On the other hand, what can be represented only by pure reason and must be counted among *ideas*, to which no object given in experience can be adequate – and a perfectly *rightful constitution* among human beings is of this sort – is the thing in itself.

If then a people united by laws under an authority exists, it is given as an object of experience in conformity with the idea of the unity of a people *as such* under a powerful supreme will, though it is indeed given only in appearance, that is, a rightful constitution in the general sense of the term exists. And even though this constitution may be afflicted with great defects and gross faults and be in need eventually of important improvements, it is still absolutely unpermitted and punishable to resist it. For if the people should hold that it is justified in opposing

[6:372]

---

[c] *Factum*. The following paragraph begins *Ein jedes Factum* (*Thatsache*). Since what is in question is, first, someone's actually taking control or seizing power, and second, an actually existing constitution, the difficulties noted above regarding the translation of *Factum* as "fact" or "deed," and of *Gewalt* as "authority" or "power" become acute.

force to this constitution, however faulty, and to the supreme authority, it would think that it had the right to put force in place of the supreme legislation that prescribes all rights, which would result in a supreme will that destroys itself.

The *idea* of a civil constitution as such, which is also an absolute command that practical reason, judging according to concepts of right, gives to every people, is *sacred* and irresistible. And even if the organization of a state should be faulty by itself, no subordinate authority in it may actively resist its legislative supreme authority; the defects attached to it must instead be gradually removed by reforms the state itself carries out. For otherwise, if a subject acts on the contrary maxim (of proceeding by unsanctioned choice), a good constitution can come into being only by blind chance. – The command "Obey the authority that has power over you" does not inquire how it came to have this power (in order perhaps to undermine it); for the authority which already exists, under which you live, is already in possession of legislative authority, and though you can indeed reason publicly about its legislation, you cannot set yourself up as an opposing legislator.

Unconditional submission of the people's will (which in itself is not united and is therefore without law) to a *sovereign* will (uniting all by means of *one law*) is a *fact*[d] that can begin only by seizing supreme power and so first establishing public right. – To permit any resistance to this absolute power[e] (resistance that would limit that supreme power) would be self-contradictory; for then this supreme power (which may be resisted), would not be the lawful supreme power which first determines what is to be publicly right or not. – This principle is already present *a priori* in the *idea* of a civil constitution as such, that is, in a concept of practical reason; and although no example in experience is *adequate* to be put under this concept, still none must contradict it as a norm.

[d] *That, die nur durch Bemächtigung der obersten Gewalt anheben kann*
[e] *Machtvollkommenheit*

The
METAPHYSICS OF MORALS
by
Immanuel Kant

Part II
Metaphysical First Principles
of the
DOCTRINE OF VIRTUE

Preface

A *philosophy* of any subject (a system of rational knowledge from concepts) requires a system of *pure rational* concepts independent of any conditions of intuition, that is, a *metaphysics*. – The only question is whether every *practical* philosophy, as a doctrine of duties, and so too the *doctrine of virtue* (ethics), also needs *metaphysical first principles*, so that it can be set forth as a genuine science (systematically) and not merely as an aggregate of precepts sought out one by one (fragmentarily). – No one will doubt that the pure doctrine of right needs metaphysical first principles; for it has to do only with the *formal condition* of choice that is to be limited in external relations in accordance with laws of freedom, without regard for any *end* (the matter of choice). Here the doctrine of duties is, accordingly, a mere *scientific doctrine* (*doctrina scientiae*).[*]

But in this philosophy (the doctrine of virtue) it seems directly contrary to the idea of it to go all the way back to *metaphysical first principles*, so as to make the concept of duty, though purified of anything empirical (any feeling), the incentive. For what sort of concept can be made of the force and herculean strength needed to subdue the vice-breeding inclinations if virtue is to borrow its weapons from the arsenal of metaphysics, a speculative subject that few know how to handle? Hence all doctrine of virtue,[a] in lecture halls, from pulpits, or in popular books, also becomes ridiculous if it is decked out in scraps of metaphysics. – But it is not useless, much less ridiculous, to investigate in metaphysics the first grounds of the doctrine of virtue; for someone, as a philosopher, has to go to the first grounds of this concept of duty, since otherwise neither certitude nor purity can be expected anywhere in the doctrine of virtue. In that case a popular teacher can indeed be content to rely on a certain *feeling* which, because of the results expected from it, is called *moral*, insofar as he insists that the following lesson be taken to heart, as the touchstone for deciding whether or not something is a duty of virtue: "How could a maxim such as yours harmonize with itself if everyone, in every case, made it a universal law?" But if it were mere feeling that made it our duty even to use this proposition as the touchstone, this

---

[*] Someone *versed in practical philosophy* is not thereby a *practical philosopher*. A practical philosopher is one who makes the *final end of reason* the principle *of his actions* and joins with this such knowledge as is necessary for it. Since this knowledge aims at action it need not be spun out into the finest threads of metaphysics, unless it has to do with a duty of right. In that case *what is mine* and *what is yours* must be determined on the scales of justice exactly, in accordance with the principle that action and reaction are equal, and so with a precision analogous to that of mathematics; but this is not necessary when it has to do with a mere duty of virtue. For what counts in the latter case is not merely knowing *what* it is one's duty to do (because of the ends all human beings have by their nature this is easily stated); it is primarily the inner principle of the will, namely that consciousness of this duty be also the *incentive* to actions. This is what is required in order to say, of someone who joins with his knowledge this principle of wisdom, that he is a *practical philosopher*.

[a] or, perhaps, "all teaching of virtue," *alle Tugendlehren*

duty would not be dictated by reason but would be taken to be a duty only instinctively, and hence blindly.

But in fact no moral principle is based, as people sometimes suppose, on any *feeling* whatsoever. Any such principle is really an obscurely thought *metaphysics* that is inherent in every human being because of his rational predisposition, as a teacher will readily grant if he experiments in questioning his pupil *socratically* about the imperative of duty and its application to moral appraisal of his actions. – The way the teacher *presents* this (his technique) should not always be metaphysical nor his terms scholastic, unless he wants to train his pupil as a philosopher. But his *thought* must go all the way back to the elements of metaphysics, without which no certitude or purity can be expected in the doctrine of virtue, nor indeed any moving force.

If one departs from this principle and begins with pathological or pure aesthetic or even moral *feeling* (with what is subjectively rather than objectively practical); if, that is, one begins with the matter of the will, the *end*, instead of [6:377] with the form of the will, the *law*, in order to determine duties on this basis, then there will indeed be no *metaphysical first principles* of the doctrine of virtue, since feeling, whatever may arouse it, always belongs to the *order of nature*. – But then the doctrine of virtue, being corrupted at its source, is corrupted alike in schools, lecture halls, and so forth. For the kind of incentive by which, as means, one is led to a good purpose (that of fulfilling every duty) is not a matter of indifference. – Hence, no matter how *metaphysics* may disgust the supposed teachers of wisdom who discourse on duty as *oracles* of *geniuses*, those same people who oppose metaphysics still have an indispensable duty to go back to its principles even in the doctrine of virtue and, before they teach, to become pupils in the classroom of metaphysics.

* * *

After it has been made so clear that the principle of duty is derived from pure reason, one cannot help wondering how this principle could be reduced again to a *doctrine of happiness*, though in such a way that a certain *moral* happiness not based on empirical causes – a self-contradictory absurdity[45] – has been thought up as the end. – It happens in this way. When a thoughtful human being has overcome incentives to vice and is aware of having done his often bitter duty, he finds himself in a state that could well be called happiness, a state of contentment and peace of soul in which virtue is its own reward. – Now a *eudaemonist* says: this delight, this happiness is really his motive for acting virtuously. The concept of duty does not determine his will *directly*; he is moved to do his duty only *by means of* the happiness he anticipates. – But since he can expect this reward of virtue only from consciousness of having done his duty, it is clear that the latter

---

[45] The primary sense of *Glück*, a component of the German word for "happiness" [*Glückseligkeit*] is "luck" or "fortune." See also 6:387.

must have come first, that is, he must find himself under obligation to do his duty before he thinks that happiness will result from his observance of duty and without thinking of this. A eudaemonist's *etiology* involves him in a *circle*; that is to say, he can hope to be *happy* (or inwardly blessed) only if he is conscious of having fulfilled his duty, but he can be moved to fulfill his duty only if he foresees that he will be made happy by it. – But there is also a *contradiction* in this subtle reasoning. For on the one hand he ought to fulfill his duty without first asking what effect this will have on his happiness, and so on *moral* grounds; but on the other hand he can recognize that something is his duty only by whether he can count on gaining happiness by doing it, and so in accordance with a *pathological* principle, which is the direct opposite of the moral principle. [6:378]

In another place (the *Berliner Monatsschrift*)[46] I have, I think, reduced the distinction between *pathological pleasure* and *moral pleasure* to its simplest terms. Pleasure that must precede one's observance of the law in order for one to act in conformity with the law is pathological and one's conduct follows the *order of nature*; but pleasure that must be *preceded* by the law in order to be felt is in the *moral order*. – If this distinction is not observed, if *eudaemonism* (the principle of happiness) is set up as the basic principle instead of *eleutheronomy* (the principle of the freedom of internal lawgiving), the result is the *euthanasia* (easy death) of all morals.

The cause of these errors is as follows. People who are accustomed merely to explanations by natural sciences[b] will not get into their heads the categorical imperative from which these laws proceed dictatorially, even though they feel themselves compelled irresistibly by it. Being unable to *explain* what lies entirely beyond that sphere (*freedom* of choice), however exalting is this very prerogative of a human being, his capacity for such an *idea*, they are stirred by the proud claims of speculative reason, which makes its power so strongly felt in other fields, to band together in a general *call to arms*, as it were, to defend the omnipotence of theoretical reason. And so now, and perhaps for a while longer, they assail the moral concept of freedom and, wherever possible, make it suspect; but in the end they must give way.

---

[b] *physiologische Erklärungen*

[46] Natorp suggests that Kant's reference is to Part I of "Theory and Practice," which was first published in the *Berliner Monatsschrift* in 1793. Another possibility, suggested by Karl Vorländer, editor of a German edition, is "On a Recently Prominent Elevated Tone in Philosophy," which appeared in that journal in 1796.

Introduction

to the Doctrine of Virtue

In ancient times "ethics" signified the *doctrine of morals* (*philosophia moralis*) in general, which was also called the *doctrine of duties*. Later on it seemed better to reserve the name "ethics" for one part of moral philosophy, namely for the doctrine of those duties that do not come under external laws (it was thought appropriate to call this, in German, the *doctrine of virtue*). Accordingly, the system of the doctrine of duties in general is now divided into the system of the *doctrine of right* (*ius*), which deals with duties that can be given by external laws, and the system of the *doctrine of virtue* (*ethica*), which treats of duties that cannot be so given; and this division may stand.

I

Discussion of the Concept of a Doctrine of Virtue

The very *concept of duty* is already the concept of a *necessitation* (constraint) of free choice through the law. This constraint may be an *external constraint* or a *self-constraint*. The moral *imperative* makes this constraint known through the categorical nature of its pronouncement (the unconditional ought). Such constraint, therefore, does not apply to rational beings as such (there could also be *holy* ones) but rather to *human beings*, rational *natural* beings, who are unholy enough that pleasure can induce them to break the moral law, even though they recognize its authority; and even when they do obey the law, they do it *reluctantly* (in the face of opposition from their inclinations), and it is in this that such *constraint* properly consists.[*] – But since the human being is still a *free* (moral) being, when the concept of duty concerns the internal determination of his will (the incentive) the constraint that the concept of duty contains can be only self-constraint (through the representation of the law alone); for only so can that *necessitation* (even if it is external) be united with the freedom of his choice. Hence in this case the concept of duty will be an ethical one.

---

[*] Yet if a human being looks at himself objectively (under the aspect of *humanity* in his own person), as his pure practical reason determines him to do, he finds that *as a moral being* [6:380] he is also holy enough to break the inner law *reluctantly*; for there is no human being so depraved as not to feel an opposition to breaking it and an abhorrence of himself in the face of which he has to constrain himself [to break the law]. – Now it is impossible to explain the phenomenon that at this parting of the ways (where the beautiful fable places Hercules between virtue and sensual pleasure), the human being shows more propensity to listen to his inclinations than to the law. For we can explain what happens only by deriving it from a cause in accordance with laws of nature, and in so doing we would not be thinking of choice as free. – But it is this self-constraint in opposite directions and its unavoidability that makes known the inexplicable property of *freedom* itself.

Impulses of nature, accordingly, involve *obstacles* within the mind of the human being to his fulfillment of duty and (sometimes powerful) forces opposing it, which he must judge that he is capable of resisting and conquering by reason not at some time in the future but at once (the moment he thinks of duty): he must judge that he *can* do what the law tells him unconditionally that he *ought* to do.

Now the capacity[a] and considered resolve to withstand a strong but unjust opponent is *fortitude* (*fortitudo*) and, with respect to what opposes the moral disposition *within us*, **virtue** (*virtus, fortitudo moralis*). So the part of the general doctrine of duties that brings inner, rather than outer, freedom under laws is a *doctrine of virtue.*

The doctrine of right dealt only with the *formal* condition of outer freedom (the consistency of outer freedom with itself if its maxim were made universal law), that is, with **right**. But ethics goes beyond this and provides a *matter* (an object of free choice), an **end** of pure reason which it represents as an end that is also objectively necessary, that is, an end that, as far as human beings are concerned, it is a duty to have. – For since the sensible inclinations of human beings tempt them to ends (the matter of choice) that can be contrary to duty, [6:381] lawgiving reason can in turn check their influence only by a moral end set up against the ends of inclination, an end that must therefore be given *a priori*, independently of inclinations.

An *end* is an object of the choice (of a rational being), through the representation of which choice is determined to an action to bring this object about. – Now, I can indeed be constrained by others to perform *actions* that are directed as means to an end, but I can never be constrained by others *to have an end*: only I myself can *make* something my end. – But if I am under obligation to make my end something that lies in concepts of practical reason, and so to have, besides the formal determining ground of choice (such as right contains), a material one as well, an end that could be set against the end arising from sensible impulses, this would be the concept of an *end that is in itself a duty*. But the doctrine of this end would not belong to the doctrine of right but rather to ethics, since *self-constraint* in accordance with (moral) laws belongs to the concept of ethics alone.

For this reason ethics can also be defined as the system of the *ends* of pure practical reason. – Ends and duties distinguish the two divisions of the doctrine of morals in general. That ethics contains duties that one cannot be constrained by others (through natural[b] means) to fulfill follows merely from its being a doctrine of *ends*, since *coercion* to ends (to have them) is self-contradictory.

---

[a] *Vermögen*
[b] *physisch*. "Natural" is also used to translate *physisch* in discussions of one's natural happiness, one's natural welfare, and one's natural perfection (as distinguished in each case from its moral counterpart).

That ethics is a *doctrine of virtue* (*doctrina officiorum virtutis*)[c] follows, however, from the above exposition of virtue when it is connected with the kind of obligation whose distinctive feature was just pointed out. – That is to say, determination to an *end* is the only determination of choice the very concept of which excludes the possibility of constraint *through natural means* by the *choice* of another. Another can indeed *coerce* me *to do* something that is not my end (but only a means to another's end), but not to *make this my end*; and yet I can have no end without making it an *end* for myself. To have an end that I have not myself made an end is self-contradictory, an act of freedom which is yet not free. – But it is no contradiction to set an end for myself that is also a duty, since I constrain myself to it and this is altogether consistent with freedom.[*] – But how is such an end possible? That is the question now. For that the concept of a thing is possible (not self-contradictory) is not yet sufficient for assuming the possibility of the thing itself (the objective reality of the concept). [6:382]

II
Discussion of the Concept of an End That Is Also a Duty[d]

One can think of the relation of end to duty in two ways: one can begin with the end and seek out the *maxim* of actions in conformity with duty or, on the other hand, one can begin with the maxim of actions in conformity with duty and seek out the end that is also a duty. – The *doctrine of right* takes the first way. What end anyone wants to set for his action is left to his free choice. The maxim of his action, however, is determined *a priori*, namely, that the freedom of the agent could coexist with the freedom of every other in accordance with a universal law.

But *ethics* takes the opposite way. It cannot begin with the ends that a human being may set for himself and in accordance with them prescribe the maxims he is to adopt, that is, his duty; for that would be to adopt maxims on empirical grounds, and such grounds yield no concept of duty, since this concept (the categorical ought) has its root in pure reason alone. Consequently, if maxims were to be adopted on the basis of those ends (all of which are self-seeking), one could not really speak of the concept of duty. – Hence in ethics the *concept of duty* will lead to ends and will have to establish *maxims* with respect to ends we *ought* to set ourselves, grounding them in accordance with moral principles.

---

[*] The less a human being can be constrained by natural means and the more he can be constrained morally (through the mere representation of duty), so much the more free he is. Suppose, for example, one so firm of purpose and strong of soul that he cannot be dissuaded from a pleasure he intends to have, no matter how others may reason with him about the harm he will do himself by it. If such a one gives up his plan immediately, though reluctantly, at the thought that by carrying it out he would omit one of his duties as an official or neglect a sick father, he proves his freedom in the highest degree by being unable to resist the call of duty.

[c] doctrine of duties of virtue

[d] *von einem Zwecke, der zugleich Pflicht ist.* For an elaboration of this phrase, see 6:384f.

[6:383]   Setting aside the question of what sort of end is in itself a duty and how such an end is possible, we have here only to show that a duty of this kind is called a *duty of virtue* and why it is called by this name.

To every duty there corresponds *a* right in the sense of an *authorization* to do something (*facultas moralis generatim*); but it is not the case that to every duty there correspond *rights* of another to coerce someone (*facultas iuridica*). Instead, such duties are called, specifically, *duties of right*. – Similarly, to every ethical *obligation* there corresponds the concept of virtue, but not all ethical duties are thereby duties of virtue. Those duties that have to do not so much with a certain end (matter, object of choice) as merely with *what is formal* in the moral determination of the will (e.g., that an action in conformity with duty must also be done *from duty*) are not duties of virtue. Only *an end that is also a duty* can be called a duty of virtue. For this reason there are several duties of virtue (and also various virtues), whereas for the first kind of duty only one (virtuous disposition) is thought, which however holds for all actions.

What essentially distinguishes a duty of virtue from a duty of right is that external constraint to the latter kind of duty is morally possible, whereas the former is based only on free self-constraint. – For finite *holy* beings (who could never be tempted to violate duty) there would be no doctrine of virtue but only a doctrine of morals, since the latter is autonomy of practical reason whereas the former is also *autocracy* of practical reason, that is, it involves consciousness of the *capacity*[e] to master one's inclinations when they rebel against the law, a capacity which, though not directly perceived, is yet rightly inferred from the moral categorical imperative. Thus human morality in its highest stage can still be nothing more than virtue, even if it be entirely pure (quite free from the influence of any incentive other than that of duty). In its highest stage it is an ideal (to which one must continually approximate), which is commonly personified poetically by the *sage*.

But virtue is not to be defined[f] and valued merely as an *aptitude*[g] and (as the prize-essay of Cochius, the court-chaplain,[47] puts it) a long-standing *habit*[h] of morally good actions acquired by practice. For unless this aptitude results from considered, firm, and continually purified principles, then, like any other mechan-
[6:384] ism of technically practical reason, it is neither armed for all situations nor adequately secured against the changes that new temptations could bring about.

Remark

Virtue = +a is opposed to *negative lack of virtue* (moral weakness = o) as its *logical opposite* (*contradictorie oppositum*); but it is opposed to vice = – a as its *real*

---

[e] *des Vermögens*   [f] *zu erklären*   [g] *Fertigkeit*   [h] *Gewohnheit*

[47] Leonhard Cochius's "*Untersuchung über die Neigungen*" was the prize essay of the Berlin Academy for 1767.

opposite (*contrarie s. realiter oppositum*);[48] and it is not only unnecessary but even improper to ask whether great *crimes* might not require more strength of soul than do great *virtues*. For by strength of soul we mean strength of resolution in a human being as a being endowed with freedom, hence his strength insofar as he is in control of himself (in his senses) and so in the state of *health* proper to a human being. But great crimes are paroxysms, the sight of which makes one whose soul is healthy shudder. The question would therefore come to something like this: whether a human being in a fit of madness could have more physical strength than when he is sane. This one can admit without attributing more strength of soul to him, if by soul is meant the vital principle of a human being in the free use of his powers; for, since the basis of great crimes is merely the force of inclinations that weaken reason, which proves no strength of soul, the above question would be tantamount to whether someone could show more strength during an attack of sickness than when he is healthy. This can be straightway denied, since health consists in the balance of all his bodily forces, while lack of health is a weakening in the system of these forces; and it is only by reference to this system that absolute health can be appraised.

III
On the Basis for Thinking of an End That Is Also a Duty

An **end** is an *object* of free choice, the representation of which determines it to an action (by which the object is brought about). Every action, therefore, has its end; and since no one can have an end without *himself* making the object of his choice into an end, to have any end of action whatsoever is an act of *freedom* on the part of the acting subject, not an effect of *nature*. But because this act which determines an end is a practical principle that prescribes the end itself (and so prescribes unconditionally), not the means (hence not conditionally), it is a categorical imperative of pure practical reason, and therefore an imperative which connects a *concept of duty* with that of an end in general.

[6:385]

Now, there must be such an end and a categorical imperative corresponding to it. For since there are free actions there must also be ends to which, as their objects, these actions are directed. But among these ends there must be some that are also (i.e., by their concept) duties. – For were there no such ends, then all ends would hold for practical reason only as means to other ends; and since there can be no action without an end, a *categorical* imperative would be impossible. This would do away with any doctrine of morals.[i]

So it is not a question here of ends the human being *does adopt* in keeping with the sensible impulses of his nature, but of objects of free choice under its

---

[i] *Sittenlehre*
[48] Compare with *Religion within the Boundaries of Mere Reason*, 6:22n.

laws, which he *ought to make* his ends. The study of the former type of ends can be called the technical (subjective) doctrine of ends; it is really the pragmatic doctrine of ends, containing the rules of prudence in the choice of one's ends. The study of the latter type of ends, however, must be called the moral (objective) doctrine of ends. But this distinction is superfluous here, since the doctrine of morals is already clearly distinguished in its concept from the doctrine of nature (in this case, anthropology) by the fact that anthropology is based on empirical principles, whereas the moral doctrine of ends, which treats of duties, is based on principles given *a priori* in pure practical reason.

IV
What Are the Ends That Are Also Duties?

They are *one's own perfection* and *the happiness of others*.

Perfection and happiness cannot be interchanged here, so that *one's own happiness* and *the perfection of others* would be made ends that would be in themselves duties of the same person.

[6:386] For *his own happiness* is an end that every human being has (by virtue of the impulses of his nature), but this end can never without self-contradiction be regarded as a duty. What everyone already wants unavoidably, of his own accord, does not come under the concept of *duty*, which is *constraint* to an end adopted reluctantly. Hence it is self-contradictory to say that he is *under obligation* to promote his own happiness with all his powers.

So too, it is a contradiction for me to make another's *perfection* my end and consider myself under obligation to promote this. For the *perfection* of another human being, as a person, consists just in this: that he *himself* is able[j] to set his end in accordance with his own concepts of duty; and it is self-contradictory to require that I do (make it my duty to do) something that only the other himself can do.

V
Clarification of These Two Concepts

A

One's Own Perfection

The word *perfection* is open to a good deal of misinterpretation. Perfection is sometimes understood as a concept belonging to transcendental philosophy, the concept of the *totality* of the manifold which, taken together, constitutes a thing. – Then again, as a concept belonging to *teleology*, it is taken to mean the

---

[j] *vermögend ist*

harmony of a thing's properties with an *end*. Perfection in the first sense could be called *quantitative* (material) perfection, and in the second, *qualitative* (formal) perfection. The quantitative perfection of a thing can be only one (for the totality of what belongs to a thing is one). But one thing can have several qualitative perfections, and it is really qualitative perfection that is under discussion here.

When it is said that it is in itself a duty for a human being to make his end the perfection belonging to a human being as such (properly speaking, to humanity), this perfection must be put in what can result from his *deeds*, not in mere *gifts* for which he must be indebted to nature; for otherwise it would not be a duty. This duty can therefore consist only in *cultivating* one's *faculties* (or natural predispositions),[k] the highest of which is *understanding*, the faculty of concepts and so too of those concepts that have to do with duty. At the same time this duty includes the cultivation of one's *will* (moral cast of mind),[l] so as to satisfy all the requirements of duty. 1) A human being has a duty to raise himself from the crude state of his nature, from his animality (*quoad actum*), more and more toward humanity, by which he alone is capable of setting himself ends; he has a duty to diminish his ignorance by instruction and to correct his errors. And it is not merely that technically practical reason *counsels* him to do this as a means to his further purposes (or art); morally practical reason *commands* it absolutely and makes this end his duty, so that he may be worthy of the humanity that dwells within him. 2) A human being has a duty to carry the cultivation of his *will* up to the purest virtuous disposition, in which the *law* becomes also the incentive to his actions that conform with duty and he obeys the law from duty. This disposition is inner morally practical perfection. Since it is a feeling of the effect that the lawgiving will within the human being exercises on his capacity to act in accordance with his will, it is called *moral feeling*, a special *sense* (*sensus moralis*), as it were. It is true that moral sense is often misused in a visionary way, as if (like Socrates' daimon) it could precede reason or even dispense with reason's judgment. Yet it is a moral perfection, by which one makes one's object every particular end that is also a duty.

[6:387]

B
The Happiness of Others

Since it is unavoidable for human nature to wish for and seek happiness, that is, satisfaction with one's state, so long as one is assured of its lasting, this is not an end that is also a duty. – Some people, however, make a distinction between moral happiness (which consists in satisfaction with one's person and one's own moral conduct, and so with what one *does*) and natural happiness (which consists

---

[k] *seines Vermögens* (*oder der Naturanlage*)   [l] *sittlicher Denkungsart*

in satisfaction with what nature bestows, and so with what one *enjoys* as a gift from without). Although I refrain here from censuring a misuse of the word happiness (that already involves a contradiction), it must be noted that the [6:388] former kind of feeling belongs only under the preceding heading, namely perfection. – For, someone who is said to feel happy in the mere consciousness of his rectitude already possesses the perfection which was explained there as that end which is also a duty.

When it comes to my promoting happiness as an end that is also a duty, this must therefore be the happiness of *other* human beings, *whose* (permitted) *end I thus* make *my own end as well*. It is for them to decide^m what they count as belonging to their happiness; but it is open to me to refuse them many things that *they* think will make them happy but that I do not, as long as they have no right to demand them from me as what is theirs. But time and again an alleged *obligation* to attend to my *own* (natural) happiness is set up in competition with this end, and my natural and merely subjective end is thus made a duty (an objective end). Since this is often used as a specious objection to the division of duties made above (in §IV), it needs to be set right.

Adversity, pain, and want are great temptations to violate one's duty. It might therefore seem that prosperity, strength, health, and well-being in general, which check the influence of these, could also be considered ends that are duties, so that one has a duty to promote *one's own* happiness and not just the happiness of others. – But then the end is not the subject's happiness but his morality, and happiness is merely a means for removing obstacles to his morality – a *permitted* means, since no one else has a right to require of me that I sacrifice my ends if these are not immoral. To seek prosperity for its own sake is not directly a duty, but indirectly it can well be a duty, that of warding off poverty insofar as this is a great temptation to vice. But then it is not my happiness but the preservation of my moral integrity that is my end and also my duty.

VI
Ethics Does Not Give Laws for *Actions* (*Ius* Does That), but Only for *Maxims* of Actions

The concept of duty stands in immediate relation to a *law* (even if I abstract from all ends, as the matter of the law). The formal principle of duty, in the [6:389] categorical imperative "So act that the maxim of your action could become a universal *law*," already indicates this. Ethics adds only that this principle is to be thought as the law of *your* own *will* and not of will in general, which could also be the will of others; in the latter case the law would provide a duty of right, which lies outside the sphere of ethics. – Maxims are here regarded as

---

^m *beurtheilen*

subjective principles which merely *qualify* for a giving of universal law, and the requirement that they so qualify is only a negative principle (not to come into conflict with a law as such). – How can there be, beyond this principle, a law for the maxims of actions?

Only the concept of an *end* that is also a duty, a concept that belongs exclusively to ethics, establishes a law for maxims of actions by subordinating the subjective end (that everyone has) to the objective end (that everyone ought to make his end). The imperative "You ought to make this or that (e.g., the happiness of others) your end" has to do with the matter of choice (an object). Now, no free action is possible unless the agent also intends an end (which is the matter of choice). Hence, if there is an end that is also a duty, the only condition that maxims of actions, as means to ends, must contain is that of qualifying for a possible giving of universal law. On the other hand, the end that is also a duty can make it a law to have such a maxim, although for the maxim itself the mere possibility of agreeing with a giving of universal law is already sufficient.

For maxims of actions can be *willful*,[n] and are subject only to the limiting condition of being fit for a giving of universal law, which is the formal principle of actions. A *law*, however, takes away what is willful[o] from actions, and this distinguishes it from any *recommendation* (where all that one requires is to know the most suitable means to an end).

VII
Ethical Duties Are of *Wide* Obligation, Whereas Duties of Right Are of *Narrow* Obligation

[6:390]

This proposition follows from the preceding one; for if the law can prescribe only the maxim of actions, not actions themselves, this is a sign that it leaves a playroom (*latitudo*) for free choice in following (complying with) the law, that is, that the law cannot specify precisely in what way one is to act and how much one is to do by the action[p] for an end that is also a duty. – But a wide duty is not to be taken as permission to make exceptions to the maxim of actions but only as permission to limit one maxim of duty by another (e.g., love of one's neighbor in general by love of one's parents), by which in fact the field for the practice of virtue is widened. – The wider the duty, therefore, the more imperfect is a human being's obligation to action; as he, nevertheless, brings closer to *narrow* duty (duties of right) the maxim of complying with wide duty (in his disposition), so much the more perfect is his virtuous action.

---

[n] *willkürlich.* LD: or perhaps "arbitary", as in the Cambridge Edition.
[o] *das Willkürliche.* LD: or perhaps "arbitrariness", as in the Cambridge Edition.
[p] *d.i. nicht bestimmt angeben könne, wie and wie viel durch die Handlung*

Imperfect duties are, accordingly, only *duties of virtue*.[q] Fulfillment of them is *merit* (*meritum*) = +a; but failure to fulfill them[r] is not in itself *culpability* (*demeritum*) –a, but rather mere *deficiency in moral worth* = o, unless the subject should make it his principle not to comply with such duties. It is only the strength of one's resolution, in the first case, that is properly called *virtue* (*virtus*); one's weakness, in the second case, is not so much *vice* (*vitium*) as rather mere *want of virtue*, lack of moral strength (*defectus moralis*). (As the word "*Tugend*"[s] comes from "*taugen*,"[t] so "*Untugend*"[u] comes from "*zu nichts taugen*."[v]) Every action contrary to duty is called a *transgression* (*peccatum*). It is when an intentional transgression has become a principle that it is properly called a *vice* (*vitium*).

Although there is nothing meritorious in the conformity of one's actions with right (in being an honest human being), the conformity with right of one's maxims of such actions, as duties, that is, **respect** for right, is *meritorious*. For one thereby *makes* the right of humanity, or also the right of human beings, one's *end* and in so doing widens one's concept of duty beyond the concept of what is [6:391] *due* (*officium debiti*), since another can indeed by his right require of me actions in accordance with the law, but not that the law be also my incentive to such actions. The same holds true of the universal ethical command, "act in conformity with duty from duty." To establish and quicken this disposition in oneself is, as in the previous case, *meritorious*, since it goes beyond the law of duty for actions and makes the law itself also the incentive.

But for this very reason these duties, too, must be counted as duties of wide obligation. With respect to them (and, indeed, in order to bring wide obligation as close as possible to the concept of narrow obligation), there is a subjective principle of ethical *reward*, that is, a receptivity to being rewarded in accordance with laws of virtue: the reward, namely, of a moral pleasure that goes beyond mere contentment with oneself (which can be merely negative) and which is celebrated in the saying that, through consciousness of this pleasure, virtue is its own reward.

If this merit is a human being's merit in relation to other human beings for promoting what all human beings recognize as their natural end (for making their happiness his own), it could be called *sweet merit*; for consciousness of it produces a moral enjoyment in which human beings are inclined by sympathy *to revel*. But *bitter merit*, which comes from promoting the true well-being of others

---

[q] *Die unvollkommenen Pflichten sind also allein Tugendpflichten.* LD: In the Cambridge Edition, this is translated as: "Imperfect duties alone are, accordingly, *duties of virtue*."

[r] *ihre Übertretung*, literally, "transgression of them." In discussing duties of virtue, notably duties of love, Kant sometimes refers to "neglect" of them, e.g., *Vernachlässigung* (6:432), *Pflichtvergessenheit* (6:458), *Verabsäumung* (6:464). Transgression of a duty of virtue is failure to adopt a maxim of promoting an end that is also a duty. More generally, when *Übertretung* occurs with "of a duty" or "of a law," I have sometimes translated it as "violating" a duty or "breaking" a law.

[s] virtue   [t] to be fit for   [u] lack of virtue   [v] not to be fit for anything

even when they fail to recognize it as such (when they are unappreciative and ungrateful), usually yields no such return. All that it produces is *contentment* with oneself, although in this case the merit would be greater still.

VIII
Exposition of Duties of Virtue as Wide Duties

I

One's Own Perfection as an End That Is Also a Duty

a) *Natural* perfection is the *cultivation* of any *capacities* whatever[w] for furthering ends set forth by reason. That this is a duty and so in itself an end, and that the cultivation of our capacities, even without regard for the advantage it affords us, is based on an unconditional (moral) imperative rather than a conditional (pragmatic) one, can be shown in this way. The capacity to set oneself an end – any end whatsoever[x] – is what characterizes humanity (as distinguished from animality). Hence there is also bound up with the end of humanity in our own person the rational will, and so the duty, to make ourselves worthy of humanity by culture in general, by procuring or promoting the *capacity* to realize all sorts of possible ends, so far as this is to be found in a human being himself. In other words, the human being has a duty to cultivate the crude predispositions of his nature, by which the animal is first raised into the human being. It is therefore a duty in itself. [6:392]

But this duty is a merely ethical one, that is, a duty of wide obligation. No rational principle prescribes specifically[y] *how* far one should go in cultivating one's capacities (in enlarging or correcting one's capacity for understanding, i.e., in acquiring knowledge or skill[z]). Then too, the different situations in which human beings may find themselves make a human being's choice[a] of the occupation for which he should cultivate his talents very much a matter for him to decide as he chooses.[b] – With regard to natural perfection, accordingly, there is no law of reason for actions but only a law for maxims of actions, which runs as follows: "Cultivate your powers of mind and body so that they are fit to realize any ends you might encounter," however uncertain you are which of them could sometime become yours.

b) The *cultivation of morality* in us. The greatest perfection of a human being is to do his duty *from duty* (for the law to be not only the rule but also the incentive of his actions). – At first sight this looks like a *narrow* obligation, and

---

[w] *aller Vermögen überhaupt*
[x] *Das Vermögen sich überhaupt irgend einen Zweck zu setzen.* LD: Gregor's translation here is controversial. Timmermann translates this phrase as: "The capacity to set oneself an end at all," and discusses the matter, in "Autonomy and Moral Regard for Ends," in Oliver Sensen (ed.), *Kant on Moral Autonomy* (Cambridge University Press, 2013), 212–24, 214f.
[y] *bestimmt*   [z] *Kunstfähigkeit*   [a] *Wahl*   [b] *sehr willkürlich*

the principle of duty seems to prescribe with the precision and strictness of a law not only the *legality* but also the *morality* of every action, that is, the disposition. But in fact the law, here again, prescribes only the *maxim of the action*, that of seeking the basis of obligation solely in the law and not in sensible impulse (advantage or disadvantage), and hence not the *action itself*. – – For a human being cannot see into the depths of his own heart so as to be quite certain, in even a *single* action, of the purity of his moral intention and the sincerity of his disposition, even when he has no doubt about the legality of the action. Very often he mistakes his own weakness, which counsels him against the venture of a misdeed, for virtue (which is the concept of strength); and how many people [6:393] who have lived long and guiltless lives may not be merely *fortunate* in having escaped so many temptations? In the case of any deed it remains hidden from the agent himself how much pure moral content there has been in his disposition.

Hence this duty too – the duty of assessing the worth of one's actions not by their legality alone but also by their morality (one's disposition) – is of only *wide* obligation. The law does not prescribe this inner action in the human mind but only the maxim of the action, to strive with all one's might that the thought of duty for its own sake is the sufficient incentive of every action conforming to duty.

2

The Happiness of Others as an End That Is Also a Duty

a) *Natural welfare. Benevolence* can be unlimited, since nothing need be done with it. But it is more difficult to *do good*,[c] especially if it is to be done not from affection (love) for others but from duty, at the cost of forgoing the satisfaction of concupiscence and of active injury to it in many cases.[d] – The reason that it is a duty to be beneficent is this: since our self-love cannot be separated from our need to be loved (helped in case of need[e]) by others as well, we therefore make ourselves an end for others; and the only way this maxim can be binding is through its qualification as a universal law, hence through our will to make others our ends as well. The happiness of others is therefore an end that is also a duty.

But I ought to sacrifice a part of my welfare to others without hope of return, because this is a duty, and it is impossible to assign determinate limits to the extent of this sacrifice. How far it should extend depends, in large part, on what each human being's true needs[f] are in view of his sensibilities, and it must be left

---

[c] *Wohlthun.* In 6:45off. Kant discusses the difference between the duty of benevolence, *Wohlwollen*, and the duty of beneficence, *Wohlthun.* Except in that passage I have often translated *Wohlthun* and its cognates by such expressions as "to do good," "to help," "a favor."

[d] *mit Aufopferung und Kränkung mancher Concupiscenz*   [e] *in Nothfällen*

[f] *wahres Bedürfniß*

to each to decide this for himself. For, a maxim of promoting others' happiness at the sacrifice of one's own happiness, one's true needs, would conflict with itself if it were made a universal law. Hence this duty is only a *wide* one; the duty has in it a latitude for doing more or less, and no specific limits can be assigned to what should be done. – The law holds only for maxims, not for determinate actions.

b) The happiness of others also includes their *moral well-being* (*salubritas* [6:394] *moralis*), and we have a duty, but only a negative one, to promote this. Although the pain one feels from the pangs of conscience has a moral source it is still a natural effect, like grief, fear, or any other state of suffering. To see to it that another does not deservedly suffer this inner reproach is not *my* duty but *his affair*; but it is my duty to refrain from doing anything that, considering the nature of a human being, could tempt him to do something for which his conscience could afterwards pain him, to refrain from what is called giving scandal. – But this concern for others' moral contentment does not admit of determinate limits being assigned to it, so that the obligation resting on it is only a wide one.

IX
What Is a Duty of Virtue?

Virtue is the strength of a human being's maxims in fulfilling his duty. – Strength of any kind can be recognized only by the obstacles it can overcome, and in the case of virtue these obstacles are natural inclinations, which can come into conflict with the human being's moral resolution; and since it is the human being *himself* who puts these obstacles in the way of his maxims, virtue is not merely a self-constraint (for then one natural inclination could strive to overcome another), but also a self-constraint in accordance with a principle of inner freedom, and so through the mere representation of one's duty in accordance with its formal law.

All duties involve a concept of *constraint* through a law. *Ethical* duties involve a constraint for which only internal lawgiving is possible, whereas duties of right involve a constraint for which external lawgiving is also possible. Both, therefore, involve constraint, whether it be self-constraint or constraint by another. Since the moral capacity[g] to constrain oneself can be called virtue, action springing from such a disposition (respect for law) can be called virtuous (ethical) action, even though the law lays down a duty of right; for it is the *doctrine of virtue* that commands us to hold the right of human beings sacred.

---

[g] *Vermögen*

But what it is virtuous to do is not necessarily a *duty of virtue* strictly speaking. What it is virtuous to do may concern only *what is formal* in maxims, whereas a [6:395] duty of virtue has to do with their matter, that is to say, with an *end* that is thought as also a duty. – But since ethical obligation to ends, to which there can be several, is only *wide* obligation – because it involves a law only for *maxims* of actions, and an end is the matter (object) of choice – there are many different duties, corresponding to the different ends prescribed by the law, which are called *duties of virtue* (*officia honestatis*) just because they are subject only to free self-constraint, not constraint by other human beings, and because they determine an end that is also a duty.

Like anything *formal*, virtue as the will's conformity with every duty, based on a firm disposition, is merely one and the same. But with respect to the *end* of actions that is also a duty, that is, what one *ought* to make one's *end* (what is material), there can be several virtues; and since obligation to the maxim of such an end is called a duty of virtue, there are many duties of virtue.

The supreme principle of the doctrine of virtue is: act in accordance with a maxim of *ends* that it can be a universal law for everyone to have. – In accordance with this principle a human being is an end for himself as well as for others, and it is not enough that he is not authorized to use either himself or others merely as means (since he could then still be indifferent to them); it is in itself his duty to make the human being as such his end.

This basic principle of the doctrine of virtue, as a categorical imperative, cannot be proved, but it can be given a deduction from pure practical reason. – What, in the relation of a human being to himself and others, *can* be an end *is* an end for pure practical reason; for, pure practical reason is a faculty of ends generally, and for it to be indifferent to ends, that is, to take no interest in them, would therefore be a contradiction, since then it would not determine maxims for actions either (because every maxim of action contains an end) and so would not be practical reason. But pure reason can prescribe no ends *a priori* without setting them forth as also duties, and such duties are then called duties of virtue.

[6:396]

X
The Supreme Principle of the Doctrine of Right[49] Was *Analytic*; That of the Doctrine of Virtue Is *Synthetic*

It is clear in accordance with the principle of contradiction that, if external constraint checks the hindering of outer freedom in accordance with universal laws (and is thus a hindering of the hindrances to freedom), it can coexist with

---

[49] i.e., the principle enunciated in §D, 6:231

ends as such. I need not go beyond the concept of freedom to see this; the end that each has may be whatever he wills. – The supreme *principle of right* is therefore an analytic proposition.

But the principle of the doctrine of virtue goes beyond the concept of outer freedom and connects with it, in accordance with universal laws, an *end* that it makes a *duty*. This principle is therefore synthetic. – Its possibility is contained in the deduction (§IX).

When, instead of constraint from without, *inner* freedom comes into play, the capacity[h] for self-constraint not by means of other inclinations but by pure practical reason (which scorns such intermediaries), the concept of duty is extended beyond outer freedom, which is limited only by the formal provision of its compatibility with the freedom of all. This extension beyond the concept of a duty of right takes place through *ends* being laid down, from which right abstracts altogether. – In the moral imperative and the presupposition of freedom that is necessary for it are found the *law*, the *capacity* (to fulfill the law), and the *will* determining the maxim; these are all the elements that make up the concept of a duty of right. But in the imperative that prescribes a *duty of virtue* there is added not only the concept of self-constraint but that of an *end*, not an end that we have but one that we ought to have, one that pure practical reason therefore has within itself. The highest, unconditional end of pure practical reason (which is still a duty) consists in this: that virtue be its own end and, despite the benefits it confers on human beings, also its own reward. (Virtue so shines as an ideal that it seems, by human standards, to eclipse *holiness* itself, which is never tempted to break the law.[*] [6:397] Nevertheless, this is an illusion arising from the fact that, having no way to measure the degree of a strength except by the magnitude of the obstacles it could overcome [in us, these are inclinations], we are led to mistake the *subjective* conditions by which we assess the magnitude for the *objective* conditions of the magnitude, itself.) Yet in comparison with *human ends*, all of which have their obstacles to be contended with, it is true that the worth of virtue itself, as its own end, far exceeds the worth of any usefulness and any empirical ends and advantages that virtue may still bring in its wake.

It is also correct to say that the human being is under obligation *to virtue* (as moral strength). For while the capacity[i] (*facultas*) to overcome all opposing

---

[*] The human being with all his faults
Is better than a host of angels without will. Haller[50]

[50] Here, and again in 6:461, Kant cites or refers to Albrecht Haller's poem "*Über den Ursprung des Übels*" (1734). Natorp's notes give the relevant portions of the poem.

[h] *Vermögen*   [i] *Vermögen*

sensible impulses can and must be simply *presupposed* in the human being on account of his freedom, yet this capacity as *strength* (*robur*) is something he must acquire; and the way to acquire it is to enhance the moral *incentive* (the thought of the law), both by contemplating the dignity of the pure rational law in us (*contemplatione*) and by *practicing* virtue (*exercitio*).

[6:398]

XI

In accordance with the principles set forth above, the schema of duties of virtue can be diagrammed in the following way:

	What is Material in Duties of Virtue		
	1.	2.	
Internal Duty of Virtue	*My own end*, which is also my duty	*The end of others*, the promotion of which is also my duty	External Duty of Virtue
	(My own *perfection*)	(The *happiness* of others)	
	3.	4.	
	The *law*, which is also the incentive	The *end*, which is also the incentive	
	On which the *morality* —	On which the *legality*	
	of every free determination of the will is based		
	What is Formal in Duties of Virtue		

[6:399]

XII
Concepts of What Is Presupposed on the Part of Feeling by the Mind's Receptivity[j] to Concepts of Duty as Such

There are certain moral endowments such that anyone lacking them could have no duty to acquire them. – They are *moral feeling, conscience, love* of one's neighbor, and *respect*[k] for oneself (*self-esteem*). There is no obligation to have these because they lie at the basis of morality, as *subjective* conditions of receptiveness to the concept of duty, not as objective conditions of morality. All of them are natural predispositions of the mind (*praedispositio*) for being affected

---

[j] *Ästhetische Vorbegriffe der Empfänglichkeit des Gemüths* LD: The first two words are challenging to translate here. Paul Guyer advocates translating them as "aesthetic preconditions" (see "Moral Feelings in the *Metaphysics of Morals*," in Denis [ed.], *Kant's Metaphysics of Morals*, 130–51, especially 130n, 137f.). Ellington has "sensitive basic concepts." For discussion, see Ina Goy, "Virtue and Sensibility," in Andreas Trampota, Oliver Sensen, and Jens Timmermann (eds.), *Kant's Tugendlehre: A Comprehensive Commentary* (Berlin: de Gruyter, 2013), 183–206, especially 185–7. Elsewhere in *The Metaphysics of Morals*, Gregor translates *Vorbegriffe* as "preliminary concepts" (6:221) and "concepts preliminary" (6:410).

[k] *Achtung.* Although I have translated *Achtung* throughout as "respect," it should be noted that Kant gives two different Latin equivalents: *reverentia* in the context of one's feeling for the moral law and for oneself as the source of the law (e.g., 6:402), and *observantia aliis praestanda* in the context of duties of virtue to other human beings (e.g., 6:449).

by concepts of duty, antecedent predispositions on the side of *feeling*.[1] To have these predispositions cannot be considered a duty; rather, every human being has them, and it is by virtue of them that he can be put under obligation. – Consciousness of them is not of empirical origin; it can, instead, only follow from consciousness of a moral law, as the effect this has on the mind.

a

Moral Feeling

This is the susceptibility to feel pleasure or displeasure merely from being aware that our actions are consistent with or contrary to the law of duty. Every determination of choice proceeds *from* the representation of a possible action *to* the deed through the feeling of pleasure or displeasure, taking an interest in the action or its effect. The state of *feeling*[m] here (the way in which inner sense is affected) is either *pathological* or *moral*. – The former is that feeling which precedes the representation of the law; the latter, that which can only follow upon it.

Since any consciousness of obligation depends upon moral feeling to make us aware of the constraint present in the thought of duty, there can be no duty to have moral feeling or to acquire it; instead every human being (as a moral being) has it in him originally. Obligation with regard to moral feeling can be only to *cultivate* it and to strengthen it through wonder at its inscrutable [6:400] source. This comes about by its being shown how it is set apart from any pathological stimulus and is induced most intensely in its purity by a merely rational representation.

It is inappropriate to call this feeling a moral *sense*, for by the word "sense" is usually understood a theoretical capacity for perception[n] directed toward an object, whereas moral feeling (like pleasure and displeasure in general) is something merely subjective, which yields no cognition. – No human being is entirely without moral feeling, for were he completely lacking in receptivity to it[o] he would be morally dead; and if (to speak in medical terms) the moral vital force could no longer excite this feeling, then humanity would dissolve (by chemical laws, as it were) into mere animality and be mixed irretrievably with the mass of other natural beings. – But we no more have a special *sense* for what is (morally) good and evil than for *truth*, although people often speak in this fashion. We have, rather, a *susceptibility* on the part of free choice to be moved by pure practical reason (and its law), and this is what we call moral feeling.

---

[1] *ästhetisch*   [m] *ästhetische Zustand*   [n] *Wahrnehmungsvermögen*
[o] *völliger Unempfänglichkeit für diese Empfindung*

b
Conscience

So too, conscience is not something that can be acquired, and we have no duty to provide ourselves with one; rather, every human being, as a moral being, *has* a conscience within him originally. To be under obligation to have a conscience would be tantamount to having a duty to recognize duties. For, conscience is practical reason holding the human being's duty before him for his acquittal or condemnation in every case that comes under a law. Thus it is not directed to an object but merely to the subject (to affect moral feeling by its act), and so it is not something incumbent on one, a duty, but rather an unavoidable fact.^p So when it is said that a certain human being *has* no conscience, what is meant is that he pays no heed to its verdict. For if he really had no conscience, he could not even conceive of

[6:401]   the duty to have one, since he would neither impute anything to himself as conforming with duty nor reproach himself with anything as contrary to duty.

I shall here pass over the various divisions of conscience and note only that, as follows from what has been said, an *erring* conscience is an absurdity. For while I can indeed be mistaken at times in my objective judgment as to whether something is a duty or not, I cannot be mistaken in my subjective judgment as to whether I have submitted it to my practical reason (here in its role as judge) for such a judgment; for if I could be mistaken in that, I would have made no practical judgment at all, and in that case there would be neither truth nor error. *Unconscientiousness* is not lack of conscience but rather the propensity to pay no heed to its judgment. But if someone is aware that he has acted in accordance with his conscience, then as far as guilt or innocence is concerned nothing more can be required of him. It is incumbent upon him only to enlighten his *understanding* in the matter of what is or is not duty; but when it comes, or has come, to a deed, conscience speaks involuntarily^q and unavoidably. Therefore, to act in accordance with conscience cannot itself be a duty; for if it were, there would have to be yet a second conscience in order for one to become aware of the act of the first.

The duty here is only to cultivate one's conscience, to sharpen one's attentiveness to the voice of the inner judge, and to use every means to obtain a hearing for it (hence the duty is only indirect).

c
Love of Human Beings

Love is a matter of *feeling*,^r not of willing, and I cannot love because I *will* to, still less because I *ought* to (I cannot be constrained to love); so a *duty to love* is an absurdity. But *benevolence* (*amor benevolentiae*), as conduct,^s can be subject to a law of duty. However, unselfish benevolence toward human beings is often

^p *Thatsache*   ^q *unwillkürlich*   ^r *Empfindung*
        ^s *als ein Thun*

172

(though very inappropriately) also called *love*; people even speak of love which is also a duty for us when it is not a question of another's happiness but of the complete and free surrender of all one's ends to the ends of another (even a supernatural) being. But every duty is *necessitation*, a constraint, even if this is to be self-constraint in accordance with a law. What is done from constraint, however, is not done from love.

To *do good* to other human beings insofar as we can is a duty, whether one loves   [6:402] them or not; and even if one had to remark sadly that our species, on closer acquaintance, is not particularly lovable, that would not detract from the force of this duty. – But *hatred of human beings* is always *hateful*, even when it takes the form merely of completely avoiding them (separatist misanthropy), without active hostility toward them. For benevolence always remains a duty, even toward a misanthropist, whom one cannot indeed love but to whom one can still do good.

But to hate vice in human beings is neither a duty nor contrary to duty; it is, rather, a mere feeling of aversion to vice, a feeling neither affected by the will nor affecting it. *Beneficence* is a duty. If someone practices it often and succeeds in realizing his beneficent intention, he eventually comes actually to love whom he has helped. So the saying "you ought to *love* your neighbor as yourself" does not mean that you ought immediately (first) to love him and (afterwards) by means of this love do good to him. It means, rather, *do good* to your fellow human beings, and your beneficence will produce love of them in you (as an aptitude^t of the inclination to beneficence in general).

Hence only the love that is *delight*^u (*amor complacentiae*) is direct. But to have a duty to this (which is a pleasure joined immediately to the representation of an object's existence), that is, to have to be constrained to take pleasure in something, is a contradiction.

d
Respect

Respect (*reverentia*) is, again, something merely subjective, a feeling of a special kind, not a judgment about an object that it would be a duty to bring about or promote. For, such a duty, regarded as a duty, could be represented to us only through the *respect* we have for it. A duty to have respect would thus amount to being put under obligation to duties. – Accordingly it is not correct to say that a human being has a *duty of self-esteem*; it must rather be said that the law within him unavoidably forces from him *respect* for his own being, and this feeling   [6:403] (which is of a special kind) is the basis^v of certain duties, that is, of certain actions that are consistent with his duty to himself. It cannot be said that he *has* a duty of respect toward himself, for he must have respect for the law within himself in order even to think of any duty whatsoever.

^t *Fertigkeit*   ^u *Liebe des Wohlgefallens*   ^v *ein Grund*

XIII
General Principles of the Metaphysics of Morals
in Handling a *Pure* Doctrine of Virtue

First. For any one duty only *one* ground of obligation can be found; and if someone produces two or more proofs for a duty, this is a sure sign either that he has not yet found a valid proof or that he has mistaken two or more different duties for one.

For any moral proof, as philosophical, can be drawn only by means of rational knowledge *from concepts* and not, as in mathematics, by the construction of concepts. Mathematical concepts allow a number of proofs for one and the same proposition because in *a priori intuition* there can be several ways of determining the properties of an object, all of which lead back to the same ground. – If, for example, someone wants to draw a proof for the duty of truthfulness first from the *harm* a lie does to other human beings and then also from the *worthlessness* of a liar and his violation of respect for himself, what he has proved in the first case is a duty of benevolence, not of truthfulness, and so a duty other than the one for which proof was required. – But it is a highly unphilosophical expedient to resort to a number of proofs for one and the same proposition, consoling oneself that the multitude of reasons makes up for the inadequacy of any one of them taken by itself; for this indicates trickery and insincerity. When different reasons are *juxtaposed*, one does not compensate for the deficiency of the others for certainty or even for probability. [6:404] Proofs must *proceed* by ground and consequent in *a single series* to a sufficient ground; only in this way can they be demonstrative. – Yet the former method is the usual device of rhetoric.

Second. The distinction between virtue and vice can never be sought in the *degree* to which one follows certain maxims; it must rather be sought only in the specific *quality* of the maxims (their relation to the law). In other words, the well-known principle (Aristotle's) which locates virtue in the *mean* between two vices is false.[*] Let good management, for instance, consist in the *mean* between two vices, prodigality and avarice: as a virtue, it cannot be represented

---

[*] The formulae commonly used in the language of classical ethics: [1] *medio tutissimus ibis*; [2] *omne nimium vertitur in vitium*; [3] *est modus in rebus, etc.*; [4] *medium tenuere beati*; [5] *insani sapiens nomen habeat, etc.*,[w] contain a superficial wisdom which really has no determinate principles. For who will specify for me this mean between the two extremes? What distinguishes *avarice* (as a vice) from thrift (as a virtue) is not that avarice carries thrift *too far* but that avarice has an *entirely different* principle (maxim), that of putting the end of economizing not in enjoyment of one's means but merely in possession of them, while denying oneself any enjoyment from them. In the same way, the vice of *prodigality* is not to be sought in an excessive enjoyment of one's means but in the bad maxim which makes the use of one's means the sole end, without regard for preserving them.

[w] [1] you will travel most safely in the middle of the road (Ovid, *Metamorphoses* II.137); [2] too much of anything becomes vice; [3] there is a certain measure in our affairs and finally fixed limits, beyond which or short of which there is no place for right (Horace, *Satires* I.i.105–6), quotation supplemented in view of Kant's note to 433; [4] happy are those who keep to the mean; [5] it is a foolish wisdom, equivalent to wickedness, that seeks to be virtuous beyond the proper measure (Horace, *Epistles* I.vi.15), quotation supplemented in view of 409 and 433n.

as arising either from a gradual diminution of prodigality (by saving) or from an increase of spending on the miser's part – as if these two vices, moving in opposite directions, met in good management. Instead, each of them has its distinctive maxim, which necessarily contradicts the maxim of the other.

For the same reason, no vice whatever can be defined^x in terms of *going further* in carrying out certain aims than there is any purpose in doing (e.g., *Prodigalitas est excessus in consumendis opibus*)^y or of not going as far as is needed in carrying them out (e.g., *Avaritia est defectus etc.*).^z Since this does not specify the *degree*, although it makes the conformity or nonconformity of conduct with duty depend entirely on it, this cannot serve as a definition.^a

Third. Ethical duties must not be determined in accordance with the capacity to fulfill the law that is ascribed to human beings; on the contrary, their moral capacity must be estimated by the law, which commands categorically, and so in accordance with our rational knowledge of what they ought to be in keeping with the idea of humanity, not in accordance with the empirical knowledge we have of human beings as they are. These three maxims for scientific treatment of a doctrine of virtue are opposed to the following ancient dicta: [6:405]

1) There is only one virtue and one vice.
2) Virtue is the observance of the middle way between opposing vices.^b
3) Virtue (like prudence) must be learned from experience.

XIV^c
On Virtue in General

Virtue signifies a moral strength of the will. But this does not exhaust the concept; for such strength could also belong to a *holy* (superhuman) being, in whom no hindering impulses would impede the law of its will and who would thus gladly do everything in conformity with the law. Virtue is, therefore, the moral strength of a *human being's* will in fulfilling his *duty*, a moral *constraint* through his own lawgiving reason, insofar as this constitutes itself an authority *executing* the law.^d – Virtue itself, or possession of it, is not a duty (for then one would have to be put under obligation to duties); rather, it commands and accompanies its command with a moral constraint (a constraint possible in accordance with laws of inner freedom). But because this constraint is to be irresistible, strength is required, in a degree which we can assess only by the

---

^x *erklärt*   ^y Prodigality is *excess* in consuming one's means   ^z Avarice is *deficiency* etc.
^a *Erklärung*
^b The first edition has *Meinungen*, "views" or "opinions," which seems to be a simple mistake for *Lastern*, "vices."
^c LD: Gregor here has followed the 1803 edition, in which this part of the text is numbered XIV and subsequent sections numbered XV–XIX. In AA, this part of the text has a smaller, unnumbered heading, and subsequent sections are numbered XIV–XVIII.
^d *einer das Gesetz ausführenden Gewalt*

magnitude of the obstacles that the human being himself furnishes through his inclinations. The vices, the brood of dispositions opposing the law, are the monsters he has to fight. Accordingly, this moral strength, as *courage (fortitudo moralis)*, also constitutes the greatest and the only true honor that the human being can win in war and is, moreover, called *wisdom* in the strict sense, namely practical wisdom, since it makes the *final end* of his existence on earth its own end. – Only in its possession is he "free," "healthy," "rich," "a king," and so forth and can suffer no loss by chance or fate, since he is in possession of himself and the virtuous man cannot lose his virtue.

[6:406] Any high praise for the ideal of humanity in its moral perfection can lose nothing in practical reality from examples to the contrary, drawn from what human beings now are, have become, or will presumably become in the future; and *anthropology*, which issues from merely empirical cognition, can do no damage to *anthroponomy*, which is laid down by a reason giving laws unconditionally. And while virtue (in relation to human beings, not to the law) can be said here and there to be meritorious and to deserve to be rewarded, yet in itself, since it is its own end it must also be regarded as its own reward.

Considered in its complete perfection, virtue is therefore represented not as if a human being possesses virtue but rather as if virtue possesses him; for in the former case it would look as if he still had a choice (for which he would need yet another virtue in order to choose virtue in preference to any other goods offered him). – To think of several virtues (as one unavoidably does) is nothing other than to think of the various moral objects to which the will is led by the one principle of virtue, and so too with regard to the contrary vices. The expression that personifies both is an aesthetic device which still points to a moral sense. – So an aesthetic of morals, while not indeed part of the metaphysics of morals, is still a subjective presentation of it in which the feelings that accompany the constraining power of the moral law (e.g., disgust, horror, etc., which make moral aversion sensible) make its efficacy felt, in order to get the better of *merely* sensible incitements.

XV
On the Principle That Distinguishes the Doctrine of Virtue from the Doctrine of Right

This distinction, on which the main division of the *doctrine of morals* as a whole also rests, is based on this: that the concept of **freedom**, which is common to both, makes it necessary to divide duties into duties of *outer freedom* and duties of *inner freedom*, only the latter of which are ethical. – Hence inner freedom must first be treated in a preliminary remark (*discursus praeliminaris*), as the condition of all *duties of virtue*, (just as conscience was treated earlier, as the condition of all duties as such).   [6:407]

Remark

*On the **Doctrine of Virtue** in Accordance with the Principle of Inner **Freedom***

An *aptitude*ᵉ (*habitus*) is a facilityᶠ in acting and a subjective perfection of *choice*. – But not every such *facility* is a *free* aptitude (*habitus libertatis*); for if it is a habitᵍ (*assuetudo*), that is, a uniformity in action that has become a *necessity* through frequent repetition, it is not one that proceeds from freedom, and therefore not a moral aptitude. Hence virtue cannot be *defined* as an aptitude for free actions in conformity with law unless there is added "to determine oneself to act through the thought of the law," and then this aptitude is not a property of choice but of the *will*, which is a faculty of desire that, in adopting a rule, also gives it as a universal law. Only such an aptitude can be counted as virtue.

But two things are required for inner freedom: being one's own *master*ʰ in a given case (*animus sui compos*), and *ruling* oneselfⁱ (*imperium in semetipsum*), that is, subduing one's affects and *governing* one's passions.ʲ – In these two states one's *character* (*indoles*) is noble (*erecta*); in the opposite case it is mean (*indoles abiecta, serva*).

XVI
Virtue Requires, in the First Place, Governing Oneself

Affects and *passions*⁵¹ are essentially different from each other. Affects belong to *feeling* insofar as, preceding reflection, it makes this impossible or more difficult. Hence an affect is called *precipitate* or *rash* (*animus praeceps*), and reason says, through the concept of virtue, that one should *get hold of oneself*. Yet this weakness in the use of one's understanding coupled with the strength of one's emotions is only a *lack of virtue* and, as it were, something childish and weak, which can indeed coexist with the best will. It even has one good thing about it: that this tempest quickly subsides. Accordingly a propensity to an affect (e.g., *anger*) does not enter into kinship with vice so readily as does a passion. A *passion* is a sensible *desire* that has become a lasting inclination (e.g., *hatred*, as opposed to anger). The calm with which one gives oneself up to it permits reflection and allows the mind to form principles upon it and so, if inclination lights upon something contrary to the law, to brood upon it, to get it rooted deeply, and so to   [6:408]

ᵉ *Fertigkeit*   ᶠ *Leichtigkeit*   ᵍ *Angewohnheit*   ʰ *seiner selbst . . . Meister . . . zu sein*
ⁱ *über sich selbst Herr zu sein*
ʲ *seine Affecten zu zähmen und seine Leidenschaften zu beherrschen*
⁵¹ On the affects and passions see *Anthropology from a Pragmatic Point of View* (7:251–82), *The Conflict of the Faculties*, Part III (7:95–116) and the *Rektoratsrede*, referred to in note 4 on 6:207.

take up what is evil (as something premeditated) into its maxim. And the evil is then *properly* evil,[k] that is, a true *vice*.

Since virtue is based on inner freedom it contains a positive command to a human being, namely to bring all his capacities and inclinations under his (reason's) control and so to rule over himself, which goes beyond forbidding him to let himself be governed by his feelings and inclinations (the duty of *apathy*); for unless reason holds the reins of government in its own hands, his feelings and inclinations play the master over him.

XVII
Virtue Necessarily Presupposes *Apathy* (Regarded as Strength)

The word "apathy" has fallen into disrepute, as if it meant lack of feeling and so subjective indifference with respect to objects of choice; it is taken for weakness. This misunderstanding can be prevented by giving the name "*moral apathy*" to that absence of affects which is to be distinguished from indifference because in cases of moral apathy feelings arising from sensible impressions lose their influence on moral feeling only because respect for the law is more powerful than all such feelings together. – Only the apparent strength of someone feverish

[6:409] lets a lively sympathy even for *what is good* rise into an affect, or rather degenerate into it. An affect of this kind is called *enthusiasm*, and the *moderation* that is usually recommended even for the practice of virtue is to be interpreted as referring to it (*insani sapiens nomen habeat[;]aequus iniqui – **ultra quam satis est virtutem si petat ipsam. Horat.**);*[1] for otherwise it is absurd to suppose that one could be *too wise, too virtuous*. An affect always belongs to sensibility, no matter by what kind of object it is aroused. The true strength of virtue is a *tranquil mind* with a considered and firm resolution to put the law of virtue into practice. That is the state of *health* in the moral life, whereas an affect, even one aroused by the thought of *what is good*, is a momentary, sparkling phenomenon that leaves one exhausted. – But that human being can be called fantastically virtuous who allows *nothing to be morally indifferent* (*adiaphora*) and strews all his steps with duties, as with mantraps; it is not indifferent to him whether I eat meat or fish, drink beer or wine, supposing that both agree with me. Fantastic virtue is a concern with petty details[m] which, were it admitted into the doctrine of virtue, would turn the government of virtue into tyranny.

---

[k] *ein qualificirtes Böse. Qualificirt* is used throughout the discussion of vices opposed to duties of love (6:458–61); it is translated as "proper."

[1] The wise man has the name of being a fool, the just man of being iniquitous, if he seeks virtue *beyond what is sufficient.* Horace (*Epistles* I.vi.15–16) LD: The Latin source contains *ferat* ["bears"] rather than *habeat* ["has"].

[m] *Mikrologie*

Remark

Virtue is always *in progress* and yet always starts *from the beginning*. – It is always in progress because, considered *objectively*, it is an ideal and unattainable, while yet constant approximation to it is a duty. That it always starts from the beginning has a *subjective* basis in human nature, which is affected by inclinations because of which virtue can never settle down in peace and quiet with its maxims adopted once and for all but, if it is not rising, is unavoidably sinking. For, moral maxims, unlike technical ones, cannot be based on habit[n] (since this belongs to the natural constitution of the will's determination); on the contrary, if the practice of virtue were to become a habit the subject would suffer loss to that *freedom* in adopting his maxims which distinguishes an action done from duty.

XVIII

Concepts Preliminary[o] to the Division of the Doctrine of Virtue

[6:410]

This principle of division must **first**, in terms of what is *formal*, contain all the conditions that serve to distinguish a part of the doctrine of morals in general from the doctrine of right and to do so in terms of its specific form. It does this by laying it down 1) that duties of virtue are duties for which there is no external lawgiving; 2) that since a law must yet lie at the basis of every duty, this law in ethics can be a law of duty given, not for actions, but only for the maxims of actions; 3) that (as follows in turn from this) ethical duty must be thought as *wide*, not as narrow, duty.

The principle of division must **second**, in terms of what is *material*, present the doctrine of virtue not merely as a doctrine of duties generally but also as a *doctrine of ends*, so that a human being is under obligation to regard himself, as well as every other human being, as his end. These are usually called duties of self-love and of love for one's neighbor; but then these words are used inappropriately, since there can be no direct duty to love, but instead to do that[p] by which one makes oneself and others one's end.

Third, with regard to the distinction of the material from the formal in the principle of duty (of conformity with law from conformity with ends),[q] it should be noted that not every *obligation of virtue*[r] (*obligatio ethica*) is a duty of virtue (*officium ethicum s. virtutis*); in other words, respect for law as such does not yet establish an end as a duty, and only such an end is a duty of virtue. – Hence there is only *one* obligation of virtue, whereas there are *many* duties of virtue; for there are indeed many objects that it is also our duty to have as ends, but there is only one virtuous disposition, the subjective determining

---

[n] *Gewohnheit*   [o] *Vorbegriffe*   [p] *zu Handlungen*, literally, "to actions"
[q] *der Gesetzmäßigkeit von der Zweckmäßigkeit*   [r] *Tugendverpflichtung*

ground to fulfill one's duty, which extends to duties of right as well although they cannot, because of this, be called duties of virtue. – Hence all the *divisions* of ethics will have to do only with duties of virtue. Viewed in terms of its formal principle, ethics is the science of how one is under obligation[s] without regard for any possible external lawgiving.

[6:411] *Remark*

But, it will be asked, why do I introduce a division of ethics into a *doctrine of elements* and a *doctrine of method*, when no such division was needed in the doctrine of right? – The reason is that the doctrine of right has to do only with narrow duties, whereas ethics has to do with wide duties. Hence the doctrine of right, which by its nature must determine duties strictly (precisely), has no more need of general directions[t] (a method) as to how to proceed in judging than does pure mathematics; instead, it certifies its method by what it does.[u] – But ethics, because of the latitude it allows in its imperfect duties, unavoidably leads to questions that call upon judgment to decide how a maxim is to be applied in particular cases, and indeed in such a way that judgment provides another (subordinate) maxim (and one can always ask for yet another principle for applying this maxim to cases that may arise). So ethics falls into a casuistry, which has no place in the doctrine of right.

Casuistry is, accordingly, neither a *science* nor a part of a science; for in that case it would be dogmatics, and casuistry is not so much a doctrine about how *to find* something as rather a practice in how *to seek* truth. So it is *woven into ethics* in a *fragmentary* way, not systematically (as dogmatics would have to be), and is added to ethics only by way of scholia to the system.

On the other hand, the *doctrine of method* of morally practical reason, which deals not so much with judgment as with reason and its *exercise* in both the *theory* and the *practice* of its duties, belongs to ethics in particular. The *first* exercise of it consists in *questioning* the pupil about what he already knows of concepts of duty, and may be called the *erotetic* method. If he knows this because he has previously been told it, so that now it is drawn merely from his memory, the method is called the *catechistic* method proper; but if it is assumed that this is already present naturally in the pupil's reason and needs only to be developed[v] from it, the method is called that of *dialogue* (Socratic method).

Catechizing, as exercise in theory, has *ascetics* for its practical counterpart.

[6:412] Ascetics is that part of the doctrine of method in which is taught not only the concept of virtue but also how to put into practice and cultivate the *capacity for* as well as the will to virtue.[w]

---

[s] *von der Art ... verbindlich zu sein* [t] *Vorschrift* [u] *sie durch die That wahr macht*
[v] *entwickelt* [w] *das Tugendvermögen sowohl als der Wille dazu*

In accordance with these principles we shall set forth the system in two parts: the *doctrine* of the *elements of ethics* and the *doctrine* of the *methods of ethics*. Each part will have its divisions. In the first part, these will be made in accordance with the different *subjects* to whom human beings are under obligation; in the second part, in accordance with the different *ends* that reason puts them under obligation to have, and with their receptivity to these ends.

XIX

The division that practical reason lays out to establish a system of its concepts in an *ethics* (the architectonic division) can be made in accordance with principles of two kinds, taken either singly or together. One sets forth *in terms of its matter* the *subjective* relation between a being that is under obligation and the being that puts him under obligation; the other sets forth in a system *in terms of its form* the *objective* relation of ethical laws to duties generally. – The *first* division is that of the *beings* in relation to whom ethical obligation can be thought; the *second* would be the division of the *concepts* of pure ethically practical reason which have to do with the duties of those beings. These concepts are, accordingly, required for ethics only insofar as it is to be a *science*, and so are required for the methodic arrangement of all the propositions found on the basis of the first division.

[6:413]

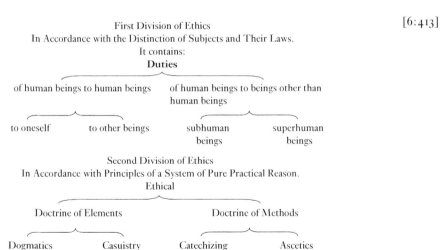

First Division of Ethics
In Accordance with the Distinction of Subjects and Their Laws.
It contains:
Duties

of human beings to human beings   of human beings to beings other than human beings

to oneself   to other beings   subhuman beings   superhuman beings

Second Division of Ethics
In Accordance with Principles of a System of Pure Practical Reason.
Ethical

Doctrine of Elements   Doctrine of Methods

Dogmatics   Casuistry   Catechizing   Ascetics

Because the latter division has to do with the form of the science, it must precede the first, as the groundplan of the whole.

I

Doctrine of the Elements of Ethics

Doctrine of the Elements of Ethics
Part I
On Duties to Oneself as Such

Introduction

§1
The Concept of a Duty to Oneself Contains (at First Glance) a Contradiction

If the I *that imposes obligation* is taken in the same sense as the I *that is put under obligation*,[a] a duty to oneself is a self-contradictory concept. For the concept of duty contains the concept of being passively constrained (I am *bound*). But if the duty is a duty to myself, I think of myself as *binding* and so as actively constraining (I, the same subject, am imposing obligation). And the proposition that asserts a duty to myself (I *ought* to bind myself) would involve being bound to bind myself (a passive obligation that was still, in the same sense of the relation, also an active obligation), and hence a contradiction. – One can also bring this contradiction to light by pointing out that the one imposing obligation (*auctor obligationis*) could always release the one put under obligation (*subiectum obligationis*) from the obligation (*terminus obligationis*), so that (if both are one and the same subject) he would not be bound at all to a duty he lays upon himself. This involves a contradiction.

§2
Nevertheless, a Human Being Has Duties to Himself

For suppose there were no such duties: then there would be no duties whatsoever, and so no external duties either. – For I can recognize that I am under obligation to others only insofar as I at the same time put myself under obligation, since the law by virtue of which I regard myself as being under obligation proceeds in every case from my own practical reason; and [6:418] in being constrained by my own reason, I am also the one constraining myself.[*]

---

[*] So when it is a question, for example, of vindicating my honor or of preserving myself, I say "I owe it to myself." Even in what concerns duties of less importance – those having to do only with what is meritorious rather than necessary in my compliance with duty – I speak in the same way, for example "I owe it to myself to increase my fitness for social intercourse and so forth (to cultivate myself)."

[a] *das verpflichtende Ich ... dem verpflichteten*

§3
Solution of This Apparent Antinomy

When a human being is conscious of a duty to himself, he views himself, as the subject of duty, under two attributes: first as a *sensible being*, that is, as a human being (a member of one of the animal species), and second as an *intelligible being* (not merely as a being that has reason, since reason as a theoretical faculty[b] could well be an attribute[c] of a living corporeal being). The senses cannot attain this latter aspect of a human being; it can be cognized only in morally practical relations, where the incomprehensible property of *freedom* is revealed by the influence of reason on the inner lawgiving will.

Now the human being as a *natural being* that has reason (*homo phaenomenon*) can be determined by his reason, as a *cause*, to actions in the sensible world, and so far the concept of an obligation[d] does not come into consideration. But the same human being thought in terms of his *personality*, that is, as a being endowed with *inner freedom* (*homo noumenon*), is regarded as a being capable of obligation and, indeed, obligation to himself (to the humanity in his own person).[e] So the human being (taken in these two different senses) can acknowledge a duty to himself without falling into contradiction (because the concept of a human being is not thought in one and the same sense).

§4
On the Principle on Which the Division of Duties to Oneself Is Based

The division can be made only with regard to objects of duty, not with regard to the subject that puts himself under obligation. The subject that is bound, as well as the subject that binds, is always the *human being only*; and though we may, in a theoretical respect, distinguish soul and body from each other, as natural characteristics of a human being, we may not think of them as different substances putting him under obligation, so as to justify a division of duties to the *body* and duties to the *soul*. – Neither experience nor inferences of reason[f] give us adequate grounds for deciding whether the human being has a soul

[6:419]

---

[b] *nach ihrem theoretischen Vermögen*   [c] *Qualität*

[d] *Begriff einer Verbindlichkeit.* LD: This replaces "concept of obligation" from the previous edition.

[e] *ein der Verpflichtung fähiges Wesen und zwar gegen sich selbst.* LD: Gregor's translation in the previous edition – "a being that can be put under obligation and, indeed, under obligation to himself" – has been criticized as overly interpretive and potentially misleading in its rendering of *Verpflichtung* (but see note j on 6:224). The revised translation agrees with Andrews Reath, "Self-Legislation and Duties to Oneself," in Mark Timmons (ed.) *Kant's Metaphysics of Morals: Interpretive Essays* (Oxford University Press, 2002), 349–70, 355. For further discussion, see Jens Timmermann, "Duties to Oneself as Such," in Trampota et al. (eds), *Kant's Tugendlehre*, 207–19, especially 216f.

[f] *Schlüsse der Vernunft*

(in the sense of a substance dwelling in him, distinct from the body and capable of thinking independently of it, that is, a spiritual substance), or whether life may not well be, instead, a property of matter. And even if the first alternative be true, it is still inconceivable that he should have a duty to a *body* (as a subject imposing obligation), even to a human body.

1) The only *objective* division of duties to oneself will, accordingly, be the division into what is **formal** and what is **material** in duties to oneself. The first of these are *limiting* (negative) duties; the second, *widening* (positive duties to oneself). Negative duties *forbid* a human being to act contrary to the **end** of his nature and so have to do merely with his moral *self-preservation*; positive duties, which *command* him to make a certain object of choice his end, concern his *perfecting* of himself. Both of them belong to virtue, either as duties of omission (*sustine et abstine*) or as duties of commission (*viribus concessis utere*), but both belong to it as duties of virtue. The first belong to the moral **health** (*ad esse*) of a human being as object of both his outer senses and his inner sense, to the *preservation* of his nature in its perfection (as *receptivity*). The second belong to his moral *prosperity* (*ad melius esse; opulentia moralis*), which consists in possessing a *capacity* sufficient for all his ends, insofar as this can be acquired; they belong to his *cultivation* (active perfecting) of himself. – The first principle of duty to oneself lies in the dictum "live in conformity with nature" (*naturae convenienter vive*), that is, *preserve* yourself in the perfection of your nature; the second, in the saying "*make yourself more perfect* than mere nature has made you" (*perfice te ut finem; perfice te ut medium*).[g]

2) There will be a *subjective* division of a human being's duties to himself, that is, one in terms of whether the subject of duty (the human being) views himself both as an **animal** (natural) and a moral being or **only as a moral** being.   [6:420]

There are impulses of nature having to do with a human being's **animality**. Through them nature aims at a) his self-preservation, b) the preservation of the species, and c) the preservation of his capacity to enjoy life, though still on the animal level only.[h] – The vices that are here opposed to his duty to himself are *murdering himself*, the unnatural use of his *sexual inclination*, and such *excessive consumption of food and drink* as weakens his capacity for making purposive use of his powers.

But a human being's duty to himself as a moral being *only* (without taking his animality into consideration) consists in what is *formal* in the consistency of the maxims of his will with the *dignity* of humanity in his person. It consists, therefore, in a prohibition against depriving himself of the *prerogative* of a moral being, that of acting in accordance with principles, that is, inner freedom, and so making himself a plaything of the mere

---

[g] perfect yourself as an end; perfect yourself as a means
[h] The second edition emends the preceding passage to read: "c) the preservation of the subject's capacity to use his powers purposefully and to enjoy ..."

inclinations and hence a thing. – The vices contrary to this duty are **lying, avarice**, and **false humility** (servility). These adopt principles that are directly contrary to his character as a moral being (in terms of its very form), that is, to inner freedom, the innate dignity of a human being, which is tantamount to saying that they make it one's basic principle to have no basic principle and hence no character, that is, to throw oneself away and make oneself an object of contempt. – The virtue that is opposed to all these vices could be called *love of honor* (*honestas interna, iustum sui aestimium*), a cast of mind[i] far removed from *ambition* (*ambitio*) (which can be quite mean). But it will appear prominently later on, under this name.

[i] *Denkungsart*

The Doctrine of Virtue
Part I
Doctrine of the Elements of Ethics
Book I
Perfect Duties to Oneself

Chapter I

A Human Being's Duty to Himself as an Animal Being

§5

The *first*, though not the principal, duty of a human being to himself as an animal being is *to preserve himself* in his animal nature.

The contrary of this is willful[a] *physical death* or killing oneself (*autochiria*), which can be thought as either total, suicide (*suicidium*), or only partial, mutilating oneself. Mutilating oneself can in turn be either *material, depriving* oneself of certain integral, organic *parts*, that is, maiming oneself, or *formal, depriving* oneself (permanently or temporarily) of one's *capacity* for the natural (and so indirectly for the moral) *use* of one's powers.

Since this chapter deals only with negative duties and so with duties of omission, the articles about duties must be directed against the *vices* opposed to duties to oneself.

First Article
Of the First Chapter
On Killing Oneself
§6

Willfully *killing* oneself[b] can be called **murdering oneself** (*homicidium dolosum*) only if it can be proved that it is in general a crime committed either against one's own person or also, through one's killing oneself, against another (as when a pregnant person takes her life).

a)[c] Killing oneself is a crime (murder). It can also be regarded as a violation of one's duty to other people (the duty of spouses to each other, of parents to their children, of a subject to his superior[d] or to his fellow citizens, and finally even as

---

[a] *willkürliche*   [b] *Die willkürliche Entleibung seiner selbst*
[c] There is no matching "b)" in the text.   [d] *Obrigkeit*

a violation of duty to God, as one's abandoning the post assigned him in the world without having been called away from it). But since what is in question here is only a violation of duty to oneself, the question is whether, if I set aside all those relations, a human being is still bound to preserve his life simply by virtue of his quality as a person and whether he must acknowledge in this a duty (and indeed a strict duty) to himself.

It seems absurd to say that a human being could wrong himself^e (*volenti non fit iniuria*). Hence the Stoic thought it a prerogative of his (the sage's) personality to depart from life at his discretion (as from a smoke-filled room) with peace of soul, free from the pressure of present or anticipated ills, because he could be of no more use in life. – But there should have been in this very courage, this strength of soul not to fear death and to know of something that a human being can value even more highly than his life, a still stronger motive for him not to destroy himself, a being with such powerful authority over the strongest sensible incentives, and so not to deprive himself of life.

A human being cannot renounce his personality as long as he is a subject of duty, hence as long as he lives; and it is a contradiction that he should be authorized to withdraw from all obligation, that is, freely to act as if no [6:423] authorization were needed for this action. To annihilate the subject of morality in one's own person is to root out the existence of morality itself from the world, as far as one can, even though morality is an end in itself. Consequently, disposing of oneself as a mere means to some discretionary end is debasing humanity in one's person (*homo noumenon*), to which the human being (*homo phaenomenon*) was nevertheless entrusted for preservation.

To deprive oneself of an integral part or organ (to maim oneself) – for example, to give away or sell a tooth to be transplanted into another's mouth, or to have oneself castrated in order to get an easier livelihood as a singer, and so forth – are ways of partially murdering oneself. But to have a dead or diseased organ amputated when it endangers one's life, or to have something cut off that is a part but not an organ of the body, for example, one's hair, cannot be counted as a crime against one's own person – although cutting one's hair in order to sell it is not altogether free from blame.

---

^e *sich selbst beleidigen könne.* In discussing perfect duties to oneself, as well as imperfect duties of respect to others, Kant often uses the terminology of the *Doctrine of Right*, as e.g., in the preceding paragraph he called killing oneself a *Verbrechen*, which in the *Doctrine of Right* was a "crime" (*crimen*). Given the context in which these terms were introduced, however, it does not always seem advisable to translate them precisely as they were used in speaking of rights.

Casuistical Questions

Is it murdering oneself to hurl oneself to certain death (like Curtius) in order to save one's country? – or is deliberate[f] martyrdom, sacrificing oneself for the good of all humanity, also to be considered an act of heroism?

Is it permitted to anticipate by killing oneself the unjust death sentence of one's ruler – even if the ruler permits this (as did Nero with Seneca)?

Can a great king who died recently[52] be charged with a criminal intention for carrying a fast-acting poison with him, presumably so that if he were captured when he led his troops into battle he could not be forced to agree to conditions of ransom harmful to his state? – For one can ascribe this purpose to him without having to presume that mere pride lay behind it.

A human being who had been bitten by a mad dog already felt hydrophobia coming on. He explained, in a letter he left, that, since as far as he knew the disease was incurable, he was taking his life lest he harm others as well in his madness (the onset of which he already felt). Did he do wrong? [6:424]

Anyone who decides to be vaccinated against smallpox puts his life in danger, even though he does it *in order to preserve his life*; and, insofar as he himself brings on the disease that endangers his life, he is in a far more doubtful situation, as far as the law of duty is concerned, than is the sailor, who at least does not arouse the storm to which he entrusts himself. Is smallpox inoculation, then, permitted?

Article II
On Defiling Oneself by Lust
§7

Just as love of life is destined by nature to preserve the person, so sexual love is destined by it to preserve the species; in other words, each of these is a *natural end*, by which is understood that connection of a cause with an effect in which, although no understanding is ascribed to the cause, it is still thought by analogy with an intelligent cause, and so as if it produced human beings on purpose. What is now in question is whether a person's use of his sexual capacity is subject to a limiting law of duty with regard to the person himself or whether he is authorized to direct the use of his sexual attributes to mere animal pleasure, without having in view the preservation of the species, and would not thereby be acting contrary to a duty to himself. – In the doctrine of right it was shown that the human being cannot make use of *another* person to get this pleasure apart from a special limitation by a contract establishing the right, by which two persons put each other under obligation. But the question here is whether the

---

[f] *vorsetzliche*
[52] Frederick the Great

human being is subject to a duty to himself with regard to this enjoyment, violation of which is a *defiling* (not merely a debasing)[g] of the humanity in his own person. The impetus to this pleasure is called carnal lust (or also simply lust). The vice engendered through it is called lewdness; the virtue with regard to this sensuous impulse is called chastity, which is to be represented here as a duty of the human being to himself. Lust is called *unnatural* if the human being is aroused to it not by a real object but by his imagining it, so that he himself creates one, contrary to [natural] purpose;[h] for in this way imagination brings forth a desire contrary to nature's end, and indeed to an end even more important than that of love of life itself, since it aims at the preservation of the whole species and not only of the individual.

[6:425]

That such an unnatural use (and so misuse) of one's sexual attribute is a violation of duty *to oneself*, and indeed one contrary to morality in its highest degree, occurs to everyone immediately, with the thought of it, and stirs up an aversion to this thought to such an extent that it is considered indecent even to call this vice by its proper name. This does not occur with regard to murdering oneself, which one does not hesitate in the least to lay before the world's eyes in all its horror (in a *species facti*).[i] In the case of unnatural vice it is as if the human being in general felt ashamed of being capable of treating his own person in such a way, which debases him beneath the beasts, so that when even the permitted bodily union of the sexes in marriage (a union which is in itself merely an animal union) is to be mentioned in polite society, this occasions and requires much delicacy to throw a veil over it.

But it is not so easy to produce a rational proof that unnatural, and even merely unpurposive,[j] use of one's sexual attribute is inadmissible as being a violation of duty to oneself (and indeed, as far as its unnatural use is concerned, a violation in the highest degree). – The *ground of proof* is, indeed, that by it the human being surrenders his personality (throwing it away), since he uses himself merely as a means to satisfy an animal impulse. But this does not explain the high degree of violation of the humanity in one's own person by such a vice in its unnaturalness, which seems in terms of its form (the disposition it involves) to exceed even murdering oneself. It consists, then, in this: that someone who defiantly casts off life as a burden is at least not making a feeble surrender to animal impulse in throwing himself away; murdering oneself requires courage, and in this disposition there is still always room for respect for the humanity in one's own person. But unnatural lust, which is complete abandonment of oneself to animal inclination, makes the human being not only an object of enjoyment

---

[g] *eine Schändung (nicht blos Abwürdigung)*   [h] *zweckwidrig*

[i] *Species facti* is the totality of those features of a deed that belong essentially to its imputability. See A.G. Baumgarten, *Initia philosophiae practicae primae*, AA 19:62.

[j] *unzweckmäßigen*

but, still further, a thing that is contrary to nature, that is, a *loathsome* object, and so deprives him of all respect for himself.

Casuistical Questions [6:426]

Nature's end in the cohabitation of the sexes is procreation, that is, the preservation of the species. Hence one may not, at least, act contrary to that end. But is it permitted to engage in this practice (even within marriage) *without taking this end into consideration?*

If, for example, the wife is pregnant or sterile (because of age or sickness), or if she feels no desire for intercourse, is it not contrary to nature's end, and so also contrary to one's duty to oneself, for one or the other of them, to make use of their sexual attributes – just as in unnatural lust? Or is there, in this case, a permissive law of morally practical reason, which in the collision of its determining grounds makes permitted something that is in itself not permitted (indulgently, as it were), in order to prevent a still greater violation? – At what point can the limitation of a wide obligation be ascribed to *purism* (a pedantry regarding the fulfillment of duty, as far as the wideness of the obligation is concerned), and the animal inclinations be allowed a latitude, at the risk of forsaking the law of reason?

Sexual inclination is also called "*love*" (in the narrowest sense of the word) and is, in fact, the strongest possible sensible pleasure[k] in an object. – It is not merely *sensitive* pleasure,[l] as in objects that are pleasing in mere reflection on them (receptivity to which is called taste). It is rather pleasure from the *enjoyment* of another person, which therefore belongs to the *faculty of desire* and, indeed, to its highest stage, passion. But it cannot be classed with either the love that is delight[m] or the love of benevolence (for both of these, instead, deter one from carnal enjoyment). It is a unique kind of pleasure (*sui generis*), and this ardor has nothing in common with moral love properly speaking, though it can enter into close union with it under the limiting conditions of practical reason.

Article III [6:427]
On Stupefying Oneself by the Excessive Use of Food or Drink
§8

Here the reason for considering[n] this kind of excess a vice is not the harm or bodily pain (diseases) that a human being brings on himself by it; for then the principle by which it is to be counteracted would be one of well-being[o] and

---

[k] *Sinnenlust*   [l] *sinnliche Lust*   [m] *zur Liebe des Wohlgefallens*   [n] *beurtheilt*
[o] *Wohlbefindens*

comfort (and so of happiness), and such a principle can establish only a rule of prudence, never a duty – at least not a direct duty.

Brutish excess in the use of food and drink is misuse of the means of nourishment that restricts or exhausts our capacity to use them intelligently. *Drunkenness* and *gluttony* are the vices that come under this heading. A human being who is drunk is like a mere animal, not to be treated as a human being. When stuffed with food he is in a condition in which he is incapacitated, for a time, for actions that would require him to use his powers with skill and deliberation. – It is obvious that putting oneself in such a state violates a duty to oneself. The first of these debasements, below even the nature of an animal, is usually brought about by fermented drinks, but it can also result from other narcotics, such as opium and other vegetable products. They are seductive because, under their influence, people dream for a while that they are happy and free from care, and even imagine that they are strong; but dejection and weakness follow and, worst of all, they create a need to use the narcotics again and even to increase the amount. Gluttony is even lower than that animal enjoyment of the senses, since it only lulls the senses into a passive condition and, unlike drunkenness, does not even arouse imagination to an *active* play of representations; so it approaches even more closely the enjoyment of cattle.

[6:428] *Casuistical Questions*

Can one at least justify, if not eulogize, a use of wine bordering on intoxication, since it enlivens the company's conservation and in so doing makes them speak more freely? – Or can it even be granted the merit of promoting what Horace praises in Cato: *virtus eius incaluit mero?*[P] – The use of opium and spirits for enjoyment is closer to being a base act than the use of wine, since they make the user silent, reticent, and withdrawn by the dream euphoria they induce. They are therefore permitted only as medicines. – But who can determine the *measure* for someone who is quite ready to pass into a state in which he no longer has clear eyes for *measuring?*[q] Mohammedanism, which forbids wine altogether, thus made a very bad choice in permitting opium to take its place.

Although a banquet is a formal invitation to excess in both food and drink, there is still something in it that aims at a moral end, beyond mere physical

---

[P] his virtue was enkindled by unmixed wine. Kant is quoting, from memory, Horace, *Odes* III. xxi.12. (LD: The line is: "*saepe mero caluisse virtus*". Kant's first edition erroneously attributes the line to Seneca; this error is corrected in the second edition.)

[q] In the second edition, the sentences "The use of opium … only as medicines" follow this sentence.

well-being:[r] it brings a number of human beings together for a long time to converse with one another. And yet the very number of guests (if, as Chesterfield says, it exceeds the number of the muses) allows for only a little conversation (with those sitting next to one); and so the arrangement is at variance with that end, while the banquet remains a temptation to something immoral, namely intemperance, which is a violation of one's duty to oneself – not to mention the physical harm of overindulgence, which could perhaps be cured by a doctor. How far does one's moral authorization to accept these invitations to intemperance extend?

[r] *Wohlleben*

Chapter II

A Human Being's Duty to Himself Merely as a Moral Being

This duty is opposed to the vices of *lying, avarice*, and *false humility* (servility).

I
On Lying
§9

The greatest violation of a human being's duty to himself regarded merely as a moral being (the humanity in his own person) is the contrary of truthfulness, *lying (aliud lingua promtum, aliud pectore inclusum gerere)*.^a In the doctrine of right an intentional untruth is called a lie only if it violates another's right; but in ethics, where no authorization is derived from harmlessness, it is clear of itself that no intentional untruth in the expression of one's thoughts can refuse this harsh name. For, the dishonor (being an object of moral contempt) that accompanies a lie also accompanies a liar like his shadow. A lie can be an external lie (*mendacium externum*) or also an internal lie. – By an external lie a human being makes himself an object of contempt in the eyes of others; by an internal lie he does what is still worse: he makes himself contemptible in his own eyes and violates the dignity of humanity in his own person. And so, since the harm that can come to others from lying is not what distinguishes this vice (for if it were, the vice would consist only in violating one's duty to others), this harm is not taken into account here. Neither is the harm that a liar brings upon himself; for then a lie, as a mere error in prudence, would conflict with the pragmatic maxim, not the moral maxim, and it could not be considered a violation of duty at all. – By a lie a human being throws away and, as it were, annihilates his dignity as a human being. A human being who does not himself believe what he tells another (even if the other is a merely ideal person) has even less worth than if he were a mere thing; for a thing, because it is something real and given, has the property of being serviceable so that another can put it to some use. But communication of one's thoughts to someone through words that yet (intentionally) contain the contrary of what the speaker thinks on the subject is an end that is directly opposed to the natural purposiveness of the speaker's capacity to communicate his thoughts, and is thus a renunciation by the speaker of his personality, and such a speaker is a mere deceptive appearance of a human being, not a human

---

^a to have one thing shut up in the heart and another ready on the tongue (Sallust, *The War with Catiline* X.5). LD: The line is "*aliud clausum in pectore, aliud in lingua promptum habere.*"

being himself. – *Truthfulness* in one's declarations is also called *honesty*[b] and, if the declarations are promises, *sincerity;*[c] but, more generally, truthfulness is called *rectitude*.[d]

Lying (in the ethical sense of the word), intentional untruth as such, need not be *harmful* to others in order to be repudiated; for it would then be a violation of the rights of others. It may be done merely out of frivolity or even good nature;[e] the speaker may even intend to achieve a really good end by it. But his way of pursuing this end is, by its mere form, a crime of a human being against his own person and a worthlessness that must make him contemptible in his own eyes. [6:430]

It is easy to show that the human being is actually guilty of many **inner** lies, but it seems more difficult to explain how they are possible; for a lie requires a second person whom one intends to deceive, whereas to deceive oneself on purpose seems to contain a contradiction.

The human being as a moral being (*homo noumenon*) cannot use himself as a natural being (*homo phaenomenon*) as a mere means (a speaking machine), as if his natural being were not bound to the inner end (of communicating thoughts), but is bound to the condition of using himself as a natural being in agreement with the declaration (*declaratio*) of his moral being and is under obligation to himself to *truthfulness*. – Someone tells an inner lie, for example, if he professes belief in a future judge of the world, although he really finds no such belief within himself but persuades himself that it could do no harm and might even be useful to profess in his thoughts to one who scrutinizes hearts a belief in such a judge, in order to win his favor in case he should exist. Someone also lies if, having no doubt about the existence of this future judge, he still flatters himself that he inwardly reveres his law, though the only incentive he feels is fear of punishment.

Insincerity is mere lack of *conscientiousness*, that is, of purity in one's professions before one's *inner* judge, who is thought of as another person when conscientiousness is taken quite strictly; then if someone, from self-love, takes a wish for the deed because he has a really good end in mind, his inner lie, although it is indeed contrary to his duty to himself, gets the name of a frailty, as when a lover's wish to find only good qualities in his beloved blinds him to her obvious faults. – But such insincerity in his declarations, which a human being perpetuates upon himself, still deserves the strongest censure, since it is from such a rotten spot (falsity, which seems to be rooted in human nature itself) that the ill of untruthfulness spreads into his relations with other human beings as well, once the highest principle of truthfulness has been violated. [6:431]

---

[b] *Ehrlichkeit*   [c] *Redlichkeit*   [d] *Aufrichtigkeit*
[e] *Gutmüthigkeit*, perhaps "kindness"

Remark

It is noteworthy that the Bible dates the first crime, through which evil entered the world, not from *fratricide* (Cain's) but from the first *lie* (for even nature rises up against fratricide), and calls the author of all evil a liar from the beginning and the father of lies. However, reason can assign no further ground for the human propensity to *hypocrisy*[f] (*esprit fourbe*), although this propensity must have been present before the lie; for, an act of freedom cannot (like a natural effect) be deduced and explained in accordance with the natural law of the connection of effects with their causes, all of which are appearances.

Casuistical Questions

Can an untruth from mere politeness (e.g., the "your obedient servant" at the end of a letter) be considered a lie? No one is deceived by it. – An author asks one of his readers, "How do you like my work?" One could merely seem to give an answer, by joking about the impropriety of such a question. But who has his wit always ready? The author will take the slightest hesitation in answering as an insult. May one, then, say what is expected of one?

If I say something untrue in more serious matters,[g] having to do with what is mine or yours, must I answer for all the consequences it might have? For example, a householder has ordered his servant to say "not at home" if a certain human being asks for him. The servant does this and, as a result, the master slips away and commits a serious crime, which would otherwise have been prevented by the guard sent to arrest him. Who (in accordance with ethical principles) is guilty in this case? Surely the servant, too, who violated a duty to himself by his lie, the results of which his own conscience imputes to him.

[6:432]

II
On Avarice
§10

By avarice in this context I do not mean *greedy avarice*[h] (acquiring the means to good living in excess of one's true needs), for this can also be viewed as a mere violation of one's duty (of beneficence) *to others*; nor, again, do I mean *miserly avarice*,[i] which is called *stinginess* or niggardliness when it is shameful but which can still be mere neglect of one's duties of love to others. I mean, rather, restricting *one's own* enjoyment of the means to good living so narrowly as to

---

[f] *Gleisnerei*   [g] *In wirklichen Geschäften*   [h] *habsüchtigen Geiz*   [i] *kargen Geiz*

leave one's own true needs unsatisfied. It is really this kind of avarice, which is contrary to duty *to oneself*, that I am referring to here.[j]

In the censure of this vice, one example can show clearly[k] that it is incorrect to define any virtue or vice in terms of mere **degree**, and at the same time prove the uselessness of the *Aristotelian* principle that virtue consists in the middle way between two vices.

If I regard *good management* as the mean between prodigality and avarice and suppose this mean to be one of degree, then one vice would pass over into the (*contrarie*) opposite vice only through the *virtue*; and so virtue would be simply a diminished, or rather a vanishing, vice. The result, in the present case, would be that the real duty of virtue would consist in making no use at all of the means to good living.

If a vice is to be distinguished from a virtue, the difference one must cognize and explain is not a difference in the *degree* of practicing moral maxims but rather in the objective *principle* of the maxims. – The *maxim of greedy* avarice (prodigality) is to get and maintain[l] all the means to good living *with the intention of enjoyment.* – The maxim of *miserly* avarice, on the other hand, is to acquire as well as maintain all the means to good living, but *with no intention of enjoyment* (i.e., in such a way that one's end is only possession, not enjoyment).

Hence the distinctive mark of the latter vice is the principle of possessing means for all sorts of ends, but with the reservation of being unwilling to use [6:433] them for oneself, and so depriving oneself of the comforts necessary to enjoy life; and this is directly contrary to duty to oneself with regard to the end.[*]

---

* The proposition, one ought not to do too much or too little of anything, says in effect nothing, since it is a tautology. What does it mean "to do too much"? Answer: to do more than is good. What does it mean "to do too little"? Answer: to do less than is good. What does it mean to say "I *ought* (to do or to refrain from something)"? Answer: that it is not good (that it is contrary to duty) to do more or less than is good. If that is the wisdom in search of which we should go back to the ancients (Aristotle), as to those who were nearer the fountainhead – *virtus consistit in medio,*[m] *medium tenuere beati, est modus in rebus, sunt certi denique fines, quos ultra citraque nequit consistere rectum* – then we have made a bad choice in turning to its oracle. Between truthfulness and lying (which are *contradictorie oppositis*) there is no mean; but there is indeed a mean betwen candor and reticence (which are *contrarie oppositis*), since one who declares his thoughts can say only what is true without telling the *whole truth.* Now it is quite natural to ask the teacher of virtue to point out this mean to me. But this he cannot do; for both duties of virtue have a latitude in their application (*latitudinem*), and judgment can decide what is to be

[j] In place of the passage "nor, again, do I mean . . . referring to here" the second edition has "I mean, rather, *miserly avarice*, which is called stinginess or niggardliness when it is shameful; and I am concerned with this kind of avarice, not as consisting in mere neglect of one's duties of love to others, but as a restricting of one's own use of the means for living well so narrowly as to leave one's true needs unsatisfied, and so as contrary to one's duty *to oneself.*" In fact, only two kinds of avarice, prodigality and miserliness, are in question.

[k] *kann man ein Beispiel von der Unrichtigkeit aller Erklärung . . . deutlich machen und zugleich die Unbrauchbarkeit. . .darthun*

[l] The second edition omits "and maintain."   [m] virtue consists in the mean

Accordingly, prodigality and miserliness are not distinguished from each other by degree; they are rather distinguished specifically, by their opposed maxims.

Casuistical Questions

Selfishness (*solipsismus*) is the basis both of the greed (insatiability in acquiring wealth) that aims at sumptuous living and of niggardliness (painful anxiety about waste); and it may seem that both of them – prodigality as well as miserliness – are to be repudiated merely because they end in poverty, though in the case of prodigality this result is unexpected and in the case of miserliness it is chosen[n] (one wills to live like a pauper). And so, since we are here speaking only of duty to oneself, it may be asked whether either prodigality or miserliness should be called a vice at all, or whether both are not mere imprudence and so quite beyond the bounds of one's duty to oneself. But miserliness is not just mistaken thrift, but rather slavish subjection of oneself to the goods of fortune,[o] which is a violation of duty to oneself since one ought to be their master. It is opposed to *liberality* of mind (*liberalitas moralis*) generally (not to generosity, *liberalitas sumptuosa*, which is only an application of this to a special case), that is, opposed to the principle of independence from everything except the law, and is a way in which the subject defrauds himself. But what kind of a law is it that the internal lawgiver itself does not know how to apply? Ought I to economize on food or only in my expenditures on external things? In old age, or already in youth? Or is thrift as such a virtue?

[6:434]

done only in accordance with rules of prudence (pragmatic rules), not in accordance with rules of morality (moral rules). In other words, what is to be done cannot be decided after the manner of *narrow* duty (*officium strictum*), but after the manner of *wide* duty (*officium latum*). Hence one who complies with the basic principles of virtue can, it is true, commit a *fault* (*peccatum*) in putting these principles into practice, by doing more or less than prudence prescribes. But insofar as he adheres strictly to these basic principles he cannot practice a *vice* (*vitium*), and Horace's verse, *insani sapiens nomen habeat* [;] *aequus iniqui*, **ultra quam satis est virtutem si petat ipsam**, is utterly false, if taken literally. In fact, *sapiens* here means only a *judicious* man (*prudens*), who does not think fantastically of virtue in its perfection. This is not an ideal which requires one to approximate to this end but not to attain it completely, since the latter requirement surpasses human powers and introduces a lack of sense (fantasy) into the principle of virtue. For really to be *too virtuous* – that is, to be too attached to one's duty – would be almost equivalent to making a circle too round or a straight line too straight. [For a translation of these Latin quotations see note on 6:404.]

[n] *willkürliche*

[o] *die Glücksgüter.* LD: The previous edition has "goods that contribute to happiness"; see 6:377 note 45.

III
On Servility
§11

In the system of nature, a human being (*homo phaenomenon, animal rationale*) is a being of slight importance and shares with the rest of the animals, as offspring of the earth, an ordinary value (*pretium vulgare*). Although a human being has, in his understanding, something more than they and can set himself ends, even this gives him only an *extrinsic* value for his usefulness (*pretium usus*); that is to say, it gives one human being a higher value than another, that is, a *price* as of a commodity in exchange with these animals as things, though he still has a lower value than the universal medium of exchange, money, the value of which can therefore be called preeminent (*pretium eminens*).

But a human being regarded as a *person*, that is, as the subject of a morally practical reason, is exalted above any price; for as a person (*homo noumenon*) he is not to be valued merely as a means to the ends of others or even to his own ends, but as an end in himself, that is, he possesses a *dignity* (an absolute inner worth) by which he exacts *respect* for himself from all other rational beings in the world. He can measure himself with every other being of this kind and value himself on a footing of equality with them.   [6:435]

Humanity in his person is the object of the respect which he can demand from every other human being, but which he must also not forfeit. Hence he can and should value himself by a low as well as by a high standard, depending on whether he views himself as a sensible being (in terms of his animal nature) or as an intelligible being (in terms of his moral predisposition). Since he must regard himself not only as a person generally but also as a *human being*, that is, as a person who has duties his own reason lays upon him, his insignificance as a *human animal* may not infringe upon his consciousness of his dignity as a *rational human being*, and he should not disavow the moral self-esteem of such a being, that is, he should pursue his end, which is in itself a duty, not abjectly, not in a *servile spirit* (*animo servili*) as if he were seeking a favor, not disavowing his dignity, but always with consciousness of his sublime moral predisposition (which is already contained in the concept of virtue). And this *self-esteem* is a duty of the human being to himself.

The consciousness and feeling of the insignificance of one's moral worth *in comparison with the* **law** is *humility* (*humilitas moralis*). A conviction of the greatness of one's moral worth, but only from failure to compare it with the law, can be called *moral arrogance* (*arrogantia moralis*). – Waiving any claim to moral worth in oneself, in the belief that one will thereby acquire a borrowed worth, is morally-false *servility* (*humilitas spuria*).

Humility *in comparing oneself with other human beings* (and indeed with any finite being, even a seraph) is no duty; rather, trying to equal or surpass others in this respect, believing that in this way one will get an even greater inner worth, is *ambition* (*ambitio*), which is directly contrary to one's duty to others. But belittling one's own moral worth merely as a means to acquiring the favor [6:436] of another, whoever it may be (hypocrisy and flattery^p)* is false (lying) humility, which is contrary to one's duty to oneself since it degrades one's personality.

True humility follows unavoidably from our sincere and exact comparison of ourselves with the moral law (its holiness and strictness). But from our capacity for internal lawgiving^q and from the (natural) human being's feeling himself compelled to revere the (moral) human being within his own person, at the same time there comes *exaltation* and the highest self-esteem, the feeling of his inner worth (*valor*), in terms of which he is above any price (*pretium*) and possesses an inalienable dignity (*dignitas interna*), which instills in him respect for himself (*reverentia*).

§12

This duty with reference to the dignity of humanity within us, and so to ourselves, can be recognized, more or less, in the following examples.

Be no man's lackey. – Do not let others tread with impunity on your rights. – Contract no debt for which you cannot give full security. – Do not accept favors you could do without, and do not be a parasite or a flatterer or (what really differs from these only in degree) a beggar. Be thrifty, then, so that you will not become destitute. – Complaining and whining, even crying out in bodily pain, is unworthy of you, especially if you are aware of having deserved it; thus a criminal's death may be ennobled (its disgrace averted) by the resoluteness with which he dies. – Kneeling down or prostrating oneself on the ground, even to show your veneration for heavenly objects, is contrary to the dignity of humanity, as is invoking them in actual images;^r for you then humble yourself, [6:437] not before an *ideal* represented to you by your own reason, but before an *idol* of your own making.

Casuistical Questions

Is not a human being's feeling for his sublime vocation, that is, his *elation of spirit* (*elatio animi*) or esteem for himself, so closely akin to *self-conceit* (*arrogantia*), the very opposite of true *humility* (*humilitas moralis*), that it would be advisable to

---

* "*Heucheln*," properly "*häuchlen*" ["to dissemble"] seems to be derived from "*Hauch*," a moaning "breath" interrupting one's speech (a sigh). "*Schmeichlen*" ["to flatter"] seems to stem from "*Schmiegen*" ["to bend"] which, as a habit, is called "*Schmiegeln*" ["cringing"] and finally, in High German, "*Schmeicheln*."

^p *Heuchelei und Schmeichelei*   ^q *inneren Gesetzgebung fähig*   ^r *in gegenwärtigen Bildern*

cultivate humility even in comparing ourselves with other human beings, and not only with the law? Or would not this kind of self-abnegation instead strengthen others' verdict on us to the point of despising our person, so that it would be contrary to our duty (of respect) to ourselves? Bowing and scraping before a human being seems in any case to be unworthy of a human being.

Preferential tributes of respect in words and manners even to those who have no civil authority – reverences, obeisances (compliments), and courtly phrases marking with the utmost precision every distinction in rank, something altogether different from courtesy (which is necessary even for those who respect each other equally) – the *Du, Er, Ihr,* and *Sie,* or *Ew. Wohledlen, Hochedeln, Hochedelgebornen, Wohlgebornen*[s] (*ohe, iam satis est!*)[t] as forms of address, a pedantry in which the Germans seem to outdo any other people in the world (except possibly the Indian castes): does not all this prove that there is a widespread propensity to servility in human beings? (*Hae nugae in seria ducunt.*)[u] But one who makes himself a worm cannot complain afterwards if people step on him.

First Section
Of the Second Chapter
On a Human Being's Duty to Himself as His Own Innate Judge
§13

Every concept of duty involves objective constraint through a law (a moral imperative limiting our freedom) and belongs to practical understanding, which provides a rule. But the internal *imputation* of a *deed,* as a case falling under a law (*in meritum aut demeritum*), belongs to the *faculty of judgment* (*iudicium*), which, as the subjective principle of imputing an action, judges with rightful force whether the action as a deed (an action coming under a law) has occurred or not. Upon it follows the conclusion of *reason* (the verdict), that is, the connecting of the rightful result with the action (condemnation or acquittal). All of this takes place before a *tribunal* (*coram iudicio*), which, as a moral person giving effect to the law, is called a *court* (*forum*). – Consciousness of an *internal court in the human being* ("before which his thoughts accuse or excuse one another") is **conscience**.   [6:438]

Every human being has a conscience and finds himself observed, threatened, and, in general, kept in awe (respect coupled with fear) by an internal judge; and this authority watching over the law in him is not something that he himself (voluntarily)[v] *makes,* but something incorporated in his being. It follows him like his shadow when he plans to escape. He can indeed stun himself or put himself

---

[s] thou, he, you (polite, plural and singular), right noble, noble highness, highborn nobility, wellborn
[t] stay, that's enough! (Horace, *Satires* I.v.12).   [u] These trifles lead to serious things.
[v] *willkürlich*

to sleep by pleasures and distractions, but he cannot help coming to himself or waking up from time to time; and when he does, he hears at once its fearful voice. He can at most, in extreme depravity, bring himself to *heed* it no longer, but he still cannot help *hearing* it.

Now, this original intellectual and (since it is the thought of duty) moral predisposition called *conscience* is peculiar in that, although its business is a business of a human being with himself, one constrained by his reason sees himself constrained to carry it on as at the bidding *of another person*. For the affair here is that of trying *a case* (*causa*) before a court. But to think of a human being who is *accused* by his conscience as *one and the same person* as the judge is an absurd way of representing a court, since then the prosecutor would always lose. – For all duties a human being's conscience will, accordingly, have to think of *someone other* than himself (i.e., other than the human being as such) as the judge of his actions, if conscience is not to be in [6:439] contradiction with itself. This other may be an actual person or a merely ideal person that reason creates for itself.*

Such an ideal person (the authorized judge of conscience) must be a scrutinizer of hearts, since the court is set up *within* the human being. But he must also *impose all obligation*, that is, he must be, or be thought as, a person in relation to whom all duties whatsoever are to be regarded as also his commands; for conscience is the inner judge of all free actions. – Now since such a moral being must also have all power (in heaven and on earth) in order to give effect to his laws (as is necessarily required for the office of judge), and since such an omnipotent moral being is called **God**, conscience must be thought of as the subjective principle of being accountable to God for all one's deeds. In fact the latter concept is always contained (even if only in an obscure way) in the moral self-awareness of conscience.

---

* A human being who accuses and judges himself in conscience must think of a dual personality in himself, a doubled self which, on the one hand, has to stand trembling at the bar of a court that is yet entrusted to him, but which, on the other hand, itself administers the office of judge that it holds by innate authority. This requires clarification, if reason is not to fall into self-contradiction. – I, the prosecutor and yet the accused as well, am the same *human being* (*numero idem*). But the human being as the subject of the moral lawgiving which proceeds from the concept of freedom and in which he is subject to a law that he gives himself (*homo noumenon*) is to be regarded as another (*specie diversus*) from the human being as a sensible being endowed with reason, though only in a practical respect – for there is no theory about the causal relation of the intelligible to the sensible – and this specific difference is that of the faculties (higher and lower) of the human being that characterize him. The first is the prosecutor, against whom the accused is granted a legal adviser (defense counsel). When the proceedings are concluded the internal judge, as a person *having power*, pronounces the sentence of happiness or misery, as the moral results of the deed. Our reason cannot pursue further his power (as ruler of the world) in this function; we can only revere his unconditional *iubeo* or *veto* ["I command" or "I forbid"].

This is not to say that a human being is entitled, through the idea to which his conscience unavoidably guides him, to *assume* that such a supreme being *actually exists* outside himself – still less that he is *bound* by his conscience to do so. For the idea is not given to him *objectively*, by theoretical reason, but only *subjectively*, by practical reason, putting itself under obligation to act in keeping with this idea; and through using practical reason, but *only in following out the analogy* with a lawgiver for all rational beings in the world, human beings are merely pointed in the direction of thinking of conscientiousness (which is also called *religio*) as accountability to a holy being (morally lawgiving reason) distinct from us yet present in our inmost being, and of submitting to the will of this being, as the rule of justice. The concept of religion is here for us only "a principle of estimating"[w] all our duties as divine commands."

[6:440]

1) In a case involving conscience (*causa conscientiam tangens*), a human being thinks of conscience as *warning* him (*praemonens*) before he makes his decision. In cases where conscience is the sole judge (*casibus conscientiae*), being most scrupulous (*scrupulositas*) where the concept of duty (something moral in itself) is concerned cannot be considered hairsplitting (a concern with petty details), nor can a real violation be considered[x] a peccadillo (*peccatillum*) and be left to the advice of a conscience that speaks at will[y] (according to the principle *minima non curat praetor*).[z] Hence ascribing a *wide* conscience to someone amounts to calling him *unconscientious*.

2) When the deed has been done the *prosecutor* first comes forward in conscience, but along with him comes a *defense counsel* (advocate); and their dispute cannot be settled amicably (*per amicabilem compositionem*) but must rather be decided with all the rigor of right. Upon this follows

3) The verdict of conscience upon the human being, *acquitting* or *condemning* him with rightful force, which concludes the case.[a] It should be noted that when conscience acquits him it can never decide on a *reward* (*praemium*), something gained that was not his before, but can bring with it only *rejoicing* at having escaped the danger of being found punishable. Hence the blessedness found in the comforting encouragement of one's conscience is not *positive* (joy) but merely *negative* (relief from preceding anxiety); and this alone is what can be ascribed to virtue, as a struggle against the influence of the evil principle in a human being.

---

[w] *ein Princip der Beurtheilung*   [x] *beurtheilt*   [y] *willkürlich*
[z] the praetor is not concerned about trifles
[a] *der den Beschluß macht*. It both concludes the case and is the conclusion [*Schluß*] of the practical syllogism discussed above, 6:438.

[6:441]

Section II
On the *First Command* of All Duties to Oneself
§14

This command is "*know*ᵇ (scrutinize, fathom) *yourself*," not in terms of your natural perfection (your fitness or unfitness for all sorts of discretionaryᶜ or even commanded ends) but rather in terms of your moral perfection in relation to your duty. That is, know your heart – whether it is good or evil, whether the source of your actions is pure or impure, and what can be imputed to you as belonging originally to the *substance* of a human being or as derived (acquired or developed)ᵈ and belonging to your moral *condition*.

Moral cognition of oneself, which seeks to penetrate into the depths (the abyss) of one's heart which are quite difficult to fathom, is the beginning of all human wisdom. For in the case of a human being, the ultimate wisdom, which consists in the harmony of a human being's will with its final end, requires him first to remove the obstacle within (an evil will actually present in him) and then to develop the original predisposition to a good will within him, which can never be lost. (Only the descent into the hell of self-cognition can pave the way to godliness.)

§15

This moral cognition of oneself will, first, dispel *fanatical* contempt for oneself as a human being (for the whole human race), since this contradicts itself. – It is only through the noble predisposition to the good in us, which makes the human being worthy of respect, that one can find one who acts contrary to it contemptible (the human being himself, but not the humanity in him). – But such cognition will also counteract that *egotistical* self-esteem which takes mere wishes – wishes that, however ardent, always remain empty of deeds – for proof of a good heart. (*Prayer*, too, is only a wish declared inwardly before someone who knows hearts.) Impartiality in appraising oneself in comparison with the law, and sincerity in acknowledging to oneself one's inner moral worth or lack of worth are duties to

[6:442] oneself that follow directly from this first command to cognize oneself.

Episodic Section
On an *Amphiboly* in Moral *Concepts of Reflection*[53], Taking What Is a Human Being's Duty to Himself for a Duty to Other Beings
§16

As far as reason alone can judge, a human being has duties only to human beings (himself and others), since his duty to any subject is moral constraint by that

---

ᵇ *Erkenne* ᶜ *beliebigen* ᵈ *erworben oder zugezogen*
[53] LD: See the *Critique of Pure Reason*, A 260–92/B 316–49.

subject's will. Hence the constraining (binding) subject must, *first*, be a person; and this person must, *second*, be given as an object of experience, since the human being is to strive for the end of this person's will and this can happen only in a relation to each other of two beings that exist (for a mere thought-entity cannot be the *cause* of any result in terms of ends). But from all our experience we know of no being other than a human being that would be capable^e of obligation (active or passive). A human being can therefore have no duty to any beings other than human beings; and if he thinks he has such duties, it is because of an *amphiboly* in his *concepts of reflection*, and his supposed duty to other beings is only a duty to himself. He is led to this misunderstanding by mistaking his duty *with regard to* other beings for a duty *to* those beings.

This supposed duty can be referred to objects *other than persons* or to objects that are indeed persons, but quite *imperceptible* ones (who cannot be presented to the outer senses). – The first (*nonhuman*) objects can be mere inorganic matter (minerals), or matter organized for reproduction though still without sensation (plants), or the part of nature endowed with sensation and choice (animals). The second (*superhuman*) objects can be thought as spiritual beings (angels, God). – It must now be asked whether there is a relation of duty between human beings and beings of these two kinds, and what relation there is between them.

§17

A propensity to wanton destruction of what is *beautiful* in inanimate nature (*spiritus destructionis*) is opposed to a human being's duty to himself; for it weakens or uproots that feeling in him which, though not of itself moral, is still a disposition^f of sensibility that greatly promotes morality or at least prepares the way for it: the disposition, namely, to love something (e.g., beautiful crystal formations, the indescribable beauty of plants) even apart from any intention to use it.

With regard to the animate but nonrational part of creation, violent and cruel treatment of animals is far more intimately opposed to a human being's duty to himself, and he has a duty to refrain from this; for it dulls his shared feeling of their suffering and so weakens and gradually uproots a natural predisposition that is very serviceable to morality in one's relations with other human beings. The human being is authorized to kill animals quickly (without pain) and to put them to work that does not strain them beyond their capacities (such work as he himself must submit to). But agonizing physical experiments for the sake of mere speculation, when the end could also be achieved without these, are to be

^e *fähig*   ^f *Stimmung*

abhorred. – Even gratitude for the long service of an old horse or dog (just as if they were members of the household) belongs *indirectly* to a human being's duty *with regard to* these animals; considered as a *direct* duty, however, it is always only a duty of the human being *to* himself.

§18

Again, we have a duty *with regard to* what lies entirely beyond the limits of our experience but whose possibility is met with in our ideas, for example, the idea of God; it is called the *duty of religion*, the duty "of recognizing all our duties *as* (*instar*) divine commands." But this is not consciousness of a duty *to God*. For this idea proceeds entirely from our own reason and we ourselves make it, whether for the theoretical purpose of explaining to ourselves the purposiveness in the universe as a whole or also for the purpose of serving as the incentive in our conduct. Hence we do not have before us, in this idea, a given being to whom we would be under obligation; for in that case its reality would first have to be shown (disclosed) through experience. Rather, it is a duty of a human being to himself to apply this idea, which presents itself unavoidably to reason, to the moral law in him, where it is of the greatest moral fruitfulness. In this (**practical**) sense it can therefore be said that to have religion is a duty of the human being to himself.

[6:444]

Duties to Oneself
Book II
On a Human Being's Imperfect Duties to Himself
(with Regard to His End)

Section I

On a Human Being's Duty to Himself to Develop and Increase His *Natural Perfection*, That Is, for a Pragmatic Purpose[a]
§19

A human being has a duty to himself to cultivate (*cultura*) his natural powers (powers of spirit, mind, and body), as means to all sorts of possible ends. – He owes it to himself (as a rational being) not to leave idle and, as it were, rusting away the natural predispositions and capacities[b] that his reason can someday use. Even supposing that he could be satisfied with the innate scope of his capacities for his natural needs[c], his reason must first show him, by principles, that this meager scope of his capacities is *satisfactory;* for, as a being capable[d] of ends (of making objects his ends), he must owe the use of his powers not merely to natural instinct but rather to the freedom by which he determines their scope. Hence the basis on which he should develop his capacities (for all sorts of ends) is not regard for the *advantages* that their cultivation can provide; for the advantage might (according to Rousseau's principles) turn out on the side of his crude natural needs[e]. Instead, it is a command of morally practical reason and a *duty* of a human being to himself to cultivate his capacities (some among them more than others, insofar as people have different ends), and to be in a pragmatic respect a human being equal to the end of his existence. [6:445]

Powers of spirit are those whose exercise is possible only through reason. They are creative to the extent that their use is not drawn from experience but rather derived *a priori* from principles, of the sort to be found in mathematics, logic, and the metaphysics of nature. The latter two are also included in philosophy, namely theoretical philosophy, which does not then mean wisdom, as the word itself would suggest, but only science. However, theoretical philosophy can help to promote the end of wisdom.

---

[a] *in pragmatischer Absicht* [b] *Naturanlage und Vermögen* [c] *natürlichen Bedürfnisse*
[d] *fähig* [e] *Naturbedürfnisses*

209

Powers of soul[f] are those which are at the disposal of understanding and the rule it uses to fulfill whatever purposes one might have, and because of this experience is their guide. They include memory, imagination, and the like, on which can be built learning, taste (internal and external embellishment), and so forth, which furnish instruments for a variety of purposes.

Finally, cultivating the *powers of the body* (gymnastics in the strict sense) is looking after the *basic stuff* (the matter) in a human being, without which he could not realize his ends. Hence the continuing and purposive invigoration of the animal in him is an end of a human being that is a duty to himself.

§20

Which of these natural perfections should take *precedence*, and in what proportion one against the other it may be a human being's duty to himself to make these natural perfections his end, are matters left for him to choose in accordance with his own rational reflection about what sort of life he would like to lead and whether he has the powers necessary for it (e.g., whether it should be a trade, commerce, or a learned profession). For, quite apart from the need to maintain [6:446] himself, which in itself cannot establish a duty, a human being has a duty to himself to be a useful member of the world, since this also belongs to the worth of humanity in his own person, which he ought not to degrade.

But a human being's duty to himself regarding his *natural* perfection is only a *wide* and imperfect duty; for while it does contain a law for the maxim of actions, it determines nothing about the kind and extent of actions themselves but allows a latitude for free choice.

---

[f] *Seelenkräfte*

Section II

On a Human Being's Duty to Himself to Increase His *Moral Perfection, That Is, for a Moral Purpose Only*[g]
§21

First, this perfection consists subjectively in the *purity* (*puritas moralis*) of one's disposition to duty, namely, in the law being by itself alone the incentive, even without the admixture of aims derived from sensibility, and in actions being done not only in conformity with duty but also *from duty*. – Here the command is "be holy." *Second*, as having to do with one's entire moral end, such perfection consists objectively in fulfilling all one's duties and in attaining completely one's moral end with regard to oneself. Here the command is "be perfect." But a human being's striving after this end always remains only a progress from *one* perfection to another. "If there be any virtue, and if there be any praise, strive for it."[h]

§22

This duty to oneself is a *narrow* and perfect one in terms of its quality; but it is wide and imperfect in terms of its degree, because of the *frailty* (*fragilitas*) of human nature.

It is a human being's duty to *strive* for this perfection, but not to *reach* it (in this life), and his compliance with this duty can, accordingly, consist only in continual progress. Hence while this duty is indeed narrow and perfect *with regard to* its object (the idea that one should make it one's end to realize), *with regard to* the subject it is only a wide and imperfect duty to himself.

The depths of the human heart are unfathomable. Who knows himself well [6:447] enough to say, when he feels the incentive to fulfill his duty, whether it proceeds entirely from the representation of the law or whether there are not many other sensible impulses contributing to it that look to one's advantage (or to avoiding what is detrimental) and that, in other circumstances, could just as well serve vice? – But with regard to perfection as a moral end, it is true that in its idea (objectively) there is only *one* virtue (as moral strength of one's maxims); but in fact (subjectively) there is a multitude of virtues, made up of several different qualities,[i] and it would probably be impossible not to find in it some lack of virtue, if one wanted to look for it (though, because of

---

[g] *in blos sittlicher Absicht*
[h] Quotations are from 1 Peter 1:16, Matthew 5:48, and Philippians 4:8.
[i] *von heterogener Beschaffenheit*

those virtues, such other qualities are not usually called vices). But a sum of virtues such that our cognition of ourselves can never adequately tell us whether it is complete or deficient can be the basis only of an imperfect duty to be perfect.

* * *

All duties to oneself regarding the end of humanity in our own person, are, therefore, only imperfect duties.

Doctrine of the Elements of Ethics
Part II
On Duties of Virtue to Others

Chapter I

On Duties to Others Merely as Human Beings
Section 1
On the Duty of Love to Other Human Beings

Division
§23

The chief division can be that into duties to others by the performance of which you also put others under obligation and duties to others the observance of which does not result in obligation on the part of others. – Performing the first is *meritorious* (in relation to others); but performing the second is fulfilling a duty *that is owed. – Love* and *respect* are the feelings that accompany the carrying out of these duties. They can be considered separately (each by itself) and can also exist separately (one can *love* one's neighbor though he might deserve but little *respect*, and can show him the respect necessary for every human being regardless of the fact that he would hardly be judged worthy of love). But they are basically always united by the law into one duty, only in such a way that now one duty and now the other is the subject's principle, with the other joined to it as accessory. – So we shall acknowledge that we are under obligation to help someone poor; but since the favor we do implies that his well-being depends on our generosity, and this humbles him, it is our duty to behave as if our help is either merely what is due him or but a slight service of love, and to spare him humiliation and maintain his respect for himself.

§24

In speaking of laws of duty (not laws of nature) and, among these, of laws for human beings' external relations with one another, we consider ourselves in a moral (intelligible) world where, by analogy with the physical world, *attraction* and *repulsion* bind together rational beings (on earth). The principle of **mutual love** admonishes them constantly to *come closer* to one another; that of the **respect** they owe one another, to keep themselves *at a distance* from one another; and should one of these great moral forces fail, "then nothingness (immorality), with gaping throat, would drink up the whole kingdom of (moral) beings like a drop of water" (if I may use Haller's words, but in a different reference).[54]

§25

In this context, however, **love** is not to be understood as *feeling*,[a] that is, as pleasure in the perfection of others; love is not to be understood as *delight* in them (since others cannot put one under obligation to have feelings). It must rather be thought as the maxim of *benevolence* (practical love), which results in beneficence.

The same holds true of the **respect** to be shown to others. It is not to be understood as the mere *feeling* that comes from comparing our own *worth* with another's (such as a child feels merely from habit toward his parents, a pupil toward his teacher, or any subordinate toward his superior). It is rather to be understood as the *maxim* of limiting our self-esteem by the dignity of humanity in another person, and so as respect in the practical sense (*observantia aliis praestanda*).

Moreover, a duty of free respect toward others is, strictly speaking, only a negative one (of not exalting oneself above others) and is thus analogous to the duty of right not to encroach upon what belongs to anyone.[b] Hence, although it [6:450] is a mere duty of virtue, it is regarded as *narrow* in comparison with a duty of love, and it is the latter that is considered a *wide* duty.

The duty of love for one's neighbor can, accordingly, also be expressed as the duty to make others' *ends* my own (provided only that these are not immoral). The duty of respect for my neighbor is contained in the maxim not to degrade any other to a mere means to my ends (not to demand that another throw himself away in order to slave for my end).

By carrying out the duty of love to someone I put another under obligation; I make myself deserving from him. But in observing a duty of respect I put only myself under obligation; I keep myself within my own bounds so as not to detract anything from the worth that the other, as a human being, is authorized to put upon himself.

On the Duty of Love in Particular
§26

Since the love of human beings (philanthropy) we are thinking of here is practical love, not the love that is delight in them, it must be taken as active

---

[a] *als Gefühl (ästhetisch)*   [b] *niemanden das Seine zu schmälern*

[54] The poem is "*Über die Ewigkeit*" (1736). Natorp's notes give the relevant portion.

benevolence, and so as having to do with the maxim of actions. – Someone who finds satisfaction in the well-being (*salus*) of human beings considered simply as human beings, for whom it is *well* when things go well for every other, is called a *friend of humanity* in general (a philanthropist). Someone for whom it is well only when things go badly for others is called an *enemy of humanity* (a misanthropist in the practical sense). Someone who is indifferent to how things go for others if only they go well for himself is *selfish* (*solipsista*). – But someone who avoids other human beings because he can find no *delight* in them, though he indeed *wishes* all of them *well*, would be *shy* of them (a misanthropist in terms of his sensibility),[c] and his turning away from them could be called anthropophobia.

§27

In accordance with the ethical law of perfection "love your neighbor as yourself," the maxim of benevolence (practical love of human beings) is a duty of all human beings toward one another, whether or not one finds them worthy of love. – For, every morally practical relation to human [6:451] beings is a relation among them represented by pure reason, that is, a relation of free actions in accordance with maxims that qualify for a giving of universal law and so cannot be selfish (*ex solipsismo prodeuntes*). I want everyone else to be benevolent toward me (*benevolentiam*); hence I ought also to be benevolent toward everyone else. But since all *others* with the exception of myself would not be *all*, so that the maxim would not have within it the universality of a law, which is still necessary for imposing obligation, the law making benevolence a duty will include myself, as an object of benevolence, in the command of practical reason. This does not mean that I am thereby under obligation to love myself (for this happens unavoidably, apart from any command, so there is no obligation to it); it means instead that lawgiving reason, which includes the whole species (and so myself as well) in its idea of humanity as such,[d] includes me as giving universal law along with all others in the duty of mutual benevolence, in accordance with the principle of equality, and *permits* you to be benevolent to yourself on the condition of your being benevolent to every other as well; for it is only in this way that your maxim (of beneficence) qualifies for a giving of universal law, the principle on which every law of duty is based.

---

[c] *ästhetischer Misanthrop*
[d] In the first edition the phrase *nicht der Mensch* ("not the human being") occurs here. It is omitted in the second edition.

§28

Now the benevolence present in love for all human beings is indeed the greatest in its *extent*,[e] but the smallest in its *degree*; and when I say that I take an interest in this human being's well-being only out of my love for all human beings, the interest I take is as slight as an interest can be. I am only not indifferent with regard to him.

Yet one human being is closer to me than another, and in benevolence I am closest to myself. How does this fit in with the precept "love your *neighbor* (your fellow human being) as yourself"? If one is closer to me than another (in the duty of benevolence) and I am therefore under obligation to greater benevolence to one than to the other but am admittedly closer to myself (even in accordance with duty) than to any other, then it would seem that I cannot, without contradicting myself, say that I ought to love every human being as myself, since the measure of self-love would allow for no difference in [6:452] degree. – But it is quite obvious that what is meant here is not merely benevolence in *wishes*, which is, strictly speaking, only taking delight in the well-being of every other and does not require me to contribute to it (everyone for himself, God for us all); what is meant is, rather, active, practical benevolence (beneficence), making the well-being and happiness of others my *end*. For in wishing I can be *equally* benevolent to everyone, whereas in acting I can, without violating the universality of the maxim, vary the degree greatly in accordance with the different objects of my love (one of whom concerns me more closely than another).

Division of Duties of Love

They are duties of A) *beneficence*, B) *gratitude*, and C) *sympathy*.

A
On the Duty of Beneficence

§29

Providing for oneself to the extent necessary just to find satisfaction in living (taking care of one's body, but not to the point of effeminacy)[f] belongs among duties to oneself. The contrary of this is depriving oneself (slavishly) of what is essential to the cheerful enjoyment of life, by *avarice*, or depriving oneself (fanatically) of enjoyment of the pleasures of life by exaggerated *discipline* of one's natural inclinations. Both of these are opposed to a human being's duty to himself.

---

[e] *Umfange*. LD: or perhaps "scope"   [f] *Weichlichkeit*

But beyond *benevolence* in our wishes for others (which costs us nothing) how can it be required as a duty that this should also be practical, that is, that everyone who has the means to do so should be *beneficent* to those in need?[g] – Benevolence is satisfaction in the happiness (well-being) of others; but beneficence is the maxim of making the same[h] one's end, and the duty to it consists in the subject's being constrained by his reason to adopt this maxim as a universal law.

It is not obvious that any such law is to be found in reason. On the contrary, the maxim "Everyone for himself, God (fortune) for us all" seems to be the most natural one.

§30   [6:453]

To be beneficent, that is, to promote according to one's means the happiness of other human beings in need[i], without hoping for something in return, is everyone's duty.

For everyone who finds himself in need[j] wishes to be helped by others. But if he lets his maxim of being unwilling to assist others in turn when they are in need[k] become public, that is, makes this a universal permissive law, then everyone would likewise deny him assistance when he himself is in need[l], or at least would be authorized to deny it. Hence the maxim of self-interest would conflict with itself if it were made a universal law, that is, it is contrary to duty. Consequently the maxim of common interest, of beneficence toward those in need, is a universal duty of human beings, just because they are to be considered fellow human beings, that is, rational beings with needs, united by nature in one dwelling place so that they can help one another.

§31

Someone who is *rich* (has abundant means for the happiness of others, i.e., means in excess of his own needs) should hardly even regard beneficence as a meritorious duty on his part, even though he also puts others under obligation by it. The satisfaction he derives from his beneficence, which costs him no

---

[g] *der Bedürftigen* LD: Dieter Schönecker suggests that Gregor's translating both *Bedürftige* and *Noth* (and their variants) with "need" is problematic, given that "one can be '*bedürftige*' without being '*in Not*'" ("Duties to Others from Love," in Trampota et al. [eds.], *Kant's Tugendlehre*, 309–41, 332 n.51). To disambiguate, the notes to this edition indicate where "need" translates *Noth*. (*Noth* is sometimes translated as "necessity", e.g., at 6:236.)

[h] *dasselbe* LD: Gregor's translation in the previous edition has "the happiness of others" here in place of "the same"; so does Ellington's. Schönecker (op cit., 333) notes that, because *Glückseligkeit* ["happiness"] is feminine, it cannot be the referent of *dasselbe*, which is neuter. *Wohlwollen* ["benevolence"], *Vergnügen* ["satisfaction"], and *Wohlsein* ["well-being"] are neuter. Schönecker holds that *Vergnügen* is the referent, which amounts substantively to the same as if *Wohlwollen* were.

[i] *in Nöthen*   [j] *in Noth*   [k] *in ihrer Noth*   [l] *in Noth*

sacrifice, is a way of reveling in moral feelings. He must also carefully avoid any appearance of intending to bind the other by it; for if he showed that he wanted to put the other under an obligation (which always humbles the other in his own eyes), it would not be a true benefit that he rendered him. Instead, he must show that he is himself put under obligation by the other's acceptance or honored by it, hence that the duty is merely something that he owes, unless (as is better) he can practice his beneficence in complete secrecy. – This virtue is greater when the benefactor's means are limited and he is strong enough quietly to take on himself the hardship he spares the other; then he is really to be considered morally rich.

[6:454] *Casuistical Questions*

How far should one expend one's resources in practicing beneficence? Surely not to the extent that he himself would finally come to need the beneficence of others. How much worth has beneficence extended with a cold hand (by a will to be put into effect at one's death)? – If someone who exercises over another (a serf of his estate) the greater power permitted by the law of the land *robs* the other of his freedom to make himself happy in accordance with his own choices, can he, I say, consider himself the other's benefactor because he looks after him paternalistically in accordance with *his own* concepts of happiness? Or is not the injustice of depriving someone of his freedom something so contrary to duty of right as such that one who willingly consents to submit to this condition, counting on his master's beneficence, commits the greatest rejection of his own humanity, and that the master's utmost concern for him would not really be beneficence at all? Or could the merit of such beneficence be so great as to outweigh the right of human beings? – I cannot do good to anyone in accordance with *my* concepts of happiness (except to young children and the insane), thinking to benefit him by forcing a gift upon him; rather, I can benefit him only in accordance with *his* concepts of happiness.

Having the resources to practice such beneficence as depends on the goods of fortune is, for the most part, a result of certain human beings being favored through the injustice of the government, which introduces an inequality of wealth that makes others need their beneficence. Under such circumstances, does a rich man's[m] help to the needy[n], on which he so readily prides himself as something meritorious, really deserve to be called beneficence at all?

B

On the Duty of Gratitude

Gratitude consists in *honoring* a person because of a benefit he has rendered us. The feeling connected with this judgment is respect for the benefactor (who puts

[m] *der Reiche*   [n] *den Nothleidenden*

218

one under obligation), whereas the benefactor is viewed as only in a relation of love toward the recipient. – Even mere heartfelt *benevolence* on another's part, without physical results, deserves to be called a duty of virtue; and this is the basis for the distinction between *active* and merely *affective*° gratitude.

[6:455]

§32

Gratitude is a duty. It is not a merely *prudential* maxim of encouraging the other to show me further beneficence by acknowledging my obligation to him for a favor he has done (*gratiarum actio est ad plus dandum invitatio*),[p] for I would then be using my acknowledgement merely as a means to my further purpose. Gratitude is, rather, direct constraint in accordance with a moral law, that is, a duty.

But gratitude must also be considered, in particular, a *sacred* duty, that is, a duty the violation of which (as a scandalous example) can destroy the moral incentive to beneficence in its very principle. For, a moral object is sacred if the obligation with regard to it cannot be discharged completely by any act in keeping with it (so that one who is under obligation always remains under obligation). Any other duty is an *ordinary* duty. – But one cannot, by any repayment of a kindness received, *rid* oneself of the obligation for it, since the recipient can never win away from the benefactor his *priority* of merit, namely having been the first in benevolence. – But even mere heartfelt benevolence, apart from any such act (of beneficence), is already a basis of obligation to gratitude. – A grateful disposition of this kind is called *appreciativeness*.

§33

As far as the *extent*[q] of this gratitude is concerned, it reaches not only to one's contemporaries but also to one's predecessors, even to those one cannot identify with certainty. It is for this reason, too, that it is thought improper not to defend the ancients, who can be regarded as our teachers, from all attacks, accusations, and disdain, insofar as this is possible. But it is a foolish mistake to attribute preeminence in talents and good will to the ancients in preference to the moderns just because of their antiquity, as if the world were steadily declining in accordance with laws of nature from its original perfection, and to despise everything new in comparison with antiquity.

[6:456]

But the *intensity*[r] of gratitude, that is, the degree of obligation to this virtue, is to be assessed by how useful the favor was to the one put under obligation and

° *affectionellen*   [p] an action of gratitude is an invitation to more of the same
[q] *Extension*   [r] *Intension*

how unselfishly it was bestowed on him. The least degree is to render *equal* services to the benefactor if he can receive them (if he is still living) or, if he cannot, to render them to others; it involves not regarding a kindness received as a burden one would gladly be rid of (since the one so favored stands a step lower than his benefactor, and this wounds his pride), but taking even the occasion for gratitude as a moral kindness, that is, as an opportunity given one to unite the virtue of gratitude with love of man, to combine the *cordiality*[s] of a benevolent disposition with *sensitivity*[t] to benevolence (attentiveness to the smallest degree of this disposition in one's thought of duty), and so to cultivate one's love of human beings.

C
Sympathetic Feeling[u] *Is Generally a Duty*

§34

Sympathetic joy and *sympathetic sadness*[v] (*sympathia moralis*) are sensible feelings of pleasure or displeasure (which are therefore to be called "aesthetic") at another's state of joy or pain (shared feeling, sympathetic feeling).[w] Nature has already implanted in human beings receptivity to these feelings. But to use this as a means to promoting active and rational benevolence is still a particular, though only a conditional, duty. It is called the duty of *humanity*[x] (*humanitas*) because a human being is regarded here not merely as a rational being but also as an animal endowed with reason. Now, humanity can be located either in the *capacity* and the *will* to *share in* others' *feelings*[y] (*humanitas practica*) or merely in the *receptivity*, given by nature itself, to the feeling of joy and sadness in common with others (*humanitas aesthetica*). The first is *free*, and is therefore called *sympathetic* [6:457] (*communio sentiendi liberalis*); it is based on practical reason. The second is *unfree* (*communio sentiendi illiberalis, servilis*); it can be called *communicable* (since it is like receptivity to warmth or contagious diseases), and also compassion,[z] since it spreads naturally among human beings living near one another. There is obligation only to the first.

---

[s] *Innigkeit*   [t] *Zärtlichkeit*   [u] *Theilnehmende Empfindung*   [v] *Mitfreude und Mitleid*
[w] *Mitgefühl, theilnehmende Empfindung*   [x] *Menschlichkeit*
[y] *Diese kann nun in dem Vermögen und Willen, sich einander in Ansehung seiner Gefühle mitzutheilen . . . .*
LD: Melissa Seymour Fahmy suggests that this passage glossing *humanitas practica* would be better rendered, "This [humanity] can be located in the capacity and will to communicate with each other in view of (with respect to) one's feelings." See "Active Sympathetic Participation: Reconsidering Kant's Duty of Sympathy," *Kantian Review* 14 (1) (2009): 31–52, 35.
[z] or "imparted suffering." The words translated as "sympathetic," "communicable," and "compassion" are, respectively, *theilnehmend, mittheilend,* and *Mitleidenschaft*. LD: Fahmy (op cit., 36) advocates translating *theilnehmend* as "participatory" rather than as "sympathetic" here.

It was a sublime way of thinking that the Stoic ascribed to his wise man[a] when he had him say "I wish for a friend, not that he might help *me* in poverty, sickness, imprisonment, etc., but rather that I might stand by *him* and rescue a human being." But the same wise man, when he could not rescue his friend, said to himself "what is it to me?" In other words, he rejected compassion.

In fact, when another suffers and, although I cannot help him, I let myself be infected by his pain (through my imagination), then two of us suffer, though the trouble really (in nature) affects only *one*. But there cannot possibly be a duty to increase the ills in the world and so to do good *from compassion*. This would also be an insulting kind of beneficence, since it expresses the kind of benevolence one has toward someone unworthy, called *pity*; and this has no place in human beings' relations with one another, since they are not to make a display of their worthiness to be happy.

§35

But while it is not in itself a duty to share the sufferings (as well the joys) of others, it is a duty to sympathize actively in their fate; and to this end it is therefore an indirect duty to cultivate the compassionate natural (aesthetic)[b] feelings in us, and to make use of them as so many means to sympathy based on moral principles and the feeling appropriate to them. – It is therefore a duty not to avoid the places where the poor who lack the most basic necessities are to be found but rather to seek them out, and not to shun sickrooms or debtors' prisons and so forth in order to avoid sharing painful feelings one may not be able to resist. For this is still one of the impulses that nature has implanted in us to do what the representation of duty alone might not accomplish.[c]

Casuistical Questions   [6:458]

Would it not be better for the well-being of the world generally if human morality were limited to duties of right, fulfilled with the utmost conscientiousness, and benevolence were considered morally indifferent? It is not so easy to see what effect this would have on human happiness. But at least a great moral adornment, benevolence[d] would then be missing from the world. This is, accordingly, required by itself, in order to present the world as a beautiful moral whole in its full perfection, even if no account is taken of advantages (of happiness).

---

[a] *des Weisen*   [b] *ästhetische*   [c] *für sich allein nicht ausrichten würde*[55]
[d] *Menschenliebe*

[55] See also Kant's assertion, in "The End of All Things" (1784), 8:337f., that if one considers not only what ought to be done but whether it actually will be done, love is an indispensable supplement to the imperfection of human nature, since unless it is added one could not count on very much being done.

Gratitude is not, strictly speaking, love toward a benefactor on the part of someone he has put under obligation, but rather *respect* for him. For universal love of one's neighbour can and must be based on equality of duties, whereas in gratitude the one put under obligation stands a step lower than his benefactor. Is it not this, namely pride, that causes so much ingratitude? seeing someone above oneself and feeling resentment at not being able to make oneself fully his equal (as far as relations of duty are concerned)?

On the Vices of Hatred for Human Beings, Directly (contrarie) *Opposed to Love of Them*

§36

They comprise the loathsome family of *envy, ingratitude,* and *malice*.[e] – In these vices, however, hatred is not open and violent but secret and veiled, adding meanness to one's neglect of duty to one's neighbor, so that one also violates a duty to oneself.

a) *Envy* (*livor*) is a propensity to view the well-being of others with distress, even though it does not detract from one's own. When it breaks forth into action (to diminish their well-being) it is called *envy proper*; otherwise it is merely *jealousy* (*invidentia*). Yet envy is only an indirectly malevolent disposition, namely a reluctance to see our own well-being overshadowed by another's because the standard we use to see how well off we are is not the intrinsic [6:459] worth of our own well-being but how it compares with that of others. – Accordingly one speaks, too, of *enviable* harmony and happiness in a marriage or family and so forth, just as if envying someone were permitted in many cases. Movements[f] of envy are therefore present in human nature, and only when they break out do they constitute the abominable vice of a sullen passion that tortures oneself and aims, at least in terms of one's wishes at destroying others' good fortune. This vice is therefore contrary to one's duty to oneself as well as to others.

b) When *ingratitude* toward one's benefactor extends to hatred of him it is called *ingratitude proper*, but otherwise mere *unappreciativeness*. It is, indeed, publicly judged to be one of the most detestable vices; and yet human beings are so notorious for it that it is not thought unlikely that one could even make an enemy by rendering a benefit. – What makes such a vice possible is misunderstanding one's duty to oneself, the duty of not needing and asking for others' beneficence, since this puts one under obligation to them, but rather preferring to bear the hardships of life oneself than to burden others with them and so incur indebtedness (obligation); for we fear that by showing gratitude we take the inferior position of a dependent in relation to his protector, which is contrary to

---

[e] *Schadenfreude*   [f] *Regungen*. LD: or perhaps "stirrings"; Ellington has "agitations."

real self-esteem (pride in the dignity of humanity in one's own person). Hence gratitude is freely shown to those who must *unavoidably* have preceded us in conferring benefits (to the ancestors we commemorate or to our parents); but to contemporaries it is shown only sparingly and indeed the very opposite of it is shown, in order to hide this relation of inequality. – But ingratitude is a vice that shocks humanity, not merely because of the *harm* that such an example must bring on human beings in general by deterring them from further beneficence (for with a genuine moral disposition they can, just by scorning any such return for their beneficence, put all the more inner moral worth on it), but because ingratitude stands love of humanity on its head, as it were, and degrades absence of love into an authorization to hate the one who loves.

c) *Malice*, the direct opposite of sympathy, is likewise no stranger to human nature; but when it goes so far as to help bring about ills or evil it makes hatred of human beings visible and appears in all its hideousness as *malice proper*. It is indeed natural that, by the laws of imagination (namely, the law of contrast), we feel our own well-being and even our good conduct more strongly when the misfortune of others or their downfall in scandal is put next to our own condition, as a foil to show it in so much the brighter light. But to rejoice immediately in the existence of such *enormities* destroying what is best in the world as a whole, and so also to wish for them to happen, is secretly to hate human beings; and this is the direct opposite of love for our neighbor, which is incumbent on us as a duty. – It is the *haughtiness* of others when their welfare is uninterrupted, and their *self-conceit* in their good conduct (strictly speaking, only in their good fortune in having so far escaped temptations to public vice) – both of which an egotist accounts to his merit – that generate this malevolent joy, which is directly opposed to one's duty in accordance with the principle of sympathy (as expressed by Terence's honest Chremes): "I am a human being; whatever befalls a human being concerns me too."[56]

[6:460]

The sweetest form of malice is the *desire for revenge*.[g] Besides, it might even seem that one has the greatest right, and even the obligation (as a desire for justice), to make it one's end to harm others without any advantage to oneself.

Every deed that violates a human being's right deserves punishment, the function of which is to *avenge*[h] a crime on the one who committed it (not merely to make good the harm that was done). But punishment is not an act that the injured party can undertake on his private authority but rather an act of a court distinct from him, which gives effect to the law of a *supreme authority* over all those subject to it; and when (as we must in ethics) we regard human beings as in

---

[g] *Rachbegierde*   [h] *wodurch...gerächt...wird*

[56] Terence, *The Self-Tormentor*, I.i.25. (LD: The line is, "*Homo sum, humani nihil a me alienum puto.*")

a rightful condition but in *accordance only with laws of reason* (not civil laws), then no one is authorized to inflict punishment and to avenge^i the wrongs sustained by them except him who is also the supreme moral lawgiver; and he alone (namely God) can say "Vengeance^j is mine; I will repay." It is, therefore, a duty of virtue not only to refrain from repaying another's enmity with hatred out of mere revenge but also not even to call upon the judge of the world for vengeance, partly because a human being has enough guilt of his own to be greatly in need of [6:461] pardon and partly, and indeed especially, because no punishment, no matter from whom it comes, may be inflicted out of hatred. – It is therefore a duty of human beings to be *forgiving* (*placabilitas*). But this must not be confused with *meek toleration* of wrongs (*mitis iniuriarum patientia*), renunciation of rigorous means (*rigorosa*) for preventing the recurrence of wrongs by others; for then a human being would be throwing away his rights and letting others trample on them, and so would violate his duty to himself.

Remark

If vice is taken in the sense of a basic principle (a vice proper), then any vice, which would make human nature itself detestable, is *inhuman* when regarded objectively. But considered subjectively, that is, in terms of what experience teaches us about our species, such vices are still *human*. As to whether, in vehement revulsion, one could call some of these vices *devilish*, and so too the virtues opposed to them *angelic*, both of these concepts are only ideas of a maximum used as a standard for comparing degrees of morality; in them one assigns a human being his place in *heaven* or *hell*, without making of him an intermediate sort of being who occupies neither one place nor the other. The question may remain open here whether Haller did not hit upon it better with his "an ambiguous hybrid of angel and beast."[57] But dividing something composite into two heterogeneous things yields no definite concept at all, and can lead us to none in ordering beings whose class distinctions are unknown to us. The first comparison (of angelic virtue and devilish vice) is an exaggeration. The second – although human beings do, alas, also fall into *brutish* vices – does not justify attributing to them a predisposition to these vices *belonging to their species*, any more than the stunting of some trees in a forest is a reason for making them a special *kind* of plant.

---

^i *rächen*   ^j *Rache*

[57] "*Über den Ursprung des Übels*"; see note 50 to Kant's note on 6:397.

Section II

On Duties of Virtue toward Other Human Beings Arising from the *Respect* Due Them

§37

Moderation in one's demands generally, that is, willing restriction of one's self-love in view of the self-love of others, is called *modesty*. Lack of *such moderation* (lack of modesty) as regards one's worthiness to be *loved* by others is called *egotism*[k] (*philautia*). But lack of modesty in one's claims to be **respected** by others is *self-conceit*[l] (*arrogantia*). The *respect* that I have for others or that another can require from me (*observantia aliis praestanda*) is therefore recognition of a *dignity* (*dignitas*) in other human beings, that is, of a worth that has no price, no equivalent for which the object evaluated (*aestimii*) could be exchanged. – Judging something to be worthless is contempt.

§38

Every human being has a legitimate claim to respect from his fellow human beings and is *in turn* bound to respect every other.

Humanity itself is a dignity; for a human being cannot be used merely as a means by any human being (either by others or even by himself) but must always be used at the same time as an end. It is just in this that his dignity (personality) consists, by which he raises himself above all other beings in the world that are not human beings and yet can be used, and so over all *things*. But just as he cannot give himself away for any price (this would conflict with his duty of self-esteem), so neither can he act contrary to the equally necessary self-esteem of others, as human beings, that is, he is under obligation to acknowledge, in a practical way, the dignity of humanity in every other human being. Hence there rests on him a duty regarding the respect that must be shown to every other human being.

§39

To be *contemptuous* of others (*contemnere*), that is, to deny them the respect owed to human beings in general, is in every case contrary to duty; for they are human beings. At times one cannot, it is true, help inwardly *looking down* on some in comparison with others (*despicatui habere*); but the outward manifestation of this is, nevertheless, an offense.[m] – What is *dangerous* is no object of contempt, and so neither is a vicious man;[n] and if my superiority to his attacks justifies my saying that I despise him, this means only that I am in no danger from him, even though

---

[k] *Eigenliebe*   [l] *Eigendünkel*   [m] *Beleidigung*   [n] *der Lasterhafte*

I have prepared no defense against him, because he shows himself in all his depravity. Nonetheless I cannot deny all respect to even a vicious man° as a human being; I cannot withdraw at least the respect that belongs to him in his quality as a human being, even though by his deeds he makes himself unworthy of it. So there can be disgraceful punishments that dishonor humanity itself (such as quartering someone, having him torn by dogs, cutting off his nose and ears). Not only are such punishments more painful than loss of possessions and life to one who loves honor (who claims the respect of others, as everyone must); they also make a spectator blush with shame at belonging to the species that can be treated that way.

Remark

On this is based a duty to respect a human being even in the logical use of his reason, a duty not to censure his errors by calling them absurdities, poor judgment, and so forth, but rather to suppose that his judgment must yet contain some truth and to seek this out, uncovering, at the same time, the deceptive illusion (the subjective ground that determined his judgment which, by an oversight, he took for objective), and so, by explaining to him the possibility of his having erred, to preserve his respect for his own understanding. For if, by using such expressions, one denies any understanding to someone who opposes one in a certain judgment, how does one want to bring him to understand that he has erred? – The same thing applies to the censure of vice, which must never break out into complete contempt and denial of any moral worth to a vicious human being; for on this

[6:464]   supposition he could never be improved, and this is not consistent with the idea of a *human being*, who as such (as a moral being) can never lose entirely his predisposition to the good.

§40

Respect for the law, which in its subjective aspect is called moral feeling, is identical with consciousness of one's duty. This is why showing respect for a human being as a moral being (holding his duty in highest esteem) is also a duty that others have toward him and a right to which he cannot renounce his claim. – This claim is called *love of honor*, and its manifestation in external conduct, *respectability* (*honestas externa*). An offense against respectability is called *scandal*, an example of disregarding respectability that might lead others to follow it. To *give* scandal is quite contrary to duty. But to *take* scandal at what is merely unconventional (*paradoxon*) but otherwise in itself good is a delusion (since one

---

° *dem Lasterhaften*

holds what is unusual to be impermissible as well), an error dangerous and destructive to virtue. – For a human being cannot carry his giving an example of the respect due others so far as to degenerate into blind imitation (in which custom, *mos*, is raised to the dignity of a law), since such a tyranny of popular mores would be contrary to his duty to himself.

§41

Failure to fulfill mere duties of love is *lack of virtue* (*peccatum*). But failure to fulfill the duty arising from the *respect* owed to every human being as such is a *vice* (*vitium*). For no one is wronged if duties of love are neglected; but a failure in the duty of respect infringes upon one's lawful claim. – The first violation is opposed to duty as its *contrary* (*contrarie oppositum virtutis*). But what not only adds nothing moral but even abolishes the worth of what would otherwise be to the subject's good is *vice*.

For this reason, too, duties to one's fellow human beings arising from the respect due them are expressed only negatively, that is, this duty of virtue will be expressed *only indirectly* (through the prohibition of its opposite). [6:465]

On Vices that Violate the Duty of Respect for Other Human Beings

These vices are A) *arrogance*, B) *defamation*, and C) *ridicule*.

A

Arrogance

§42

Arrogance (*superbia* and, as this word expresses it, the inclination to be always *on top*) is a kind of *ambition* (*ambitio*) in which we demand that others think little of themselves in comparison with us. It is, therefore, a vice opposed to the respect that every human being can lawfully claim.

It differs from **pride proper**[p] (*animus elatus*), which is *love of honor*, that is, a concern to yield nothing of one's human dignity in comparison with others (so that the adjective "*noble*" is usually added to "pride" in this sense); for arrogance demands from others a respect it denies them. – But *pride* itself becomes a fault and an offense when it, too, is merely a demand upon others to concern themselves with one's importance.

---

[p] LD: There is no modifier (such as *qualificirt*) accompanying *Stolz* ["pride"]. Gregor's addition of "proper" here presumably reflects her reading of the paragraph as a whole.

Arrogance is, as it were, a solicitation on the part of one seeking honor for followers, whom he thinks he is entitled to treat with contempt. It is obvious that this is *unjust* and opposed to the respect owed to human beings as such; that it is *folly*, that is, frivolity in using means to something so related to them as not to be worth being taken as an end; that someone arrogant is even a *conceited ass*,[q] that is, that he shows an offensive lack of understanding in using such means as must bring about, on the part of others, the exact opposite of his end (for the more he shows that he is trying to obtain respect, the more everyone denies it to him). –

[6:466] But it might not be so readily noticed that someone arrogant is always *mean* in the depths of his soul. For he would not demand that others think little of themselves in comparison with him unless he knew that, were his fortune suddenly to change, he himself would not find it hard to grovel and to waive any claim to respect from others.

B
Defamation

§43

By defamation (*obtrectatio*) or backbiting I do not mean *slander* (*contumelia*), a *false* defamation to be taken before a court; I mean only the immediate inclination, with no particular aim in view, to bring into the open something prejudicial to respect for others. This is contrary to the respect owed to humanity as such; for every scandal given weakens that respect, on which the impulse to the morally good rests, and as far as possible makes people skeptical about it.

The intentional *spreading* (*propalatio*) of something that detracts from another's honor – even if it is not a matter of public justice, and even if what is said is true – diminishes respect for humanity as such, so as finally to cast a shadow of worthlessness over our race itself, making misanthropy (shying away from human beings) or contempt the prevalent cast of mind, or to dull one's moral feeling by repeatedly exposing one to the sight of such things and accustoming one to it. It is, therefore, a duty of virtue not to take malicious pleasure in exposing the faults of others so that one will be thought as good as, or at least not worse than, others, but rather to throw the veil of benevolence[r] over their faults, not merely by softening our judgments but also by keeping these judgments to ourselves; for examples of respect that we give others can arouse their striving to deserve it. – For this reason, a mania for spying on the morals of others (*allotrio-episcopia*) is by itself already an offensive inquisitiveness on the

---

[q] The distinction between being "foolish" and being "a conceited ass" is, as in *Anthropology from a Pragmatic Point of View* (7:210), that between *Thorheit* and *Narrheit*.
[r] *Menschenliebe*

part of anthropology, which everyone can resist with right as a violation of the respect due him.

C   [6:467]
Ridicule

§44

Wanton faultfinding and *mockery*, the propensity to expose others to laughter, to make their faults the immediate object of one's amusement, is a kind of malice.[s] It is altogether different from *banter*, from the familiarity among friends in which one makes fun of their peculiarities that only seem to be faults but are really marks of their pluck in sometimes departing from the rule of fashion (for this is not *derision*). But holding up to ridicule a person's real faults, or supposed faults as if they were real, in order to deprive him of the respect he deserves, and the propensity to do this, a mania for *caustic* mockery (*spiritus causticus*), has something of fiendish joy in it; and this makes it an even more serious violation of one's duty of respect for other human beings.

This must be distinguished from a jocular, even if derisive, brushing aside with contempt an insulting attack of an adversary (*retorsio iocosa*), by which the mocker (or, in general, a malicious[t] but ineffectual adversary) is himself made the laughing stock. This is a legitimate defense of the respect one can require from him. But when the object of his mockery is really no object for wit but one in which reason necessarily takes a moral interest, then no matter how much ridicule the adversary may have uttered and thereby left himself open to laughter it is more befitting the dignity of the object and respect for humanity either to put up no defense against the attack or to conduct it with dignity and seriousness.

Remark

It will be noticed that under the above heading virtues were not so much commended as rather the vices opposed to them censured. But this is already implicit in the concept of the respect we are bound to show other human beings, which is only a *negative* duty. I am not bound to *revere*[u] others (regarded merely as human beings), that is, to show them *positive* high esteem.[v] The only reverence[w] to which I am bound by nature is reverence for law as such (*revere legem*); and to revere[x] the law, but not to revere other   [6:468]

---

[s] *Bosheit*   [t] *schadenfroher*   [u] *verehren*   [v] *Hochachtung*   [w] *Achtung*

[x] *verehren*. Kant may well have in mind the duty not to give scandal. However, the second edition changes this sentence to read "To obey the law also with regard to other human beings, but not to . . ."

human beings in general (*reverentia adversus hominem*) or to perform some acts of reverence for them, is a human being's universal and unconditional duty toward others, which each of them can require as the respect originally owed others (*observantia debita*).

The different forms of respect to be shown to others in accordance with differences in their qualities or contingent relations – differences of age, sex, birth, strength, or weakness, or even rank and dignity, which depend in part on arbitrary arrangements – cannot be set forth precisely[y] and classified in the *metaphysical* first principles of a doctrine of virtue, since this has to do only with its pure rational principles.

---

[y] *ausführlich*. LD: This replaces "in detail" from the previous edition.

Chapter II

On Ethical Duties Of Human Beings toward One Another with Regard to Their *Condition*

§45

These (duties of virtue) do not really call for a special chapter in the system of pure ethics; since they do not involve principles of obligation for human beings as such toward one another, they cannot properly constitute a *part* of the *metaphysical* first principles of a doctrine of virtue. They are only rules modified in accordance with differences of the *subjects* to whom the principle of virtue (in terms of what is formal) is *applied* in cases that come up in experience (the material). Hence, like anything divided on an empirical basis, they do not admit of a classification that could be guaranteed to be complete. Nevertheless, just as a passage from the metaphysics of nature to physics is needed – a transition having its own special rules – something similar is rightly required from the metaphysics of morals: a transition which, by applying the pure principles of duty to cases of experience, would *schematize* these principles, as it were, and present them as ready for morally practical use. – How should one behave, for example, toward human beings who are in a state of moral purity or depravity? toward the cultivated or the crude? toward the learned or the unschooled, and toward the learned in so far as they use their science as members of polite society or outside society, as specialists in their field (scholars)? toward those whose learning is pragmatic or those in whom it proceeds more from spirit and taste? How should people be treated in accordance with their differences in rank, age, sex, health, prosperity or poverty, and so forth? These questions do not yield so many different *kinds* of ethical *obligation*[a] (for there is only *one*, that of virtue as such), but only so many different ways of *applying* it (corollaries). Hence they cannot be presented as sections of ethics and members of the *division* of a system (which must proceed *a priori* from a rational concept), but can only be appended to the system. Yet even this application belongs to the complete presentation of the system.

[6:469]

---

[a] *Arten der ethischen Verpflichtung*

Conclusion of the Elements of Ethics

On the Most Intimate Union of Love with Respect in *Friendship*

§46

Friendship (considered in its perfection) is the union of two persons through equal mutual love and respect. – It is easy to see that this is an ideal of each participating and sharing sympathetically in the other's well-being through the morally good will that unites them, and even though it does not produce the complete happiness of life, the adoption of this ideal in their disposition toward each other makes them deserving of happiness; hence human beings have a duty of friendship. – But it is readily seen that friendship is only an idea (though a practically necessary one) and unattainable in practice, although striving for friendship (as a maximum of good disposition toward each other) is a duty set by reason, and no ordinary duty but an honorable one. For in his relations with his neighbor how can a human being ascertain whether one of the elements requisite to this duty (e.g., benevolence toward each other) is *equal* in the disposition of each of the friends? Or, even more difficult, how can he tell what relation there is in the same person between the feeling from one duty and that from the other [6:470] (the feeling from benevolence and that from respect)? And how can he be sure that if the *love* of one is stronger, he may not, just because of this, forfeit something of the other's *respect*, so that it will be difficult for both to bring love and respect subjectively into that equal balance required for friendship? – For love can be regarded as attraction and respect as repulsion, and if the principle of love bids friends to draw closer, the principle of respect requires them to stay at a proper distance from each other. This limitation on intimacy, which is expressed in the rule that even the best of friends should not make themselves too familiar with each other, contains a maxim that holds not only for the superior in relation to the inferior but also in reverse. For the superior, before he realizes it, feels his pride wounded and may want the inferior's respect to be put aside for the moment, but not abolished. But once respect is violated, its presence within is irretrievably lost, even though the outward marks of it (manners) are brought back to their former course.

Friendship thought as attainable in its purity or completeness (between Orestes and Pylades, Theseus and Pirithous) is the hobby horse of writers of romances. On the other hand Aristotle says: My dear friends, there is no such thing as a friend! The following remarks may draw attention to the difficulties in perfect friendship.[58]

---

[58] *Nicomachean Ethics*, IX.10–11 and *Eudemian Ethics*, VII.12.

From a moral point of view it is, of course, a duty for one of the friends to point out the other's faults to him; this is in the other's best interests and is therefore a duty of love. But the latter sees in this a lack of the respect he expected from his friend and thinks that he has either already lost or is in constant danger of losing something of his friend's respect, since he is observed and secretly criticized by him; and even the fact that his friend observes him and finds fault with him[b] will seem in itself offensive.

How one wishes for a friend in need[c] (one who is, of course, an active friend, ready to help at his own expense)! But still it is also a heavy burden to feel chained to another's fate and encumbered with his needs. – Hence friendship cannot be a union aimed at mutual advantage but must rather be a purely moral one, and the help that each may count on from the other in case of need[d] must not be regarded as the end and determining ground of friendship – for in that case one would lose the other's respect – but only as the outward manifestation [6:471] of an inner heartfelt benevolence, which should not be put to the test since this is always dangerous; each is generously concerned with sparing the other his burden and bearing it all by himself, even concealing it altogether from his friend, while yet he can always flatter himself that in case of need[e] he could confidently count on the other's help. But if one of them accepts a *favor* from the other, then he may well be able to count on equality in love, but not in respect; for he sees himself obviously a step lower in being under obligation without being able to impose obligation in turn. – Although it is sweet to feel in possession of each other in a way that approaches fusion into one person, friendship is something so *delicate* (*teneritas amicitiae*) that it is never for a moment safe from interruptions if it is allowed to rest on feelings, and if this mutual sympathy and self-surrender are not subjected to principles or rules preventing excessive familiarity and limiting mutual love by requirements of respect. Such interruptions are common among uncultivated people, although they do not always result in a *split* (for the rabble fight and make up). Such people cannot part with each other, and yet they cannot be at one with each other since they need quarrels in order to savor the sweetness of being united in reconciliation. – But in any case the love in friendship cannot be an affect; for emotion is blind in its choice, and after a while it goes up in smoke.

§47

Moral friendship (as distinguished from friendship based on feeling)[f] is the complete confidence of two persons in revealing their secret judgments and

---

[b] The context of "even the fact" would make *gemeistert* ["finds fault with"] seem a misprint for *gemustert* ["examines"].
[c] *in der Noth*   [d] *im Falle der Noth*   [e] *im Falle der Noth*   [f] *ästhetischen*

feelings[g] to each other, as far as such disclosures are consistent with mutual respect.

The human being is a being meant for society (though he is also an unsociable one), and in cultivating the social state he feels strongly the need to *reveal* himself to others (even with no ulterior purpose). But on the other hand, hemmed in and cautioned by fear of the misuse others may make of his disclosing his thoughts, he finds himself constrained *to lock up* in himself a [6:472] good part of his judgments (especially those about other human beings). He would like to discuss with someone what he thinks about his associates, the government, religion, and so forth, but he cannot risk it: partly because the other person, while prudently keeping back his own judgments, might use this to harm him, and partly because, as regards disclosing his faults, the other person may conceal his own, so that he would lose something of the other's respect by presenting himself quite candidly to him.

If he finds someone intelligent[h] – someone who, moreover, shares his general outlook on things – with whom he need not be anxious about this danger but can reveal himself with complete confidence, he can then air his views. He is not completely *alone* with his thoughts, as in a prison, but enjoys a freedom he cannot have with the masses, among whom he must shut himself up in himself. Every human being has his secrets and dare not confide blindly in others, partly because of a base cast of mind in most human beings to use them to one's disadvantage and partly because many people are indiscreet or incapable of judging and distinguishing what may or may not be repeated. The necessary combination of qualities is seldom found in one person (*rara avis in terris, nigroque simillima cygno*),[i] especially since the closest friendship requires that a judicious and trusted friend be also bound not to share the secrets entrusted to him with anyone else, no matter how reliable he thinks him, without explicit permission to do so.

This (merely moral friendship) is not just an ideal but (like black swans) actually exists here and there in its perfection. But that (pragmatic) friendship, which burdens itself with the ends of others, although out of love, can have neither the purity nor the completeness requisite for a precisely determinant maxim; it is an ideal of one's wishes, which knows no bounds in its rational concept but which must always be very limited in experience.

A *friend of human beings*[j] as such (i.e., of the whole race) is one who takes an affective interest[k] in the well-being of all human beings (rejoices with them) and will never disturb it without heartfelt regret. Yet the expression "a *friend* of

---

[g] *Empfindungen*   [h] *der Verstand hat*
[i] a bird that is rare on earth, quite like a black swan (Juvenal, *Satires* II.vi.165). LD: In AA, "*et nigro*" appears rather than "*nigroque*"; the latter, which appears in the second edition, is correct.
[j] *Menschenfreund*   [k] *ästhetischen Antheil*

human beings" is somewhat narrower in its meaning than "one who merely loves human beings" (a *philanthropist*).[1] For the former includes, as well, thought and consideration for the *equality* among them, and hence the idea that in putting others under obligation by his beneficence he is himself under obligation, as if all were brothers under one father who wills the happiness of all. – For, the relation of a protector, as a benefactor, to the one he protects, who owes him gratitude, is indeed a relation of mutual love, but not of friendship, since the respect owed by each is not equal. Taking to heart the duty of being benevolent as a friend of human beings (a necessary humbling of oneself), serves to guard against the pride that usually comes over those fortunate enough to have the means for beneficence.

[6:473]

Appendix

On the Virtues of Social Intercourse (*virtutes homileticae*)

§48

It is a duty to oneself as well as to others not to *isolate* oneself (*separatistam agere*) but to use one's moral perfections in social intercourse (*officium commercii, sociabilitas*). While making oneself a fixed center of one's principles, one ought to regard this circle drawn around one as also forming part of an all-inclusive circle of those who, in their disposition, are citizens of the world – not exactly in order to promote as the end what is best for the world[m] but only to cultivate what leads indirectly to this end: to cultivate a disposition of reciprocity – agreeableness, tolerance, mutual love and respect (affability and propriety, *humanitas aesthetica et decorum*) – and so to associate the graces with virtue. To bring this about is itself a duty of virtue.

These are, indeed, only *externals* or by-products (*parerga*), which give a beautiful illusion resembling virtue that is also not deceptive since everyone knows how it must be taken. *Affability, sociability, courtesy, hospitality,* and *gentleness* (in disagreeing without quarreling) are, indeed, only tokens; yet they promote the feeling for virtue itself by a striving to bring this illusion as near as possible to the truth. By all of these, which are merely the manners one is obliged to show in social intercourse, one binds others too; and so they still promote a virtuous disposition by at least making virtue *fashionable*.[n]

[6:474]

But the question arises whether one may also keep company with those who are vicious. One cannot avoid meeting them, without leaving the world; and besides, our judgment about them is not competent. – But if the vice is a scandal,

---

[1] *Menschenliebenden (Philanthrop)*   [m] *das Weltbeste*   [n] *beliebt*

that is, a publicly given example of contempt for the strict laws of duty, which therefore brings dishonor with it, then even though the law of the land does not punish it, one must break off the association that existed or avoid it as much as possible, since continued association with such a person deprives virtue of its honor and puts it up for sale to anyone who is rich enough to bribe parasites with the pleasures of luxury.

II
Doctrine of the Methods of Ethics

Doctrine of the Methods of Ethics

Section I

Teaching Ethics[a]

§49

The very concept of virtue already implies that virtue must be acquired (that it is not innate); one need not appeal to anthropological knowledge based on experience to see this. For a human being's moral capacity would not be virtue were it not produced by the *strength* of his resolution in conflict with powerful opposing inclinations. Virtue is the product of pure practical reason insofar as it gains ascendancy over such inclinations with consciousness of its supremacy (based on freedom).

That virtue can and must be *taught* already follows from its not being innate; a doctrine of virtue is therefore *something that can be taught*.[b] But since one does not acquire the power to put the rules of virtue into practice merely by being taught how one ought to behave in order to conform with the concept of virtue, the Stoics meant only that virtue cannot be *taught* merely by concepts of duty or by exhortations (by paraenesis), but must instead be *exercised* and cultivated by efforts to combat the inner enemy within the human being (asceticism); for one *can* not straightway do all that one *wants* to do, without having first tried out and exercised one's powers. But the *decision* to do this must be made all at once and completely, since a disposition (*animus*) to surrender at times to vice, in order to break away from it gradually, would itself be impure and even vicious, and so could bring about no virtue (which is based on a single principle).

§50

As for the method of teaching (for every scientific doctrine must be treated *methodically*; otherwise it would be set forth *chaotically*), this too must be *systematic* and not *fragmentary* if the doctrine of virtue is to be presented as a *science*. But it can be set forth either by *lectures*, when all those to whom it is directed merely *listen*, or else by *questions*, when the teacher asks his pupils what he wants to teach them. And this erotetic method is, in turn, divided into the method of **dialogue** and that of **catechism**, depending on whether the teacher

---

[a] *Die ethische Didaktik.* In the "second division of ethics," 6:413, this was called "Catechizing," although in 6:411 two methods, catechizing and dialogue, were distinguished.
[b] *eine Doctrin*

addresses his questions to the pupil's *reason* or just to his *memory*. For if the teacher wants to question his pupil's reason he must do this in a dialogue in which teacher and pupil question and answer each other *in turn*. The teacher, by his questions, guides his young pupil's course of thought merely by presenting him with cases in which his predisposition for certain concepts will develop (the teacher is the midwife of the pupil's thoughts). The pupil, who thus sees that he himself can think, responds with questions of his own about obscurities in the propositions admitted or about his doubts regarding them, and so provides occasions for the *teacher* himself to *learn* how to question skillfully, according to the saying *docendo discimus*.[c] (For logic has not yet taken sufficiently to heart the challenge issued to it, that it should also provide rules to direct one in *searching* for things, i.e., it should not limit itself to giving rules for *conclusive* judgments but should also provide rules for *preliminary* judgments [*iudicia praevia*], by which one is led to thoughts. Such a theory can be a guide even to the mathematician in his discoveries, and moreover he often makes use of it.)

§51

For the beginning pupil the first and most essential instrument for *teaching*[d] the doctrine of virtue is a moral *catechism*. This must precede a religious catechism; it cannot be interwoven, merely as an interpolation, in the teachings of religion but must rather be presented separately, as a self-subsistent whole; for, it is only by pure moral principles that a transition from the doctrine of virtue to religion can be made, since otherwise the professions of religion would be impure. – For their own part, even the worthiest and most eminent theologians have hesitated [6:479] to draw up a catechism for teaching statutory religion (which they would personally answer for), though one would have thought this the least that could be expected from the vast treasury of their learning.

But a pure *moral* catechism, as the basic teaching of duties of virtue, involves no such scruple or difficulty since (as far as its content is concerned) it can be developed from ordinary human reason, and (as far as its form is concerned) it needs only to be adapted to rules of teaching suited for the earliest instruction. The formal principle of such instruction does not, however, permit Socratic *dialogue* as the way of teaching for this purpose, since the pupil has no idea what questions to ask; and so the teacher alone does the questioning. But the answer which he methodically draws from the pupil's reason must be written down and preserved in definite words that cannot easily be altered, and so be committed to the pupil's *memory*. So the way of *teaching by catechism* differs from both the *dogmatic* way (in which only the teacher speaks) and the way of *dialogue* (in which both teacher and pupil question and answer each other).

---

[c] by teaching we learn   [d] *doctrinale Instrument*

§52

The *experimental* (technical) means for cultivating virtue is *good* example on the part of the teacher (his exemplary conduct) and *cautionary* example in others, since, for a still undeveloped human being, imitation is the first determination of his will to accept maxims that he afterwards makes for himself. – To form a habit is to establish a lasting inclination apart from any maxim, through frequently repeated gratifications of that inclination; it is a mechanism of sense rather than a principle of thought (and one that is easier to *acquire* than *to get rid of* afterwards). – As for the power of examples[*] (good or bad) that can be held up to the propensity for imitation or warning, what others give us can establish no maxim [6:480] of virtue. For, a maxim of virtue consists precisely[c] in the subjective autonomy of each human being's practical reason and so implies that the law itself, not the conduct of other human beings, must serve as our incentive. Accordingly, a teacher will not tell his naughty pupil: take an example from that good (orderly, diligent) boy! For this would only cause him to hate that boy, who puts him in an unfavorable light. A good example (exemplary conduct) should not serve as a model but only as a proof that it is really possible to act in conformity with duty. So it is not comparison with any other human being whatsoever (as he is), but with the idea (of humanity), as he ought to be, and so comparison with the law, that must serve as the constant standard of a teacher's instruction.

Remark
Fragment of a Moral Catechism

The teacher elicits from his pupil's reason, by questioning, what he wants to teach him; and should the pupil not know how to answer the question, the teacher, guiding his reason, suggests the answer to him.

1. Teacher: What is your greatest, in fact your whole, desire in life?
   Pupil: (is silent)
   Teacher: That *everything* should *always* go the way you would like it to.
2. Teacher: What is such a condition called?
   Pupil: (is silent)

---

[*] "Instance" [*Beispiel*], a German word, is commonly used as synonymous with "example" [*Exempel*], but the two words really do not have the same meaning. To take something as an *example* and to bring forward an *instance* to clarify an expression are altogether different concepts. An example is a particular case of a *practical* rule, insofar as this rule represents an action as practicable or impracticable, whereas an *instance* is only a particular (*concretum*), represented in accordance with concepts [6:480] as contained under a universal (*abstractum*), and is a presentation of a concept merely for theory.

[c] *gerade*

Teacher: It is called *happiness* (continuous well-being, enjoyment of life, complete satisfaction with one's condition).

3. Teacher: Now, if it were up to you to dispose of all happiness (possible in the world), would you keep it all for yourself or would you share it with your fellow human beings?

Pupil: I would share it with others and make them happy and satisfied too.

4. Teacher: Now that proves that you have a good enough *heart*; but let us see whether you have a good *head* to go along with it. – Would you really give a layabout soft cushions so that he could pass his life away in sweet idleness? Or would you see to it that a drunkard is never short of wine and whatever else he needs to get drunk? Would you give a swindler a charming air and manner to dupe other people? And would you give a violent man[f] audacity and strong fists so that he could crush other people? Each of these things is a means that somebody wishes for in order to be happy in his own way.

[6:481]

Pupil: No, I would not.

5. Teacher: You see, then, that even if you had all happiness in your hands and, along with it, the best will, you still would not give it without consideration to anyone who put out his hand for it; instead you would first try to find out to what extent each was *worthy* of happiness. But as for yourself, would you at least have no scruples about first providing yourself with everything that you count in your happiness?

Pupil: I would have none.

Teacher: But doesn't it occur to you to ask, again, whether you yourself are worthy of happiness?

Pupil: Of course.

Teacher: Now the force in you that strives only toward happiness is *inclination;* but that which limits your inclination to the condition of your first being worthy of happiness is your *reason;* and your capacity to restrain and overcome your inclinations by your reason is the freedom of your will.

6. Teacher: As to how you should set about sharing in happiness and also becoming at least not unworthy of it, the rule and instruction in this lies in your *reason* alone. This amounts to saying that you need not learn this rule for your conduct from experience or be taught it by others. Your own reason teaches you what you have to do and directly commands you to do it. Suppose, for example, that a situation arises in which you could get a great benefit for yourself or your friend by making up a subtle *lie* that would harm no one: what does your reason say about it?

Pupil: That I ought not to lie, no matter how great the benefits to myself and my friend might be. Lying is *mean* and makes a human being *unworthy* of happiness. – Here is an unconditional necessitation through a command

[f] *dem Gewaltthätigen*

(or prohibition) of reason, which I must obey; and in the face of it all my
inclinations must be silent.

Teacher: What do we call this necessity, which reason lays directly upon
a human being, of acting in conformity with its law? [6:482]

Pupil: It is called *duty*.

Teacher: So a human being's observance of his duty is the universal and
sole condition of his worthiness to be happy, and his worthiness to be
happy is identical with his observance of duty.

7. Teacher: But even if we are conscious of such a good and active will in us,
by virtue of which we consider ourselves worthy (or at least not unworthy)
of happiness, can we base on this a sure hope of sharing in happiness?

Pupil: No, not on this alone. For it is not always within our power to
provide ourselves with happiness, and the course of nature does not of
itself conform with merit. Our good fortune in life (our welfare in general)
depends, rather, on circumstances that are far from all being in our
control. So our happiness always remains a wish that cannot become
a hope, unless some other power is added.

8. Teacher: Has reason, in fact, any grounds of its own for assuming the
existence of such a power, which apportions happiness in accordance
with a human being's merit or guilt, a power ordering the whole of nature
and governing the world with supreme wisdom? that is, any grounds for
believing in God?

Pupil: Yes. For we see in the works of nature, which we can judge,
a wisdom so widespread and profound that we can explain it to ourselves
only by the inexpressibly great art of a creator of the world. And with
regard to the moral order, which is the highest adornment of the world, we
have reason to expect a no less wise regime, such that if we do not make
ourselves *unworthy of happiness*, by violating our duty, we can also hope to
share in happiness.

In this catechism, which must be carried out through all the articles of virtue and
vice, the greatest care must be taken to base the command of duty not on the
advantages or disadvantages that follow from observing it, whether for the one it
is to put under obligation or even for others, but quite purely on the moral
principle. Only casual mention should be made of advantages and disadvantages,
as of a supplement which could really be dispensed with but which is serviceable,
merely as an instrument, for the taste of those who are weak by nature. It is the [6:483]
shamefulness of vice, not its *harmfulness* (to the agent himself), that must be
emphasized above all. For unless the dignity of virtue is exalted above everything else in actions, the concept of duty itself vanishes and dissolves into mere
pragmatic precepts, since a human being's consciousness of his own nobility

then disappears and he is for sale and can be bought for a price that the seductive inclinations offer him.

Now when this is wisely and carefully developed out of a human being's own reason, with regard for the differences in age, sex, and rank which he gradually encounters, then there is still something that must come at the end, which moves the soul inwardly and puts him in a position in which he can look upon himself only with the greatest wonder at the original predisposition dwelling within him, the impression of which is never erased. – When, namely, at the end of his instruction his duties are once more, by way of summary, recounted in their order (recapitulated); and when, in the case of each of them, his attention is drawn to the fact that none of the pains, hardships, and sufferings of life – not even the threat of death – which may befall him because he faithfully attends to his duty can rob him of consciousness of being their master and superior to them all, then the question is very close to him: what is it in you that can be trusted to enter into combat with all the forces of nature within you and around you and to conquer them if they come into conflict with your moral principles? Although the solution to this question lies completely beyond the capability of speculative reason[g], the question arises of itself; and if he takes it to heart, the very incomprehensibility in this cognition of himself must produce an exaltation in his soul which only inspires it the more to hold its duty sacred, the more it is assailed.

In this catechistic moral instruction it would be most helpful to the pupil's moral development to raise some casuistical questions in the analysis of every duty and to let the assembled children test their understanding by having each say how he would solve the tricky problem put to him. – The advantage of this is not only that it is a *cultivation of reason* most suited to the capacity of the undeveloped [6:484] (since questions about what one's duty is can be decided far more easily than speculative questions), and so is the most appropriate way to sharpen the understanding of young people in general. Its advantage lies especially in the fact that it is natural for a human being to *love* a subject which he has, by his own handling, brought to a science (in which he is now proficient); and so, by this sort of practice, the pupil is drawn without noticing it to an *interest* in morality.

But it is most important in this education not to present the moral catechism mixed with the religious one (to combine them into one) or, what is worse yet, to have it follow upon the religious catechism. On the contrary, the pupil must always be brought to a clear insight into the moral catechism, which should be presented with the utmost diligence and precision.[h] For otherwise the religion that he afterwards professes will be nothing but hypocrisy; he will acknowledge duties out of fear and feign an interest in them that is not in his heart.

[g] *das Vermögen der speculativen Vernunft*
[h] *Ausführlichkeit.* LD: The translation here replaces "thoroughness" from the previous edition.

Section II

Ethical Ascetics

§53

The rules for practicing virtue (*exercitiorum virtutis*) aim at a frame of mind that is both *valiant* and *cheerful* in fulfilling its duties (*animus strenuus et hilaris*). For, virtue not only has to muster all its forces to overcome the obstacles it must contend with; it also involves sacrificing many of the joys of life, the loss of which can sometimes make one's mind gloomy and sullen. But what is not done with pleasure but merely as compulsory service has no inner worth for one who attends to his duty in this way and such service is not loved by him; instead, he shirks as much as possible occasions for practicing virtue.

With regard to the principle of a vigorous, spirited, and valiant practice of virtue, the cultivation of virtue, that is, moral *ascetics*, takes as its motto the *Stoic* saying: accustom yourself *to put up with* the misfortunes of life that may happen and *to do without* its superfluous pleasures (*assuesce incommodis et desuesce commoditatibus vitae*).[j] – This is a kind of *regimen*[k] for keeping a human being [6:485] healthy. But *health* is only a negative kind of well-being: it cannot itself be felt. Something must be added to it, something which, though it is only moral, affords an agreeable enjoyment to life. This is the ever-cheerful heart, according to the idea of the virtuous Epicurus. For who should have more reason for being of a cheerful spirit, and not even finding it a duty to put himself in a cheerful frame of mind and make it habitual, than one who is aware of no intentional transgression in himself and is secured against falling into any? (*hic murus aheneus esto etc., Horat.*)[l] On the other hand monkish ascetics, which from superstitious fear or hypocritical loathing of oneself goes to work with self-torture and mortification of the flesh, is not directed to virtue but rather to fantastically purging oneself of sin by imposing punishments on oneself. Instead of morally *repenting* sins (with a view to improving), it wants to do *penance* by punishments chosen and inflicted by oneself. But such punishment is a contradiction (because punishment must always be imposed by another); moreover, it cannot produce the cheerfulness that accompanies virtue, but rather brings with it secret hatred for virtue's command. – Ethical gymnastics, therefore, consists only in combating natural impulses sufficiently to be able to master them when a situation comes up in which they threaten morality; hence it makes one valiant and cheerful in the consciousness of one's restored freedom. To *repent* of something and to impose a *penance* on oneself (such as a fast) not for

---

[i] *gehen auf die zwei Gemüthsstimmungen hinaus, wackeren und fröhlichen Gemüths. . .zu sein*
[j] accustom yourself to the inconveniences and disaccustom yourself to the conveniences of life
[k] *Diätetik*   [l] let this be our wall of bronze, etc. Horace (*Epistles* I.i.60).

hygienic but for pious considerations are, morally speaking, two very different precautionary measures. To repent of a past transgression when one recalls it is unavoidable, and, in fact, it is even a duty not to let this recollection disappear; but doing penance, which is cheerless, gloomy, and sullen, makes virtue itself hated and drives adherents away from it. Hence the training (discipline) that a human being practices on himself can become meritorious and exemplary only through the cheerfulness that accompanies it.

Conclusion [6:486]

Religion^m as the Doctrine of Duties to God Lies Beyond the Bounds of Pure Moral Philosophy

Protagoras of Abdera began his book with the words: "*As for whether there are gods or not, I do not know what to say.*"* For this the Athenians drove him off his land and from the city and burned his books before the public assembly. (Quintilian, *Institutio Oratoria*, Book III, Chapter 1).[59] – In doing this the Athenian judges, as *human beings*, did him a great *wrong*. But as *officials of the state* and judges they proceeded quite *rightly* and consistently; for how could someone swear an oath unless it had been decreed publicly and lawfully, *on high authority* (*de par le Sénat*), that there are gods?**

But granting this belief and admitting that *religion* is an integral part of the [6:487] general *doctrine of duties*, the problem now is to determine the boundaries of the *science* to which it belongs. Is it to be considered a part of ethics (for what is in question here cannot be the rights of human beings against one another), or must it be regarded as lying entirely beyond the bounds of a purely philosophic morals?

The *formal aspect* of all religion, if religion is defined^n as "the sum of all duties *as* (*instar*) divine commands," belongs to philosophic morals, since this definition expresses only the relation of reason to the *idea* of God which reason makes for itself; and this does not yet make a duty of religion into a duty *to* (*erga*) God, as a being existing outside our idea, since we still abstract from his existence. – The ground on which a human being is to think of all his duties in keeping with this *formal aspect* of religion (their relation to a divine will given *a priori*) is only subjectively logical. That is to say, we cannot very well make obligation

---

* "*De Diis, neque ut sint, neque ut non sint, habeo dicere.*"

** Later on, however, a great and wise moral lawgiver completely forbade the taking of oaths as something absurd and, at the same time, almost bordering on blasphemy; however, from a political point of view people still maintain that this device is quite indispensable as a means serving the administration of public justice, and liberal interpretations of that prohibition have been thought up in order to soften it. – Although it would be absurd to swear in earnest that there is a God (because one must already have postulated this in order to be able to take an oath at all), the question still remains: whether an oath would not be possible and valid if someone swears only in case there is a God (like Protagoras, deciding nothing about it)? – In fact, every oath that has been taken both sincerely and circumspectly may well have been taken in just this sense. – For if someone is willing simply to swear that God exists, his offer, it might seem, involves no risk for him, whether he believes in God or not. If there is a God (the deceiver will say), then I have hit the mark; if there is no God, then neither is there anyone to call *me* to account, and by such an oath I run no risk. – But *if there is a God*, then is there no danger of being caught in a lie deliberately told just in order to deceive him?

^m *Religionslehre*   ^n *erklärt*

[59] Natorp suggests that the reference is probably to Cicero, *On the Nature of the Gods* I.xxiii.63.

(moral constraint) intuitive for ourselves without thereby thinking of *another's* will, namely God's (of which reason in giving universal laws is only the spokesman).– – But this duty *with regard to* God (properly speaking, with regard to the idea we ourselves make of such a being) is a duty of a human being to himself, that is, it is not objective, an obligation to perform certain services for another, but only subjective, for the sake of strengthening the moral incentive in our own lawgiving reason.

But as for the *material aspect* of religion, the sum of duties *to* (*erga*) God, that is, the service to be performed for him (*ad praestandum*), this would be able to contain special duties as divine commands which do not proceed only from reason giving universal laws, so that they would be cognizable by us only empirically, not *a priori*, and would therefore belong only to revealed religion. They would therefore also have to assume the existence of such a being, not merely the idea of him for practical purposes, and to assume it not at will° but rather as something that could be set forth as given directly (or indirectly) in experience. But such a religion would still comprise no part of a *purely philosophic morals*, no matter how well-grounded it might otherwise be.

So *religion* as the doctrine of duties *to* God lies entirely beyond the bounds of [6:488] purely philosophic ethics, and this serves to justify the author of the present ethical work for not having followed the usual practice of bringing religion, conceived in that sense, into ethics, in order to make it complete.

We can indeed speak of a "Religion *within the Bounds* of Mere Reason"[60] which is not, however, derived *from* reason alone but is also based on the teachings of history and revelation, and considers only the *harmony* of pure practical reason with these (shows that there is no conflict between them). But in that case as well religion is not *pure*; it is rather religion *applied* to a history handed down to us,[P] and there is no place for it in an *ethics* that is pure practical philosophy.

Concluding Remark

All moral relations of rational beings, which involve a principle of the harmony of the will of one with that of another, can be reduced to *love* and *respect*; and, insofar as this principle is practical, in the case of love the basis for determining one's will can be reduced to another's *end*, and in the case of respect, to another's *right*. – If one of these is a being that has only rights and no duties to the other (God) so that the other has only duties and no rights against him, then the principle of the moral relation between them is

---

° *willkürlich*   P *auf eine vorliegende Geschichte angewandte*
60 See *Die Religion innerhalb der Grenzen der bloßen Vernunft* (1793), in AA 6. (LD: It is titled *Religion within the Boundaries of Mere Reason* in the Cambridge Edition.)

transcendent. (On the other hand, the moral relation of human beings to human beings, whose wills limit one another, has an *immanent* principle.)

The divine end with regard to the human race (in creating and guiding it) can be thought only as proceeding from *love*, that is, as the *happiness* of human beings. But the principle of God's will with regard to the *respect* (awe) due^q him, which limits the effects of love, that is, the principle of God's right, can be none other than that of *justice*. To express this in human terms, God has created rational beings from the need, as it were, to have something outside himself which he could love or by which he could also be loved.

But in the judgment of our own reason, the claim that divine *justice* makes upon us is not only as great but even greater (because the principle is a limiting one), and the claim is that of *punitive* justice. – For, there is no place for *reward* (*praemium, remuneratio gratuita*) in justice toward beings who have only duties and no rights in relation to another, but only in his love and beneficence (*benignitas*) toward them;^61 – still less can a claim to *compensation* (*merces*) be made by such beings, and *compensatory justice*^r (*iustitia brabeutica*) in the relation of God to human beings is a contradiction.

But in the idea of an exercise of justice by a being who is above any interference with his ends there is something that cannot well be reconciled with the relation of human beings to God: namely, the concept of a *wrong*^s that could be done to the infinite and inaccessible ruler of the world; for what is in question here is not human beings' violations of each other's rights, on which God, as the punishing judge, passes sentence, but of a violation supposed to be done to God himself and his right. The concept of this is *transcendent*, that is, it lies entirely beyond the concept of any punitive justice for which we can bring forward any instance (i.e., any instance among human beings) and involves extravagant^t principles that cannot be brought into accord with those we would use in cases of experience and that are, accordingly, quite empty for our practical reason.

Here the idea of divine punitive justice is personified. There is no particular judging being that exercises it (for then this being would come into conflict with principles of right); instead it is *justice* – as if it were a substance (otherwise called *eternal* justice) which, like the *fate* (destiny) of the ancient philosophical poets, is above even Jupiter – that pronounces on rights in accordance with an iron, inevitable necessity which we cannot penetrate further. – Now some instances of this.

Punishment (according to Horace)^62 does not let the criminal out of its sight as he strides proudly before it; rather, it keeps limping after him until it

[6:489]

---

^q *der schuldigen Achtung (Ehrfurcht)*   ^r *belohnende Gerechtigkeit*   ^s *Läsion*
^t *überschwengliche*
^61 It seems inappropriate to speak of a "reward" [*Belohnung*] as having a place in love and beneficence. Perhaps Kant is referring to a reward that was "promised in the law" (6:227).
^62 *Odes* III.ii.31–2. (LD: The lines are: "*raro antecedentem scelestum, deservit pede Poena claudo.*")

[6:490]

catches him. – Blood innocently shed cries out for vengeance. – Crime cannot remain unavenged; if punishment does not strike the criminal, then his descendants must suffer it, or if it does not befall him during his lifetime, then it must take place in a life after death,* which is accepted and readily believed in expressly so that the claim of eternal justice may be settled. – I will not allow *blood-guilt* to come upon my land by granting pardon to an evil, murdering duelist for whom you intercede, a wise ruler once said. – *Guilt for sins* must be expiated, even if a complete innocent should have to offer himself to atone for it (in which case the suffering he took upon himself could not properly be called punishment, since he himself had committed no crime). All of this makes it clear that this judgment of condemnation is not attributed to a *person* administering justice (for the person could not pronounce in this way without doing others wrong), but rather that *justice* by itself, as a transcendent principle ascribed to a supersensible subject, determines the right of this being. All of this conforms, indeed, with the *formal aspect* of this principle, but it conflicts with the *material aspect* of it, the *end*, which is always the *happiness* of human beings. – For, in view of the eventual multitude of criminals who keep the register of their guilt running on and on, punitive justice would make the *end* of creation consist not in the creator's *love* (as one must yet think it to be) but rather in the strict observance of his *right* (it would make God's right itself, located in his *glory*,ᵘ the end). But since the latter (justice) is only the condition limiting the former (benevolence), this seems to contradict principles of practical reason, by which the creation of a world must have been omitted if it would have produced a result so contrary to the intention of its author, which can have only love for its basis.

[6:491]

From all this it is clear that in ethics, as pure practical philosophy of internal lawgiving, only the moral relations of *human beings* to *human beings* are comprehensible by us. The question of what sort of moral relation holds between God and human beings goes completely beyond the bounds of ethics and is altogether incomprehensible for us. This, then, confirms what was maintained above: that ethics cannot extend beyond the limits of human beings' duties to one another.

---

* It is not even necessary to bring the hypothesis of a future life into this, in order to present that threat of punishment as completely fulfilled. For a human being, considered in terms of his morality, is judged as a supersensible object by a supersensible judge, not under conditions of time; only his existence is relevant here. His life on earth – be it short or long or even everlasting – is only his existence in appearance, and the concept of justice does not need to be determined more closely since belief in a future life does not, properly speaking, come first, so as to let the effect of criminal justice upon it be seen; on the contrary, it is from the necessity of punishment that the inference to a future life is drawn.

ᵘ *in der Ehre Gottes*

I.   DOCTRINE OF THE ELEMENTS OF ETHICS.

Part I
On a Human Being's *Duties to Himself.*

Book I
On a Human Being's *Perfect Duties to* Himself.
Chapter I
On a Human Being's Duties to Himself as an *Animal Being.*
Chapter II
On a Human Being's Duties to Himself Merely as a *Moral* Being.
Section I
On a Human Being's Duties to Himself as His Own Innate *Judge.*
Section II
On the First Command of All Duties to Oneself.
Episodic Section.
On an Amphiboly in Moral *Concepts of Reflection* with Regard to Duties to Oneself.

Book II [6:493]
On a HumanBeing's *Imperfect* Duties to Himself with Regard to His End.
Section I
On the Duty to Oneself to Develop and Increase One's Natural Perfection.
Section II
On the Duty to Oneself to Increase One's Moral Perfection.

DOCTRINE OF THE ELEMENTS OF ETHICS.

Part II
On Ethical *Duties to Others.*
Chapter I
On Duties to Others *Merely as Human Beings.*
Section I
On the *Duty of Love* to Other Human Beings.
Section II
On the *Duty of Respect* for Others.
Chapter II
On Duty to Others in Accordance with *Differences in Their Condition.*
Conclusion of the Doctrine of Elements.
On the Most Intimate Union of Love with Respect in Friendship.

Index

Cambridge Texts in the History of Philosophy

Titles published in the series thus far

Aquinas *Disputed Questions on the Virtues* (edited by E.M. Atkins and Thomas Williams)

Aquinas *Summa Theologiae, Questions on God* (edited by Brian Davies and Brian Leftow)

Aristotle *Eudemian Ethics* (edited by Brad Inwood and Raphael Woolf)

Aristotle *Nicomachean Ethics Revised Edition* (edited by Roger Crisp)

Arnauld and Nicole *Logic or the Art of Thinking* (edited by Jill Vance Buroker)

Augustine *On the Free Choice of the Will, On Grace and Free Choice, and Other Writings* (edited by Peter King)

Augustine *On the Trinity* (edited by Gareth Matthews)

Bacon *The New Organon* (edited by Lisa Jardine and Michael Silverthorne)

Berkeley, *Philosophical Writings* (edited by Desmond M. Clarke)

Boyle *A Free Enquiry into the Vulgarly Received Notion of Nature* (edited by Edward B. Davis and Michael Hunter)

Bruno *Cause, Principle and Unity and Essays on Magic* (edited by Richard Blackwell and Robert de Lucca with an introduction by Alfonso Ingegno)

Cavendish *Observations upon Experimental Philosophy* (edited by Eileen O'Neill)

Cicero On *Moral Ends* (edited by Julia Annas, translated by Raphael Woolf)

Clarke *A Demonstration of the Being and Attributes of God and Other Writings* (edited by Ezio Vailati)

Classic and Romantic German Aesthetics (edited by J.M. Bernstein)

Condillac *Essay on the Origin of Human Knowledge* (edited by Hans Aarsleff)

Conway *The Principles of the Most Ancient and Modern Philosophy* (edited by Allison P. Coudert and Taylor Corse)

Cudworth *A Treatise Concerning Eternal and Immutable Morality with A Treatise of Freewill* (edited by Sarah Hutton)

Descartes *Meditations on First Philosophy, with selections from the Objections and Replies* (edited by John Cottingham)

Descartes *The World and Other Writings* (edited by Stephen Gaukroger)

Fichte *Attempt at a Critique of All Revelation* (edited by Allen Wood, translated by Garrett Green)

Fichte *Foundations of Natural Right* (edited by Frederick Neuhouser, translated by Michael Baur)

Fichte *The System of Ethics* (edited by Daniel Breazeale and Günter Zöller)

Greek and Roman Aesthetics (edited by Oleg V. Bychkov and Anne Sheppard)

Hamann *Philosophical Writings* (edited by Kenneth Haynes)

Heine *On the History of Religion and Philosophy in Germany and Other Writings* (edited by Terry Pinkard, translated by Howard Pollack-Milgate)